Treasures for Scholars Worldwide

哈佛燕京圖書館文獻叢刊第十五種
Harvard-Yenching Library Reprint Series, No. 15

美國哈佛大學
哈佛燕京圖書館藏
鋼和泰未刊往來書信集

The Unpublished Correspondence
of Alexander von Staël-Holstein
in the Harvard-Yenching Library, Harvard University

鄒新明 編

下

GUANGXI NORMAL UNIVERSITY PRESS
廣西師範大學出版社
·桂林·

北京大學出版社
PEKING UNIVERSITY PRESS
·北京·

目　錄

序號	書信人	信件擬目	頁碼
117	E. Denison Ross	01　E. Denison Ross to Alexander von Staël-Holstein, Sept. 1, 1927	1
		02　Alexander von Staël-Holstein to E. Denison Ross	2
		此信日期不詳。	
118	Brice J. Sachs	01　Brice J. Sachs to Alexander von Staël-Holstein, Mar. 4, 1929	3
		此信原放在 "Sachs, Paul 來" 信封內，寫信人與 Paul Sachs 應不是一個人，故單獨列出。	
119	Paul J. Sachs	01　Alexander von Staël-Holstein to Paul J. Sachs, Feb. 25, 1930	5
		02　Paul J. Sachs to Alexander von Staël-Holstein, Mar. 25, 1930	7
120	Kenneth J. Saunders	01　Kenneth J. Saunders to Alexander von Staël-Holstein, Dec. 7, 1930	8
		02　Kenneth J. Saunders to Alexander von Staël-Holstein, Dec. 7, 1930	10
121	Catherine Scholer	01　Catherine Scholer to Alexander von Staël-Holstein, Nov. 2, 1928	11
		此信原置於"Embassies (and Legations) (Letters from-) 來"信封內，僅署 11 月 2 日，信開頭說："I am so sorry that I will not have the pleasure to which I had looked forward, of seeing you in America."又說："do not expect to reach America till March, when I fear you will be gone!" 説明寫信時鋼和泰已經在美國。鋼和泰在美國的時間大致在 1928 年 9 月到 1929 年 5 月之間，故此信可以推定寫於 1928 年 11 月 2 日。	

序號	書信人	信件擬目	頁碼
122	K. M. Sen	01　K. M. Sen to Alexander von Staël-Holstein, Jun. 26, 1924	14
		02　Alexander von Staël-Holstein to K. M. Sen, 1925?	16
		此信無日期，第二頁説："Mr. Yü who studies Sanskrit and Tibetan with me is a very good pupil……"，Sen 在 1924 年 6 月 26 日給鋼和泰的信中説："I hope you find in Mr. Yü a very good worker." 故此信應爲對 Sen 1924 年 6 月 26 日一信的回復。鋼和泰在此信開頭説："I am rather late in thanking you for your letter." 第三頁又説："The Chinese civil war has upset things very much……Moreover the train service between Shanghai and Peking ceased many months ago ……"，這裏的内戰可能是指於 1924 年 9 月爆發的第二次直奉戰争，考慮到鋼和泰説回信很晚，又説内戰使京滬鐵路停運好幾個月，此信大致寫於 1925 年初。	
123	Kurakichi Shiratori	01　Kurakichi Shiratori to Alexander von Staël-Holstein, Jul. 21, 1916	19
124	Lawrence Sickman	01　Lawrence Sickman to Alexander von Staël-Holstein, Jun. 9, 1931	24
125	Osvald Sirén	01　Alexander von Staël-Holstein to Osvald Siren, Oct. 2, 1922	25
		此信寫於鋼和泰1922年12月致戴何都一信第二頁的另一半。	
		02　Alexander von Staël-Holstein to Osvald Siren, Jan. ?, 1930	26
		此信無日期，於此信寫於同一頁的另一封德文信的時間爲 1930 年 1 月 17 日，故大致推定此信寫於 1930 年 1 月。	
		附 01　Alexander von Staël-Holstein to Dcotor, Jan.17, 1930	26
		此信與鋼和泰大約 1930 年 1 月寫給喜仁龍的信在同一頁，德文，收信人僅爲 "Doctor"，具體不詳，暫繫於此。	
126	George E. Sokolsky	01　George E. Sokolsky to Alexander von Staël-Holstein, May 2, 1924	27
		02　George E. Sokolsky to Alexander von Staël-Holstein, Jun. 28, 1924	28
		03　George E. Sokolsky to Alexander von Staël-Holstein, Aug. 7, 1924	29

序號	書信人	信件擬目	頁碼
		附 01　Alexander von Staël-Holstein to Someone	30
		此信寫於鋼和泰 1924 年 6 月 28 日致索克思一信的背面，日期不詳。因收信人無法辨識，暫繫於此。	
127	John Leighton Stuart	01　John Leighton Stuart to Alexander von Staël-Holstein, Jun. 13, 1929	31
		此信日期僅寫爲"June Thirteenth", 開頭説："I am greatly distressed that an engagement in Tientsin which I cannot postpone will prevent my attendance at your wedding next Monday." 據 *North China Standard* 1929 年 6 月 18 日關於鋼和泰婚禮的報道，鋼和泰 1929 年 6 月結婚，故此信當寫於 1929 年。另，此信説鋼和泰將在 6 月 13 日之後的下一個周一結婚，可以確定鋼和泰結婚日爲 1929 年 6 月 16 日。	
		02　John Leighton Stuart to Alexander von Staël-Holstein, Jun. 15, 1929	33
		附 01　Hu Shih to John Leighton Stuart, Jun. 10, 1929	34
		此信爲鋼和泰抄録的司徒雷登 1929 年 6 月 15 日給他的信中所附胡適致司徒雷登信，原件退給司徒雷登，故繫於此信後。	
		03　Alexander von Staël-Holstein to John Leighton Stuart, Jul. 16, 1929	35
		04　Alexander von Staël-Holstein to John Leighton Stuart, Jul.?, 1929	36
		此信無日期，信中開頭説："Many thanks for your kind congratulations and for sending me Dr. Hu's letter. I shall return the letter to you in a few days." 司徒雷登 1929 年 6 月 13 日給鋼和泰的信中説："Now the less I wish you my heartish good wishes and extend congratulations on this happy occasion. I shall hope before very long to meet your bride and offer my felicitations to her in person." 司徒雷登 1929 年 6 月 15 日給鋼和泰的信中説："The enclosed letter has just come from Dr. Hu Shih." 故此信當爲對司徒雷登這兩封信的回復。另鋼和泰 1929 年 7 月 16 日給司徒雷登的信末説："I enclose Dr. Hu's Letter." 此信説幾天後將把胡適的信退給司徒雷登，故此信大致寫於 1929 年 7 月。	
		05　John Leighton Stuart to Alexander von Staël-Holstein, Feb. 2, 1932	41
		06　John Leighton Stuart to Alexander von Staël-Holstein, Jun. 26, 1934	42

序號	書信人	信件擬目	頁碼
128	S. Tachibana	01　S. Tachibana to Alexander von Staël-Holstein, Sept. 23, 1917	43
129	Teng Ping (Ruyin)	01　Teng Ping to Alexander von Staël-Holstein, Monday	45
		此信日期僅署爲 "Monday"，具體日期不詳。	
		02　Alexander von Staël-Holstein to Teng Ping, Monday, 1929	46
		此信無日期。信中説："Dear Dean Teng, I hear that you have asked my assistant Lin to lecture at the National University. ……I have advised him to undertake no task whatever which might interfere with his work here, at least during his first year at Peking." 這裏鋼和泰的助手 Mr. Lin 應指林藜光，林 1929 年到中印研究所任研究助理，故此信當寫於 1929 年。	
130	F. W. Thomas	01　Alexander von Staël-Holstein to F. W. Thomas, Jul. 12, 1921	47
		此信無日期，開頭説："Exactly five months ago (on the 12, 2, 21) I despatched a registered letter……"，故可推定，此信寫於 1921 年 7 月 12 日。	
		02　F. W. Thomas to Alexander von Staël-Holstein, Aug. 3, 1921	51
		03　F. W. Thomas to Alexander von Staël-Holstein, Nov. 24, 1921	57
		04　F. W. Thomas to Alexander von Staël-Holstein, Feb. 23, 1922	59
		05　Alexander von Staël-Holstein to F. W. Thomas, Jul. 11, 1922	62
		此信兩份，一爲草稿，一爲寫於北京大學信箋上的正式信。	
		06　F. W. Thomas to Alexander von Staël-Holstein, Feb. 18, 1926	66
		07　Alexander von Staël-Holstein to F. W. Thomas, 1926	70
		此信無日期，信末説："I am replying under separate cover to your kind letter dated February 18, 1926." 故此信當寫於 1926 年 2 月 18 日之後，具體時間不詳。	

序號	書信人	信件擬目	頁碼
08		F. W. Thomas to Alexander von Staël-Holstein, Sept. 8, 1927	72
09		F. W. Thomas to Alexander von Staël-Holstein, Sept. 8, 1927	76
10		Alexander von Staël-Holstein to F. W. Thomas, Autumn?, 1927	80
		此信無日期。開頭說:"Many thanks for your letter and for the most interesting article on the language of Ancient Khotan. ...... your article which appeared in Jacobi's Festschrift." Thomas 1927 年 9 月 8 日致鋼和泰的信中說:"I am sending you a copy of my Jacobi Festschrift paper ......", 此信當爲對 Thomas 1927 年 9 月 8 日一信的回復,大致推定爲 1927 年秋季。	
11		Alexander von Staël-Holstein to F. W. Thomas, 1929	84
		此信無日期,第二頁說:"Has Mrs. Thomas received my Christmas Card ?...... In April 1929 I hope to return to Peking......",故此信大致寫於 1929 年初。	
12		Alexander von Staël-Holstein to F. W. Thomas, 1933	86
		此信無日期,第四頁說:"Please do induce somebody to publish a few encouraging words about my efforts in the Journal of the R. A. S. if you should be too busy to do so yourself. I suppose that the encouraging words cannot appear in the October number, but if they appear in the January number they will reach America in time for the early spring meeting of the authorities on whose decision my fate depends." 鋼和泰 1934 年 8 月 16 日致 Thomas 的信中說:"I am indeed obliged to you for your letter and for sending me a reprint of the review, which appeared just in time for the American Trustee's meeting. I am sure that the Trustees have been greatly impressed......",且此句注釋說:"In April 1934 the Trustees passed our budget without further diminishing the appropriation for the Sino-Indian Institute ......"。綜上,此信當寫於 1933 年,具體日期不詳。	
13		Alexander von Staël-Holstein to F. W. Thomas, Aug. 16, 1934	92
14		Alexander von Staël-Holstein to F. W. Thomas, Summer ? 1936	93
		此信無日期,開頭說:"I am greatly obliged to you for the passport......",鋼和泰 1936 年 7 月 5 日曾爲護照之事致信胡適,	

序號	書信人	信件擬目	頁碼
		信中説："At this rate of progress I shall certainly have to wait for the passports until the summer is over and therefore I thought of asking some of my foreign friends in Nanking for assistance." 兩封信所談到的或許是同一件事，故大致推定此信寫於1936年暑期。	
		附 01 Alexander von Staël-Holstein to Someone	94
		此信無頭無日期，收信人不詳，原放在 "Thomas, F. W. 回發" 信封内，暫繫於此。	
131	Mr. Thomas	01 Alexander von Staël-Holstein to Mr. Thomas, 1936	96
		此信在鋼和泰1935年4月2日致Lattimore書信的背面，信中説："Many thanks for the passports!" 鋼和泰1936年7月5日給胡適的信中還提到passport未解決的事情，此信當在此後。大致推定爲1936年。	
132	Daniel V. Thompson Jr.	01 Daniel V. Thompson Jr. to Alexander von Staël-Holstein, Jan. 23, 1925	97
		02 Daniel V. Thompson Jr. to Alexander von Staël-Holstein, Feb. 12, 1925	98
		此信日期僅署爲 "Thursday, Feb. 12"，結合其他兩封信年代，查萬年曆，1925年2月12日爲周四，故此信寫於1925年2月12日。	
		03 Daniel V. Thompson Jr. to Alexander von Staël-Holstein, Mar. 26, 1925	99
		04 Alexander von Staël-Holstein to Daniel V. Thompson Jr., 1925	100
		此信無日期，開頭説："When the events of May and June made it desirable, that all foreigners should be able to leave China at rather short notice I decided to sell my collection. I had the enclosed photographs of a part of my collection made and sent a set of them together with a short description to Professor Woods of Harvard." 信中提到的 "events of May and June" 似指1925年的 "五卅運動"。查Woods 1925年10月21日給鋼和泰的回信，開頭説："You were very good to send me the photographs of the Buddhist statuettes. The Curator of the university Museum was much interested, but he has undertaken some purchases which go beyond his resources for the present." 故此信當寫於1925年，大致在6月到10月之間。	
133	Tien Hungtu	01 Tien Hungtu to Alexander von Staël-Holstein, Mar. 6, 1933	104

序號	書信人	信件擬目	頁碼
		02 Tien Hungtu to Alexander von Staël-Holstein, May 11, 1934	105
		03 Tien Hungtu to Alexander von Staël-Holstein, May 3, 1935	106
		04 Alexander von Staël-Holstein to Tien Hungtu, Jun. ?, 1935	107
		此信無日期，與鋼和泰 1935 年 6 月 25 日致陳寅恪的信寫在同一頁，且信中提到 29 日星期六，查萬年曆，1935 年 6 月 29 日確係周六。故大致推定此信寫於 1935 年 6 月。此信收件人 Mr. Tien，信中提到鋼和泰將與他一起到燕大，大致推定爲田洪都。	
		05 Alexander von Staël-Holstein to Tien Hungtu, Oct.?, 1935	109
		此信無日期，信中說："May I ask you now to lend me the first number of the third volume of the ……?" 田洪都 1935 年 10 月 28 日給鋼和泰的信中說："We beg to inform you that the book 佛教學雜誌第三卷第一期 you want to borrow from us is also not owned by either the National Library of Peiping or the College of Chinese Studies Library." 兩封信所說的卷期一致，田洪都這封信應爲對此信的回復。故大致推定此信寫於 1935 年 10 月。	
		06 Tien Hungtu to Alexander von Staël-Holstein, Oct. 28, 1935	110
134	V. K. Ting	01 V. K. Ting to Alexander von Staël-Holstein, Apr. 23, 1921	111
		02 V. K. Ting to Alexander von Staël-Holstein, Apr. 28, 1921	112
		03 V. K. Ting to Alexander von Staël-Holstein, May 16, 1921	114
		04 V. K. Ting to Alexander von Staël-Holstein, May 21, 1921	116
		05 V. K. Ting to Alexander von Staël-Holstein, Mar. 10, 1924	118
		06 Alexander von Staël-Holstein to V. K. Ting, Mar. 21, 1924	119
		此信無日期，無結尾。開頭說："Many thanks for your kind	

序號	書信人	信件擬目	頁碼
		note. I feel very much honored by the fact, that Mr. Liang has written an introduction to the Kāçyapaparivarta."丁文江 1924 年 3 月 10 日給鋼和泰的信中説："Mr. Liang Chi Chao has written a preface to the book as requested."故此信當爲對丁文江 1924 年 3 月 10 日一信的回復。另，丁文江同年 3 月 29 日給鋼和泰的信，應爲對此信的回復，該信開頭説："Your letter dated 21st March was received some time ago ……"，故可推定，此信寫於 1924 年 3 月 21 日。	
		07 V. K. Ting to Alexander von Staël-Holstein, Mar. 29, 1924	120
		08 Alexander von Staël-Holstein to V. K. Ting, Sept. 9, 1926	122
		09 Alexander von Staël-Holstein to V. K. Ting, Sept.?, 1926	124
		此信無日期。信中説："I am very glad to hear that the Commercial Press have at last set a definite term for the publication of my book…… I am also very much obliged to you for having obtained the Press' promise of sending me sixty free copies."鋼和泰 1926 年 9 月 9 日给丁文江的信中説："Under these circumstances I am of course very anxious that the Kāçyapaparivarta should appear as soon as possible. …… May I ask you to hurry the Commercial Press, so that the book might appear before the end of this month? Please also try and get me as many free copies (fifty, or seventy five?) as possible."由此可以推定，此信應爲鋼和泰對丁文江回復自己 1926 年 9 月 9 日書信之後的回復。時間大致在同年 9 月底或 10 月。	
135	G. Ch. Toussaint	01 G. Ch. Toussaint to Alexander von Staël-Holstein, Jan. 6, 1933	125
		02 G. Ch. Toussaint to Alexander von Staël-Holstein	127
		此信日期不詳。	
		03 G. Ch. Toussaint to Alexander von Staël-Holstein	128
		此信日期不詳。	
136	Yinkoh Tschen	01 Yinkoh Tschen to Alexander von Staël-Holstein, Jan. 30, 1931	129

序號	書信人	信件擬目	頁碼
02		Alexander von Staël-Holstein to Yinkoh Tschen, Dec. ?, 1933	130
		此信無日期，信中提到下周六爲12月9日，查萬年曆，結合鋼和泰與陳寅恪的交往，當爲1933年，此年12月9日爲周六。此信寫於12月9日所在周的上一周，故大致在1933年12月初前後。	
03		Alexander von Staël-Holstein to Yinkoh Tschen, Mar. 28, 1935	131
04		Alexander von Staël-Holstein to Yinkoh Tschen, May?, 1935	132
		此信無日期，信中説取消5月11日（周六）的課程。結合陳寅恪與鋼和泰的交往，查萬年曆，可能的時間是1929年或1935年。此二年的5月11日都是周六。1929年5月前後鋼和泰正從哈佛返回北平，故此信應寫於1935年。考慮到此信大致應該是5月11日之前幾天通知陳寅恪取消課程，可以大致推定此信寫於1935年5月。	
05		Alexander von Staël-Holstein to Yinkoh Tschen, Jun. 25, 1935	133
06		Alexander von Staël-Holstein to Yinkoh Tschen, Summer ?, 1935	134
		此信無日期，信中提及爲哈佛燕京學社出版Woods紀念集約稿之事。鋼和泰1935年5月14日給趙元任的信向趙約稿，也是爲此事。故此信當寫於1935年。信中説陳寅恪和胡適將於8月15日前交稿，則此信大致寫於1935年暑期。	
07		Alexander von Staël-Holstein to Yinkoh Tschen, Aug. 15, 1935	135
08		Alexander von Staël-Holstein to Yinkoh Tschen, 1929、1930、1933、1935、1936？	136
		此信無日期，鋼和泰在信中説自己將去日本。鋼和泰1930年3月10日寫給Eliot的信提到記得1929年5月在奈良的情形，并説當年7月底將去日本。鋼和泰1936年7月給胡適的信中説："According to a Japanese Estonian convention, Estonian citizens travelling in Japan require no visés. I know this from my personal experience in 1933 and in 1935." 説明鋼和泰可能在1933或1935年去過日本或日本占據的中國的某地。另據鋼和泰1936年7月5日給胡適的信中説："We can then stay at 大連 or go on to Japan and return to Peking via 大連." 説明鋼和泰1936年也有計劃去日本。故此信可能寫於1929、1930、1933、1935、1936年。	

序號	書信人	信件擬目	頁碼
		附 01　Alexander von Staël-Holstein to someone	136
		此信與上一封信同在一頁，收信人不能辨識，暫繫於此。	
		09　Alexander von Staël-Holstein to Yinkoh Tschen	137
		此信日期不詳。	
		10　Alexander von Staël-Holstein to Yinkoh Tschen	138
		此信日期不詳。	
		11　Alexander von Staël-Holstein to Yinkoh Tschen ?, May ?, 1930 ?	139
		此信收信人爲 Doctor，與陳寅恪往來書信同放在 "Chen (Tschen) Prof. 回發" 信封中，暫繫於此。并此信無日期，信中提到 5 月 15 日是周四，大致是 1930 年，這一年 5 月 15 日是周四。大致推斷此信寫於 1930 年 5 月。	
		12　Alexander von Staël-Holstein to Someone	140
		此信無日期，無收信人。寫於鋼和泰 1935 年 8 月 15 日致陳寅恪一信的背面，暫繫於此。	
137	Tucci	01　Alexander von Staël-Holstein to Tucci, Aug. 17, 1934	141
		02　Alexander von Staël-Holstein to Tucci	144
		此信日期不詳。	
138	Vogel	01　Alexander von Staël-Holstein to Vogel, Jul. 25, 1933	145
		02　Alexander von Staël-Holstein to Vogel, Nov. 27, 1933	148
		03　Alexander von Staël-Holstein to Vogel	149
		此信日期不詳。	
139	M. Walleser	01　M. Walleser to Alexander von Staël-Holstein, Jan. 23, 1928	150
		02　M. Walleser to Alexander von Staël-Holstein, May. 16, 1928	151
		與前一封信同放在 "Walleser, M. 來" 信封内，内另有資料八頁，暫繫於此。	

序號	書信人	信件擬目	頁碼
		03 Alexander von Staël-Holstein to M. Walleser, Jul. 28, 1933	160
140	James R. Ware	01 Alexander von Staël-Holstein to James R. Ware, Sept. 2, 1934	161
		02 Alexander von Staël-Holstein to James R. Ware, Sept. 19, 1934	163
		03 Alexander von Staël-Holstein to James R. Ware, Dec. 26, 1934	165
		04 James R. Ware to Alexander von Staël-Holstein, Jul. 30, 1935	166
		05 Alexander von Staël-Holstein to James R. Ware, Jul. 31, 1935	167
		06 Alexander von Staël-Holstein to James R. Ware, Aug. 31, 1935	168
		07 James R. Ware to Alexander von Staël-Holstein, Oct. 23, 1935	170
		08 Alexander von Staël-Holstein to James R. Ware, 1935?	171
		此信無日期。開頭說:"Before you left Peking I told you about a Kanjur volume." Ware1935年寫給鋼和泰的信7月的地址爲北京，10月的地址爲麻省劍橋，故此信可能寫於1935年。另，第二頁寫於第一頁背面，似與此信無關，暫繫於此。	
		09 Alexander von Staël-Holstein to James R. Ware, Jan. 28, 1936	173
		10 James R. Ware to Alexander von Staël-Holstein, Oct. 2, 1936	174
		11 James R. Ware to Alexander von Staël-Holstein, Oct. 13, 1936	175
		12 Alexander von Staël-Holstein to James R. Ware, Nov. 12, 1936	176
		此信原無日期，開頭:"Dear Professor Ware, The Tibetan Lalitavistara can, as far as I know, not be procured in Peking, but I have sent two copies of the Tibetan Saddharmapundarika to Prof.	

序號	書信人	信件擬目	頁碼
		Clark and one to prof. Edgerton." 據 Ware 1937 年 1 月 25 日給鋼和泰的信："The copies of the Tibetan Saddharmapundarika, which you mention in your letter of November 12th, have been duly received by Professors Clark and Edgerton." 可知 Ware 1937 年 1 月 25 日一信當爲對鋼和泰此信的回復，故此信當寫於 1926 年 11 月 12 日。	
		13　James R. Ware to Alexander von Staël-Holstein, Jan. 25, 1937	177
		附 01　Harvard Yenching Institute to Alexander von Staël-Holstein, Apr. 22, 1936	178
		此信放在 "Ware, James R. 來" 信封内，暫繫於此。	
141	Langdon Warner	01　Langdon Warner to Alexander von Staël-Holstein, Apr. 17, 1929	179
		此信原僅署月日，信中説："The ills of poor old China can not be expected to more deeply either the fortunate bridegroom or the abstracted scholar ……"，説明鋼和泰已準備結婚，鋼和泰 1929 年 6 月結婚，故此信當寫於 1929 年。	
		附 01　Helen B. Chapin to Langdon Warner, Mar. 28, 1929	183
		02　Langdon Warner to Alexander von Staël-Holstein, Oct. 16, 1929	186
		03　Alexander von Staël-Holstein to Langdon Warner, Dec.?, 1929	190
		此信無日期，信中説："I am deeply touched by your kind congratulations and by the wonderful article in the New York Times." Warner 1929 年 10 月 16 日給鋼和泰的信末説："My wife joins me in sending to you and the bride very good wish …… P. S. I was delighted with the sympathetic and understanding article about you and your activities which I saw in the N. Y. Times." 故此信應爲對 Warner 1929 年 10 月 16 日一信的回復，考慮到鋼和泰信末還有 "Wishing you and Mrs. Warner a very happy New Year" 等語，故大致推斷此信寫於 1929 年 12 月。	
		04　Langdon Warner to Alexander von Staël-Holstein, Oct. 1, 1930	191
		05　Langdon Warner to Alexander von Staël-Holstein, Jan. 15, 1931	195

序號	書信人	信件擬目	頁碼
06		Alexander von Staël-Holstein to Langdon Warner, Jul. 7, 1931	199
07		Langdon Warner to Alexander von Staël-Holstein, Jul. 14, 1931	201
08		Langdon Warner to Alexander von Staël-Holstein, Jul. 18, 1931	203
09		Alexander von Staël-Holstein to Langdon Warner, Aug. ?, 1931	205
		此信無日期，開頭説："Many thanks for your note dated July 18th from which I learn that you will reach Cambridge towards the end of this month ……"，Warner 1931 年 7 月 18 日寫給鋼和泰信箋爲 Harvard University, Fogg Art Museum 的信中説："As my collotype illustrations can not be done till after Sept. 1st at best, I've decided to dash home at once ……"，據兩封信的内容，此信當寫於 1931 年 8 月。	
10		Langdon Warner to Alexander von Staël-Holstein, Sept. 28, 1931	209
11		Langdon Warner to Alexander von Staël-Holstein, Sept. 29, 1931	211
		此電報僅有月日，電文説："Collection arrived." Warner 1931 年 9 月 28 日給鋼和泰的信開頭説："Your boxes arrived yesterday ……"，故此信電報的年代當爲 1931 年。	
12		Alexander von Staël-Holstein to Langdon Warner, Oct.?, 1931?	212
		此信無日期，開頭説："Many thanks for your letter dated Sept. 1931. I am so glad to hear that you have safely returned to Cambridge, and I am very much obliged to you for having seen my collection through the customs." Warner 1931 年 9 月 28 日給鋼和泰的信中説："Your boxes arrived yesterday (12 of them) and are to be examined by the customs ……"，故此信應爲對 Warner 1931 年 9 月 28 日一信的回復，可能寫於 1931 年 10 月。	
13		Alexander von Staël-Holstein to Langdon Warner, 1931?	214
		此信無日期，信中説："I am very much obliged to you for writing: 'I will do my best to sell the collection in America.'" 鋼和泰另一封給 Warner 的信日期大約爲 1931 年 10 月的信中説："I am very much obliged to you for having seen my collection	

序號	書信人	信件擬目	頁碼
		through the customs. What has happened to the cataloges?" 鋼和泰想賣掉一部分收藏，大致可以推測此信寫於 1931 年。另，信開頭說："Your kind note dated Sept. 3rd reached me …… towards the end of that month. I delayed my reply ……"，故此信可能寫於 10 月或之後。	
		14 Langdon Warner to Alexander von Staël-Holstein, Jan. 18, 1933	218
		15 Langdon Warner to Alexander von Staël-Holstein, Jan. 12, 1934	224
		16 Langdon Warner to Alexander von Staël-Holstein, Feb. 9, 1934	230
		17 Alexander von Staël-Holstein to Langdon Warner, Sept. 1, 1934	232
		18 Langdon Warner to Alexander von Staël-Holstein, Oct. 1, 1934	239
		19 Alexander von Staël-Holstein to Langdon Warner, Feb. 14, 1935	243
		20 Alexander von Staël-Holstein to Langdon Warner, Feb. 14, 1935	248
		21 Langdon Warner to Alexander von Staël-Holstein, Mar. 9, 1935	249
		22 Alexander von Staël-Holstein to Langdon Warner, Oct. 22, 1935	251
		23 Langdon Warner to Alexander von Staël-Holstein, Feb. 17, 1936	253
		24 Langdon Warner to Alexander von Staël-Holstein, Feb. 17, 1937	255
		此信年代 36 旁有鉛筆書 "7"，或此信寫於 1937 年。	
142	Friedrich Weller	01 Friedrich Weller to Alexander von Staël-Holstein, Jan. 19, 1930	259
		02 Friedrich Weller to Alexander von Staël-Holstein, Jul. 26, 1930	260

序號	書信人	信件擬目	頁碼
		03 Friedrich Weller to Alexander von Staël-Holstein, Aug. 22, 1930	263
		04 Friedrich Weller to Alexander von Staël-Holstein, Aug. 28, 1930	264
		05 Friedrich Weller to Alexander von Staël-Holstein, Nov. 23, 1930	266
		06 Friedrich Weller to Alexander von Staël-Holstein, Dec. 16, 1930	268
		07 Friedrich Weller to Alexander von Staël-Holstein, Aug. 10, 1931	269
		08 Friedrich Weller to Alexander von Staël-Holstein, Aug. 15, 1931	273
		09 Friedrich Weller to Alexander von Staël-Holstein, Jan. 16, 1932	274
		第二頁可能爲 Weller 給鋼和泰《大寶積經迦葉品梵藏漢六種合刊》一書的評論，寫於 1931 年 9 月 13 日，暫繫於此。	
		10 Friedrich Weller to Alexander von Staël-Holstein, Jul. 16, 1932	276
		11 Friedrich Weller to Alexander von Staël-Holstein, Jul. 26, 1932	278
		12 Friedrich Weller to Alexander von Staël-Holstein, Mar. 30, 1933	280
		13 Friedrich Weller to Alexander von Staël-Holstein, Apr. 16, 1933	281
		14 Friedrich Weller to Alexander von Staël-Holstein, Jun. 12, 1933	288
		15 Friedrich Weller to Alexander von Staël-Holstein, Jul. 14, 1933	290
		16 Friedrich Weller to Alexander von Staël-Holstein, Aug. 25, 1933	292

序號	書信人	信件擬目	頁碼
		17 Friedrich Weller to Alexander von Staël-Holstein, Sept. 16, 1933	294
		18 Friedrich Weller to Alexander von Staël-Holstein, Dec. 26, 1933	296
		此信月份誤作"13"。	
		19 Friedrich Weller to Alexander von Staël-Holstein, Apr. 30, 1934	297
		20 Friedrich Weller to Alexander von Staël-Holstein, Oct. 2, 1934	299
		21 Friedrich Weller to Alexander von Staël-Holstein, May 5, 1935	302
		22 Friedrich Weller to Alexander von Staël-Holstein, Jun. 4, 1935	304
		23 Friedrich Weller to Alexander von Staël-Holstein, Jan. 1, 1936	306
		24 Friedrich Weller to Alexander von Staël-Holstein, Feb. 20, 1936	308
		25 Friedrich Weller to Alexander von Staël-Holstein, Feb. 4, 1937	310
		26 Alexander von Staël-Holstein to Friedrich Weller	312
		此信日期不詳。最後一頁與此信無關，爲鋼和泰所寫，原放在"Weller, Friedrich 來"信封内，暫繫於此。	
143	Wen Yu	01 Wen Yu to Alexander von Staël-Holstein, Jun. 9, 1936	316
144	Mdez Wickremasinghe	01 Mdez Wickremasinghe to Alexander von Staël-Holstein, Jul. 31, 1931	317
145	Wilfort	01 Alexander von Staël-Holstein to Mr. Wilfort, Nov. ?, 1936	318
		此信無日期，原放在"Ware, James 回發"信封内，寫於鋼和泰 1936 年 11 月 12 日致 Ware 一信下半頁，時間應該相近，故暫定爲 1936 年 11 月。	

序號	書信人	信件擬目	頁碼
146	U. Wogihara	01 U. Wogihara to Alexander von Staël-Holstein, Jun. 28, 1916	319
		02 U. Wogihara to Alexander von Staël-Holstein, Oct. 13, 1916	321
		03 U. Wogihara to Alexander von Staël-Holstein, Oct. 22, 1916	323
		04 U. Wogihara to Alexander von Staël-Holstein, Dec. 10, 1916	325
		05 U. Wogihara to Alexander von Staël-Holstein, Feb. 25, 1917	328
147	Wong Wenhao	01 Wong Wenhao to Alexander von Staël-Holstein, Jun.15, 1925	329
		02 Wong Wenhao to Alexander von Staël-Holstein, Jun.17, 1925	331
		此信與翁文灝同月 15 日寫給鋼和泰的信內容基本相同，僅多出信末的附言。	
		03 Wong Wenhao to Alexander von Staël-Holstein, Jun.29, 1925	333
		04 Alexander von Staël-Holstein to Wong Wenhao, Summer, 1925	334
		此信寫於翁文灝 1925 年 6 月 17 日致鋼和泰一信的背面，應爲對翁文灝一信的回復，無日期，從翁文灝同年 7 月的回信致謝看，此信大致應在 1925 年六七月間。	
		05 Alexander von Staël-Holstein to Wong Wenhao, Jul.?, 1925	335
		此信無日期，應爲對翁文灝 1925 年 6 月請教鋼和泰的三封信的回復，從翁文灝同年 7 月的回信致謝看，此信大致應在 1925 年 7 月初。	
		06 Wong Wenhao to Alexander von Staël-Holstein, Jul.8, 1925	338
		07 Wong Wenhao to Alexander von Staël-Holstein, Jul. 14, 1925	340

序號	書信人	信件擬目	頁碼
		08 Alexander von Staël-Holstein to Wong Wenhao, 1925	341
		此信無年代，寫於鋼和泰 1925 年夏寫給 Sohtsu G. King 書信的背面，時間應比較接近，暫定爲 1925 年。收信人 Dr. Wong 應爲翁文灝。	
148	Y. W. Wong	01 Y. W. Wong to Alexander von Staël-Holstein, Apr. 20, 1922	342
		02 Y. W. Wong to Alexander von Staël-Holstein, May 6, 1922	343
		03 Alexander von Staël-Holstein to Commercial Press, May 18, 1922	344
		此信無日期。信中説："I am in receipt of your letters dated April 20th and May 6th, 1922. ……I enclose the second proofs of pages 18–59 of the 大寶積經, which I have signed." 查商務印書館致鋼和泰書信，5 月 6 日之後的書信爲 6 月 14 日，信中説："In reply to your favour dated 18th ult., we beg to inform you that we have already corrected the second proofs of pages 18–59 as shown ……"，"18th ult." 意即上月 18 日，故可推定，此信寫於 1922 年 5 月 18 日。	
		04 Y. W. Wong to Alexander von Staël-Holstein, Jun. 14, 1922	346
		05 Y. W. Wong to Alexander von Staël-Holstein, Oct. 4, 1922	347
		06 Commercial Press to Alexander von Staël-Holstein, Dec. 20, 1922	348
		07 Commercial Press to Alexander von Staël-Holstein, Dec. 31, 1922	349
		08 Alexander von Staël-Holstein to Commercial Press, Feb.-Sept.?, 1923	350
		此信無日期，信中説："Many thanks for the second proofs of the pages 106–143"，并説："I also offer you my apologies for the delay which was caused by my illness." 查商務印書館給鋼和泰的書信，1922 年 12 月 31 日寄給鋼和泰的是一校 122—143 頁，此後商務給鋼和泰的信的日期爲 1923 年 9 月 29 日，寄的是一校 170—188 頁，再後是 1923 年 11 月 23 日，寄的是二校 144—188 頁。則此信大致應在 1923 年 1 月至 9 月間，考慮鋼和泰此信中因病推遲校對，大致推斷此信寫於 1923 年 2—9 月間。	

序號	書信人	信件擬目	頁碼
09		Y. W. Wong to Alexander von Staël-Holstein, Sept. 29, 1923	352
10		Y. W. Wong to Alexander von Staël-Holstein, Nov. 23, 1923	353
11		Alexander von Staël-Holstein to Commercial Press, Dec.?, 1923	354
		此信無日期，開頭説："I enclose the second proofs of pages 144-188 of the Ta-Pao-chi-ching corrected and signed by myself." 查商務印書館致鋼和泰書信，1923 年 11 月 23 日的信中説："Under separate cover we beg to send you 5 copies of the 2nd proofs of the Pao-chi-ching, from page 144 to 188 ……"，故此信爲鋼和泰對商務印書館 1923 年 11 月 23 日一信的回復，大致應在 1923 年 12 月前後。《年譜簡編》推測爲 1924 年 1 月。	
12		Y. W. Wong to Alexander von Staël-Holstein, Sept. 29, 1924	356
13		Alexander von Staël-Holstein to Commercial Press, Mar. 1, 1925	357
14		Y. W. Wong to Alexander von Staël-Holstein, Mar. 24, 1925	358
15		Alexander von Staël-Holstein to Commercial Press, Aug. 31, 1925	359
16		Alexander von Staël-Holstein to Commercial Press, Sept. 19, 1925	362
17		Alexander von Staël-Holstein to Commercial Press, Sept. 26, 1925	364
18		Baen E. Lee to Alexander von Staël-Holstein, Oct. 2, 1925	366
		《年譜簡編》僅辨識出 B. E. Lee，也未能考證出此人爲李培恩。	
19		Alexander von Staël-Holstein to Commercial Press, Oct. 7, 1925	367
20		Alexander von Staël-Holstein to Commercial Press, Feb. 18, 1926	368

序號	書信人	信件擬目	頁碼
		21　Y. W. Wong to Alexander von Staël-Holstein, Jun. 18, 1926	370
		22　Alexander von Staël-Holstein to Commercial Press, Jul. 8, 1926	371
		23　Y. W. Wong to Alexander von Staël-Holstein, Aug. 28, 1926	373
		24　Alexander von Staël-Holstein to Commercial Press, Sept. 8, 1926	374
		25　Y. W. Wong to Alexander von Staël-Holstein, Sept. 18, 1926	376
		26　Y. W. Wong to Alexander von Staël-Holstein, Dec. 15, 1926	377
149	James H. Woods	01　James H. Woods to Alexander von Staël-Holstein, Feb. 10, 1921	378
		02　James H. Woods to Alexander von Staël-Holstein, Feb. 19, 1921	379
		03　James H. Woods to Alexander von Staël-Holstein, Jun. 3, 1921	380
		04　Alexander von Staël-Holstein to James H. Woods, 1924	381
		此信無日期，開頭說："Dear Professor Woods, About three years ago you asked me to send you one copy of the best Chinese translation of the Vajracchedikā and one copy of the Tibetan translation of the same work." Woods 1921 年 2 月 19 日致鋼和泰的信中說："Will you allow me to ask whether some one of the pundits whom you know could secure me a Tibetan copy of the Vajracchedikā printed separately in a small volume? I should also be glad if a similar small copy could be found in Chinese." 故此信當寫於 1924 年。	
		05　James H. Woods to Alexander von Staël-Holstein, Oct. 21, 1925	382
		06　Alexander von Staël-Holstein to James H. Woods, Jan.?, 1929	383
		此信無日期，開頭說："On December 20th I told Dean Chase	

序號	書信人	信件擬目	頁碼

that I thank you all very much indeed and that I will accept the Peking position ……", 信中所説的 "Peking position" 應指哈佛燕京學社聘請鋼和泰主持中印研究所。鋼和泰寫此信時可能還在哈佛，從鋼和泰在哈佛的時間看，信中的 12 月祇能是 1928 年 12 月，此信寫於此時間之後，故大致應在 1929 年初。

07		James H. Woods to Alexander von Staël-Holstein, May 10, 1929	388
08		James H. Woods to Alexander von Staël-Holstein, Jul. 24, 1929	389
09		Alexander von Staël-Holstein to James H. Woods, Sept. ? 1929	390

此信無日期，從行文看似是電文，因與此信起草在同一頁的另一封信寫於 1929 年 9 月 4 日，此信可能大致寫於 1929 年 9 月前後。此外，鋼和泰此信寄給 Woods 的地址爲 Empress France，與 Woods 1929 年 9 月 6 日給鋼和泰的信所留的地址相同，爲客輪的名字。信中提到 9 月 21 日或 22 日到北平，與鋼和泰此信中請 Woods 電告到北平日期相呼應。

10		James H. Woods to Alexander von Staël-Holstein, Spet. 6, 1929	391
11		James H. Woods to Alexander von Staël-Holstein, Sept. 11, 1929	394
12		Alexander von Staël-Holstein to James H. Woods, Sept.?, 1929	396

此信無日期，開頭説："I am very glad to hear from Damiéville that you will proceed to China without stopping in Japan." Woods 1929 年 9 月 6 日的信中説："Our plans are slightly changed. Instead of taking the P. O. boat Mantua to Shanghai arrives there about Sept. 21, we wil take the N. Y. K. boat from Kobe on Sept 16 and arrive at Tiensin about September 20. I do not know whether we can catch the train to Peking on the same day.or on the next day the 21st. We should be obliged to you if you could reserve a room with two beds and a bath at the Wagon Lib." 鋼和泰此信中説："Shall I reserve rooms for you at the Hotel de Pékin or at the Hôtel des Wagons-Lits？" 據此，此信當寫於 1929 年 9 月前後。

附 01		James H. Woods to John Leighton Stuart, Oct. 3, 1929	397

此信爲 Woods 致司徒雷登書信的抄送件，最後一頁爲鋼和泰鉛筆抄録資料，暫繫於此。

序號	書信人	信件擬目	頁碼
13		Alexander von Staël-Holstein to James H. Woods, Oct. 3, 1929	400
14		Alexander von Staël-Holstein to James H. Woods, Oct. ?, 1929	401
		此信無日期，與此信在同一頁的鋼和泰致袁同禮的信寫於1929年10月初，同頁另一封鋼和泰致 de Tscharuer 夫婦的法文信寫於10月8日，故可大致推定此信寫於1929年10月初。	
15		James H. Woods to Alexander von Staël-Holstein, Oct. 22, 1929	402
16		Alexander von Staël-Holstein to James H. Woods, Oct. 24, 1929	403
17		James H. Woods to Alexander von Staël-Holstein, Nov. 14, 1929	405
18		Alexander von Staël-Holstein to James H. Woods, Nov.?, 1929	408
		此信無開頭，無日期，信中說："……1/12 part of the sums allotted to 'Sino-Indian Studies' should be paid to me by Yenching on August 1st 1929. But August 1st, September 1st, October 1st passed without any funds reaching me from Yenching." 又說："On Wednesday November 6th Professor Porter promised me in your presence to send me the long delayed cheque for my representation expenses at once. This promise was made days ago." 故此信大致寫於1929年11月。另，此信最後一頁寫於第三頁背面，暫繫於此。	
19		Alexander von Staël-Holstein to James H. Woods, Dec. 5, 1929	412
20		Alexander von Staël-Holstein to James H. Woods, Dec. 10, 1929	414
21		Alexander von Staël-Holstein to James H. Woods, Dec. 22, 1929	422
22		Alexander von Staël-Holstein to James H. Woods, 1929	426
		此信無日期，信中提到與 Woods 等人在 Wagons-Libs 開會，地點應是 Woods 在北京入住的酒店，Woods 1929年9月下旬到北平，故此信大致寫於1929年10月或之後。	

序號	書信人	信件擬目	頁碼
23		Alexander von Staël-Holstein to James H. Woods, Dec. ?, 1929	430
		此信無首頁，無日期，信中説："On November 6th Professor Porter definitely promised in your presence to pay me certain sums ……As I already wrote you he paid me the accumulated sums for July August and September on November 18th …… I thought that he might let me have the October November and December sums together at the end of December, but he has not done so." 鋼和泰 1929 年 12 月 10 日給 Woods 的信中説："Professor Porter promised on November 6th at the Wagons Lits Hotel in your presence to send me a cheque covering my representation expenses for four months at once." 故此信大致寫於 1929 年 12 月底或 1930 年初。	
24		Alexander von Staël-Holstein to James H. Woods, Winter, 1929	433
		此信無頭尾，無日期，信中説："During the academic year 1929/1930 I conducted the following classes"，説明此信至少寫於 1929—1930 學年之後，信中又説："Since my return to Peking, eighteen months ago"，據《年譜簡編》，鋼和泰 1929 年 5 月從哈佛回北平，故此信大致寫於 1930 年 11 月底前後。	
25		Alexander von Staël-Holstein to James H. Woods, Jan. 4, 1930	435
26		Alexander von Staël-Holstein to James H. Woods, Feb.?, 1930	438
		此信無日期，開頭説："Only a few lines to thank you for having spoken to President Stuart about our funds. He has wired to Professor Porter who called here with the telegram a few days ago. As a result of that telegram Pankrat off received his January cheque which had evidently been forgotten, on Feburary 5th." 由此大致可以推斷，此信寫於 1929 年底或 1930 年初鋼和泰致 Woods 抱怨博晨光撥給經費不及時一信之後，大致在 1930 年 2 月或之後。	
27		James H. Woods to Alexander von Staël-Holstein, Nov. 30, 1930	440
28		Alexander von Staël-Holstein to James H. Woods, Dec.?, 1930	443
		此信無日期，信末説："My wife and I send you and Mrs. Woods our best New Year's greetings." P. S. 説："I shall regard it as a great favour if you will send me a deferred (LCO) telegram indicating in a few words that the fire of your indignation (Kopāgni) is	

序號	書信人	信件擬目	頁碼
		no longer blazing as fiercely as it did on November 30th 1930." 第一頁又説: "Please do forgive me! Your annoyance is principally due to my failure to indicate the title of the Chinese Vajracchedikā Commentary." 故此信或爲對 Woods 1930 年 11 月 30 日發怒一信的回復，時間大致在 1930 年 12 月。	
29		James H. Woods to Alexander von Staël-Holstein, Apr. 19, 1931	461
30		Alexander von Staël-Holstein to James H. Woods, Nov. 18, 1931	463
		此信包括手寫草稿和打印件兩份。	
31		Alexander von Staël-Holstein to James H. Woods, Nov.?, 1931	488
		此信無日期，開頭説: "On account of the Manchurian crisis great excitement reigns everywhere in China"，這裏的 "Manchurian crisis" 應指 1931 年的 "九一八事變"。信中又説: "send you my best Christmas greetings"，加之此信背面鋼和泰寫給 Woods 夫人的信的日期爲 1931 年 11 月 21 日，故可大致推定此信寫於 1931 年 11 月底前後。	
32		James H. Woods to Alexander von Staël-Holstein, Dec. 28, 1931	489
33		James H. Woods to Alexander von Staël-Holstein, Jan. 18, 1932	491
34		Alexander von Staël-Holstein to James H. Woods, Mar. 2, 1933	493
		此信無日期，開頭説: "On February 28th 1933 I wrote a long letter which was primarily intended for you. I despatched it to-day on March 2nd 1933." 故此信寫於 1933 年 3 月 2 日。	
35		Alexander von Staël-Holstein to James H. Woods, Feb. 27, 1934	494
36		James H. Woods to Alexander von Staël-Holstein, Dec. 4, 1934	495
37		Alexander von Staël-Holstein to James H. Woods	498
		此信日期不詳。	

序號	書信人	信件擬目	頁碼
		38　Alexander von Staël-Holstein to James H. Woods	499
		此信日期不詳，無開頭結尾。	
		39　Alexander von Staël-Holstein to James H. Woods	500
		此信日期不詳，無開頭結尾。	
		附 01　Alexander von Staël-Holstein to Comte, 1929	500
		此信寫於鋼和泰大約 1929 年 9 月致 Woods 一信的背面，無日期，時間大致接近，故暫定爲 1929 年。收信人無姓名，僅署爲 "Comte"，暫繫於此。	
		附 02　Alexander von Staël-Holstein to Mrs. Woods, Nov. 21, 1931	501
		此信寫於鋼和泰 1931 年 11 月致 Woods 一信的背面，收件人爲 Woods 夫人，暫繫於此。	
		附 03　Alexander von Staël-Holstein to Mr. & Mrs. Birkhoff, Bingham, Chases Kinder, Lattimore, Garder	502
		此信日期不詳，放在 "Woods, James H. 回發" 信封内，暫繫於此。	
150	Wrangell	01　Baron Wrangell to Alexander von Staël-Holstein, Jul. 4, 1917	503
		02　Baron Wrangell to Alexander von Staël-Holstein, Feb. 3, 1918	507
		03　Baron Wrangell to Alexander von Staël-Holstein, Nov. 11, 1928	511
		04　Alexander von Staël-Holstein to Baron Wrangell, Nov.?, 1933	513
		此信無日期，德文，開頭説："Meine besten Dank für Ihren Brief von 17 XI 33"，意即謝謝對方 1933 年 11 月 17 日的來信，大致推斷此信寫於 1933 年 11 月底前後。	
151	Dr. Yasumura	01　Alexander von Staël-Holstein to Dr. Yasumura, Jun. 20, 1934	515

序號	書信人	信件擬目	頁碼
152	Yü Daochuan	01　Alexander von Staël-Holstein to Yü Daochuan, Jun. 19, 1925	518
		此信寫於 John C. Ferguson 1925 年 6 月 13 日致鋼和泰一信的背面，收信人爲 "Mr. Yü"，從時間和書信內容判斷，應爲于道泉。	
		02　Yü Daochuan to Alexander von Staël-Holstein, Autumn, 1925	519
		此信無日期，此信的內容説明自己陷於困頓之中。于道泉 1925 年 10 月 6 日的信中開頭説："I received your letter with ten dollars this morning. Thank your so very much for your kindness; but since my impudence of that day has given you enough trouble, I do not wish to give you more, so I send the money back by post." 此信當在此之前。大約九十月間。	
		03　Yü Daochuan to Alexander von Staël-Holstein, Oct. 6, 1925	524
153	T. K. Yu	01　T. K. Yu, to Alexander von Staël-Holstein, Feb. 26, 1930	529
		02　T. K. Yu, to Alexander von Staël-Holstein, Oct. 29, 1932	530
154	Yuan Tungli	01　Alexander von Staël-Holstein to Yuan Tungli, 1926?	531
		此信無日期，信中説："I have distributed most of the sixty copies of the commentary which I received from the Commercial Press." 信中提到的商務印書館出版的書應指《大寶積經迦葉品梵藏漢六種合刊》，此書出版於 1926 年，信中開列了鋼和泰寄贈給一些學者、學術機構的清單，大致推斷此信寫於 1926 年底前後。	
		02　Yuan Tungli to Alexander von Staël-Holstein, Jun. 13, 1929	533
		03　Alexander von Staël-Holstein to Yuan Tungli, Oct. ?, 1929	534
		此信與鋼和泰 1929 年 10 月致 James H. Woods 寫在同一頁，無日期，信中説："I have much pleasure in accepting your kind invitation for Wednesday October 9th"，查萬年曆，1929 年 10 月 9 日为周三，故此信大致寫於 1929 年 10 月初。	
		04　Yuan Tungli to Alexander von Staël-Holstein, Mar. 7, 1930	535

序號	書信人	信件擬目	頁碼
		05 Yuan Tungli to Alexander von Staël-Holstein, Jun. 17, 1932	536
		06 Alexander von Staël-Holstein to Yuan Tungli, Jul. 18, 1932	537
		07 Alexander von Staël-Holstein to Yuan Tungli, Aug. 28, 1933	538
		08 Alexander von Staël-Holstein to Yuan Tungli, Aug.?, 1933	539
		此信無日期，信中説："I now do know of a scholar who will be able to continue Mr. Lin's indexing work in Peking"，這裏的"Mr. Lin"應指林藜光，林藜光1933年底到巴黎任東方語言學校 (l'École des Langues Orientales de Paris) 中文講師。信中删掉的内容有"I shall wish him 'bon voyage' at the station"等語，説明林藜光此時尚未離開北平。另，此信背面鋼和泰寫給 Mrs. Creel 的信，日期大致爲1933年8月，故此信大致寫於1933年8月前後。	
		09 Alexander von Staël-Holstein to Yuan Tungli, 1933?	540
		此信寫於鋼和泰1933年5月24日致 Father Mostaert 一信的背面，無日期，大致寫於1933年。收信人原寫爲"Professor Yuan"，信中提到"Ching Hua Yin Shu Chü"即清華印書處，袁同禮曾任清華圖書館館長，此 Professor Yuan 或即爲袁同禮。	
		10 Alexander von Staël-Holstein to Yuan Tungli, Jul. 10, 1936	541
		11 Alexander von Staël-Holstein to Yuan Tungli	542
		此信日期不詳。	
155	Erwin Zach	01 Erwin Zach to Alexander von Staël-Holstein, Jun. 23, 1936	543
156	Letters Unidentified	01 Alexander von Staël-Holstein to Someone, Feb. 28, 1917	544
		此信收信人無法辨識。	
		02 Someone to Alexander von Staël-Holstein, Oct. 19, 1927	546
		此信寫信人簽名無法辨識。	

序號	書信人	信件擬目	頁碼
		03 Alexander von Staël-Holstein to Someone, Sept. 2, 1929	550
		此信收信人寫爲"Monsieur et Collègue"，具體不詳。	
		04 Someone to Alexander von Staël-Holstein, May 3, 1932	551
		此信寫信人簽名無法辨識。	
		05 Someone to Someone，Dec. 28	552
		此信收信人、寫信人不能辨識，日期僅見月日。暫繫於此。	
157	顧頡剛	01 顧頡剛致鋼和泰，1933 年 12 月 2 日	556
		此信非鋼和泰親筆。	
		02 顧頡剛致鋼和泰，1934 年 1 月 22 日	557
		此信僅署月日，信中説擬將鋼和泰一篇論文發表在《燕京學報》第 15 期，此期 1934 年 6 月出版，故此信當寫於 1934 年 1 月 22 日。	
158	國立北京大學研究所國學門	01 國立北京大學研究所國學門致鋼和泰，1923 年 11 月 4 日	558
		02 國立北京大學研究所國學門致鋼和泰，1924 年 1 月 15 日	559
		此信僅署月日，信中請鋼和泰辨別一種文字拓片屬何種文字，另國學門 1924 年 5 月 13 日給鋼和泰的信中也有類似的内容，故暫定此信爲 1924 年。	
		03 國立北京大學研究所國學門致鋼和泰，1924 年 5 月 13 日	561
159	黄文弼	黄文弼致鋼和泰，8 月 11 日	563
		此信僅署月日，無年代。	
160	梅光羲	01 梅光羲致鋼和泰，1928 年 6 月 9 日	565
161	容庚	01 容庚致鋼和泰，1934 年 9 月 12 日	572
		此信僅署月日,無年代。信中提到 9 月 19 日周三，查萬年曆，當爲 1934 年。	

序號	書信人	信件擬目	頁碼
162	周用　梁寶羅	01　周用、梁寶羅致鋼和泰，1930年10月2日	573
		此信僅署10月2日，無年代，信中説："日昨無意中在《海潮音》雜誌看見先生主持的中印研究院的相片"，查《海潮音》，當指1930年第11卷第5期刊載的《太虛法師應剛俄泰博士邀觀中印研究院攝影》（編者注：鋼和泰之名原文作"剛俄泰"），故大致推定此信寫於1930年10月2日。	
163	山室三良	01　山室三良致鋼和泰，1936年11月26日	576
		此信僅署月日，信中提到北平近代科學圖書館將於12月5日舉行開幕典禮，查北平近代科學圖書館成立於1936年，故此信當寫於1936年。	
164	新駒	01　新駒致鋼和泰，8月3日	577
		此信僅署月日，年代不詳，寫信人姓名不全。	
		附01　Beim Pantschen Lama	578
		此爲Erwin Rousselle所寫關於班禪的文章，原放在"Rousselle, Erwin 來"信封内，疑爲作者寫給鋼和泰的信所附，書信遺失。暫繫於此。	

書信人簡介

117 E. Denison Ross（1871—1940）

英國東方學家、語言學家。早年就讀於倫敦大學學院（University College London），後留學巴黎、斯特拉斯堡學習東方語言，特別是阿拉伯語和波斯語。1896—1901年任倫敦大學學院波斯語教授。1901年任加爾各答伊斯蘭大學（Calcutta Madrasah）校長。1914年回英國，任大英博物館印刷與繪畫部助理。1916—1937年任東方研究學院（School of Oriental Studies）首任院長，同時兼任倫敦大學波斯語教授，1938年退休。1940年被聘爲英國情報局駐伊斯坦布爾顧問。曾任英國皇家亞洲學會主席、中國學會主席。

118 Brice J. Sachs

生平不詳。

119 Paul J. Sachs（1878—1965）

美國博物館學家。1900年畢業於哈佛大學，畢業後參與家族生意。1914年被聘爲哈佛大學福格藝術博物館（Fogg Art Museum）副館長。1916—1917年被聘爲衛斯理學院（Wellesley College）藝術講師。1917年被聘爲哈佛大學藝術系助理教授，1927年被聘爲教授，1942年獲哈佛大學榮譽博士學位，1945年退休，1948年獲榮譽退休教授稱號。1929年參與創辦紐約現代藝術博物館，并長期擔任執行董事、榮譽董事。1932—1965年曾任波士頓美術博物館董事會董事。

120 Kenneth J. Saunders（1883—1937）

美國佛教學者。曾任教於加州大學，從事佛教研究。曾參加印度宗教研究會，游歷東亞，訪問斯里蘭卡、日本、中國西藏等地名刹。著有《佛教的終極理想》（*Buddhist Ideals*）、《亞洲的福音》（*The*

Gospel for Asia)、《佛教心靈》(The Heart of Buddhism)、《東西方終極理想》(The Ideals East and West)、《佛教故事》(The Story for Buddhism)等。

121 Catherine Scholer

生平不詳。

122 K. M. Sen（？—1906）

Kshiti Mohan Sen，印度學者，早年就讀於印度貝拿勒斯梵文學校，精通梵文和許多現代印度語言，并成爲印度宗教文本專家。主要研究梵文和古代、中世紀印度文化，曾在泰戈爾創辦的學院任教。著有《印度中世紀神秘主義》、《印度教》等。

123 Kurakichi Shiratori（1865—1942）

白鳥庫吉，日本東洋史權威、漢學家。1883 年入大學預備科。1997 年入東京帝國大學史學科，1890 年畢業，後任學習院教授、歷史地理課課長。1901 年到歐洲游學，入柏林大學學習中國學，後到匈牙利留學，1903 年回國。次年兼任東京帝國大學文科大學史學科助教授。1906 年游歷朝鮮和中國東北。1909 年創辦《東洋學報》。1910 年組織學術團體到中國東北進行實地調查。1911 年任東京帝國大學教授，兼學習院教授。1912 年代理學習院院長。1914 年被任命爲東宫學問所官員。1919 年當選帝國學士會會員。1922 年出訪歐美各國，接受法國授予的文化功勞紀念勛章。1923 年任東洋文庫理事兼研究部長。1925 年從東京大學退休，爲名譽教授。1934 年任日本民族學會首任理事長。主要研究整個亞洲各民族的語言和歷史，特別是中亞細亞、中國東北和蒙古歷史，主要著作有《西洋歷史》、《西域史研究》、《音譯蒙文元朝秘史》、《神代史的新研究》、《支那古代史批判》，有《白鳥庫吉全集》。

124 Lawrence Sickman（1907—1988）

美國藝術史家、漢學家。1930 年畢業於哈佛大學，後獲哈佛燕京學社獎學金到中國游學，曾在鋼和泰主持的中印研究所學習梵文和漢文佛典。1931 年任職於内爾森—阿特金斯藝術博物館（Nelson—Atkins Museum of Art），1935 年任該館東方藝術部主任。二戰後曾到日本服務。1953—1977 年任内爾森—阿特金斯藝術博物館館長。著有《中國的藝術與建築》（The Art and Architecture of China）等。

125 Osvald Sirén（1879—1959）

喜仁龍，瑞典學者。1900 年、1929 年兩度來華，拍攝北京和其他各地的名勝古迹編輯出版。著有《北京的城墻和城門》（*The Walls and Gates of Peking*）、《中國雕塑》（*Chinese Sculpture*）、《中國繪畫史》（*Histoire de la Peinture Chinoise*）、《中國園林》（*Gardens of China*）等。

126 George E. Sokolsky（1893—1963）

索克思，美國新聞專欄作者。1917 年畢業於哥倫比亞大學，畢業後到俄羅斯，爲《俄羅斯日報》撰稿。1918 年來華，任《華北明星報》（*North China Star*）副編輯。後任直隸警察廳廳長顧問、上海美國同學會顧問。1920 年任中華共同通訊社（China Bureau of Public Information）經理。1921—1924 年任職於上海商報印刷有限公司。曾擔任孫中山政治顧問。後任美國報紙駐上海通訊員。1928 年任《遠東時報》（*Far Eastern Review*）副編輯。1935 年回國。著有《世界史大綱》（*An Outline of Universal History*）、《中東鐵路見聞》（*The Story of Chinese Eastern Railway*）、《亞洲的導火綫》（*The Tinder Box of Asia*）等。

127 John Leighton Stuart（1876—1962）

司徒雷登，美國來華傳教士、教育家。1876 年生於杭州。1887 年返美求學。1896 年畢業於漢普登悉尼學院，獲文學士學位。1902 年獲弗吉尼亞州南長老會協和神學院神學士學位。1904 年來華，在杭州傳教。1908—1919 年任教於南京金陵神學院。1919 年參與創辦燕京大學，任校長。1929 年改任校務長。1941 年太平洋戰争爆發後，曾被日軍囚禁北平。1946 年出任美國駐華大使。1949 年 8 月離開中國。1962 年卒於華盛頓。著有《在華五十年——司徒雷登回憶錄》。

128 S. Tachibana（1886—1931）

或 Seiji Tachibana，橘靜二，曾任教於早稻田大學。

129 Teng Ping（Ruyin）

生平不詳。

130 F. W. Thomas（1867—1956）

Frederick William Thomas，英國印度學家、藏學家。早年就讀於劍橋大學，師從考威爾（Edward Byles Cowell）學習梵文。1898—1927 年任印度辦公室圖書館（Indian Office Library）館長。1927—1937 年任牛津大學波登梵文講座教授（Boden Professor of Sanskrit）。著有《與中國新疆有關的西藏文本和文獻》（*Tibetan literary texts and documents concerning Chinese Turkestan*）《藏東北古代民族文獻》（*Tibetan literary texts and documents concerning Chinese Turkestan*）等。

131 Mr. Thomas

生平不詳。

132 Daniel V. Thompson Jr.

生平不詳。據信箋，上世紀 20 年代曾隨哈佛大學福格博物館考察隊來華，到過北京和甘肅平凉等地。

133 Tien Hungtu

田洪都，早年畢業於武昌文華圖書館專科學校。1929—1941 年任燕京大學圖書館主任。1948 年任教於武昌文華圖書館專科學校，後任訓導主任。

134 V. K. Ting（1887—1936）

丁文江，字在君。江蘇泰興人。1902 年留學日本。1904 年轉赴英國，就讀於劍橋大學。1911 年畢業於格拉斯哥大學。同年回國，不久任教於上海南洋中學。1913 年任工商部礦政司地質科科長。1916 年與章鴻釗、翁文灝等創建農商部地質調查所，任所長。1921 年任北票煤礦總經理。1922 年發起成立中國地質學會。後曾任淞滬辦公署總辦。1931 年任北京大學地質學教授。1934 年任中央研究院總幹事。1936 年初赴湖南考察，不幸煤氣中毒逝世。

135 G. Ch. Toussaint

全名 Gustave Charles Toussaint，法國藏學家，生平不詳。最重要的譯著是《蓮花遺教》，還與巴考、托馬斯合譯《敦煌吐蕃歷史文書》。

136 Yinkoh Tschen（1890—1969）

陳寅恪，江西修水人，生於湖南長沙。1902 年官費留學日本。1907 年入上海吳淞復旦公學。1910 年至 1924 年先後留學於柏林大學、蘇黎世大學、巴黎大學、哈佛大學。1925 年任清華學校國學研究院教授，後任清華大學歷史、中文、哲學三系合聘教授。1930 年後兼任中央研究院理事、歷史語言研究所研究員兼第一組組長、故宮博物院理事、清代檔案編委會委員等職。抗戰爆發後，先後在西南聯大、香港大學、廣西大學、燕京大學任教。1945 年夏應邀訪問牛津大學。1946 年回清華大學任教。1948 年當選中央研究院院士。新中國成立後，任教於嶺南大學、中山大學。1955 年被選爲中國科學院哲學社會科學部學部委員。著有《隋唐制度淵源略論稿》、《元白詩箋證稿》等。主要論文集有《寒柳堂集》、《金明館叢稿》初、二編。

137 Tucci

疑爲 Giuseppe Tucci（1895—1984），意大利東方學家、藏學家、考古學家、探險家。羅馬大學畢業後入伍（1915—1919）。精通梵文、藏文、中文，二十幾歲即被聘爲中國歷史與文明教授。1921 年翻譯出版《孟子》。曾在印度兩所大學講授中文、藏文、意大利文，八次組織和指導西藏探險，并曾指導兩次尼泊爾探險。1930 年在那不勒斯大學教授中文，兩年後任教於羅馬大學，講授印度、東亞哲學。創辦意大利中東與遠東研究所。曾多次到西藏、尼泊爾。1936 年到日本演講。1948—1978 年任所長，1950 年在該所創辦著名英文漢學雜誌《東方與西方》。意大利科學院院士，中亞遠東協會會長。主要研究領域爲佛教、藏學、印度哲學和文化，以及亞洲的各種宗教和文化。著有《印度與西藏》、《西藏畫卷》、《印度哲學史》、《西藏哲學史》等。

138 Vogel

似爲 Claus Vogel，德國藏學家，曾任教於哥廷根大學印藏學系。著有《印度詞典編纂學》(*Indian Lexicography*) 等。

139 M. Walleser（1847—1953）

全名 Max Walleser，德國印度學、佛教學者。大學畢業後重視印度思想，致力於佛學研究。1918 年應聘爲海德堡大學印度學教授。通曉西藏語，承認漢譯佛典的價值，成爲西歐利用此類典籍的先驅者之一。曾對《大乘無量壽宗要經》進行梵藏漢三種譯本研究，并將全經譯爲德文刊行。

140 James R. Ware（1901—？）

魏魯男，美國漢學家。1925 年畢業於賓夕法尼亞大學，獲碩士學位。1929 年成爲哈佛燕京學社第一位研究生，同年來華學習，1932 年返美。1933 年起任教於哈佛大學，歷任講師、助理教授、教授。爲亞洲文物學會會員。主要研究六朝史。著有《六朝時期的中國》等，譯有《孔子語錄》、《孟子語錄》、《莊周語錄》，以及陳寅恪《韓愈與唐代小説》等。

141 Langdon Warner（1881—1955）

美國東方學家。1903 年畢業於哈佛大學。1904 年到俄屬土耳其斯坦探險，由此引發對東方的興趣，主要研究日本、中國佛教雕塑，以及遠東陶瓷。1906—1909 年任波士頓美術博物館助理館長，1909—1913 年任該館副館長。1912—1915 年任哈佛大學美術講師。1915 年被克利夫蘭博物館派往中國。1917—1923 年任費城賓夕法尼亞博物館館長。1922 年任哈佛大學福格藝術博物館亞洲研究員，并曾任東方部主任。1923 年爲哈佛大學到敦煌探險。1925 年再度率隊到中國西部探險。曾在弗瑞爾美術館的創建中做出重大貢獻。1924 年在争取鋁業大王霍爾的基金創辦哈佛燕京學社的談判中也起到積極的作用，并自 1928 年到 1950 年任哈佛燕京學社教育委員會委員。1938—1939 年任舊金山博覽會東方藝術主任。著作有《推古朝日本雕塑》（*Japanese Sculpture of the Suiko Period*）、《佛教壁畫》（*Buddhist Wall-Painting*）、《漫長古老的中國道路》（*The Long Old Road in China*）、《日本雕塑家的工藝》（*The Craft of the Japanese Sculptor*）、《日本的不朽藝術》（*The Enduring Art of Japan*）等。

142 Friedrich Weller（1889—1958）

德國梵文和佛教學者。曾在鋼和泰主持的中印研究所工作，著有《大寶積經藏文本索引》。1938—1958 年任萊比錫大學梵文教授、印度學院院長。對於研究與佛教有關的印度文、藏文、中文、蒙古文和索格底文碑文做出了重要貢獻。翻譯出版了一些佛教碑文。

143 Wen Yu（1901—1985）

聞宥，字在宥，號野鶴。江蘇松江人。1913年小學畢業，因家貧，就業於上海申報館，同時在震旦大學進修。1920年前後曾任職於《民國日報》，與錢病鶴稱"雙鶴"。後就職於商務印書館編輯部，兼持志大學國文教員。曾加入南社、創造社。1921年主編《禮拜花》小說周刊。1925年主編《中國畫報》。曾爲鴛鴦蝴蝶派的重要成員，有小說數部。1929年任廣州國立中山大學文史科副教授，後任教授。不久任國立青島大學（1932年改爲國立山東大學）中文系教授、北平燕京大學中文系副教授，兼國立北平大學女子文理學院講師，從事民族語言文字研究。1937年去成都，任國立四川大學中文系教授。次年任國立雲南大學中文系教授兼主任。同時兼國立西南聯合大學名譽講師。1940年起任成都華西協合大學中文系教授，兼系主任、中國文化研究所所長、博物館館長等。後兼國立四川大學歷史系教授。1952年任四川大學中文系教授、文科研究所研究員，兼西南民族學院教授。1955年起，任中央民族學院教授。從事字喃、彝文、羌語、古銅鼓研究與教學。曾當選法國遠東博古學院通訊院士、聯邦德國德意志東方文學會會員、土耳其國際東方研究會會員、中國民族語言學會理事、中國民族古文字研究會名譽會員等。著有《古銅鼓圖録》《四川大學歷史博物館所藏古銅鼓考》《四川漢代畫像選集》、《聞宥論文集》等。

144 Mdez Wickremasinghe（1865—1937）

全名 MartinodeZilva Wickremasinghe，錫蘭（今斯里蘭卡）碑銘研究家，編有《大英博物館藏僧伽羅語手稿目録》(*Catalogue of the Sinhalese manuscripts in the British Museum*)。

145 Wilfort

生平不詳。

146 U. Wogihara（1869—1937）

荻原雲來，日本梵文和佛教學者，和歌縣人。1883年受戒，1895年畢業於東京淨土宗學校。兩年後任該校教授。1899年赴德留學，在斯特拉斯堡大學師從伊·羅曼（E. Leumann）學習梵文，1905年獲哲學博士學位。同年回國，後任東京宗教大學教授。後歷任豐山大學校長、東京大學講師。1920年住持東京淺草誓願寺，1922年獲文學博士稱號。1926年任大正大學文學部聖語研究室主任，次年任僧正，後出講立正大學。著有《實習梵語學》、《印度的佛教》，編有《漢譯梵和大辭典》。

147 Wong Wenhao（1886—1971）

翁文灝，字詠霓，地質學家。浙江鄞縣人。13歲考中秀才，後就讀於上海震旦學校。1908年赴比利時留學，1912年獲魯汶大學博士學位。1913年回國，任農商部地質調查所講師，後升任教授，兼北京大學、清華學校教授。1916年任地質調查所礦產股股長，1921年代理所長，1926年任所長。1928年創辦清華大學地學系，任系主任。1931年任清華大學代理校務。1934年任中國地理學會第一任會長。1935年後從政，歷任國民政府行政院秘書長，資源委員會主任委員，行政院副院長、院長，總統府秘書長等職。1948年當選中央研究院院士。1949年底遷居法國，1951年回國，曾任全國政協委員、中國國民黨革命委員會中央常委，中國地質學會副會長、會長，國際地質學會副會長。著有《中國礦產志略》、《甘肅地震考》、《地震》等。

148 Y. W. Wong（1888—1979）

王雲五，原名王之瑞，字岫廬。原籍廣東中山，生於上海。早年隨父在上海半工半讀，後入同文館補習英文。1907年任教於上海中國公學。1912年1月任孫中山南京臨時政府總統府秘書，兼教育部科長。4月到北京，任教育部主任秘書兼專門司司長。1913年辭職，到國民大學任教。1914年兼全國煤油礦經理處編譯股股長。1921年任上海商務印書館編譯所所長。抗戰期間被聘為國民政府國民參政會參政員，國防最高委員會憲政實施協進會常務委員。抗戰勝利後，辭去商務印書館任職，任國民政府經濟部部長。後歷任國民政府委員、行政院副院長、行政院政務委員兼財政部長。1948年辭職，赴英國劍橋大學講學。1951年由香港赴臺灣，創辦華國出版社，并任國民黨"行政院"設計委員會委員等職。後任"考試院"副院長、"行政院"副院長等職。1964年任臺灣商務印書館董事長。1979年病逝於臺北。

Baen E. Lee，即李培恩（1889—1958），浙江杭州人，生於傳教士家庭。1910年畢業於育英書院。後就讀於上海東吳大學。畢業後留學美國，先後獲芝加哥大學商學碩士、紐約大學文學博士學位。1922年回國，任商務印書館英文編輯、商科函授學校主任，兼東南大學、暨南大學教授。1928年任之江大學文理學院院長，後任校長。

149 James H. Woods（1864—1935）

美國希臘和印度哲學學者。1887年入哈佛大學，主修哲學和英語寫作。畢業後先後在牛津大學和劍橋大學學習神學和教會歷史。之後去德國，先後在斯特拉斯堡大學和柏林大學學習古代和中世紀史、語言學，獲得博士學位後回哈佛大學任教兩年，講授人類學和語言學。後重返歐洲，師從歐洲印度研究奠基人保羅·多伊森（Paul Deussen）。在印度進行深入研究之後，於 1903 年回哈佛大學，任教於哲學系，先後任講師和教授，1934 年退休。曾對爭取查爾斯·霍爾基金成立哈佛燕京學社貢獻很大，并任學社理事會成員。翻譯有多種巴利文和梵文經典，著有《宗教的實踐與科學：比較宗教學方法的研究》（*Practice and Science of Religion: A Study of Method in Comparative Religion*）、《佛教意識的整合》（*Integration of Consciousness in Buddhism*）等。

150 Wrangell

或爲 Baron Georges Wrangell，生平不詳。

151 Dr. Yasumura

或爲 Giichi Yasumura，安村義一，生平不詳。

152 Yü DaoChuan（1901—1992）

于道泉，字伯源。山東臨淄（今屬淄博市）人。1920 年畢業於山東省立甲種工業學校，同年考入齊魯大學化學系，後轉社會學系。1924 年畢業。同年由泰戈爾推薦到北京大學，擔任鋼和泰梵文課翻譯，并隨其學習梵文和藏文。1926 年兼任北海圖書館蒙藏滿文古籍編目工作。1927 年被聘爲中央研究院歷史語言研究所助理研究員。1934 年被派出國進修，先後在法德英等國學習和工作，1949 年回國。新中國成立後，被聘爲北京大學東方語言系教授。1952 年院系調整，調入中央民族學院，籌建全國第一個藏語文學教研機構。主要著作有《第六代達賴喇嘛倉央嘉措情歌》、《達賴喇嘛于根敦珠巴以前之轉生》、《藏漢對照拉薩口語詞典》等。

153 T. K. Yu（1876—1962）

俞同奎，字星樞。浙江德清人，生於福建福州。早年入福州英華書院。畢業後赴蘇州隨叔祖父俞樾攻讀國文。1902 年考取京師大學堂師範館。1904 年赴英留學，就讀於利物浦大學，1906 年畢業，獲碩士學位。後到德國、法國、意大利、瑞士等國游學深造，1907 年參與發起"中國化學會歐洲支會"，任臨時書記。1910 年回國,任京師大學堂格致科教授兼化學門研究所主任。1914 年任北京大學教科書編委會化學主編。1919 年,北京大學廢門改系,任化學系首任系主任、教授會主任。後任北京大學教務長。1920 年任北京工業專門學校校長。1922 年與陳世璋發起成立中國化學工業會,創辦《中華化學工業會會志》,任總編纂。1923 年任國民政府教育部就業委員會主任,次年辭職,同年任"清室善後委員會"委員。1925 年,故宮博物院成立,任理事兼總務處長。1933 年底,任國民政府全國經濟委員會技正。1938 年任液體燃料管理委員會長沙辦事處主任,次年任該委員會昆明辦事處主任,負責管理滇越路油料進口事宜。1946 年調任河北平津區燃料管理委員會主任,兼平津液體燃料管理處主任,同年調回故宮博物院工作。1947 年任教育部北平文物管理委員會秘書。新中國成立後,任北京文物管理委員會秘書,1956 年該委員會改組爲文化部古代建築修整所,任所長。

154 Yuan Tungli(1895—1965)

袁同禮,字守和。河北徐水人。1913 年考入北京大學預科,1916 年畢業,到清華學校圖書館參考部工作。1920 年赴美國哥倫比亞大學留學,獲文學士學位,後入紐約州立圖書館專科學校。1924 年歸國,任廣東嶺南大學圖書館館長,次年改任北京大學圖書館主任。1926 年任北海圖書館圖書部主任。1929 年任北平圖書館副館長,主持館務,1942 年任館長。1944 年赴英美考察,并以中國代表身份參加舊金山聯合國第一次會議。1949 年應美國國會圖書館邀請,赴美重訂國會圖書館藏中國善本圖書目錄。1951 年任斯坦福大學研究所編纂主任。1953 年赴歐洲,研究漢學西文書目。1957 年任職於美國國會圖書館編目部。1964 年赴歐洲調查中國流散海外藝術珍品,編製目錄,在德國生病返美醫治,1965 年 2 月逝世。

155 Erwin Zach(1872—1942)

奧地利外交家、漢學家。主要從事中國文學的研究和翻譯。生於維也納。早年就讀於維也納大學,學習數學和中文等課程,1895 年因病遷居荷蘭萊頓,參加施古德(Gustaaf Schlegel)的漢語班,并開始學習滿語和藏文。1901—1907 年在奧匈帝國駐華領事館工作。1909 年獲維也納大學哲學博士學位。後在香港、橫濱、新加坡等地任外交官。1919 年奧匈帝國解體,改任荷蘭駐印度支那外交官。其間翻譯《文選》和杜甫、李白的詩集。1942 年因搭乘的荷蘭船隻遭日軍攻擊遇難。

157 顧頡剛(1893—1980)

原名誦坤,字銘堅。江蘇蘇州人。1920 年畢業於北京大學哲學門,留校任圖書館編目員。1922

年任商務印書館編輯。1923 年提出"層累地造成的中國古史"學說。1926 年編成《古史辨》第一册，成爲"古史辨"學派創建人。同年任厦門大學教授。次年轉任廣州中山大學教授。1929 年回北平，先後任燕京大學國學研究所導師、研究員，歷史系教授、主任，主編《燕京學報》。1934 年創辦《禹貢》半月刊，1936 年創辦禹貢學會。抗戰期間先後任雲南大學、成都齊魯大學、重慶中央大學教授，主編多種學術雜誌。1948 年當選中央研究院院士。新中國成立後，任復旦大學教授、中國科學院歷史研究所研究員、中國史學會理事、中國民間文藝研究會副主席、全國政協委員。主要著作有《中國上古史研究講義》、《秦漢的方士與儒生》、《中國疆域沿革史》、《吴歌甲集》等。

158 國立北京大學研究所國學門

成立於 1922 年，蔡元培校長任國學門委員會委員長，沈兼士任國學門主任，其他成員包括胡適、李大釗、顧孟餘、馬裕藻、朱希祖、錢玄同、周作人等。聘請王國維、陳垣、鋼和泰、伊鳳閣、陳寅恪、柯劭忞等人爲導師。國學門編輯出版有《國學季刊》，胡適任主任編輯。

159 黄文弼（1893—1966）

字仲良，湖北漢川人，考古學家。1918 年畢業於北京大學哲學門。後任北京大學研究所國學門講師、副教授，曾協助沈兼士籌辦古物陳列室。1927 年參加斯文·赫定與中方組建的西北科學考察團，帶領一支考古小分隊在吐魯番盆地、塔里木盆地和羅布泊地區進行考古調查和重點發掘。第一次考古結束後回北平，任女師大等校教授。1933 年再度赴新疆考察。抗戰期間任西北聯大、四川大學等校教授。1943 年第三次赴新疆考察。後任北平研究院史學研究所研究員。新中國成立後，任中國科學院考古研究所研究員。1957 年第四次赴新疆考察。1965 年當選全國政協委員。主要從事新疆考古，對新疆羅布泊歷史變遷、吐魯番高昌墓葬文物，以及塔里木盆地歷史地理、民族研究都有很高的成就，著作有《高昌磚集》、《高昌陶集》、《羅布淖爾考古記》、《吐魯番考古記》、《塔里木盆地考古記》等。

160 梅光羲（1878—1947）

字擷芸。江西南昌人。中國近代佛教學者。光緒二十三年（1887）中舉，二十五年（1899）與友人創辦明達學堂，後捐候補道。二十八年（1902）任京師大學堂藏書樓提調，次年改任湖北農務局會辦，後任武漢高等學堂監督。三十年（1904）入日本東京振武學校陸軍科學習，1906 年入早稻田大學政治經濟部學習法律。三十四年（1908）回國後入張之洞兩廣總督幕。辛亥革命後先後任職於教育部、交通部，1918—1925 年任山東省高等監察廳廳長。1928 年任安徽蕪湖地方法院院長，次年調任南京最高法院檢察署檢察官。1930 年任江西省高等法院院長，此後歷任中央司法院編譯專員、中央司法院法規研究委員會專任委員，1940 年辭職。曾游學於楊文會祇洹精舍，與歐陽竟無同學。晚年在長安寺佛學社講《大乘起信論》、《唯識要義》。著有《相宗新舊兩譯不同論》、《相宗綱要》、《相宗綱要續編》、《高僧傳節要》、《大乘相宗十法論》等。

161 容庚（1894—1983）

原名肇庚，字希白，號頌齋。廣東東莞人。古文字學家。少年隨舅父習小學。1914 年就讀於東莞中學。1921 年任東莞中學教員。1922 年入北京大學研究所國學門爲研究生，1926 年畢業。先後任北京大學講師、燕京大學講師、副教授、教授，主編《燕京學報》。1927 年任北平古物陳列所鑒定委員。1934 年倡議成立考古學社，出版《考古社刊》。抗戰勝利後任廣西大學教授，1946 年改任嶺南大學中文系主任，主編《嶺南學報》。新中國成立後，任中山大學中文系教授、全國政協委員、廣東政協常委。著有《金文編》、《金文續編》、《秦漢金文錄》、《商周彝器通考》、《殷周青銅器通論》等。

162 周用　梁寶羅

生平不詳。從書信内容看，曾就讀於北京大學，并上過鋼和泰的印度學課程。

163 山室三良（1905—？）

日本學者。1933 年畢業於九州帝國大學法文學部，後留學北京，入清華大學研究院。1936 年受日本外務省委託創立北京近代科學圖書館，任館長。戰後任九州大學副教授、教授。

164 新駒

生平不詳。

SCHOOL OF ORIENTAL STUDIES, LONDON INSTITUTION.

Director:
E. DENISON ROSS, C.I.E., PH.D.

Telephone: LONDON WALL, 6792.

Telegrams: SOSLINST, PHONE, LONDON.

In reply, please quote

FINSBURY CIRCUS,
LONDON, E.C. 2.

1st September, 1927.

My dear von Staël-Holstein,

It was very nice to find that you had not forgotten me during all this long period. From time to time I have had news of you from mutual friends, but all too little. I am delighted to possess a copy of your Kaçyapaparivarta and will certainly give it a notice in our School Bulletin. It is a fine work you have done and I hope it may be adopted here as a text-book, for we have quite a number of students who take Chinese and Tibetan or Sanskrit and Chinese. I myself hope to revive my small knowledge of these languages by stealing hours for the perusal of your text, but I am unfortunately very much occupied with my administrative work and writing articles on Islamic subjects for encyclopaedias, which on the whole is very dull work. I do wish there were a chance of your coming to England; the only mutual friend we see is Stcherbatsky and he has not been for some time, but I am in regular correspondence with him.

The English translation of Barthold's Turkestan is just about to appear and will, I feel, create a great sensation as so few people have known enough Russian to realise how important this work is and it has now been brought up to date by Barthold himself.

I hope if you have anything in the way of an article you wish to have printed you will remember our Bulletin. I should love to put in something from your pen.

With kindest regards,

Yours very sincerely,

E Denison Ross

Dear Sir Denison,
~~You probably know that~~
Mr. Korostowetz has, for many years, been ~~Russian~~ the Imperial Russian Minister in China, Mongolia ~~~~ Persia etc. ~~I think that his book of on Mongolia~~
He is, of course, exceptionally well informed on all matters concerning the political life of Asia in general, but his knowledge about Mongolia is quite unique, because he was the only foreign representative there at the time. Mr. Korostovetz, ~~who~~ who will personally hand you this letter, has written an english book ~~about~~ on Mongolia, which contains a great amount ~~of inform~~ exclusive information, and he is in quest of a publisher. ~~I hope~~ Will you be so kind as to assist him in finding one?

With kind regards
Yours sincerely A. v. Staël-Holstein.

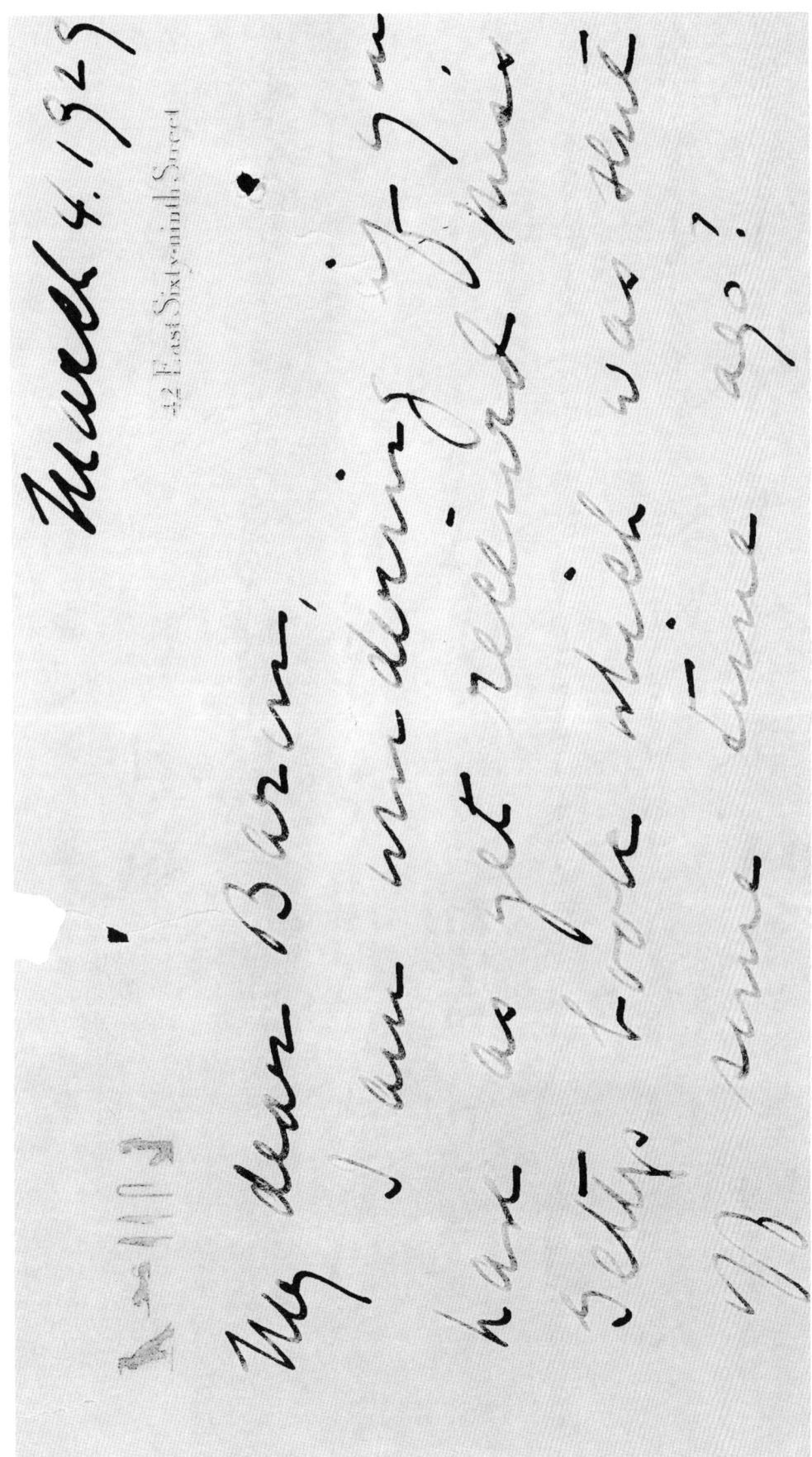

No 1113

March 4. 1925

42 East Sixty-ninth Street

My dear Baron,

I am wondering if you have as yet received my Seelye book which was sent some time ago?

A/B

indeed I mean it is at Easter present?. And when are you coming again to New York? Hoping it may be soon. I am with cordial greetings Yours, Brice P. Facen

Ex-Austrian Legation, Peking, February 25th 1930.

My dear Professor Sachs,

Some time ago Professor Sirén showed me some of the photographs (wonderful) he had collected during his recent travels in China and elsewhere. He wants to reproduce them in an enlarged edition of his well-known work on Chinese sculpture, and he is preparing a new work which will be a work of iconography for any art-lover, a work of study. I think that such an enlarged edition would be very well received by all those interested in the history of Chinese art and especially in iconography. The material which is accessible at present is far from being sufficient and the originals are very disappointing, melting away, being sold for a few dollars to tourists (this new exploitation alone) the heads have been knocked off the statues in the far flung parts during the last few years. Professor Sirén thinks that the Harvard University Press might be interested in his book and asks me to write to you on the subject. Professor Sirén's work will contain 1000 plates, reproducing about 1930 sp- ecimens, with descriptive notes and a short history of the evolution of style. Professor Sirén writes

(as follows
to me)

Professor Sirén is leaving Peking for Stockholm (to the known Royal University) about a fortnight.
May I ask to be kindly remembered to Mrs. and Miss Sachs?
I remember the many charming hours spent at your house last winter with very great pleasure.
Believe me yours sincerely and gratefully
AvHolstein

HARVARD UNIVERSITY
FOGG ART MUSEUM
CAMBRIDGE, MASS., U.S.A.

March 25, 1930

Baron A. von Stael Holstein
Austrian Legation
Peking, China

My dear Baron:

I appreciate your kind lines of the 25th ult. in regard to Professor Siren's book. I do not think that the Harvard Press has funds available to undertake the important publication in question. I shall, however, take it up at the next meeting of the Harvard University Press, and in the meantime I have sent forward your letter to Dean Chase to see whether he has any funds that could possibly used for such a purpose.

My ladies appreciate your kind greetings. We also recall with pleasure your delightful visits at Shady Hill and we trust that at an early day we may greet you and the Baroness.

Believe me to be, with cordial regards,

Sincerely yours,

Paul J. Sachs.

IONA
TERRACE DRIVE
HONOLULU, HAWAII

7. XII. 30

My dear Baron,

This tomb of a Korean King of the Silla Dynasty may be of interest to you.

Will you remember that Mr Crane is willing to finance D.T. Suzuki for 3 or 4 months at Yenching, & that he would like to come in the spring or fall of 1932 when I may also be there?

And can you send me way of getting Bruno Petzold who knows Tendai & T'ien-tai Buddhism to universities to Peking? He has 2 books soon to be published on Buddhist systems: Oxford Press.
His address is:

  10 Higashi Toriisaka
   AZABU
    TOKYO.

All good wishes to you & to Madame la Baronne
  Yours Cordially
  Kenneth Saunders.

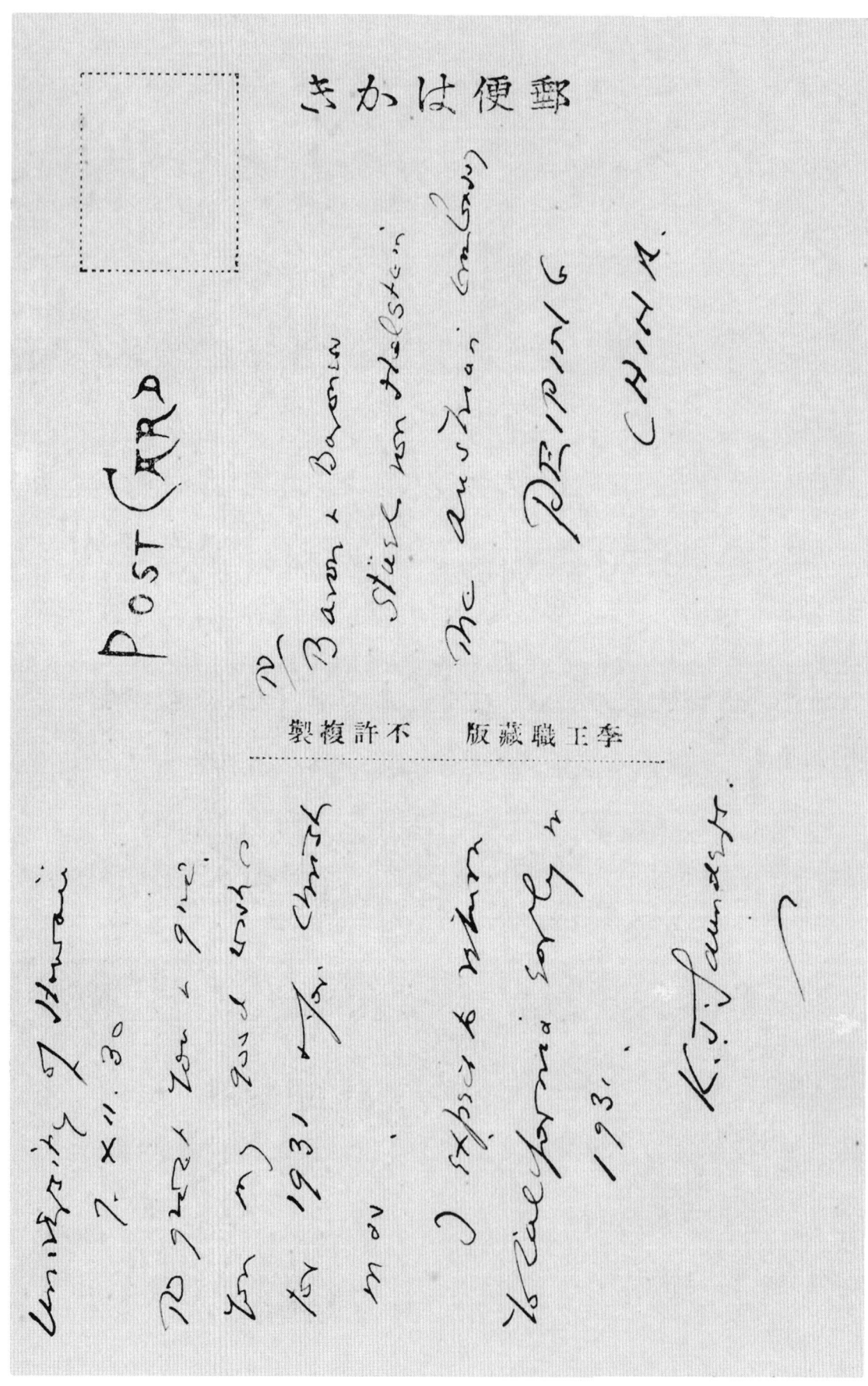

Deutsche Botschaft
Tokio.

November 2nd

My dear Baron Staël-Holstein —

I am so sorry that I will not have the pleasure, to which I had looked forward, of seeing you in America. My plans have changed and I am now sailing direct for Europe via Suez on the 18th of this month, and do not expect to reach America till March, when I fear you will be gone! — I do hope that you are enjoying your stay and that you will have time when you are in New York, to see my uncle. He is looking forward with the greatest pleasure and interest to meeting you. He returns to town from the country about the last of this month. Also, if you are in Washington and are not too rushed with more important engagements. The sister whom you met two years ago in Peking, would be delighted to see you. Her address is 3028 N Street Mrs. E. R. Finkenstaedt — My other sister is meeting me in Europe.

Peking seems to be rather quiet to judge from letters received recently. Mrs. Hussey has returned but many others are away. — My husband is staying on here till the new Ambassador arrives, when I hope he will be able to leave to join me. I shall be in Paris all of January — should you chance to be there, it would be too nice to see you. My address is c/o Guaranty Trust Co. as I do not yet know where I shall stay. Many, many good wishes for Christmas and a very happy new year —
With the sincere hope that it is only "auf wiedersehen"
Catherine Scholes

S.S. Suwa MARU
Shanghai
29th June/24

My Dear Baron,

We have tendered Govt of China - but we cannot go and meet you. This makes us sad. Someday we will be able to meet and work together for a longer period - This is my hope.

I hope you find in me for a very good worker and "Chela". Gisanda has been promised a South-Mungfu to South America to visit them so he has dropped his

To Baron A. Von Stael Holstein

all offers to visit in his programme. Even Javad Suzo Chien — he will not do this time.

Please write to me in my University address — the work you are doing. The "Ratnakuta" and the commentary whenever you are doing any) the passage of difficulty.

We are paying more than shore of China with but wishes to you all.

Yours in le
K. M. Sen
S. Kantiniketan (Bengal, India)

Dear Professor Sen

I am rather late in thanking you for your letter, but I have been thinking of my dear Sabhramacari nearly every day, whenever my glance fell on the Gaṇeśa मूर्ति statue which you so kindly presented to me about eight months ago, which occupies the place of honour above my writing desk.

I was very sorry to hear that the Gurudeva had been ill in South America and I hope that he has safely returned to शान्तिनिकेतन Śāntiniketana by now. Please give him my compliments and tell him that his visits to my house with his परिवार are gratefully remembered by me as the most fortunate events of 1924. In October I expected the Śāstrī who was to come here to arrive from Śāntiniketana, but he did not come which I regretted very much.

But now the situation is changed. On the 23rd of November a fire occurred at my house and six rooms were entirely destroyed by it. ~~Under these circumstances I think it rather providential. The rooms have not~~

Under these circumstances I think it rather providential that the Sāstrī did not come, as I cannot put him up at my house until the damage is repaired. ~~They cannot build~~ The reconstruction will take some months and cannot be commenced before the spring on account of the ~~cold weather~~ frost which renders the masons' work impossible at this time of year.

Mr. Yü who ~~is studying~~ studies Sanskrit and Tibetan with me ~~at present~~, is a very good pupil and we ~~are~~ ~~at present reading the Kāśyapaparivarta (Mahāratnakūṭa-dharmaparyāya) in Sanskrit, Tibetan and Chinese.~~ ~~We have also made the acquaintance of some very learned Tibetan lamas who are natives of Tibet at present temporarily residing~~

A number of other circumstances of a more general character which would have interfered with the Sastri's comfort, had he arrived in China. The Chinese civil war has upset things in this part of the world very much and the state of the country is still far from quiet which seriously interferes with every scientific activity. Moreover the train service between Shanghai and Peking ceased many months ago and there is very little hope of its being resumed in the near future.

Mr. Jü sends you his compliments and I wish my dear Sabratmacevin a very happy New Year.

Yours sincerely
v. Stäel Holstein.

Ochiaimura, July 21, 1916

Dear Baron von Staël Holstein:

At my first meeting with you on 9th of this month, I have told you that the name Liao-yue-chi 11月氏 occurs in the two Buddhistic books named Shi-ron 倶舎論 and Dai-chi-do-ron 大智度論 (Mahāprajñāpāramitā-śāstra), but on seeing my note-book I found out that Liao-yue-chi is mentioned only in Dai-chi-do-ron which was translated by Kumārajīva into Chinese

d. 9. 402-405. In this book (佚2, fol. 23).
Lico-yue-chi is stated together with the nations
such as Andhra 安陀羅, Cabala 迦跋羅, Luli
厲利, Parthia 安息, Syria 大秦, etc. The text is
as follows:
蝶主優安陀羅羯若婆提(裸國也)厲利邊國(小)
月支川修利, 安息大秦等在此邊國.
("On the frontiers of my own country lie the
nations such as Andhra, Cabala (**naked** nation),
Toxara (Lia-yue-chi), Luli, Su-zi, Ta-ts'in etc."

I will make further researches in the Buddhistic books to get more informations about Ārya-gue-chi.

With kind regards, I am,
most sincerely
A. Shira Torri

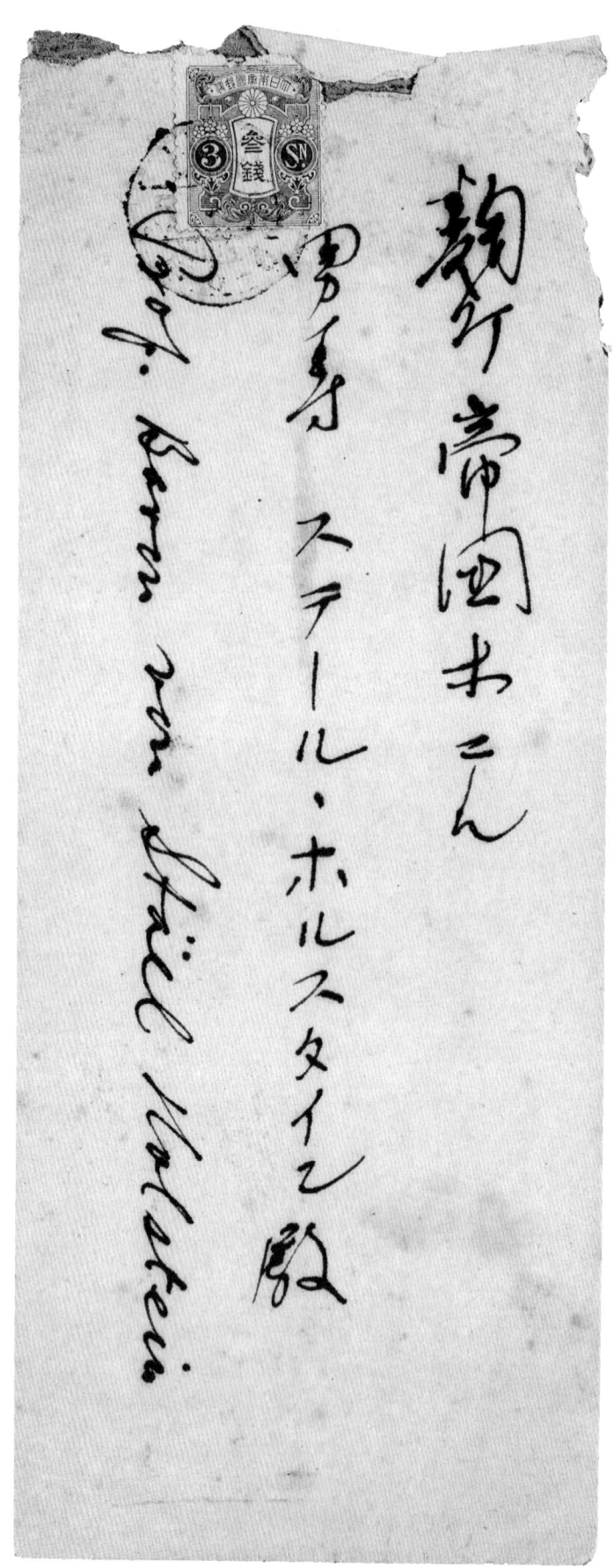

鞠町帝国ホテル
男爵 スタール・ホルスタイン 殿
Prof. Baron von Staël Holstein

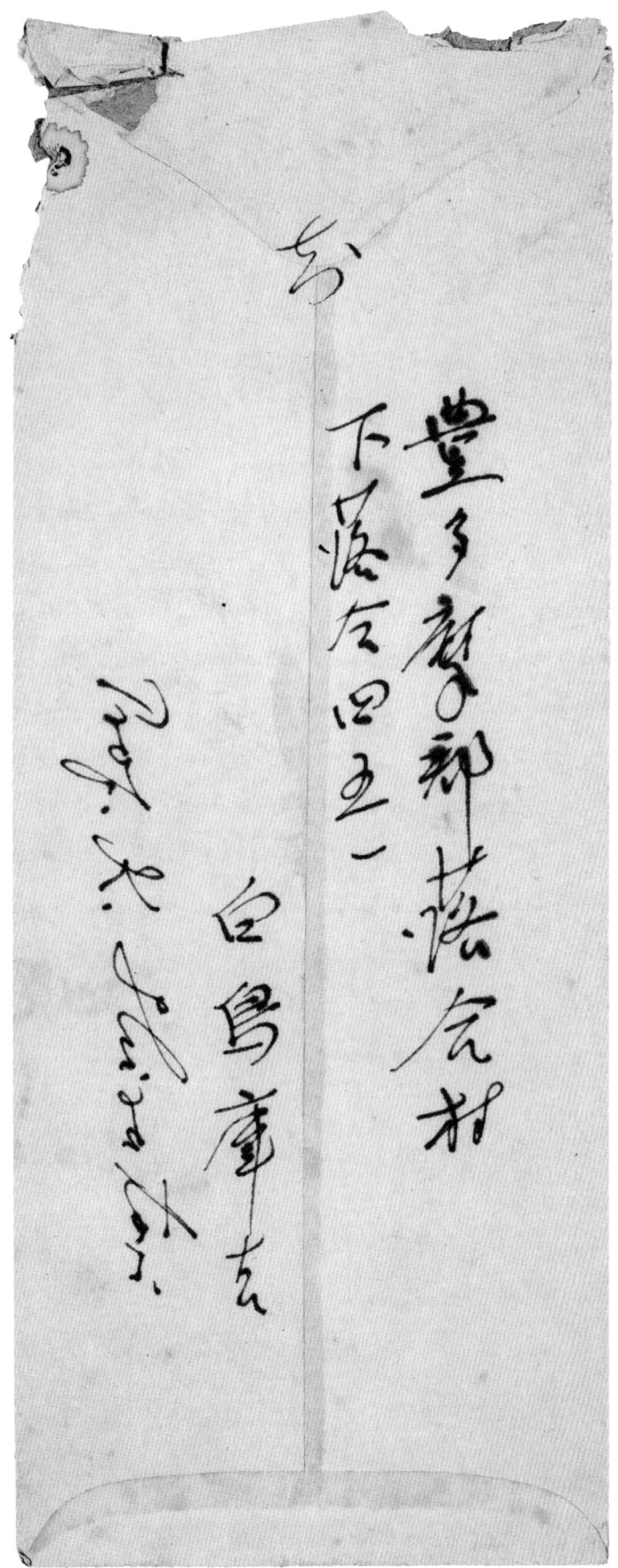

460 East Cliff
Pei Tai Ho
June 9, 1931

Dear Baron von Staël Holstein,

On my return here I found a wire from Mr. Warner saying that Mr. Edward Forbes is not coming to China. In that case if H. Ex Cameron Forbes does not take the pictures, I think it would be best to send them to Mr. Lin 14 Nan Po Yen and have him pack them and send them by post. I have already written him instruction in case you send him the three pictures. I think they should leave as soon as possible.

With all best wishes for a pleasant summer, I am,

Sincerely yours,
Laurence Sickman

Peking October 2nd 1929

Dear Professor Sirén,

Unfortunately I am busy tomorrow morning, but I shall call at your hotel on Wednesday at 10 a.m.

Yours sincerely

[second part of letter:]

...the grammar at all. I think that Curtis's grammar is by far the best of all existing grammars on the subject and I would be very grateful to you for getting me a copy. Hoping to see you soon back again at Peking I remain yours most sincerely A. Staël-Holstein

Peking, den 17. Januar 1930

Dear Professor Sirén,

A few days ago my wife was suddenly taken ill and had to be transported to the German hospital where she still is. If you do not mind we will postpone our conference for some days, because my presence is constantly required at the hospital, and I hope there, and I should like to postpone our conference for a few days. The doctors tell me that my wife will soon be able to return home, and I hope that we will have our talk. You do not mind the short delay which is due to the anxiety which I still feel.

Believe me yours very sincerely
[signature]

[German postscript:]
Der beiliegende titulierte Brief nach hat nochmalig in meinem Hause von Dr. Khampo, dem Vikar des Panchen Lama, in Peking, verfaßt und unterzeichnet.
In diesem Briefe werden Sie und Dr. Hummel Gesandter Ch'ing An Shih El[?] Amy Shun[?] das Jadelan [?] am Sonntag den 19. Januar, ich und Dr. Hung Lo Ssu und Li Hu Si[?] am Montag, den 20. Januar Abends, zum Thee eingeladen.
Es wird auch Richthofen Ta Ts'un[?] und Li Hu Si[?] Abend aus die Einladung angenommen.
D.i. Aufzug wird morgen überbracht werden.
In der Hoffnung Sie Mittwoch zu der morgen übertracht[?] werden
sehr geehrter
[signature] v. Stael-Holstein

索克思

GEORGE E. SOKOLSKY
SHANGHAI, CHINA.

Box 1194

May 2, 1924

My dear Baron Holstein:

Would you mind again looking over this chapter of my book for mistakes in fact. You will find many typographical errors which have been corrected for the printer, but I am very worried lest I have got some of the facts twisted, which is always liable to happen when journalists become historians.

How are you enjoying Tagore's visit to Peking? How is Dr. Esser? Do his enthusiasm still keep him busy? My best regards to him. I have ordered Mencken's book on the American language for you, which I hope will soon arrive.

Faithfully yours,

Geo. E. Sokolsky

GEORGE E. SOKOLSKY
SHANGHAI, CHINA.

P. O. Box 1184

June 28, 1924.

My dear Baron Holstein:-

    You were so kind as to go through my chapter on the Ayrans that I wonder whether you would care to trouble yourself with a review of the few pages I am herewith enclosing. I should like to be sure that I have them right.

    With best wishes,

Faithfully yours,

G. E. Sokolsky

Baron A. Von Stael Holstein,
Peking Club,
Peking,
China.

Encls: 1

索克思

GEORGE E. SOKOLSKY
SHANGHAI, CHINA.
P.O.Box 1184

August 7, 1924

Dear Baron von Holstein:

    I write to thank you so much for your kindess in correcting some of my chapters. Apparently, I was more in error in some things than I knew. Progress on the book is satisfactory, although it will not be ready in September as I had hoped.

    My wife has not been well although she is now improving. Her appendix troubled her and she had to undergo an operation which fortunately was successful. She is now devoting herself entirely to a fattening course in the hope of weighing about 100 pounds. She sends her best wishes to you.

    Again please accept my thanks for your help.

    Yours sincerely,

[signature]

Baron A. von Stael Holstein,
Peking Club,
Peking,
China.

Dear Dr. Hummling

I enclose a cheque for M$ 140,40 and the corrected (in red ink) policy. I have added an s to the word house because there are several houses in my compound. The most important curios I possess are more than two hundred bronze and wooden statuettes (mostly Buddhist images) and more than one hundred pictures (also mainly Buddhist). The items which I value highest are the following: a complete set of the eight Buddhist jewels (wood, XVI or XVII century) a complete set of the Buddhist world guardians (four pieces, wood, XVII or XVIII century) the god of war (Kuan) and his two attendants (wood, XVII century) a life size Tibetan picture of a living Buddha, and four large Tibetan pictures representing scenes from the life of the Buddha.

Believe me yours sincerely,

A. Stäel Holstein.

YENCHING UNIVERSITY

THE PRESIDENT'S HOUSE

My dear Baron,

I am greatly distressed that an engagement in Tientsin which I cannot postpone will prevent my attendance at your wedding next Monday. I had understood you to say it would be on Sunday and had been scrupulously reserving that day! None the less I wish you my heartiest good wishes and extend congratulations on this happy occasion. I shall hope before very long to meet your bride and offer my felicitations to her in person.

Very cordially yours,

Leighton Stuart

June thirteenth

YENCHING UNIVERSITY June 15, 1929

THE PRESIDENT'S HOUSE

My dear Baron

The enclosed letter has just come from Dr. Hu Shih. Kindly let me have your comments when convenient.

Yours cordially
J. Leighton Stuart

Copy of letter dated Shanghai June 10th, 1929
written by Dr. Hu to Pres. Stuart.

Some six or seven years ago the Baron and I were interested in an offer of the Kanjur for sale, and we wanted to buy it for the Libr. of the Nat. Univ. But the Univ. was without money at that time, and fearing that we might miss the rare opport. of obtaining the Kanjur, I asked the Com. Pr. to advance the money ($1200.00 I think). But the C. Pr. being a joint stock comp., had no way of loaning us the money to buy books for some other institution; so they gave us the money to buy the Kanjur for the Comm. Pr. with the understanding that the Baron might retain the collection in Peking for a length of time for the convenience of his research work. // // I have approached the Comm. Pr. several times with the request that some research institution in Peking be allowed to pay back the advanced money with interest and keep the Kanjur in Peking for the benefit of the Tib. scholars. But the Comm. Pr. people have thrown open their Tungfang Library to the public and are very anxious to ship the Kanjur to Shanghai to be housed in the Library. That is where the matter stands now. Being the original borrower of the money, I am a little embarrassed to press the request too strongly. Kindly consult the Baron and decide on what steps to be taken in this matter.

Austrian Legation, Peking, July 16th 1929.

My dear President,

The Yenching water tower is really a beauty and ~~I am very glad~~ we are much obliged to you for sending ~~me~~ us such an excellent ~~town~~ colour photograph of it. ~~All I am~~ The other picture ~~as well as the wonderful frames~~ is also ~~very pretty~~ delightful, and ~~so the~~ my wife as well as myself thank you very much indeed for your charming presents. ~~The~~ We think the carving of the frames ~~is very~~ extremely artistic. ~~indeed~~ I enclose Dr. Hu's letter.

Believe me yours most sincerely

My dear President Stuart,

Many thanks for your kind congratulations and for sending me Dr. Hu's letter. ~~Shall~~ I shall return the latter to you in a few days. In the mean time I ~~will~~ shall try to ~~convince~~ make it clear to the Commercial Press ~~through certain~~ that the Kanjur will be nothing but a "white elephant" at Shanghai where there is not one Tibetan scholar, and that it is quite indispensable here. ~~We cannot do~~ Without that collection of Tibetan books I cannot accomplish the ~~task~~ work which I have promised to do during the next few years. ~~I propose to make a~~ I intend preparing a detailed inventory (catalogue raisonné) of all the sacred texts of Mahāyāna Buddhism ~~which are available~~ at the present moment ~~in Sanskrit Chinese Tibetan and Mongolian~~. Only comparatively few ~~of these works have~~ come down to us in the original Sanskrit, because Mahāyāna Buddhism has been practically extinct in India for many centuries. The great majority of the texts ~~exist only in translations of which the Chinese~~ But

In addition to purely religious and philosophical matters those texts contain much historical material connected with the history of India Tibet Central Asia and China. That historical material has never been systematically collected, because an international staff of scholars is necessary for accomplishing the task.

and only comparatively few of the texts in question have come down to us in the original Sanskrit. Mahāyāna Buddhism has been practically extinct in India for many centuries. In most cases we are confronted by with translations only. Most of the Chinese translations are older than the Tibetan and Mongolian versions, but they are written in a language which is not always easily understood by the scholars of modern China. Therefore the Tibetan and Mongolian translations have frequently to be consulted in order to obtain a clear understanding of the ancient writings.

The Tibetan and Mongolian versions if studied without referring alike to the Chinese parallels are equally unsatisfactory, and only a comparative investigation of all the sources in the various languages can assure success. Much traditional information which is not available either in China Tibet or Mongolia has been preserved in Japan. Furthermore modern Japanese scholars have done much research work in the field of Buddhist history. Consequently I need the services of a Japanese Buddhist scholar in addition to those of Chinese Tibetan and Mongolian assistants to help me, and the necessary funds have already been granted by the authorities at Cambridge, Massachusetts. Some of the assistants are already here, while others are on their way to Peking. Owing to American liberality Sino-Indian studies will thus be placed on a broader basis here than anywhere else in the world and I hope that greater results will be achieved in I shall be able to justify the confidence placed

~~in me by the trustees~~ and I hope to be able to justify the confidence with which the trustees have honoured me. ~~One of the trustees Professor Woods Professor Woods is Dr. Woods and professor of philosophy and Dr. Clark professor of philosophy and of Sanskrit, as well as Dr. Sachs professor of Fine Arts at Harvard have most~~ I have found many friends and supporters at Harvard ~~in Cambridge Mass~~ (professors Woods, Clark, Lanman, ~~Sachs,~~ Blake etc. ~~etc. etc.~~) but I will never forget very that you and professor Porter so kindly made the ~~french~~ arrangements for my second trip to Cambridge Mass. ~~Harvard~~ which I had already visited ~~been~~ there in 1912. During my second stay ~~at Harvard~~ I conducted Sino-Indian and Tibetan courses in addition to some instruction in Buddhist iconography at Harvard University.

Believe me yours most gratefully

A. Staël-Holstein.

That confidence ~~is~~ I owe primarily to the recommendations of yourself ~~and of~~ of professor Porter, ~~and of a number of other scholars~~, and I thank you from all my heart for arranging my trip to Cambridge. ~~xxxx~~ During the last academic year I conducted Sino-Indian and Tibetan courses in addition to some instruction in Buddhist iconography in Harvard University.

燕京大學
YENCHING UNIVERSITY
PEIPING, CHINA.

OFFICE OF THE PRESIDENT

TELEGRAPH ADDRESS
"YENTA"

February 2, 1932

Baron A. Stael Holstein
Former Austrian Legation
P E I P I N G

My dear Baron:

Your note with the accounts came duly to hand, and I shall have these filed with our Treasurer for such reference as may be necessary.

I am still puzzling as to whether I ought to make the trip to Hongkong and then to the States or not in view of the very much disturbed conditions in Shanghai.

If I leave Saturday, I shall probably be so very much rushed that it would be difficult to find time to call on you for a word of farewell, though I shall still keep this in mind and accomplish it if possible. If I abandon the plan, or postpone the date of leaving, I shall hope to have a visit with you in the near future.

With cordial regards-

Very sincerely yours,

J. Leighton Stuart

JLS/P

YENCHING UNIVERSITY
PEIPING, CHINA.

OFFICE OF THE PRESIDENT

TELEGRAPH ADDRESS
"YENTA"

June 26, 1934

Baron de Stael-Holstein
ex-Austrian Legation
Peiping

My dear Baron Stael-Holstein:

I am sorry that your ill health prevented your being present at our graduateion exercises yesterday. I always feel that it adds distinction to these occasions to have you in our academic procession. Let me thank you also for your courtesy in sending me your most recent publication. I shall look forward to reading it in the near future. This letter gives me the occasion of saying what has been frequently in my thoughts of late - which is that I should like to have a visit with you. Could you and the Baroness come out to my home sometime this summer? Or if the heat and your state of health make this too much of a burden, I shall find the opportunity to call on you.

With cordial regards,

Very sincerely yours,

JLS C

Tokyo, Sept. 23, '17.

My dear Prof. Baron Holstein,

I am in receipt of your kind letter and very thankful to you for it. I have been unable to identify the Chinese name I have asked you about and am at a loss what to do with it.

Last time you mentioned that a friend of yours who is in Peking had ordered a set of the Chinese Tripiṭaka from a Japanese bookseller in Kyōto or somewhere else, and that he had not yet received the scriptures. I am told that complete sets of the Tripiṭaka are now very rare, and that the bookseller may possibly be looking for a set among the monasteries in provinces. As you yourself have experienced last time, some Bouddhist books are very few, some are out of print. I wish you would tell your friend that the Kyoto bookseller would not mean to cheat him, but that ~~no~~ it is possible he might be hunting out one. When he is successful in his search, he will surely send it to him.

I hope you will return to our country in the near future.

Yours sincerely,
S. Tachibana

京師圖書館用箋

Monday

Dear Baron Stäel

I hope that you remember to put in that Philosophies (roots) of Nāgārjuna 龍樹樹 (Aśvaghoṣa 馬鳴, Vasubandhu 世親 or 天親 and (maybe Kumārajīva 鳩摩羅) well many other great teachers known to Chinese in your new list. Also the Sutras as 法華經, 金剛經 (its original Sanskrit, I word, he has been mentioned once in 陰陽二名 Academy, then 金剛) is still existed) 般若經 心經 and many others must be put in the list. Do you think these are important. We shall happily meet you on Wednesday

Yours sincerely Jeng Ping Kuijia.

Enclosed a few titles for your choosing.

Dear Dean Pong,

I hear that you have asked my assistant Lin to lecture at the National University. Please blame me, not him, for declining your kind invitation. I have advised him to undertake no task whatsoever which might interfere with his work here, at least during this his first year at Peking. Later on when he will have perfected his Sanskrit and acquired some knowledge of Tibetan, he might be able to accept invitations such as yours.

Believe me yours sincerely
JPhilStahlstein.

My dear Thomas, Exactly five months ago (on the 12/2/21) I dispatched a registered letter to your address. The letter contained in that letter I asked you to be so kind as to cash the enclosed certain cheque for £24/... / and to buy some books for me. I ventured to do so — because there are no International book sellers in Peking you asked you to ... could be fruitful with an order for scientific books. Having received no reply whatever I wired the bank to inquire by telegram whether the cheque had been cashed in London. The answer was that the cheque was still outstanding. From that I concluded that the letter must have gone astray and I renew my request and I ...

another cheque for the same amount, I am working at our edition of the Kāśyapaparivarta 經 in Jansen's (after a Ms. found in Khotan). I publish the Tibetan text together with the Sanskrit and four different Chinese translations the oldest of which has been during the Han period. It is very small part of the work has already been printed. I must add since writing this to the above that it is taking me in spite of very many hours which I cannot get here in running the text and the notes I must of course correct a number of books which cannot be found in Peking and I hope to get those books not later than the month of June from London. You can (me—you wrote a fortnight arrangement it to me for me when I learnt that the letter has got lost and that I would have to wait yet least another four months for the books.

It is really too bad! Besides the books which I want in connexion with my edition there are some others which I want for my work as a professor at the University of my country T. Bull.

You be so kind as to buy the books on the warm paper (the usual cheap Chinese paper one mixed with straw than rice paper) and send them to my address (The Peking Club, Peking, North China) as soon as possible. Please do not wait until all the books are assembled but ask the bookseller to send them one by one as soon as possible. I have already lost five months through the neglegence of the P.U.T. I have paid my subscription as a member of the P.U.T. but the journal has not been sent to me since 1916. Please do ask the secretary to send me the journal for the last five years, if possible. Through the society although they must be in possession of my address have sent me absolutely nothing. It seems as if the whole world had conspired in order to keep me in the darkness of avidyā, or do they think that I have already entered the state of 無有 (agatosa)? I have of course lost all my money through this calamity to the State — and it is only owing to the fact my august aunt [anumati] I am still in māptagrīvah [human] all the [dhama] [accounts in my care few members of the borough of 道 [dharma] and arhs] are practically identical and the arhat (dhama) does not lead me far away from the first named parts.

TELEGRAMS, "AQUILÆ, LONDON".
TELEPHONE Nos REGENT 4024 & 4025.

August 3. 1921

ROYAL SOCIETIES CLUB,
ST. JAMES'S STREET,
S.W.1.

My dear von Staël-Holstein

Your letter of February 12 reached me in India, or rather, I think, in Tibet, & it gave me much pleasure by the certainty, which I had not before, of your being safe & well. I had often inquired in various quarters for news of you, the postcard which you sent me years ago from Japan having contained no more indication beyond your signature. Now Stcherbatskoi has also reappeared, having been allowed to visit the countries of Western Europe on behalf of the Petrograd Academy, & I have news welcome, even if not very cheering, of most of my Russian friends.

It is now about a month since I returned to England after an absence of about 8 months. My 6½ months in India, Nepal, & Tibet were very instructive and enjoyable. I covered a wide stretch of country, & have added solidity to my knowledge of things Indian. You had attained this, & more experience many years ago.

Since my return I have found myself fully occupied with arrears of business in the Library, & not a little new business, while domestically I am faced with the problem of discovering a new house, which in these post-bellum times is a problem of world-wide difficulty. Hence I hope you will forgive my not having yet discharged your commission as regards purchase of books. But a fair instalment of the list shall be sent out to you by the next mail. I am afraid that the cost of the whole will greatly exceed, as prices now are, the amount of your draft.

To-day I have seen Wickrema-singhe, who was anxious to know your address & was much relieved to hear of your present circumstances

You say that you are in Peking 'for good'. I hope that you will not be there longer than you find it agreeable & interesting, & that, if you are staying on for some time, I may possibly be moved to visit you there. In the meanwhile I think you will be rendering good service to scholarship there; &, if you can be induced to devote a part of your energies to the projected Buddhist Dictionary, it will be good news to the Association of Asiatic Societies, which has that matter in hand. Let me explain a little further.

In Europe we are awaiting definite news from our Japanese friends, Takakusu & others, who were to be mainly responsible for the first part of our task, an amplified Nanjio. From your favourable situation you might be able to learn what circumstance is delaying their coöperation or to kindle their activity. And for China you might become a pivot of our enterprize & control our operations in that great sphere. From the R. As. Soc. Journal, which I am arranging to be sent to you, you will be able to learn in detail the circumstances of the project.

I am glad that you are going on with the Kāśyapaparivarta & are also investigating Chinese characters, which I suppose may furnish a key to many things in Central Asia. I hope by the time this reaches you to have completed my translation of the Dinakari to supplement that of the Siddhānta-muktāvalī which I have had ready so many years. It will be a great relief to have go to the end of the enormously difficult text.

Please expect a further letter from me before long. I am heartily glad to have heard from you again. With kind regards,

Yours sincerely,

F. W. Thomas.

Library

November 24. 1921

My dear von Stael Holstein,

I am writing a hasty letter to send you the enclosed list of books which I have managed to secure & send to you on various dates. From this you will be able to see how much of your commission I have discharged & how much of your money I have spent. By the next mail or so I shall send you the receipts. In the meanwhile I am trying to secure the remaining books from Harrassowitz, &c. but I suspect that some of them will have to come from India or

them to be sent to you direct.

Stcherbatskoi is still here, but we have no further news of d'Oldenbourg. Were you aware that Mironow is in Kharbin, in fact quite in your vicinity, relatively speaking?

I am overwhelmed in work. So I will now add nothing more, except my kind regards, in which my wife would wish to join (I am at present living for a time as a bachelor in London), + my hope that we may meet during the coming year.

Yours sincerely,
Baron von Staël Holstein

The Library
India Office
London S.W.1.
Feb. 23. 1922.

My dear von Staël-Holstein,

I am writing just a line to thank you for your long & interesting letter of Nov. 9 — Dec. 6 & also to acknowledge receipt of the £250, which I have passed on to my bankers, pending further instruction from you.

I sent on to M. Senart a copy of that part of your letter which relates to the Buddhist Dictionary. I hope that we may soon begin to make some progress with the preparation of that work.

Your Kāśyapa-parivarta will be well based indeed.

I have still to send you the receipts for the books which I have purchased & sent to you. But I will keep them still a little while in order to take a note of them

Stcherbatskoi is here: he seems very well, & we are reading some philosophy with a Swāmī.

I need not say that I am full of engagements & a slave to official duties, callers & correspondents. But I hope to write to you again before

very long.
With kind regards,
Yours sincerely,
F. W. Thomas.

THE NATIONAL UNIVERSITY OF PEKING
PEKING CHINA

Department of Indian and Central Asian Philology.

July 11th 1922

Baron A. von Staël-Holstein, Ph. D.
Director of Researches.

My dear Thomas,

Many thanks for your kind note of February 23rd 1922. I am very glad to learn that you are well and that you work with Stcherbatzkoy. I shall write to the latter and address the letter % The India Office Library. Mironov is in Kharbin and writes to me from time to time. He intends going to India as he has received an offer from a Jaina community who want the services of a European Sanscritist. My edition of the Kāçyapaparivarta progresses very slowly; only 78 pages (about 1/3 of the whole text) have been printed so far. The proofs have to travel from Shanghai to Peking and back which takes up a great amount of time. I intend publishing a translation of the text, based upon Sthiramati's commentary which exists only in a good Tibetan and in a very bad Chinese translation. I am also preparing an English translation of a part of Asanga's Sutralamkāra with extracts from the commentaries of Arvabhāva and Sthiramati. Both commentaries exist only in Tibetan. There is a very learned Tibetan Lama here whom I consult from time to time. Unfortunately he has to travel about a good deal and is not always available.

The enclosed list of books is a rough copy of the list you sent me in November 1921. Besides the books mentioned in the list I have received the following books, the prices of which I ignore, from you: Pāṇini, ed. Böhtlingk, an Indian edition of the Siddhāntakaumudī and Finot's edition of the Rāṣṭrapāla-paripṛcchā. I am very much obliged to you for sending me all those books and I thank you very much for your kindness. In future I shall be able to get my books through a bookseller without encroaching upon my learned friends' time, because an up-to-date bookshop has been established here a few months ago (Vetch, la Librairie Française) which does business with Luzac, Harrassowitz etc. I am very glad to learn from your note that you have received on my behalf the two hundred and fifty pounds from Mr. Hartmann. May I ask you to send that money and the rest (if any) of my 1921 remittance (24 pounds, 8 shillings and 9 pence) to Peking by telegram? If you send the money through the Hongkong & Shanghai Banking Corporation "Stael Holstein" will suffice and no indication of my Peking address is necessary, as I am well known at the Peking office of the Hongkong and Shanghai Banking Corporation. Please do not forget to deduct all telegram charges and the cost of sending the books to Peking, which must be considerable, before sending me the money. I have asked Mr. Vetch to get some copies of the Siddhāntamuktāvalī and of the Dinakarī, translated by you, for my pupils and for myself. I am sure that we shall profit enormously from your translation.

Believe me yours gratefully

AStaelHolstein.

P. S. Please ask the London Times to send their daily edition to the following address: Baron A. von Staël-Holstein % the Peking Club, Peking, China and pay my subscription from September 1st 1922 up to December 31st 1922. Excuse my troubling you once more in spite of the assurances given in this letter.

Your last letter was addressed % the National University, Peking. % the Peking Club, Peking is preferable, because the personnel of the latter are acquainted with the languages of Europe, while the staff of the University, except a few professors, know nothing but Chinese.

Idem.

Nanning July 11th 1922

My dear Thomas!

Many thanks for your kind note of February 23. 1922. I am very glad to learn that you are well and that you were with Stcherbatsky. I shall write to the latter and address the letter ℅ the India Office library. Misprov Vissilenko and works to me from time to time. He intends going to India as he has recognised offer from a Jaina community who are looking for a European sanskritist as an instructor. Vidyabhusana progresses very slowly, only about half of the whole has been printed so far. The pages of the text (about 80 pages) have to travel from Shanghai to Peking and back which takes up a great amount of time. Sthiramati's commentary reflects alike only in a bad Chinese translation. I am also preparing an English translation of Vasubandhu's Trimsika based upon the Commentaries of Asvabhava and Sthiramati. Both commentaries exist only in Tibetan. There is a very learned Lama here whose services I avail from time to time. Unfortunately he has to travel about a good deal and is not always available. The enclosed list of books is a rough copy of the list you sent from Tun in November 1921. Besides the books mentioned I have received all the following books, the prices of which I ignore: Panini, ed. Kielhorn, with an Introduction of the Siddhāntakaumudī and Finot's edition of the Muṣṭopālapariprcchā. I am very much obliged to you for sending me all those books. It is so kind of you and I thank you very much for your kindness. In future I shall be able to get my books through a bookseller, because an up-to-date bookshop has been established here a few months ago (Vetch, la Librairie Française) which corresponds with Luzac, Harrassowitz etc. I am very glad to learn that you have received the two hundred and fifty pounds from Mr. Harfmann. May I ask you to send that money and the rest of my 1921 remittance to Peking by telegram? If you can send the money through the Hongkong and Shanghai Bank Peking address "von Staël-Holstein" will suffice and not indication of my Peking address is necessary. Please do not forget to deduct all telegram charges and the cost of sending the books to Peking which must be considerable. Mr. Vetch to get some copies of the Siddhāntakaumudī and of the Dīnakarī for my pupils and for myself. We will surely learn very much from your translation.

Believe me yours gratefully
Staël-Holstein

Please ask the London Times to send their daily edition to Baron A. von Staël-Holstein c/o the Peking Club, Peking, China and pay my subscription from November 1st 1922 up to December 31st 1922. Because my friends gave me no more in spite of the assurances given in their letters to the following address.

Your last letter was addressed c/o the National University Peking; c/o the Peking Club Peking is preferable, because the personnel of the latter are acquainted with the languages of Europe, while the staff of the University, except a few professors, know nothing but Chinese.

February 18. 1926
6, GRANVILLE ROAD,
SEVENOAKS.

My dear von Stael-Holstein,

It is a very long time that I have been owing you a letter; &, though I have constantly intended to write, that is hardly a justification. You know, however, the sort of pressure of engagements amid which I lived even in pre-War times; &, if you will only multiply that by 2 or 3, you will, I dare-say, partly realize what excuse I have for not writing. I must confess, that I am almost as bad in regard to other correspondents.

Probably I never sent the copy of Dasgupta's 'History of

Indian Philosophy" & Keith's
~~the~~ books, as proposed in your
letter of June 23. 1924? If so,
please let me know, & I will
then certainly repair the error.
Are there any other omissions of the
same nature?

I congratulate you upon being
enshrined in the new edition of
the ~~Chinese~~ Tripitaka: perhaps
I shall have a humble place as
being mentioned in your notes
to the edition of the Ganḍī-
-stotra.

By this post I am sending
you a copy of my last paper
on Khotan, up to date: for
there are some more to appear.
What an age since we discussed

2 18/2/26

the Kuśanas at Chaldon. Perhaps you saw my last heresy re the name Kuśana in the J.R.A.S. for 1925.

If you have not received my translation of the Sid-dhānta-muktāvalī & com-mentary, the reason is that it is, alas! still only type-written & not yet printed: it awaits only a few notes. As regards Stcherbatsky's "Central Con-ception of Buddhism", if you have not received it, please let me know, & it shall then be sent at once.

No doubt you receive all the books which so numerously emerge from the Press. The Fest-schrift for Jacobi should appear soon (with an article by me on the Khotanese language). There is also in preparation a volume in honour of Lanman to which also likewise I have contributed. At present I am busy in preparation for a lecture, also on Chinese Turkestan, at the R.A.S. A really deplorable activity!

I shall look forward to your Kāśyapa-parivarta, & I hope it will soon appear. With kind regards + remembrances from us both.

Yours very sincerely,
F. W. Thomas

My dear Thomas,

The translator of the Nyāyas ~~Bidhhāntamuvāt avah~~ ~~simply is rarely~~ must know the

~~am sure you know the~~

"The development of the logical method in Ancient China" by Hu Shih, Professor of Philosophy at the National University of Peking. The bearer of this letter is the author of that important work and I am sure that you will be glad to make his

I am sure that the
~~The~~ translator of the Nyāyapraveśa interpretatī-
vrtī will be glad to know the
author of "the development of the
logical method in ancient China"
~~Professor~~ by Hu Shih, Professor of Philosophy at the National University
~~Dr. Hu Shih,~~ The bearer of this of Peking.
                Professor Hu Shih,
letter is ~~the author~~, and I
am proud to be able to intro-
duce you to one another.
Professor Hu Shih is also a very
good friend of mine.
I am replying under separate
cover to your kind letter dated
February 18, 1926.
    Yours very sincerely
         A v StaëlHolstein.

6 Granville Road
Sevenoaks
Kent
September 8. 1927

My dear von Stael-Holstein,

First let me thank you very heartily for sending me a copy of your wonderful Kāçyapa-parivarta, which must really constitute a 'record' in the editing of an oriental text. I am sure that no one would regard the list of corrigenda as long for such a work, even if he were unaware of the special difficulties mentioned in your note. Most of us would have been content with making out the Sanskrit text, or at the most with adducing the Tibetan

Your four Chinese versions are, of course, beyond me; but I can readily believe that they will be helpful to Indianists better equipped, as well as to the scholars of Chinese & Japanese Buddhism.

I have read the Sanskrit text, which shows some interesting marks of antiquity, & will be very useful as a landmark.

Your very original paper on Some divine metamorphoses also brings together a number of considerations unknown to most of us & rather enlightening in their ensemble. I will try & send by a later post any observations on the Tibetan 'letter', in which, of course, I accord with your rendering tnotes.

I must hasten to thank you for so kindly sending me the fac-simile of the Tibetan document from Central Asia. No doubt you are publishing the text & translation yourself: otherwise I would offer to incorporate it in a projected article dealing with Tibetan documents from Khotan (the Hu-then, of course, & your document, & others). In any case, I could send you some notes upon it, if it is not too late for you. I see that you ask me to publish the Tibetan text, & I gratefully accept the proposal. As you may imagine, I have been very busy in getting free from the I.O. Library, London, & preparing for Oxford, where

I look forward to a blessed time, when we have succeeded in getting there. It would be delightful if we could welcome you there at the International Congress of Orientalists in 1928: and why not?

My wife sends kind regards. I will write again, concerning your letter, by the next mail. I must also send some literature. In haste Yours very sincerely,

F. W. Thomas

6 Granville Road
Sevenoaks
Kent

Sept. 8. 1927

My dear von Stael Holstein,

after posting my letter I found that there is another mail for Peking to-morrow, & so I am resuming my letter to you.

The Tibetan letters which you have sent are highly interesting to me, as you may see from the July number of the J.R.A.S., where I have published some rather similar documents from Tun-huang. Unfortunately the article is in 'miscellanea', & I shall not have a supply of copies. If I get one, it shall be sent to you. The travellers from Hu-then, Hu-then in your documents seem to have had a bad time, their camels dying en route, & they themselves only escaping with their lives — ma.si.tram. tco.bo. The. bo hi.spya.nar.mchis. Who this co.bo (jo.bo) The.bo Lha. rgyal.po is remains to be ascertained: perhaps you can say. The document contains several phrases which I have had to deal with elsewhere.

I congratulate you upon the important iconographic material which you have discovered. It is good news that you are able to arrange for the publication, & certainly I shall lose no time in replying to Professor Porter, when he writes to me concerning your Sino-Indian Research Institute. With you in Peking

& our Japanese friends in communication with us in Europe we shall have really a magnificent instrument for international research in the field of Buddhism & Central Asia. I expect that before long I shall be writing to you for help. I have got a new (long) Chinese text in Tibetan characters & have also the same in Chinese writing.

After re-reading your text & translation of the Pan-chen's passport & your notes, I am not ambitious of making any further contribution to the interpretation of it, which in fact seems perfect. I do not think that any other scholar would have been able to produce anything approaching your full interpretation of the document.

I am sending you a copy of my Jacobi Festschrift paper, & will try to find something else that may have an interest for you (all my letters & literary possessions are at present in much disorder). As regards Kur-shan, my idea was that it means 'western mountain' & was a territorial designation (like other Khotan names in -shan) in which the -shan was a Chinese equivalent of a local si or shi, meaning 'mountain'. If this is so, it will not, I think, conflict with your views. Of course it will be said that the Kuṣānas are known to us too early for such a semi-Chinese designation. But? I hope that life is agreable in Peking, even now. That you make it highly interesting needs no saying. It will always be a delight to have your news. With our united kind remembrances,
Yours very sincerely,
F. W. Thomas

My dear Thomas,

Many thanks for your letter and for the most interesting article on the language of ancient Khotan. There does not seem to be any doubt as to the fact that before the language 于闐 appeared on the scene another language was used in Khotan, spoken in the country, and I congratulate you most heartily on your discovery. Your article which appeared in Festschrift Windisch I have never seen, and will probably never see. Your article (non-iranian manuscript) in Jacob's Festschrift. But you give the name Kuṣana in 三 (J.R.A.S. 1925, page 110) I have read with great interest seen 貴霜 and I note with great interest that Hu-ṣi and Hur-ṣi have the same meaning as Kuṣana. There can be no doubt that 月氏 (月支) pronounced Ṅghuar-ṣi in western China (comp. J.R.A.S. 1917, page 8) has been Kuṣa and that K-U-Ṣ(A-N-O) Guṣana Kuṣa and Kuṣa (comp. Kuan-tsi name Kuzan most characters J.R.A.S. 1915, page 86 and also J.R.A.S. year 2 page 2 where Lévi shows that Hsiun-tang

a special set of characters by Chinese writers to name Kuzan most characters ? where Lévi shows that Hsiun-tang were the forms of the name current in India. Can one in face of these facts still contend that Kuṣaṇa and FJt have nothing (at all) to do with one another, though phonologically and typographical [typographically?] correspond in India? Name Kuṣi (of which Kuṣana may very well be an abbreviation) postology and and (of which Kuṣa must have been regarded as the stem by the grammarians of the language No 2) might be a transcription of FJt, which is an exceedingly fitting name for a warlike race, meaning Candra-vaṃśa. I think I have seen Kṣatriya or another FJt ruler described as belonging to the lunar race, but I do not just now remember the reference, because I have very few books here. I am still firmly convinced that KOPANO represents the genitive pl. of FJt, but I admit (Schme Comp. SBB Kgl. Pr. Ak. d. W. 1914, pages 643 sqq) (proper noun) that Kuṣāna may have arisen as a substantive derived from the stem Kuṣa. FJt may of course also be a Chinese transcription

I think that your interesting discovery
my view as to the correlation of 月氏王 is
I still consider both expositions as constructs very strongly supports
all three must mean and 䓗(or kuśara) which
"King of the Kuṣiḥ-㗔" The existence
of 㗔 the stem ("The grammarians of the language of course
regarded kuśa 㗔 as the stem of the nom. sg. kuṣe and
the stem kuṣāna whose existence cannot be denied
as a patronymic derived from kuśa.) Do not you think
that "N.N. King of the Kuṣī" ¹¹ (䓗 ᴜᴥ 䓗 des admittedly (from: King of 月氏, not 月氏
The evidence of there kuṣāna can now no longer ˢᵒ) is a much more
plausible origin legend (at a comparatively late period)
be denied; it may very well be regarded as a comparatively
late patronymic derived from the stem kuśa (which
The grammarians of the language N°.2 must have
regarded as underlying the 月氏 nom. sg. kuṣe). If there
are visible testis. "Gabiana" instead of Asiana (or Asiani
at least Gabiana Asiani).

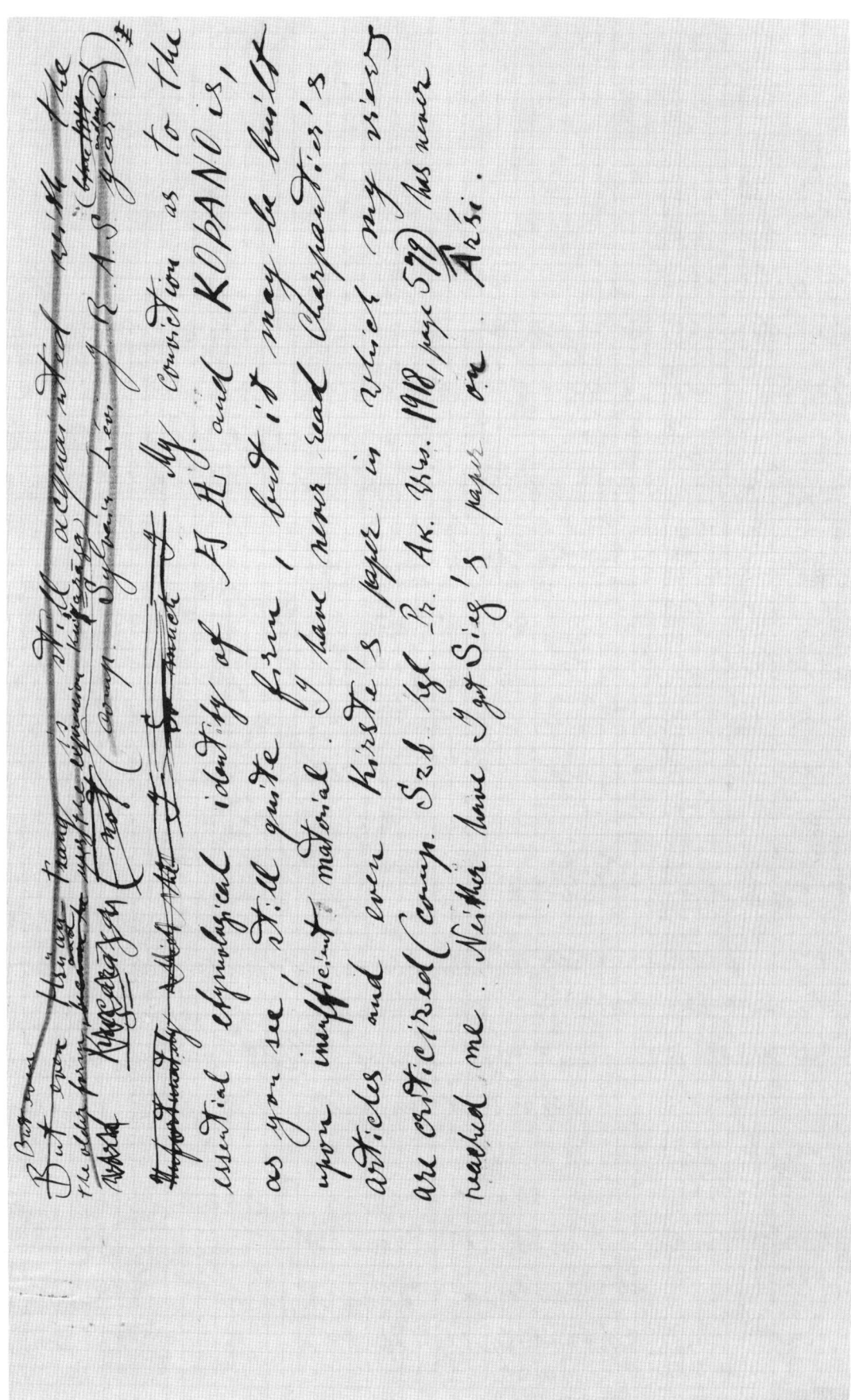

But now Hsüan-tsang transcribed *Kikana* with *a* characters, still the plain form misrepresents *kiṣkaṣa* (comp. Sylvain Lévi, J.R.A.S. 1915)⸺

Importantly I think that there is not much ground for my conviction as to the essential chronological identity of F.H. and KOPANO is, as you see, still quite firm, but it may be built upon insufficient material. I have never read Charpentier's articles and even Kirste's paper in which my views are criticised (comp. Szb. Kgl. Pr. Ak. Wiss. 1918, page 579) has never reached me. Neither have I got Sieg's paper on Arṣi.

My dear Thomas,

I am very pleased to learn from Professor Freimann, that the document ~~part of which I sent you~~ from Tun Huang which I bought in Peking some time ago is of some geographical interest. ~~Both the Tibetan lines. The~~ The entire obverse of the document (which is one roll) ~~contains~~ is inscribed with ~~an entirely~~ uninter[esting] a section of the Chinese Prajñāpāramitā - without the slightest interest. ~~They I~~ A part of the reverse contains: first the ~~Tibetan lines~~ lines in Language N⁰ 2 (photographs sent to Konow) and then the Tibetan lines, photographs of which were sent to you. ~~Before giving the roll away~~ ~~Quite lately~~ I discovered that not all the Tibetan lines had been photographed, ~~There is very much blank~~ on account of the great amount of space left blank between the second Tibetan document and the enclosed five lines.

~~My~~ About two months ago I presented the entire roll to the Harvard University Library. ~~My~~ Professor Blake, the director, ~~knows~~ that I had sent photographs of the reverse to various

European authorities for publication, and the question of copyright does not arise. It would be well, however, to mention in your publication that the roll has been presented to Harvard in the autumn (or as they say here: in the fall) of 1928.

Has Mrs. Thomas received my Christmas card?

In April (1929) I hope to return to Peking (c/o the Peking Club).

Believe me yours sincerely

A. Staël-Holstein.

My dear Thomas,

Many thanks for your letter and I am so glad to hear that you are well and that a thaw, although I am awfully sorry to say that I cannot find the Album here in Peking. I would very much like to read your article which it contains and to learn something about King Piratinda. I think you and know have made splendid use of the photographs which I sent you some years ago, and I have studied your articles (Prof. Melvianed Documents from Pun-Huang) with the greatest interest to the limits of my knowledge of friends. I am glad I am not abandoned my original intention of publishing the documents myself. I shall send you in a few days snatching you cought agarnts to every a number of books and articles. May I ask you to keep

Since 1929 I am a professor of Central Asian philology in Harvard University, the authorities of which have so far allowed me to live in Peking.* I like this city very much and I hope that I shall be allowed to stay here for a few years longer. In order to obtain a further extension of my leave I must, however, be able to prove that my work is appreciated in Europe. This by European philologists.** The latter

* I preside here over the Sino-Indian Institute, which depends entirely upon American liberality, Professor Keller.

** My far eastern efforts have been almost entirely ignored by the philologists of the West. In England, at any rate, no one seems to have quoted them. (The new text edition of the Saddharmapuṇḍarīka which appeared in 1926, etc

*** My edition of the 145 pages preserved in 1925, has been almost completely ignored by the philologists of Europe, and I shall feel very much obliged to you indeed, if you will save the commentary edition as well as my recent articles from a similar fate.

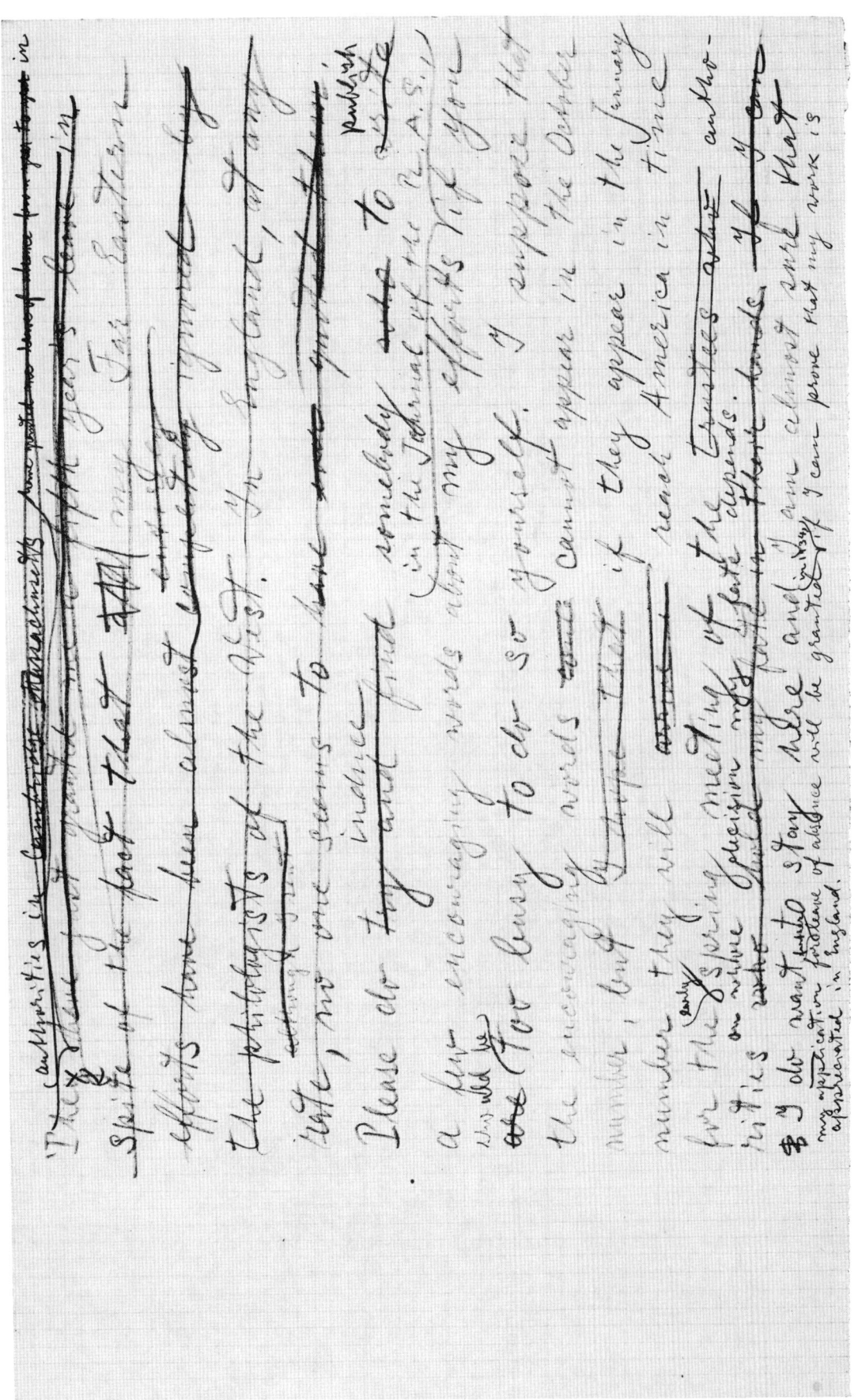

Seeing the books and articles, which I send you, though, it is not mere vanity which makes me ask for a printed appreciation of my work, but dire necessity.

I think I may claim that my bilingual edition of the commentary represents a useful innovation, and I hope that it will prove of some use to the students of Mahāyāna Buddhism.

Registered A.B.

To Professor F. W. Thomas
161 Woodstock Road
Oxford
England
Via America

16. Aug. 34

My dear Dear Thomas,

I am very much obliged indeed to you for the kind sending me your last letter and for sending me a reprint of your review, which appeared just in time for the American Trustees' meeting. I am sure that the Trustees have been very much impressed by the fact that you appreciate my efforts, and I thank you very much for your great service the kind words which you published in the J.R.A.S.

* In April 1934 the Trustees passed our budget without further diminishing the appropriation for the Sino-Indian Institute, which had been reduced by over 40% in 1932.

Dear Mr. Thomas,

I am ~~very~~ greatly obliged to you for the passport. It was very kind and I thank you very much for having obtained it for me. In a few days we shall start for our summer cruise.

Believe me yours sincerely and gratefully

Manuscript (Tibetan translation of the second [struck] (Tamil-ajnisūtra) copies of the) Aparimitāyuḥsūtra (or Aparimitāyurjñānasūtra) in Peking. If there exists an all show, they are supposed to have been found in one of the Tun Huang caves and not first they contain many amount spellings (as my instead of the y etc.) and the photographic reproduction of the [struck] I enclose the last page of one of the copies, [struck] of the [struck]

If you are [struck] that the Kinsha [struck] that you are interested in these manuscripts I shall be happy to send you photographic reproductions of all the pages of one of the three copies of the Tibetan translation of the Aparimi- tāyuḥsūtra for publication or for private study.

Not long ago I acquired twelve bronze statuettes representing the twelve animals of the Chinese 'Zodiac', and I enclose a photograph of the bronze tiger. I hope not ~~establishing~~ the May I annex it not know the name ~~of the Riga~~ (~~well~~-known country woman who rides on the tiger (~~my~~ young lady "young lady"). The other of Riga who went for a ride on a tiger"). Before clemons return seven animals for hear ~~unidentifiable~~ Pt. before clemons return one cannot identify. Do you know anything about these clemons? I am ordering the Album here from Europe, because I am very anxious to read your paper on 'Dvādaśanāʒas'.
May I ask to be kindly remembered to Mrs. Thomas?
Believe me yours very sincerely and gratefully
AvStaël-Holstein

Dear Mr. Phenius,

Many thanks for the passports! I am especially grateful to you for having got them in record time. Now we can get to Shanghai — shan't we? — start our journey, without any need not fear any complications with the Chinese authorities.

Believe me yours sincerely
MvStaël-Holstein.

CHINA EXPEDITION
FOGG ART MUSEUM
HARVARD UNIVERSITY

                                          Tung T'sung Pu Hutung, 60
                                          P E K I N G, 23 January, 1925

Baron von Holstein
Pi Kuan Hutung, P E K I N G

Dear Sir:-

        I am taking the liberty of sending you a copy of a photograph which I recently made at the Ellora Caves, in India. Dr. Ferguson told me that you might be willing to decipher and translate the fragments of inscription which can be made out on the painting, and which I hope may cast some light on the subject of the picture. Perhaps you may be able to give me some light on this and some other photographs of material which has not previously been photographed or studied.

        If you have a little time in the next few days, I should be very glad to call on you at your convenience, and should greatly appreciate any help you can give me.

                                          Faithfully yours,

                                          Daniel V. Thompson Jr.

CHINA EXPEDITION
FOGG ART MUSEUM
HARVARD UNIVERSITY

T'ou T'iaou Hutung, 5
Thursday, Feb. 12

Dear Baron von Holstein:-

  I am sending you the latest and largest prints from the photographs with inscriptions, and if you will let me know whether you are free, I should be very glad to call on you tomorrow morning, at any time you suggest, to hear what you can tell me about the things.

  We expect to start for the West on Monday. Mr. Warner will however remain in Peking for a little while, and hopes to see more of you and of your interesting collection.

Faithfully yours,

D V Thompson Jr.

CHINA EXPEDITION
FOGG ART MUSEUM
HARVARD UNIVERSITY

P'ing Liang, Kansu
26, March, 1925

Dear Baron von Holstein:-

    I seize this opportunity, which I am sorry to say, is almost the first which has presented itself since I received your very kind contributions on the eve of my departure from Peking, to thank you for your most generous interest in my problem of the Ellora inscriptions, and in my desire to learn Sanskrit.

    Your observations on the puzzling inscription I have, as Mr. Warner has doubtless told you, incorporated as a note in my article on the paintings, which I hope will appear before long. I am very gre atly obliged to you for your help in the matter, and only regret that I could not put more worthy material at your disposal.

    Your sheets of Sanskrit paradigms have been, and are, the greatest help to me in my attempts to penetrate the complexities of Macdonell, while bumping along in a Peking Cart! When I return to Peking, I hope to see much more of you than I was able, during this last brief visit, and to get hints from you for my further progress, en amateur, along these lines.

    Our trip proceeds well: we are making good time, and have made one or two important finds as well, so we are all content. We all regret that Mr. Warner could not be with us, but are making the best of things in his absence.

    With renewed thanks for your many courtesies, I am

            Very faithfully yours,

            [signature: O. R. Thompson Jr.]

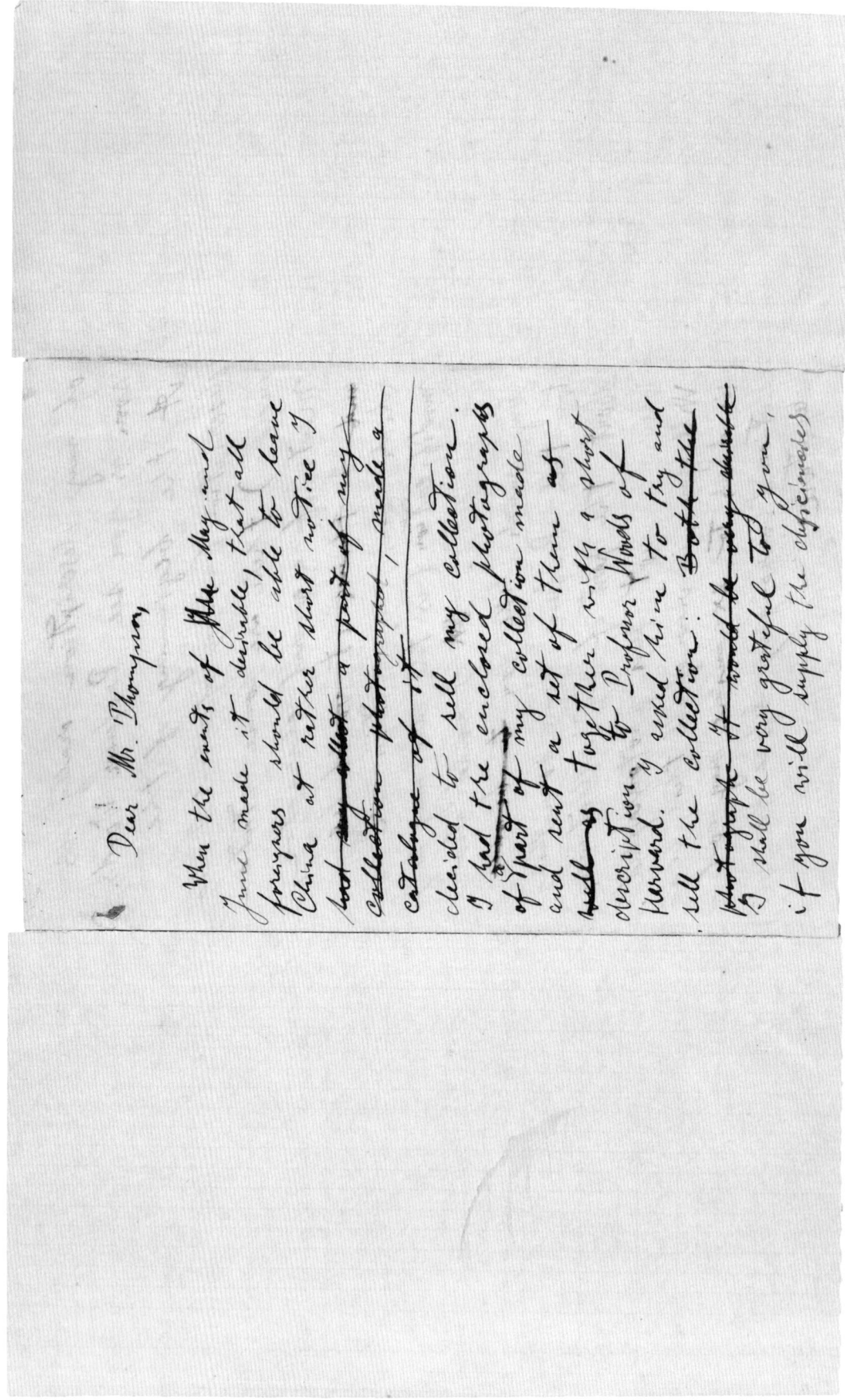

Dear Mr. Thompson,

When the events of May and June made it desirable, that all foreigners should be able to leave China at rather short notice I had also collected a part of my collection photographs, made a catalogue of it decided to sell my collection. I had the enclosed photographs of part of my collection made and sent a set of them together with a short description to Professor Woods of Harvard. I eared him to try and sell the collection. Both the photographs it would be very desirable shall be very grateful to you, if you will supply the deficiencies)

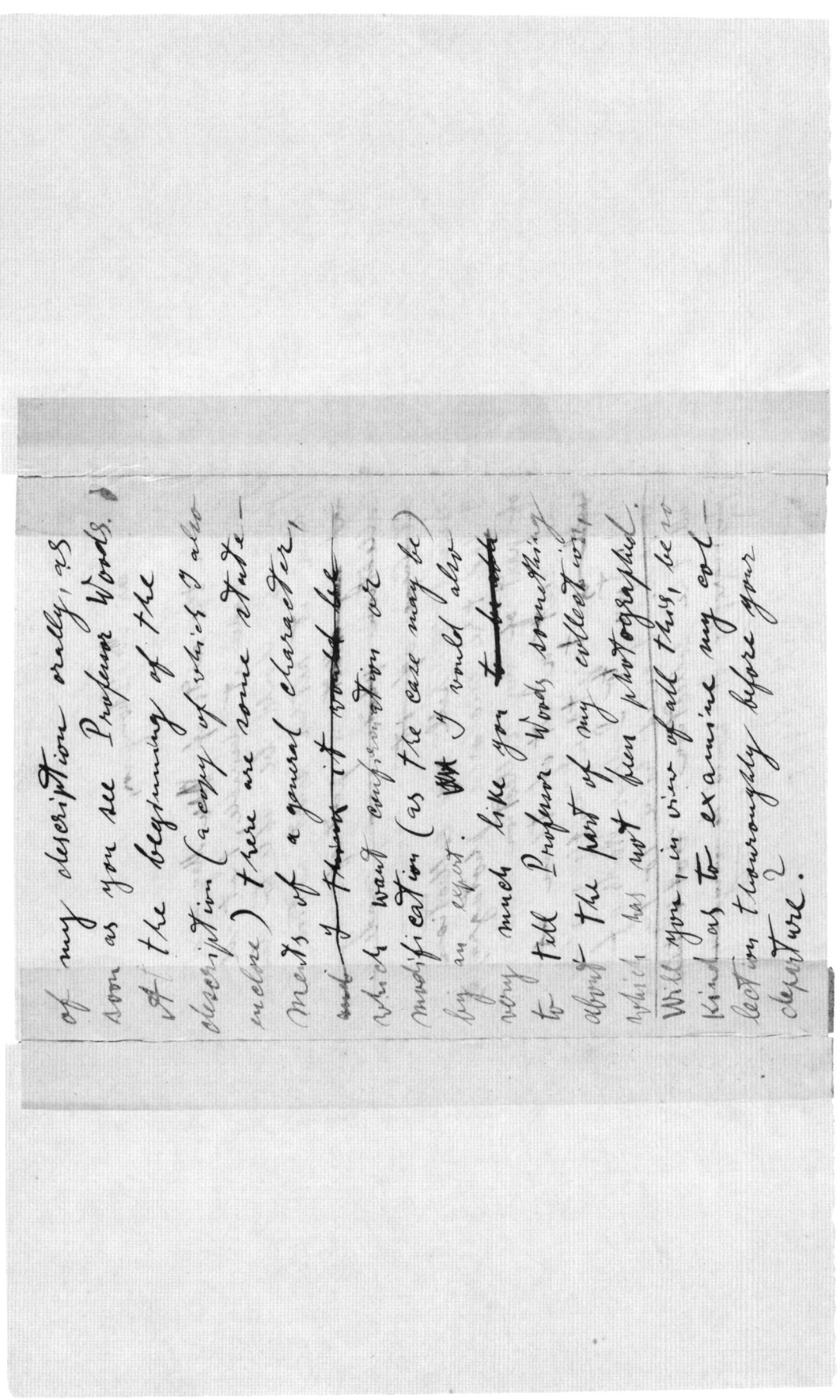

of my description orally, as soon as you see Professor Woods. At the beginning of the description (a copy of which I also enclose) there are some statements of a general character, and I think it would be which want confirmation or modification (as the case may be) by an expert. But I would also very much like you to [crossed out] to tell Professor Woods something about the part of my collection which has not been photographed. Will you, in view of all this, be so kind as to examine my collection thouroughly before your departure?

I have not spoken to anyone about my intention of selling the collection and I do not want anyone to know about it. The fact that I contemplate to know (that I contemplate) should also be kept absolutely secret leaving China seems to me that

It would mean disaster if people were to know now about my plans (as my bonus would not be allowed to be given Russia, my leave of absence, to which I am entitled, would not be granted etc). Therefore, please do not let anyone (not even Mr. Warner) know about this letter.

When may I expect you here? I have no engagements except tomorrow (Thursday) at 6 p.m. (I suppose).

YENCHING UNIVERSITY
(INCORPORATED IN 1889 AS PEKING UNIVERSITY)
Peiping, China.

THE UNIVERSITY LIBRARY

TELEGRAPH ADDRESS:
"YENTA"

March 6, 1933.

Prof. Alexander von Stael-Holstein,
Austrian Legation, Peiping.

Dear Sir:

    At the request of Prof. William Hung I am sending you herewith Vol. 32 of the Harvard Oriental Series, the last volume in the set which has just been received from Harvard as a gift to the Yenching University Library.

    Kindly sign one copy of this communication and return to me as a receipt.

Yours very truly,

Tien Hungtu,
Librarian.

燕京大學圖書館

YENCHING UNIVERSITY LIBRARY

PEIPING, CHINA.

ADDRESS CORRESPONDENCE
AND SHIPMENTS TO THE
LIBRARIAN

TELEGRAPH ADDRESS
"YENTA"

May 11, 1934.

Mr. Alexander von Stael-Helstein,
Austrian Legation,
Peiping.

Dear Mr. von Stael-Holstein:

The University Library acknowledges with thanks the receipt of:

On a Peking edition of the Tibetan Kanjur which seems to be unknown in the West.
A commentary to the Kacyapaparivarta.
On a Tibetan text translated into Sanskrit under Ch'ien Lung (XVIII cent.) and into Chinese under Tao Kuang (XIX cent.).
On two Tibetan pictures representing some of the spiritual ancestors of the Dalai Lama and of the Panchen Lama.
On a Peking, a St. Petersburg, and a Kyoto reconstruction of a Sanskrit stanza transcribed with Chinese characters under the Northern Sung dynasty.

Yours sincerely,

Tien Hung-tu,
Librarian.

YENCHING UNIVERSITY LIBRARY
PEIPING, CHINA.

ADDRESS CORRESPONDENCE
AND SHIPMENTS TO THE
LIBRARIAN

TELEGRAPH ADDRESS
"YENTA"

May 3, 1935.

Baron A. Von Stael-Holstein,
Austrian Legation,
Peiping.

Dear Baron,

We write to thank you for sending us your work; On Two Recent Reconstructions of a Sanskrit Hymn Transliterated With Chinese Characters in the X Century A. D., for the Exhibition on April 27.

We regret to say that we had not been able to have it printed in the special number as it came late. We, however, will accession and catalogue it for general use with your other works in this Library.

Sincerely yours,

Tien Hungtu,
Librarian.

Dienstag den 25. Juni 1935.

Lieber Professor Dieny!

Soeben ~~eingegangen~~ bin ich von meiner Reise zurückgekehrt. Jetzt ~~~~ werde ich wieder in Peking sein und hoffe sehr, Sie nicht hier anzutreffen, ~~sollten~~ Darf ich Sie Sonnabend den 29. Juni um eine gewohnte Zeit erwarten?

Herzliche Grüsse
von Ihnen ergebenen

AvStaël-Holstein.

Dear Mr. Dieny,
I have returned from my journey and I shall be very pleased if you will come to see me on Saturday the 29th at 3 o'clock.

I am delighted to hear that you will go to Mukden with me. I shall start from I shall leave the Wutherian Legation at 9.15 to-morrow morning and I I think we shall have to leave the Austrian Legation at 9.15 to-morrow morning.

Looking forward to seeing you at here at that time I remain yours sincerely

MikailAlstein.

Sehr verehrter Herr Doctor,

Ihr grosses Werk

Dear Mr. Pien,

Herewith I return to you with many thanks the two numbers of the which you so kindly lent me.

May I ask you now to lend me number 1 of the first number of the of the 2. I shall be very grateful to you if you will give the number to my coolie the bearer of this letter.

Believe me yours sincerely

YENCHING UNIVERSITY LIBRARY
PEIPING, CHINA.

ADDRESS CORRESPONDENCE
AND SHIPMENTS TO THE
LIBRARIAN

TELEGRAPH ADDRESS
"YENTA"

Oct. 28, 1935.

Dear Prof. Von Stael-Holstein:

We beg to inform you that the book 佛教學雜誌第三卷第一期 you want to borrow from us is also not owned by either the National Library of Peiping or the College of Chinese Studies Library. An order has been sent to the Isseido Co. in Tokyo for a set of it. According to Japanese bibliographical information this magazine is pretty rare now.

We regret very much that we cannot help you this time.

Very sincerely yours,

Tien Hung-tu,
Librarian.

農商部地質調查所
The Geological Survey
Ministry of Agriculture and Commerce

Peking 23 April 1921
(China).

Baron de Staël-Holstein,
Pikuan Hutung,
Peking E.

Dear Baron Staël-Holstein,

Mr. Kao, the Editor-in-Chief of the Commercial Press, came to see me this morning and he gave me a few proofs which I enclose herewith. He told me the following points:

1. The special characters are being made, but as we hurried them several times they have set a few pages with ordinary type in order to save time. These are sent in order that we may decide upon the form. The whole will of course be reset with proper characters.

2. There are two sets of proofs. Please tell them which is the best. Any alteration in the form must be told to them now.

3. As you now can see the size of the page and the number of characters, please tell them, if you can, the exact number of pages. They calculate according to the information I supplied them that the proofs sent represent about 1/90 of the whole. Is this correct?

4. When every thing is settled they will want to have the beginning of the book at once.

5. All proofs will be sent to you.

Kindly answer as soon as possible.

Yours sincerely,

V. K. Ting

28 April 1921
Peking –

Dear Baron Staël-Holstein,

Mr Liang chi chao has just given me additional evidence from Chinese sources on the time of Kanishka which seems to confirm my view: –

1. In the preface to the first translation of <u>Vibhasa</u>, in the time of Pei liang (北凉, about 430 a.d.) the monk Tao Yen says the Vibhasa was made by order of Kanishka <u>more than</u> 600 years after the death of Buddha

2. In his preface to the translation of "the Acts of

Buddha (佛行經)", the famous Tao-an says: "Monk Saṃgharakṣa, the author of the book, lived 700 years after the death of Buddha, and became the teacher of Kanishka when he went to Gāndhāra."

These agree wonderfully well with the date I have given in my last letter. Both these authors lived in the 5th century, only 250 200 years after Kanishka's time.

Have you made any progress in the copying of the Khotanese chronicle?

Yours sincerely,
V. Staël-Holstein

16 May 1921
Peking

Dear Baron Staël-Holstein,

I have heard from Mr Kao of the Commercial Press that all the special characters are being made and that there will be no doubt whatsoever that they will print the book.

Mr Liang Chi Chao has written asking you to supply him with a short list of literature on Kanishka. I shall be grateful if you can send the same to me as soon as possible.

Have you succeeded in

copying the Khotanese chronicle?

With kind regards
yours sincerely,
V. K. ling

21 May 1921
Peking

Dear Baron Staël-Holstein,

Thank you very much for your letter of yesterday. My typist is away on leave and as soon as he is back I will set him to work at once.

I am afraid there was a slight misunderstanding. What Mr Liang wanted was merely a <u>list of literature</u>. Do you think there is anything more than the references you have given?

I am very sorry I am unable to come to you today, but will be glad to do so on Tuesday, when I am to lunch with M. Grave and can see you after lunch.

With kind regards,
Yours sincerely,
V. K. Ting

The Peipiao Coal Mining Co., Ltd.,
HEAD OFFICE.

TELEGRAPHIC ADDRESS: 4384.
TELEPHONE: 3055.
38 Via Principe di Udine
ITALIAN CONCESSION.

Tientsin, 10 March 1924

Dear Baron Stäel,

Mr. Leang chi chao has written a the preface to the book as requested. It is being copied. Shall I send it to you or to the Commercial Press direct to save you trouble?

Mr. Leang points out a serious error on the title page. "失譯附秦錄勘同編又" is not correct, but the word 錄 must be inserted after 勘同. He thinks that the alteration must be made if at all possible.

He further suggests that the words "大寶積經" be added before 普門菩薩會, but this is not so important.

Please let me know your opinion,

Yours sincerely,

V. K. Ting

My dear Dr. Tsing!

Many thanks for your kind note. I felt very much honored by the fact that Mr. Wang has written an introduction to the Kāśyapaparivarta. Please send it to me. If you will be so kind as to send it to me I shall forward it to Shanghai together with my English introduction. I shall ask the printers (see the english also) after that the Chinese one. (see enclosure) I propose to have only one title page and mentioning the Chinese and Tibetan titles merely in the introduction. I shall be pleased to insert the words 釋迦佛說 大寶積經卷一百十二第四十三會普明etc. As to the phrase 大寶積經斷句編入 I think I shall ought to print it as it is, because

The Peipiao Coal Mining Co., Ltd.,

TELEGRAPHIC ADDRESS: 4384.
TELEPHONE: 3055.

HEAD OFFICE.

38 VIA PRINCIPE DI UDINE
ITALIAN CONCESSION.

Tientsin, March 29, 1924

Baron A. Staël-Holstein,
Pikuan Hutung,
Peking E.

My dear Baron,

Your letter dated 21st March was received sometime ago, but Mr. Liang did not come back to Tientsin until yesterday. He has written a short note giving the reasons for inserting the second Lu 錄 and the following is roughly the substance.

The original title as appeared in the Ta Pao Chi Ching was; 失譯附秦錄勘同錄編入 which may be explained as follows;

"失譯" = the translator unknown.

"附秦錄" = seen only in the collection of the translations of the Tsing.

"勘同錄編入" = now edited according to the same book (錄)

Thus the second Lu has an important meaning and, if omitted, the whole sentence would be unintelligible. Mr. Liang does not understand the reason why the Japanese altered the title when they fully knew the original text, but he supposes that they made a serius blunder in this way. There is a well known book called 至元法寶勘同 which is often shortened as 勘同 in quotations. The Japanese perhaps thought that the words 勘同 in Tapaochiching referred to the same thing, but this 勘同 was made in the Yuan dynasty and therfore has nothing to do with the present case at all.

I enclose also the Chinese introduction by Mr. Liang.

Please forward it to the Commercial Press to be printed.

I hope to come up to Peking sometime next month when I will discuss the points in your long letter. I will give you a definite answer then.

With best regards,

Yours sincerely,

4 Li-Kuan Hu-T'ung, Peking. Sept 9th 1926.

My dear Dr. Ting,

Everyday I ~~use~~ let me congratulate. Please accept my sincerest congratulations on the occasion of your appointment as governor of Shanghai and be assured of the great pleasure with which I read of your successes in almost every morning's paper.

The ~~Hořejsapomata~~ Is what ~~buffelships~~ Namely Bones are to a philologist

The position of a country depends on international politics ~~depends~~ upon it's armies (farmies) and what ~~letations~~ notations are to a world power, books are to a philologist. Under these circumstances I am of course very anxious that the Hořejšapomata should appear as soon as possible. After a great many misunderstandings and innumerable delays (24) ~~I~~ dispatched the manuscript of my index duction by the first of September 1st 1925 and received the first proof sheets on January 27th 1926) The book is now ready and every page is signed. May I ask you to hurry the Commercial Press,

To
His Excellency
Dr. V. K. Ting
governor of Greater Shanghai
Shanghai

and took or that the book might appear M before the end of this month. Please also try and get me as many free copies (fifty, or seventy five?) as possible. This is the first book of its kind which has ever appeared in China and I should like to present it to very many friends in Europe, and America.

With kind regards yours sincerely [signature]

I am very anxious to know when the book will appear. The question as to when the book will appear naturally interests me very much, but I am not likely to hear from the Commercial Press soon, if I have merely two months to reply to my last letter containing many important questions. I sent them a letter, written by Dr. [?] on July 9th, and, although I enclosed a letter asking for a telegraphic reply, I only received an answer on July 30th. Will you be so kind as to inquire at the Commercial Press and let me know as soon as possible?

Dear Dr. Ting,

Many thanks for your kind letters dated September ~~th~~ and ~~th~~ respectively. ~~I am very much obliged to you for having~~ ~~I am~~ I do appreciate the fact that ~~you~~ in spite of the great number of more important ~~engagements~~ ~~affairs~~ things ~~duties~~ which ~~I suppose claim~~ your attention at present, you have found ~~the~~ time for answering my letter so promptly. I am very glad to hear that ~~it~~ the Commercial Press have at last set a definite term for ~~publishing~~ the publication of my book and I hope that they will be punctual for once. I am also very much obliged to you for having obtained the Press' promise of sending me sixty free copies. I am ~~still~~ not quite certain ~~uncertain~~ about my departure for Europe, but I think that I shall leave in April.

Hoping to see you ~~soon in Peking~~ again soon ~~they at Shanghai if not earlier at Peking~~ I remain

yours sincerely

A v Staël Holstein

Shanghaï, 6 janvier/33.

Mon cher ami,

Je reçois tout ensemble vos aimables souhaits et les trois beaux articles dont vous avez bien voulu me faire l'envoi. Laissez-moi vous remercier très amicalement et vous offrir mille vœux pour vous et les vôtres. Le Padma va paraître d'ici un mois : vous en recevrez, bien entendu, un exemplaire.

Sans doute aurai-je le plaisir de vous voir dans quinze ou vingt jours, car j'ai à me rendre à

Tientsin prochainement, et je pousserai jusqu'à Pékin.

J'ai eu le plaisir de voir ici Pelliot, que vous avez certainement vu depuis qu'il est à Pékin.

Mes respectueux hommages, je vous prie, à la Baronne de Staël, et ma plus amicale poignée de main.

G. Ch. Toussaint

Légation de France
en Chine
—*—

Cher Baron,

Voici, de retour, avec tous mes remerciements, votre excellente étude sur les Kuṣa. Je tiens pour démontré que le thème est simplement Kuṣa (ou peut-être Kuṣi गोस la langue n° 2). Le nom 拘尸 (ịṅḥ) dans le मुञाळकार d' अखघोष parachève la démonstration.

Ci-joint l'Analyse du 口丌2. 2口丆.

Très amusante la phrase où il est question d'une "maladresse du lapicide".

Tout amicalement.
J. Ch. Toussaint

Mon cher Baron

Je propose :

Nāgara et Sindhu, c'est-à-dire Gmaçānas saisis par les Asuras
Meru et Kulūta, autrement dit Upaçmaçānas
saisis par la suite des Asuras Nāga du Nāgaloka
et Asura venus des cavernes cachées du Meru
avaient les fosons du Nāgaloka
—
Nouveau problème. Que peut signifier
"Ritta matam ma Ritta", qui revient
plusieurs fois comme un refrain à la fin
des strophes décrivant l'arrogance de Ritra ?
Je tâcherai de venir ce doir.
Bien amicalement
L. B. Poussain

January 30, 1931

Dear Baron,

I have to accompany my wife to go to P. M. U. C. this morning unexpectedly. Please excuse me for not being able to come to you.

Sincerely yours,

Yinkoh Tscheng

Lieber Professor Tscheu,

Es freut mich sehr, dass ich Sie nächsten Sonnabend (den 9. December) hier erwarten darf, und dass wir unsere gemeinsamen Studien auch in diesem Jahre fortsetzen können und 16

Ich schlage vor, dass wir den Commentar die Lecture des Commentars zu § I fortsetzen, und 13 war von chos dari chos smra ba la (Seite 21, Zeile 15) bis chos kyi bstan te (Seite 25, Zeile 13).

Herzliche Grüsse von Ihrem ergebenen

W. Walleser

Peking den 28. März 1935.

Lieber Professor Pelliot,

Aus dem gemeinsamen Besuch, den wir Herrn Huang im Kuo Hsüeh Hsin abstatten wollten, wird für's Erste nichts. Herr Huang ist nämlich nicht in Peking, und, wenn er hierher zurück- kehrt, ist unbekannt.

Ich würde Sie am Sonnabend (den 30. März) früh erwarten.

Viele Grüsse von Ihrem ergebenen

A. Stael-Holstein.

An Herrn Professor Pelliot
Tsinghua

Lieber Professor Tschen,

Es tut mir sehr leid, dass unsere Sonntag- Lecture morgen (Sonnabend den 11. Mai) ausfallen muss. Ich will Sonntag auf einige Wochen nach Paryfung fahren und habe noch sehr viel vorzubereiten und zu tun. Ich hoffe, dass Sie mir gestatten werden, Ihnen später, sobald ich wieder zurück gekehrt sein werde, mit meinen Vorträgen und ich hoffe, dass auch Sie dann bereit sein werden, une re gemeinsamen Studien wieder aufzunehmen.

Herzliche Grüße
von Ihrem ergebenen A. v. Müllstein.

Dienstag den 25. Juni 1935.

Lieber Professor Pelliot,

Soeben habe ich wieder einige Seiten zurückerhalten. Jetzt bin ich wieder in Peking und hoffe sehr, Sie recht bald wiederzusehen. Sollte es Ihnen Dienstag den 2. Juli zum Sonnenuntergang um die gewohnte Zeit erwarten?

Herzliche Grüsse
von Ihrem ergebenen
Staël-Holstein

Dear Mr. Dien,

I have returned from my journey and I shall be very pleased if you will come to see me on Saturday the 29th at 3 o'clock

Lieber Professor Tschen,

Ich muss vor meiner Abreise den Harvard-Tientsin über den Woods Memorial Volume berichten.
Ich habe ihnen schon geschrieben, dass Ihr werter Dr. Hu Shih's steht not auf Sicherheit dass auf keinen Fall das Ihr Artikel und z derjenige Dr. Hu Shih's vor dem 15. August fertig sein werden. Darf ich Sie nun bitten mir mitzuteilen, wie es um den Beitrag Professor P'ang's steht. Wird Professor P'ang's Artikel auch vor dem 15. August fertig sein? Ich habe meine Abfahrt verschoben, müssen und reise erst Dienstag. Herzliche Grüsse von Ihnen ergebenen

AvonStaël-Holstein

Peking, den 16. Januar 1935

Lieber Professor Pelliot,

Beifolgend sende ich Ihnen den ersten Theil meines Artikels für's "Woods" Memorial Volume. Wollen Sie die Güte haben, ihn durchzulesen und besonders meine Übersetzung der kaiserlichen Vorrede sorgfältig mit dem chinesischen Original zu vergleichen, dessen photographische Reproduktion ich auch beilege. Ich hoffe, dass Sie mir erlauben werden, den zweiten Sommer mit Ihnen zu discutieren.

Mit den besten Grüssen
Ihr ergebener
A. Staël-Holstein.

Lieber Professor Tschen,

Es thut mir sehr leid, dass Ihre Gesundheit noch immer nicht vollständig wiederhergestellt ist. Hoffentlich erholen Sie sich gut im Ch'ing Tao. Ich reise morgen nach Japan.

Professor Lüders schrieb mir:

3 Professor: Ich schicke Ihnen beiliegend die Photographie des Knabens Burniak. Professor V. Soedens Bemerkungen sind auf der Rückseite notiert.

Herzliche Grüsse von Ihnen ergebenen
Walter v. Stein

Lieber Professor Tschen,

Ich muss nun meiner Strauss den Harvard-Leuten über den Woods Memorial Volume berichten.

Ich habe ihnen schon geschrieben, dass Prof. Hu Shih sicher aber auf Sicherheit abernt behaven strifton, dass Ihr Artikel und 2 derjenige Dr. Hu Shih's vor dem 15. August fertig sein werden. Darf ich Sie nun bitten mir mitzuteilen, wie es um den Beitrag Professor Pland's steht. Wird Professor Pland's Artikel auch vor dem 15. August fertig sein?

Ich habe meine August vorschrieben meinen nuch nune erst Dienstag. Herzliche Grüsse von Ihrem ergebenen A. v. Staël-Holstein

Lieber Herr Tschen,

Neunzehn japanische Zen-Mönche, die jetzt auf einer Informationsreise durch China begriffen sind, wollen mich morgen (Freitag) früh besuchen. Ihre Zeit ist sehr beschränkt, und sie können ihren Besuch unmöglich auf einen anderen Tag verlegen. Daher bitte ich Sie, am Sonntag früh um acht, anstatt morgen (Freitag), 12 u. 1/2 12 zu kommen. Sollte Ihnen der Sonntag nicht passen, so kommen Sie, bitte, am nächsten Freitag um acht Uhr.

Herzliche Grüsse von Ihrem ergebenen

v. Heilbostein

Hochverehrter Herr Doctor,

Meine Frau hat hat sich dem November keine einzige Einladung angenommen, und kann Ihr Ihrem geschätzten Bedauern am Donnerstag (den 15. Mai) nicht bei Ihnen speisen. Ich nehme aber Ihre freundliche Einladung für meine Person mit dem grössten Danke an.

Mit den besten Grüssen

Ihr ergebener
AvStaël-Holstein

Hochverehrte gnädige Frau

Ihre gütige Einladung nehme ich mit dem besten Dank an und werde am Dienstag den 20. Mai um 1.15 bei Ihnen erscheinen.

Es wird Ihnen die Hand küssen Ihr ganz ergebener
AvStaël-Holstein

The lCaṅ-skya Hu-thug-thu —

The lCaṅ-skya Hu-thug-thu mentioned here was Rol-pah̩i-rdo-rje [Lalitavajra]. The personal name of the lCaṅ-skya Hu-thug-tu mentioned here was Rol-pah̩i-rdo-rje [Lalitavajra]. Under the auspices of this Rol-pah̩i-rdo-rje the bsTan-h̩gyur was translated into Mongol in A.D. 1744(?)

Nach Schulem. (pag. 140) Chung hua Bol ch. geb. 1/1/14 nach pag. 209 A.D. 1744(?) geschrieben. Huth 290 flgg.

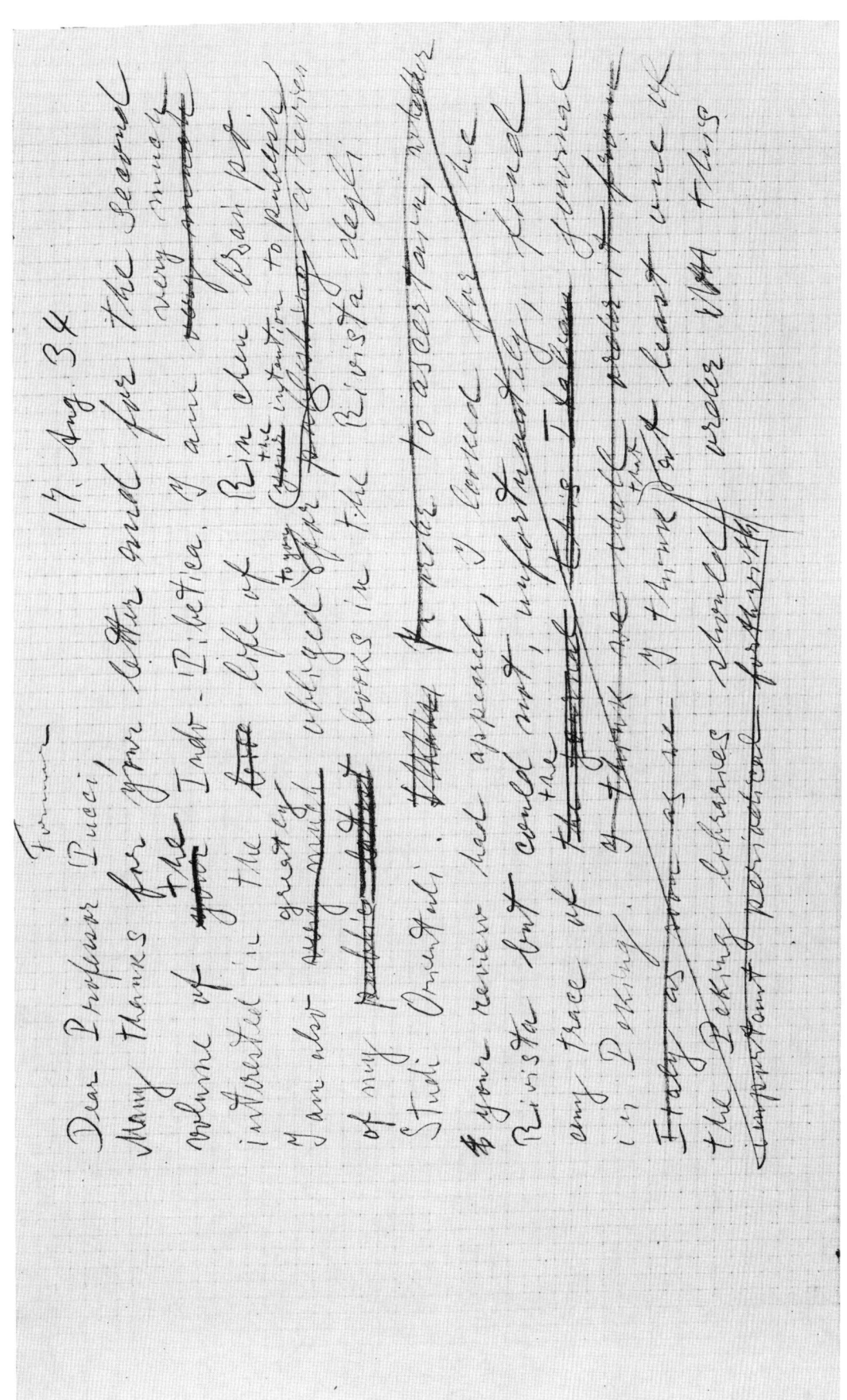

Firenze 17. Aug. 34

Dear Professor Pucci,

Many thanks for your letter and for the second volume of your Indo-Tibetica. I am very much interested in the life of Rin chen bzan po. I am also greatly obliged to you for the intention to publish of my probable a review of my probable papers in the Rivista degli Studi Orientali. After to ascertain whether ↑ your review had appeared, I looked for the Rivista but could not, unfortunately, find any trace of the journal this Ikeda journal in Peking. I think we shall probably leave Italy as soon as we I think that learnt une ↑ the Peking Libraries should order lich things important periodical forthwith.

My Dear von Staël — Have you ever heard of a book entitled
Amitābha (according to and of its commentary
(ཟླ་བ?) entitled འོད་ཟེར་ཅན་ (according to
my Jäng's spelling)? I have written several
times to India and to Tibet for these books,
but in vain. I shall willingly pay any price
for these two, for the photographic reproductions
of them.

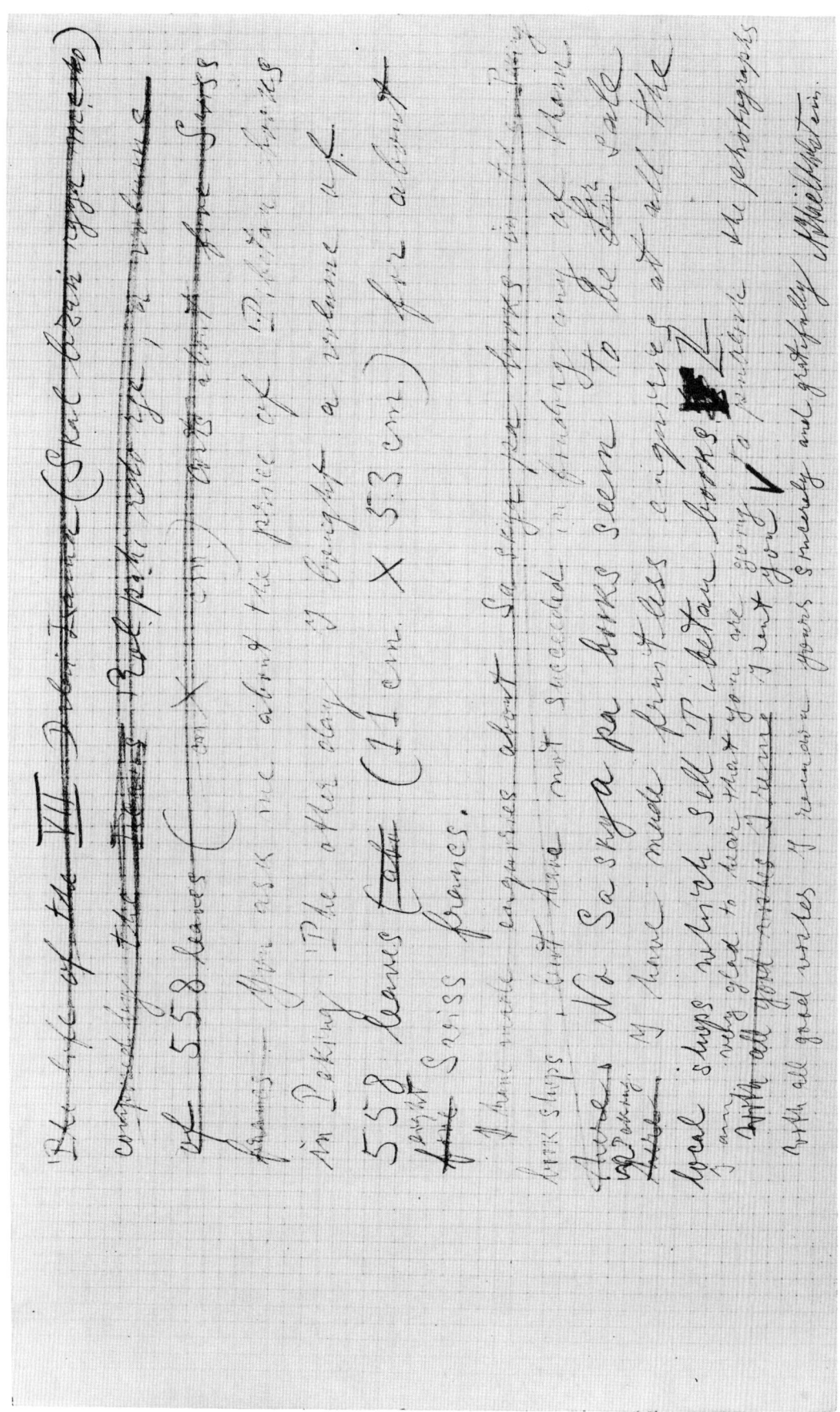

Tucci

Peking
Hochgeehrter Herr Professor,

Für die gütige Zusendung der Indo-Tibetica danke ich Ihnen bestens. Ich habe den Band nicht nur ausserordentlich gründlich studiert und sehr viel für mich Wichtiges daraus gelernt. Besonders habe ich mich gefreut Sie ernste Photographien (ohne welche retouchieren?) veröffentlichen werden. Die anliegenden Photographien werden Sie vielleicht interessieren — es ist kaum möglich [...] zu einem gesunden an [...] finden, [...]

In dem nächsten Tagen werde ich nach 五台 (= Aśramakāsthāna), wo sich acht buddhistische Dengelöster befinden. In diesem Berge (eine Tagestunde von Peking) ist es viel ruhiger als in der Stadt.
Mit nochmaligem Dank verbleibe ich Ihr ganz ergebener
Es ist mysteriös nur ohne Stahlhofen ... v. Stael-Holstein

Former Austrian Legation Peking, July 25th 1933.

My dear Professor Vogel,

Many thanks for your letter dated February 19th 1933. I also remember with much pleasure the weeks which we spent together at Simla and Lahore in 1903. I feel as if those weeks belonged to an entirely different kalpa; the world has certainly experienced a period of thorough prakṛya since we went for walks in the Ladies' Mile.

Since 1929 I am ~~I am sending you under separate cover a copy of~~ my edition of the commentary of the Kāśyapaparivarta. The I published the text of the Kāśyapaparivarta in 1926, but my that edition has, like any other Far Eastern imprint efforts, been almost entirely neglected by the philolo- gists of the West. Please do induce somebody to publish a few encouraging words about my efforts, it you should be too busy to do so yourself. I shall be very grateful for a printed appreciation of my work, because it must be able to prove to the authorities of Cambridge Massachusetts that my ~~MSS for Sanskrit publications~~ ~~are regarded as potential~~ ~~(it must before the end of this year) which I could submit~~ to the authorities of Cambridge Massachusetts upon whom my fate depends Harvard University. Since 1929 I am a professor of Central Asian philology in Harvard University, the authorities of which have so far allowed me to live in Peking *. I like this city very much, and I hope that I shall be allowed to stay here for a few more years. In order to obtain an extension of my leave, which has to be renewed every year, I must, however, ~~I provide hereunto~~ am in charge of the Sino-Indian Institute ~~which~~ depends entirely upon American liberality. Professor Zeller………

* Sino-Indian Institute of Peking

be able to prove that my work is appreciated in Europe. Please do help me in doing this. You could certainly help me in doing this by letting me have a few (in print) a short review of my editions or of the articles which appeared in 1932. Seeing books and articles, which I have sent you through the press, was not an easy task, because the Chinese compositors were entirely unacquainted with character marks etc. But now the ice is broken, and the bringing out of our next publications (we have a number of books and papers almost ready for the press) will be less difficult.

It is not mere vanity which makes me ask for a printed appreciation of my work, but dire necessity.

Believe me yours sincerely AvStaëlHolstein.

Former Austrian Legation, Peking, November 23rd 1933.

My dear Professor Vogel,

I am very greatly obliged to you ~~that~~ (kind) for your letter dated October 12th 1933 found return of yesterday, and for ~~many thanks~~ your kindly and for learn that a review will appear in Het Museum. It ~~is~~ I shall be very grateful if you will send me a reprint of the review. But may I ask you to have it registered? ~~Very many~~ Letters & addressed etc to Peking, which are not registered, frequently ~~do not~~ often fail to reach their destination. I ~~am sorry~~ regret to say that I have never yet seen the "Annual Bibliography of Indian Archaeology" but I am very anxious to get acquainted with this periodical. Wishing you a very happy New year I remain yours gratefully ~~very gratefully~~ [signature]

P.S. Do not trouble ~~you~~ to send reprints of the review to America. Why? got a copy of it ~~from~~ I shall have it mitographed and found copies of it to my American friends ~~the~~ & Americans.

Dolcin

Vogel

Lieber Herr Professor,

Für die freundliche Übersendung Ihrer neuen Professor Radin im Museum & meinen Publicationen gewidmet hat, bin ich in erster Linie Ihnen Ihm zu Danke verpflichtet. Ich habe Übersetzt davon, dass Professor Radin es hat mich sehr gefreut Professor Radin, den nunlich einige Tage hier verbrachte, persönlich kennen zu lernen.

Auch für die gütige Übersendung der Annual Bibliography of Indian Archaeology für the year 1927 bin ich Ihnen zu herzlichem Danke. Ich habe nemlich interessiere mich selbst auch sehr für Archäologie.

Heidelberg, den 29. Januar 1929
Goethestr. 12

Hochgeehrter Herr!

Gelegentlich einer heute stattgehabten Vorbesprechung zwecks Begründung einer „Gesellschaft für Buddhismus-Kunde" wurde der einstimmige Beschluß gefaßt, Sie zu bitten, das -- mit keiner Verpflichtung oder Verantwortung verbundene -- Amt eines Ehrenbeirats (Honorary Councillor) der Gesellschaft übernehmen zu wollen.

Zugleich beehre ich mich, Sie zu der laut Beschluß am 15. März d.J. nachm. 3 Uhr in meiner Wohnung (Heidelberg, Goethestr. 12) stattfindenden Gründungsversammlung einzuladen.

Es liegen diesem Schreiben bei:
1) eine Kopie des Protokolls der heutigen Vorbesprechung.
2) eine Kopie des Statutenentwurfs.
3) ein informatorischer Aufsatz, um dessen weitere Verbreitung in interessierten Kreisen höflichst gebeten wird.

Mit ausgezeichneter Hochachtung
ganz ergebenst

M. Walleser

Herrn Dr. Baron v. Staël-Holstein
Professor d. Universität
Peking

Heidelberg, den 16. März 1928

Hochgeehrter Herr Baron,

Ich bin beauftragt Ihnen mitzuteilen, daß gelegentlich der gestern hier stattgehabten Gründungsversammlung der „Gesellschaft für Buddhismuskunde" der einstimmige Beschluß gefaßt wurde, Sie zu bitten, das Amt eines Ehrenbeirats der Gesellschaft übernehmen zu wollen.
Es liegen diesem Schreiben bei:
1). eine Kopie des Protokolls der Gründungsversammlung,
2). eine Kopie der auf derselben gefaßten Resolution,
3). eine berichtigte Kopie des Statutenentwurfs;

Mit ausgezeichneter Hochachtung
ganz ergebenst
M. Walleser

Herrn Baron Dr. v. Stael-Holstein
Professor d. Univ. Peking

~~ENTWURF~~

STATUTEN

der

GESELLSCHAFT FÜR BUDDHISMUSKUNDE

§ 1. Zweck der am ~~Februar~~ *15. März* 1928 in Heidelberg begründeten „Gesellschaft für Buddhismuskunde" ist, die wissenschaftliche Erforschung des Buddhismus zu pflegen und zu fördern.

§ 2. Den angegebenen Zweck sucht die Gesellschaft zu erreichen durch :

1. Herausgabe von Texten, Übersetzungen und wissenschaftlichen Abhandlungen,

2. Unterhaltung einer buddhistischen Bibliothek, im Falle ausreichender Mittel auch eines an die Bibliothek anzugliedernden Forschungsinstituts.

§ 3. Die Mitgliedschaft wird erworben durch einen vorauszuzahlenden jährlichen Beitrag von 12 Mark. Dafür wird ein „Jahrbuch der Gesellschaft für Buddhismuskunde" unentgeltlich und portofrei geliefert. Außerdem steht den Mitgliedern die Benutzung der Bibliothek der Gesellschaft zu noch bekanntzugebenden Bedingungen zu. Außerordentlich erwünscht sind freiwillige höhere Beiträge und sonstige Zuwendungen der Mitglieder.

§ 4. Man gilt als Mitglied von dem 1. Januar des Jahres an, für das man sich angemeldet hat. Der Austritt ist nur am Ende des Jahres zulässig und ist dem Vorstand vorher anzuzeigen.

§ 5. Mit der Zahlung des Beitrags säumige Mitglieder verlieren ihre aus der Mitgliedschaft erwachsenden Rechte und können, wenn sie auch der Mahnung des Vorstandes nicht nachkommen, aus den Listen der Gesellschaft gestrichen werden.

§ 6. Das Geschäftsjahr des Vereins beginnt mit dem 1. Januar und endigt mit dem 31. Dezember.

§ 7. Mitglieder, die, gleichviel ob freiwillig oder unfreiwillig, ausscheiden, haben keinen Anspruch auf das Vermögen der Gesellschaft.

§ 8. Der Vorstand besteht aus dem Vorsitzenden, der durch Majoritätsbeschluß der Mitgliederversammlung gewählt wird, einem stellvertretenden Vorsitzenden und einem Schriftführer.

§ 9. Es ist Sache des Vorsitzenden, die zu veröffentlichenden Arbeiten zu bestimmen und alle die Veröffentlichung betreffenden Abmachungen zu regeln. Er vertritt die Gesellschaft gerichtlich und außergerichtlich.

§ 10. Der stellvertretende Vorsitzende wird jährlich von den ortsanwesenden Mitgliedern der Gesellschaft gewählt. Kommt keine Wahl zu stande, so gilt das älteste ortsanwesende Mitglied der Gesellschaft als solcher.

§ 11. Für die Länder, in denen besondere Interessen für die Gesellschaft vorhanden sind (Japan, Indien etc.), sollen ~~durch den Vorstand~~ Ehrenbeiräte gewählt werden.

§ 12. Der Schriftführer hat über Einnahmen und Ausgaben Buch zu führen und die Korrespondenzen zu erledigen. Er wird durch den Vorsitzenden bestimmt. Seine Tätigkeit kann entsprechend vergütet werden. Das Amt des Schriftführers kann stellvertretungsweise durch den Vorsitzenden ausgeübt werden.

§ 13. Da die überwiegende Zahl der Mitglieder voraussichtlich außerhalb Deutschlands domiziliert ist, wird von der Abhaltung von Mitgliederversammlungen außer der Gründungsversammlung abgesehen. Der Vorstand wird daher eventuelle, von zehn Mitgliedern unterschriebene Anträge auf schriftlichem Wege zur allgemeinen Kenntnis und [nach weiteren 2-3 Monaten zur] Abstimmung bringen. ~~Letztere soll nicht vor Ablauf des nachfolgenden Vierteljahres und nicht nach Ablauf desselben erfolgen.~~ Über das Ergebnis der Abstimmung soll Beurkundung durch den Vorstand erfolgen und den Mitgliedern auf schriftlichem Wege alsbald Mitteilung gemacht werden.

§ 14. Der Vorsitzende führt bei Versammlungen der Gesellschaft und des Vorstandes den Vorsitz. Bei Stimmengleichheit entscheidet die Stimme des Vorsitzenden.

§ 15. Ist nach Ablauf von 5 Jahren die Zahl von 100 Mitgliedern nicht erreicht, so steht dem Vorsitzenden ohne weiteres das Recht zu, im Falle der vorherigen Eintragung in das Vereinsregister die Streichung des Vereins mit Wirkung vom Schluß des Geschäftsjahres ab zu veranlassen. Etwaige Kassenüberschüsse sind für die Erweiterung der Bibliothek zu verwenden und diese der am Wohnsitze des Vorsitzenden befindlichen Universitätsbibliothek oder, falls hier eine solche nicht vorhanden sein sollte, einer von dem Vorsitzenden zu bestimmenden deutschen Universitäts- oder Staatsbibliothek zur geschlossenen Aufbewahrung zu überantworten.

§ 16. Für den Fall der Auflösung des Vereins erklärt sich der Vorsitzende als persönlich für die Geschäftsführung und Liquidierung haftbar.

§ 17. Falls nach Ablauf von 5 Jahren der Bestand der Gesellschaft als hinreichend gesichert erscheint, so soll sie zunächst als für weitere 10 Jahre bestehend betrachtet werden.

§ 18. Im Falle eines früheren Ablebens des Begründers und Vorsitzenden soll die sofortige Liquidierung der Gesellschaft vollzogen werden, falls nicht für diesen Fall von dem Vorsitzenden ein anderes Mitglied der Gesellschaft mit der Geschäftsführung betraut sein und sich dieses als persönlich für die Geschäftsführführung und eventuelle Liquidierung haftbar erklären sollte.

§ 19. Alle Einzahlungen erfolgen auf das Konto der Gesellschaft bei der Rheinischen Creditbank Filiale Heidelberg (Postscheckkonto Karlsruhe N° 519).

"Gesellschaft für Buddhismus-Kunde" (Society for Buddhist Lore)
to be founded at Heidelberg.

Repeatedly the German Ambassador in Japan Dr. W. Solf has pointed out the opportunity of a more intense occupation of European scholars with Buddhism, especially Mahayana-Buddhism. This advisability has surely never been earnestly disputed by competent scientists, and it seems exclusively to be traced back to the indifference on the side of the Berlin officials, if those instigations which lastly go back to a memorandum, composed by Dr. B. Petzold and forwarded to the Prussian Minister of Education (cf. Young East II p. 271), have been till now without any success. In which direction these steps towards a profounder exploration and a more exact knowledge of Buddhism have got to lie, has been sufficiently shown by His Exc. Dr. Solf: establishment of an Institute for Buddhist Research and "exchange professors" between Japan and the Western countries (Young East I p. 384). As it must be supposed that these propositions have been without any visible result, it is obvious to consider a non-official institution, independent on and therefore not to be influenced by government, but notwithstanding capable of presenting all advantages which a government-institute could afford. Now these are the same exigencies to which the "Gesellschaft für Buddhismus-Kunde" seeks to correspond, taking up the following points in its programme:

1) Publication of Buddhist texts, translations and monographs in a Yearbook which is to bring at the same time to the members of the Society any important or interesting communications on the Society and its activity.

2) Establishment of a Buddhist library the real success of which, however, would in the main depend on voluntary contributions and donations.

3) Systematical courses for those active members to whom the courses held at the University are not convenient in consequence of the higher number of participants required there, under conditions which do not exceed those charged by the University.

Every one interested in the purposes of the Society is heartily invited to join it as a member. The annual subscription which has to be paid in advance (scil. in the first three months of the year) on the account of the Society (Rheinische Creditbank Filiale Heidelberg) is twelve marks for which the Yearbook will be sent postfree. The size of the Yearbook will, of course, depend chiefly on the number of the subscribers; so it will be the common interest of all to do their best to win as many members for the Society as possible.

Copies of the Rules of the Society may be had on application from the undersigned.

Heidelberg

Goethestr. 12   Prof. Dr. M. Walleser.

Abschrift

Protokoll der am 28. Januar 1928 stattgehabten vorläufigen
Besprechung wegen Begründung einer
„Gesellschaft für Buddhismus-Kunde"

1) Anwesend sind die Herren Walleser, Tomomatsu, Saeado, Gochale,
   Kitayama, Zinegref.
2) Herr Walleser legt den Entwurf der Statuten einer zu begründenden
   „Gesellschaft für Buddhismuskunde" vor. Er wird einstimmig
   angenommen.
3) Herr Walleser beauftragt, Se. Exzellenz Herrn Botschafter Dr. Solf,
   Tokio, um die Übernahme des Ehrenpräsidiums der Gesellschaft
   zu bitten. Herr Walleser wird beauftragt, bei Herrn Dr. Solf
   deshalb anzufragen.
4) Gemäß § 11 des Statutenentwurfs werden von Herrn Walleser als
   Ehrenmitglieder vorgeschlagen:
       In Birma: Herr Shwe Zan Aung (Rangoon)
       China: Herr Baron von Staël-Holstein (Peking)
       Ceylon: Herr Wanatiloka
       Japan: die Herren Takakusu, Watanabe, Yasui (Tokio)
       Indien: die Herren Tucci, Barua
       Rußland: Herr Stcherbatsky (Leningrad)
       Siam: der siamesische Gesandte in Berlin.
   Diese Vorschläge werden einstimmig angenommen.
   Herr Walleser wird beauftragt, die gewählten Herren hiervon
   in Kenntnis zu setzen und ihr Einverständnis zu erbitten.
   Herr Walleser wird ferner beauftragt, den genannten Herren
   zu übersenden: 1) eine Abschrift des vorliegenden Protokolls,
   2) ein Tonto des Statutenentwurfs zur Kenntnisnahme und Begut-
   achtung, 3) einen informatorischen Artikel, 4) ein Begleit-
   schreiben
5) Die Gründungsversammlung soll am 15. März 1928 nachm. 3 Uhr in der
   Wohnung von Herrn Walleser stattfinden. Die genannten Herren
   sind hierzu einzuladen.

Heidelberg, 29. Januar 1928   (gez.)   M. Walleser
                                             Ch. Saeado
                                             E. Tomomatsu
                                             J. Kitayama
                                             W. Zinegref
                                             V. Gochale

Für die Richtigkeit

Ch. Sakado   M. Walleser

Heidelberg, Januar 1928
Goethestr. 12

An

Beiliegend beehre ich mich, den Entwurf der Statuten einer in Heidelberg zu begründenden „Gesellschaft für Buddhismus-Kunde" ganz ergebenst zur Durchsicht zu unterbreiten, mit der Bitte, im Falle der allgemeinen Zustimmung zu den Zielen und Tendenzen der Gesellschaft die Ihnen erforderlich erscheinenden Änderungen vermerken zu wollen.

Die Gründung eines Institutes ist durch die besonderen Verhältnisse an der Universität Heidelberg notwendig geworden, indem hier seit einigen Semestern Vorlesungen und Übungen nur noch bei einer Beteiligung von mindestens drei Hörern stattfinden können. Bei der starken Spezialisierung der Buddhismus-Forschung, die sich aus der Verschiedenheit der Kultur- und Sprachgebiete — indisch, chinesisch, tibetisch, japanisch — ergibt, ist es untunlich, wenn nicht gar unausführbar, gemeinsame Studien ohne starke Beeinträchtigung der individuellen Interessen zu betreiben. Aus der Notwendigkeit einer besonderen Studiums- und Forschungsstätte, also eines wissenschaftlichen Instituts, ergibt sich aber auch die der Errichtung einer buddhistischen Bibliothek, die umso unentbehrlicher ist, als eine solche in Deutschland bis jetzt überhaupt nicht existiert. Diese ist aber ohne erhebliche Zuwendungen von Büchern oder Geldmitteln nicht wohl denkbar.

Ist aber die Zweckmäßigkeit eines besonderen Lehr- und Forschungsinstituts für den Buddhismus erkannt, so ergibt sich ohne weiteres als nächste Forderung die Finanzierung einer Zeitschrift oder — als den vorerst bescheideneren Zielen des Instituts besser entsprechend — eines Jahrbuchs, in welchem die aus dem Institut hervorgehenden Arbeiten publiziert werden. Diese Forderung ist um so dringender, als die Druckkosten seit dem Krieg auf etwa das Dreifache des früheren Betrags gestiegen sind und daher die Publizierung wissenschaftlicher Arbeiten nur noch durch besondere staatliche Zuwendungen („Notgemeinschaft der deutschen Wissenschaft") angängig ist, die aber für die Zwecke des Instituts aus verschiedenen Gründen nicht in Betracht kommen.

Unter diesen Umständen glaubt der Unterzeichnete, auf das wohlwollende Verständnis und Entgegenkommen vor allem derjenigen Kreise rechnen zu dürfen, denen das Interesse für die wissenschaftliche Erforschung des Buddhismus in besonderem Maße obliegt, also den Kultgemeinschaften und prominenten Vertretern des Buddhismus in Japan und sonstigen überwiegend buddhistischen Ländern.

Es würde ihm zur besonderen Ehre und Freude gereichen, wenn diese Teilnahme dadurch zum Ausdruck käme, daß sich möglichst viele Teilnehmer aus den Ihnen nahestehenden Kreisen als Mitglieder der geplanten „Gesellschaft für Buddhismus-Kunde" anmeldeten. In diesem Sinne beehrt sich der Unterzeichnete, ganz ergebenst zum Beitritt aufzufordern.

Prof. D. M. Walleser

ENTSCHLIESSUNG

der Gesellschaft für Buddhismuskunde

zu Heidelberg, 15. März 1928.

 Die Gesellschaft für Buddhismuskunde nimmt dankend zur Kenntnis, daß in Heidelberg als einziger deutscher Universität ein Lehrauftrag für indische und ostasiatische Religionswissenschaft besteht, und gibt der Erwartung Ausdruck, daß er auch weiterhin erhalten bleibe. Sie glaubt umso eher hierauf rechnen zu dürfen, als mit Hinsicht auf die Honorierung des Lehrauftrags nur bei einer Mindestzahl von drei Teilnehmern die der Universität erwachsenen Kosten des Lehrauftrags als durch die allgemeinen Semestergebühren der Teilnehmer, zumal wenn diese nicht ohne das Bestehen des obigen Lehrauftrags nach Heidelberg gekommen wären, nahezu gedeckt betrachtet werden können, während bei mehr als drei Teilnehmern sich ein finanzielles Plus dadurch ergibt, daß der Zuwachs an Semestergeldern die Kosten des Lehrauftrags übersteigt.

 Andererseits erscheint es mit besonderer Hinsicht auf die fernausländischen Teilnehmer nicht angängig, daß Vorlesungen und Übungen, die im Vorlesungsverzeichnis angezeigt sind, infolge Nichterreichung der Mindestzahl von drei Teilnehmern nicht abgehalten werden können, und nimmt dankend zur Kenntnis, daß Herr Prof. Walleser auch in diesen Falle zur Abhaltung der angezeigten Übungen und Vorlesungen bereit ist, falls diese in einem besonderen, von der Gesellschaft zu errichtenden Institut auf Grund einer generellen finanziellen Regelung abgehalten werden könnten, welche im Einvernehmen mit der Universität zu treffen wäre.

 Der Vorstand wird beauftragt, sich deshalb mit den maßgebenden Instanzen in Verbindung zu setzen und eine grundsätzliche Regelung herbeizuführen.

 Sollte eine Regelung auf der Grundlage des obigen Vorschlags nicht angängig sein, soll der Vorstand die Angelegenheit dem Beirat unterbreiten und mit dessen Unterstützung versuchen, ein selbständiges Institut für Buddhismuskunde zu errichten.

Vorsitzender: Schriftführer:

P r o T o k o l l

der

Gründungsversammlung der Gesellschaft für Buddhismuskunde
zu Heidelberg am 15 März 1928

1) Anwesend sind die Herren Vailleser, Saeato, Tomomatsu, Matsumoto, Gokhale, Wolff, Zinegraf.
2) Die Anwesenden erklären sich mit den im Statutenentwurf niedergelegten Zielen und Aufgaben der Gesellschaft einverstanden. Die Statuten werden mit den in dem beiliegenden Entwurf vermerkten Änderungen genehmigt.
3) Die Gründung der Gesellschaft auf Grund der Statuten wird einstimmig beschlossen.
4) Als Vorstandsmitglieder werden gewählt:
   Vorsitzender: Herr Vailleser,
   Stellvertretender Vorsitzender: Herr Saeato,
   Schriftführer: Herr Gokhale.
5) Als Ehrenbeiräte werden vorbehaltlich ihres Einverständnisses gewählt:
   für Birma: Herr Chos Tai Jung,
   Ceylon: Herr Wanatilloka,
   China: Herr Baron v. Stael-Holstein,
   Deutschland: die Herren Geiger und Beumann,
   Indien: die Herren Barua und Tucci,
   Japan: die Herren Masuda, Taeaeusu, Watanabe, Yoshihara,
   Nepal: Herr Hemaraja Sarman,
   Rußland: Herr Stcherbatsky,
   Siam: Herr Phra Vitraecurmeshita.
6) Herr Botschafter Dr. Solf, Exzellenz, soll nach seiner Rückkehr nach Deutschland gebeten werden, den Ehrenvorsitz der Gesellschaft zu übernehmen, bejahendenfalls auch um die Genehmigung der Bezeichnung der Gesellschaft als „Solf-Gesellschaft für Buddhismuskunde".
7) Der Vorstand wird beauftragt, sich wegen Regelung von Übungskursen in einem eventuell von der Gesellschaft zu errichtenden Institut mit der Universitätsbehörde in Verbindung zu setzen (Entschließung.

           (gez.) V. Vailleser
               Ch. Saeato
               V. Gokhale
               S. Tomomatsu
               S. Wolff
               T. Matsumoto
               V. Zinegraf

Für die Richtigkeit
V. Gokhale

Former Austrian Legation, Peking, den 28. Juli 1933.

Hochgeehrter Herr Professor,

Für die freundliche Zusendung des 19. Bandes des Materialien danke ich Ihnen bestens. Ihre Übersetzung ist für mich von grossem ~~Nutzen~~ Bedeutung, und ich habe schon Gelegenheit ~~gehabt~~ ~~für meine Vorarbeit zu der Kōyōpapanmokḥi~~ sehen ~~für meine Vorarbeit zu der Kōyōpapanmokḥi~~ Ausgabe der Kōyōpapanmokḥi Auszüge daraus verwerthet zu sehen bei der Zusammenstellung des Vorworts zu meiner letzten Publication verwerthen können.

Seit 1929 ... zu listen.

Vielleicht

Peking September 2nd 1934.

Dear Dr. Ware,

Many thanks for your letter (and for the doctor's thesis which I have studied with the greatest interest.

Only a few days ago I had occasion to occupy myself again with great profit while analyzing a Tibetan inscription. I am very happy to know that you are now firmly established at Cambridge, and I expect many good results from your collaboration with Professor Eliséev.

My former pupils Yü and Lin are now both in Paris, where they continue their studies under Lévi, Bacot and Pelliot. For a long time there is among the Pekingese in Buddhistic history interest of the Pekingese in Buddhistic studies seems to be growing, and we ought to have hopes of collaboration of youngish Chinese with a number of young Chinese scholars quite promising Chinese scholars. In a few weeks we are to spend a learned Brahman who goes in for Sino-Indian studies, is expected to spend the winter here and I hope that he will take part to join Ischen and myself in our [?] (Prince Rinpa-max-chien) for Buddhist words. Believe me yours sincerely [Stcherbatsky?]

Peking, September 19th 1934.

Dear Dr. Ware,

According to the book entitled "Who's Who in America" (Chicago, 1932) Professor [James R.] Ware will be seventy years old on November 24th 1934. I presume that you are in constant touch communication with him and venture to ask you to send him the ~~inserted~~ attached my congratulations tablet which I have sent to your address ~~my congratulations~~ are inserted in Chinese on his next birthday. My words are inserted in Chinese on the silver tablet which I have sent to your address through the Pacific Storage and Packing Company of Peking. They ~~tell me that~~ assume me ~~customs dues whatever~~ ~~have anything~~ to pay ~~to either~~ upon receipt of the tablet. I hope that you have received ~~anything~~ the letter which I sent you in September. May I ask you to announce the receipt of the tablet by the following ~~cable~~ deferred cable: Staël Anneno Peking arrived (no signature is necessary). I enclose ~~the a draft~~ three dollars for the ~~cable~~ deferred ~~cable~~ telegram. With many anticipated thanks I am yours sincerely [Staëlholstein]

P.S. I feel very guilty for troubling you with this tablet. But it is seen no other way of assuring its arrival at 29 Jabra Street on November 24th. Please excuse me.

Yours,
[signature]

Rue Lanchester,
No. 65
M 6

Peking, December 26th 1934.

Dear Dr. Ware,

Many thanks for your letter dated October 17th 1934. I mightily appreciate your kind offices, and I entirely agree with your plan. Please ask a Boston jeweller to remove the dent in the plaque and to mount it on a mahogany frame. I shall pay the bill as soon as it comes to hand. Professor Woods has already thanked me (in a letter from Honolulu) for the plaque, and I will probably want to see it, when the artist returns to Cambridge next spring. My wife joins me in wishing you a happy New Year, and I remain yours gratefully

AvStaël-Holstein.

HARVARD-YENCHING INSTITUTE

1 Fang Chia Yuan,
Peiping, East City,
July 30, 1935.

Cher Maitre:

In accordance with our conversation of yesterday I report as follows regarding the money which you advanced me to pay some Institute expenses here in Peiping:

The check for G$500 which you gave me was exchanged for S$1253.92, that is, each silver dollar cost G$0.3987. Of this sum I have spent S$960.70. The balance of S$293.22 I am herewith returning to you as the equivalent of G$116.91. In a letter dated today I have asked Professor Blake to have a sum of G$383.09 deposited to your credit with The Kidder Peabody Trust Company, Boston, Mass., and to telegraph you as follows: STAEL AMEXCO PEIPING DEPOSITED. Thus the G$500 which you loaned me will have been returned to you in full without interest.

Respectfully yours,

James R. Ware.

July 31st 1935

Dear Dr. Ware,

I entirely agree with your arrangements and I thank you very much for your cheque (two hundred ninety three Peking dollars and twenty-two cents).

Cordially yours
Alexander Stäel Holstein.

Peiping August 31st 1935.

Dear Dr. Ware,

I shall be very much obliged to you if you will effect the following changes in my article. Please replace the original version of note 9 (which you have) by the new version (which I enclose), and change the words "the Emperor would never" (Note 24) into "The Emperor Ch'ien Lung would never". Tsehun, whom I quote in note 24 told me today that he prefers the new version to the old one.

I highly appreciate the interest you take in my object and
I thank you very much for your kind letter.
I went to see you this afternoon in order to tell you personally how awfully sorry I am that I cannot after all dine with you on the 11th. Unfortunately you were not in.

Hoping that you I hope you will allow me to explain to you on some future occasion why I must forgo the pleasure of joining your party on Monday.

Believe me yours sincerely

HARVARD-YENCHING INSTITUTE

18 Bates St.,
Cambridge, Mass.,
Oct. 23, 1935.

Cher Maître:

I received your letter some time ago and am making the necessary changes in the manuscript of your article.

Periodicals and the Transactions of learned societies may not be sent away from the library, consequently I was forced to have Oldenberg's article photographed. I have paid the cost? $1.50. If there is anything else that I can do for you, do not hesitate to call upon me. The Kanjur and Tanjur arrived safely and in excellent condition. As soon as the shelves are ready, they will be unpacked. Everybody here, particularly Clark, is very pleased with these books.

I often think of you and your wife and the pleasant moments I enjoyed with you at Peiping.

Very sincerely yours,

James R. Ware

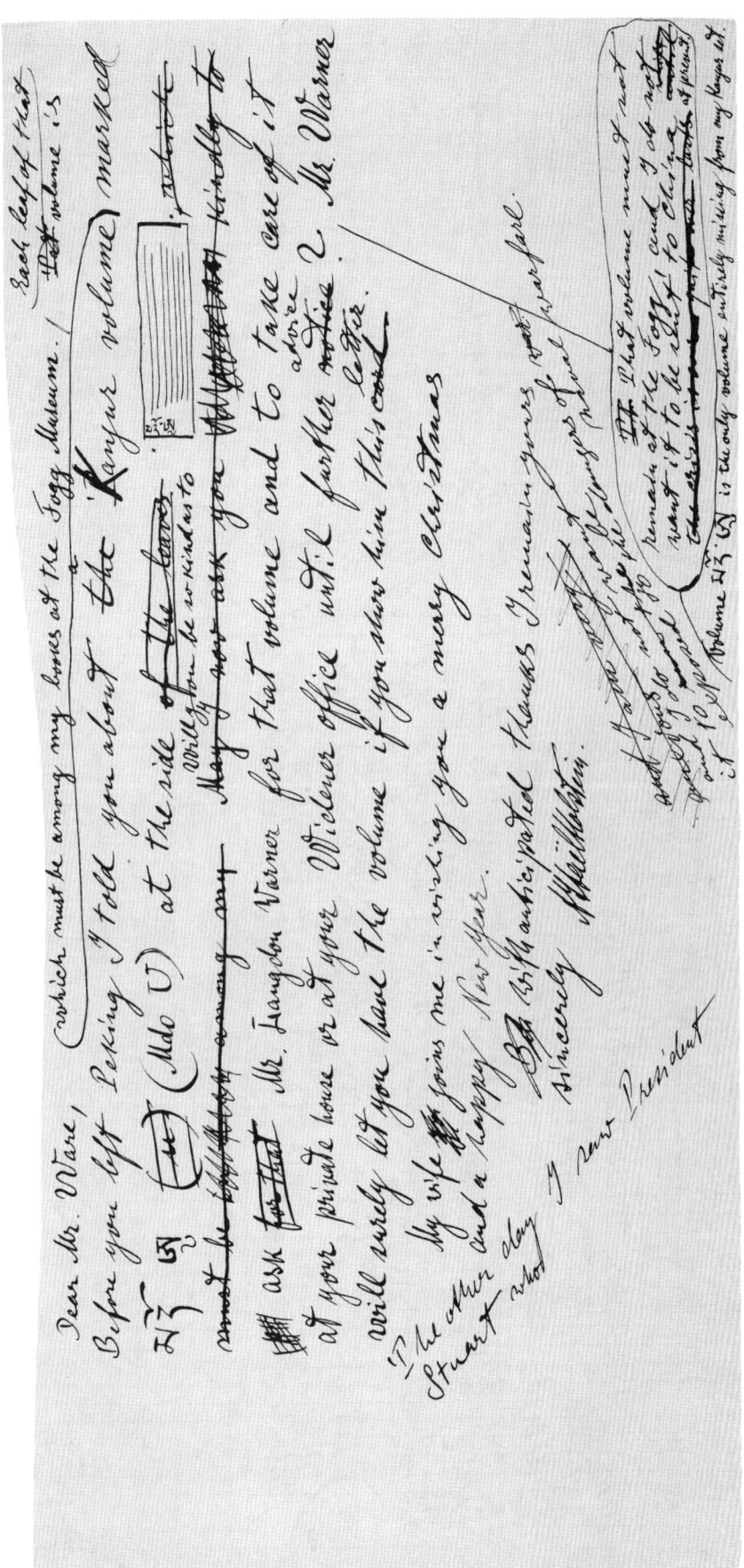

Am 29. Aug. 1932 folgende Fragen durch Mrs Manner an Langdon Warner abgeschickt:

Please ask Mr. Langdon Warner
1) Whether the catalogue of my collection has been found at the Fogg Museum. Answer: one yes, or: one no
2) Whether Mr. Langdon Warner will ever answer the letter which I wrote him in October 1931. Answer: two yes, or: two no.

Peking, January 28th 1936.

Dear Dr. Ware,

I am very much obliged to you for the Mahāyāna films.

It was very kind of you to have the ~~bushely~~ obliged to you for the Mahāmayuri-films. Now I can go on with my study of ~~the~~ I Ching's method of transliterating Indian texts. Thank you very much.

I am so glad to hear that the Staël-thair volumes have safely arrived at Cambridge and that you are pleased with them. My wife and I thank you and Mrs. Ware for your kind New Year's wishes, which ~~are~~ we heartily reciprocate.

I am greatly interested in two collections of [?]

Believe me yours sincerely

AvStaël-Holstein.

P.S.
I enclose a cheque for two dollars.
Holstein.

HARVARD-YENCHING INSTITUTE

HARVARD JOURNAL OF ASIATIC STUDIES
S. ELISSÉEFF, EDITOR

17 BOYLSTON HALL
CAMBRIDGE, MASSACHUSETTS

October 2, 1936

Cher maître:

This is just another short note to ask for an additional favor. Tibetan studies seem to be growing here in the United States, but there is a lamentable lack of texts. Edgerton of Yale, along with his colleague Sapir, now seem to be as keenly interested as Clark here at Harvard. Will you please buy and mail to
> Professor Franklin Edgerton
> 174 Blake Road
> Hamden, Connecticut

one copy of the best edition of the Tibetan Saddharma-pundarika published at Peiping, and if possible one copy also of the Tibetan Lalitavistara.

Will you also buy and ship to
> Professor Walter E. Clark
> 85 Dunster St.
> Cambridge, Mass

two copies of this same Tibetan Saddharma pundarika, and also one copy of the Lalitavistara if it is available. The bill for these books, you might please send to me, and I will see that you are reimbursed. I do not need to remind you that your help in this matter will be greatly appreciated.

With best wishes to you, Madame, and the two youngsters, I remain

Respectfully yours,

James R. Ware

Your article on Avalokita is in press and should appear in November.

HARVARD-YENCHING INSTITUTE

HARVARD JOURNAL OF ASIATIC STUDIES
S. ELISSÉEFF, EDITOR

17 BOYLSTON HALL
CAMBRIDGE, MASSACHUSETTS

October, 13, 1936.

Cher Maître:

      This is just a post scriptum to my letter dated Oct. 2.

      Instead of sending just one of each text to Edgerton will you please send THREE copies of each.

      With renewed assurances of the gratitude and best wishes of all of us, I remain

Respectfully yours,

James R. Ware

James R/ Ware

Dear Professor Ware

The Kalistan is, as far as I know, not to be procured in Peking; but I have sent two copies of the Tibetan Saddhūvinā pindārtha to Prof. Clark and one to Prof. Edgerton. Many thanks for your reprints. They impress me as highly useful.

Yours sincerely
A v Staël-Holstein

Lieber Herr Wilgust,

Meinen besten Dank für die interessanten Photographien! Ihren Neffen wird es sich hoffentlich sehr über sie freuen. Es thut mir sehr leid, dass ich Sie nicht gesehen habe, als Sie so freundlich waren, bei uns vorzusprechen. Herzlichen Gut wünschen Ihnen Frau und Tochter
A v Staël-Holstein

HARVARD-YENCHING INSTITUTE

HARVARD JOURNAL OF ASIATIC STUDIES
S. ELISSÉEFF, EDITOR

17 BOYLSTON HALL
CAMBRIDGE, MASSACHUSETTS
January 25, 1937

Baron Alexander von Staël-Holstein
Former Austrian Legation
Peiping, China

Cher Maître:

The copies of the Tibetan Saddharmapundarika, which you mention in your letter of November 12th, have been duly received by Professors Clark and Edgerton. Meanwhile Prof. Clark has also received from you two additional copies of this same text in another edition. None of us have had the time to compare these two different editions, so if you know or can find out anything regarding them, it would be appreciated if you would let us know. Since there are these two different editions, will you please send to Prof. Franklin Edgerton, 174 Blake Rd., Hamden, Connecticut, two additional copies of the Tibetan Saddharmapundarika in the first edition, namely that characterized by large format. Will you also please send him three copies of the edition in the smaller format.

We acknowledge that we now owe you $15.00 for books, plus $8.00 for packing and mailing. We hope that it will be agreeable to you for us to wait until Prof. Edgerton has received these five additional books before remitting. If there is any error in our calculations, please do not hesitate to advise us.

With best wishes to you and yours for the New Year, I remain

Most respectfully yours,

James R. Ware

W:E

HARVARD-YENCHING INSTITUTE

HARVARD JOURNAL OF ASIATIC STUDIES
S. ELISSÉEFF, EDITOR

17 BOYLSTON HALL
CAMBRIDGE, MASSACHUSETTS

April 22, 1936

Baron Alexander von Stael-Holstein debtor to the Harvard
Journal of Asiatic Studies for 100 reprints   12pp.
                                          cuts 10pp.
                                                    $11.10

HARVARD UNIVERSITY
FOGG ART MUSEUM
CAMBRIDGE, MASS., U.S.A.

April 14th

Dear Baan,

I was delighted to hear from you — and in such a merry vein. The ills of poor old Clinica can not be expected to move deeply either the fortunate bridegroom or the abstracted scholar — which are only two of your many facets.

As for your fresh translation of "timeo Danaos" — I am impressed with your erudition and delighted to find that the French Schoolboy was wrong, as I had always suspected. You remember that he rendered that phrase: —

"J'estime les Danois et leurs dents ferrées."

We have had a delightful visit from your President Stuart. Of course I met him only by chance as he avoided me as the

Devil avoids holy water. It amused me to ask him why he hadn't looked me up — as I had a room at his disposal and had hoped he would at least dine. This seemed rather to embarrass him because he remembered, as I did, how intimate he was with me when I was in China and he thought — (though I assured him it wasn't true) that I held the Harvard-Yenching money bags. He now has persuaded himself that I am a ruthless ruffian who loots the priceless treasures of dear old China and robs her of her birthright, which she values so highly.

He was asked to meet Sir Aurel Stein and told him that Yenching feared contamination by possible association with his name. He also said that Stein would be "doing very wrong" if he tried to do any work in China without first consulting the Committee for the Preservation of China's monuments etc. etc. Stein innocently asked if they had government standing. On finding that they were self-appointed he rather sternly replied that he failed to understand how Stuart

HARVARD UNIVERSITY
FOGG ART MUSEUM
CAMBRIDGE, MASS., U.S.A.

could suggest any such improper interference on his (Stein's) part with a matter that must rest entirely with the British & American representatives and with the Nanking Gov't. I believe that Hung & Stuart were prepared to make trouble about Stein's proposed trip, but I very much hope that their teeth are drawn. I must ask you as a personal favor, not to speak of this matter or of Stein's plans. Much harm might be done by Peking gossip. If you hear any talk about it — among Chinese or foreigners — I should be very grateful for a note from you.

My young friend Sickman has won his Harv-Yen. Fellowship through hard work. He is not the most brilliant person in the world but he is a very willing and conscientious worker. I hope you will give him some good advice when he arrives. You will, no doubt, find that he is less addicted to Tibetan & Sanscrit than to art — but that is small harm as we need various tastes and talents represented over there.

I hope very much that you were not so disgusted with Cambridge that you utterly refuse to come back with Madm. le Baronne — to whom my felicitations & respectful hommages. Surely you realize that you need not be sentenced again to imprisonment in the Business School across the river.

I hope to take my 14 year old daughter to walk in Dorsetshire this summer & then to push on (alone) to see von le Coq's treasures in Berlin and perhaps revisit the Hermitage & some of the Provincial Russian Museums.

Please be sure to let me know if I can be of any service to you in Cambridge

and believe me
  Always most sincerely yours
   Langdon Warner

DEPARTMENT OF
ASIATIC ART

MUSEUM OF FINE ARTS
BOSTON, MASS.

March 28, 1929

Dear Mr. Warner:

In response to your question asked on the telephone yesterday morning, I beg to give you the reasons for my identification of your picture as the Arhat Dharmatrata.

Only one painting of Hsüan Chuang is known to me, the famous Sung painting illustrated in Masterpieces Selected from the Fine Arts of the Far East, by S. Tajima and S. Omura, (published by the Shimbi Shoin, Tokyo), vol. VIII, Plate XXXIV. In this case, although the package of books and the canopy, from which a vessel hangs, are points of likeness between this representation and those of Dharmatrata, the absence of the tiger and of the Buddha Amitābha on a cloud, are points of difference. Hsüan Chuang will also be seen to wear a necklace of skulls, as Dharmatrata apparently did not, and to carry a scroll in the left hand instead of Dharmatrata's flask, although both carry a fly-whisk in the right.

The representation of which I spoke to you may be found on page 88, No. 209, of Das Pantheon des Tschangtscha Hutuktu, by Eugen Pander, a reprint (sonderabdruck) of the publication of

Langdon Warner, Esq.   - 2 -   March 28, 1929

the Museum für Völkerkunde, Berlin, 1910, where it is labelled
in Chinese, 達摩多羅 Ta-mo-to-lo or Dharmatala, a name
often given to the 17th Arhat Dharmatrata, as noted by Pander,--
and in Tibetan, which I cannot read, but which Pander read as
Dharmatrata. Placed as the picture is, in a list of the 18
Arhat, in which it forms the 17th, there seems no reason to
doubt that it represents Dharmatrata. The Museum possesses a
series of Tibetan paintings of Arhat of the Yüan dynasty, one
of which represents Dharmatrata. The figure, carrying books
on his back, a canopy over his head, is accompanied by a tiger;
above sits Amitābha, red of color, on a cloud, just as in
Pander's book. The main figure carries also fly-whisk and
flask, as in the other labelled representation. There is also
a drawing in the British Museum, Thousand Buddhas, Plate XXXIII,
which, having the tiger and the Buddha Amitābha, I should think
was probably intended for Dharmatrata. In short, I am inclined
to think that the presence of the Buddha Amitābha on a cloud
and of the tiger, constitute pretty good evidence for Dharmatrata.
The presence of the Buddha, without the tiger, is not, of course,
so conclusive, but, in the absence of any particular evidence in
the other direction, I should think that Dharmatrata was, perhaps, the better guess. The figure in your Museum, as I remember it, somewhat resembles the drawing in the British Museum,
and both of them are nearer to the Tibetan representations of
Dharmatrata than to the painting of Hsüan Chuang. Absolute

Langdon Warner, Esq.   - 3 -   March 28, 1929

certainty, however, is something *at present* out of reach, seeing that the inscription quite misses the point, and, so far as I can see, has no bearing one way or another on the identification.

                Sincerely yours,

                Helen B. Chapin
                Assistant in the Department

Langdon Warner, Esq.
The Fogg Art Museum
Cambridge
    Massachusetts

HBC/PL

HARVARD UNIVERSITY
FOGG ART MUSEUM
CAMBRIDGE, MASS., U.S.A.

October 10th 29

My dear Staël-Holstein

I was much delighted and surprised to receive your wedding announcement and to read of your happiness. Permit me to congratulate you with all my heart and to felicitate the Baroness, whom I hope to have the honor of meeting.

Perhaps even, you may bring her to Cambridge if she is not too much frightened by your accounts

of the barbarians whose tribal laws
forbid the use of intoxicants, but who
retire to their caves and indulge in their
orgies secretly, hoping that their gods
may not see them. At any rate she
need not fear living at the Business School
for it, mercifully, will be closed to ladies.
Hearing that there is really some hope that
you are to be with us again I am refraining
from sending my modest wedding token to
Peking and hoping that it may prove of some
use during your next stay in Cambridge.
As I wrote you before, the dinner given in
your honor proved to be Hamlet acted without
the Prince of Denmark and my guests all
lamented your absence very much.
The Fogg Museum pursues its plodding way
without much change. My great excitement is
the coming of Sir Aurel Stein to lecture next
December, and the presence here of my friend
Yanagi a Japanese scholar who is helping me

HARVARD UNIVERSITY
FOGG ART MUSEUM
CAMBRIDGE, MASS., U.S.A.

with my work. He is a never-failing delight and a source of inspiration to the students. Priest writes that he will soon be back — you must have been seeing a great deal of him in Peking. I only hope that his Museum were generous in providing him with funds for purchase.

Now that Hovod is with you, I imagine that Harvard-Yenching is somewhat at a standstill in Cambridge. Holles is gone to Cleveland to curate at the Museum & his place as Secretary is being taken by young Plumer — a nice chap on a year's leave from the Chinese Customs. Laufer hasn't yet made up his mind — as far as I know — whether he will come to Cambridge or not. I judge that he shares your healthy and natural dread of falling under the control of certain persons whom you know. The Yen Ching library has been moved into more commodious quarters of its own and I think you will be pleased with all that has happened.

My wife joins me in sending to you and the bride every good wish, and in looking forward to seeing you both in Cambridge next year.

Always Sincerely yours

Langdon Warner

P.S. I was delighted with the sympathetic and understanding article about you and your activities which I saw in the N.Y. Times. Surely the Esthonian Government must recognize scholarship if it is recognized in America! Hollis's description of your house & of the scholars & cocktails found there seemed particularly just & vivid. I wish I might drop in this very afternoon.

L.W.

My dear Warner,

Iconographically speaking I am an orthodox hanaist and never look at heretical images. Therefore I cannot express any opinion on the enclosed representations of Buddhas etc. I have, however, tried to explain ~~trans~~ the inscriptions.

Wishing you and Mrs. Warner a very happy New Year, I remain yours sincerely ~~most~~ Sthael Holstein

P.S. I am deeply touched by your kind congratulations and by the wonderful article in the New York Times. I shall express my gratitude in a long letter very soon.
Johann.

HARVARD UNIVERSITY
FOGG ART MUSEUM
CAMBRIDGE, MASS., U.S.A.

October first '30

My dear Stael

In all these months you have been often in my thoughts and now that the College year has begun, and I am entirely too busy for anything beyond College work, I must send you a short line. Of course I defer to your judgement in the matter of your translation of "Timeo Danaos et dona ferentes". As a youth in Paris I translated it for a FRENCH boy (who seemed perfectly satisfied with my rendering): "J'estime les Danois, et leurs dents ferrées."
Cambridge is much as you left it except that I seem to detect more and better liqueur about the place. My own wine – made in the cellar – is

much better than some French vin ordinaire that I have tasted, and it keeps me contented. The great groups of buildings that constitute the new "Houses" of Harvard are growing rapidly, and two of them are already in use. They are opposite your old quarters on the Cambridge side of the river, and I must say are pretty handsome. The huge smoke-stacks that you will remember by the bridge have been demolished to make place for another group, and still other buildings are being erected between the back of Widener library and the noisy street.

We hear less of Harvard-Yenching now that your beloved colleague Hung has rejoined you. But I am glad to hear that Prof. de Vargas is to give a course on "The Cultural Renaissance in China" during the 2nd half year. I have never had the pleasure of meeting him but look forward to doing so.

I regret to report that my own course has grown to such a size that I am now among the ranks of "popular lecturers" — a most unexpected and not

HARVARD UNIVERSITY
FOGG ART MUSEUM
CAMBRIDGE, MASS., U.S.A.

/3

entirely welcome change. If I can raise money enough there is just a chance of my coming to Nara next March for 6-8 months to work on Tempyo Sculpture. The thing has been hanging about my neck for more than a dozen years and I'm most anxious to finish and bring it out.

Can we hope for you in Cambridge next year? I wonder if you could persuade Madame to like us? At any rate I very much hope that you will bring her over and make the experiment.

Laurence Sickman, by this time has reached Peking and no doubt has paid his call on you. Be good to him for I consider him a most conscientious student. It may prove that he does not shine in Tibetan and Sanscrit — in which case he can confine himself to Chinese and especially to the history of Chinese art. I do not know much about the young man (Shuster), with whom he is living — but I understand that he is brilliant. Perhaps you will be good enough to write me your opinion so that I shall know what to expect from him.

I hope very much that your home affairs in Europe are somewhat brighter than formerly — Howard Hollis's account in the New York Times seemed to me an eminently just one. I understand from him that it was translated and reprinted in Europe.

Please give my sincere regards to Madame and tell her that we look forward eagerly to her coming to Cambridge before long. My wife joins me in sending her best wishes to you.

Always sincerely yours,
Langdon Warner

Please remember me to Lucius Porter.

HARVARD UNIVERSITY
FOGG ART MUSEUM
CAMBRIDGE, MASS., U.S.A.

January 15ᵗʰ '31

Dear Staël

That is indeed a plump and charming son with a real sparkle of his father's geniality. I protest, however, that he ought not to be dressed in Lama's robes and compelled to have his head shaved just because of parental leanings towards Tantric devil-worship.

There is a tremendous flutter in the dove-cotes of Cambridge because of the attack on Stein's good name and the attempt to stop his work made by the Peking Society for the Preservation of Chinese Antiquities. While I am heartily in favor of the professed aims of that Society I regret that they do not realize how upright and how scholarly the person is whom they have singled out for attack. They would do well, in their own interest, to encourage instead of to prevent his work. They would find his behavior impeccably correct and his word as good as his bond. It surprises me much more that Pres. Stuart and Roger Greene and Lucius Porter have been infected by the same idea about Stein. They imply that he behaved in a disingenuous manner by not consulting the Peking Committee though advised to by Stuart & Dean Donham in Cambridge. As a matter of fact he was bound to do precisely what he was told by the British & American Ministers in whose hands his case was placed. He could not have acted otherwise without gravely embarrassing them in their dealings with Nanking.

I do not know what the outcome of it all will be though I fear the cause of Science will receive another set-back. The Cambridge group invited me to one luncheon last week to discuss the matter but I don't know their final decision.

HARVARD UNIVERSITY
FOGG ART MUSEUM
CAMBRIDGE, MASS., U.S.A.

From my point of view there was nothing to do but to stand fast behind our accredited agent. Seeing that they didn't agree & I could do no good I declined the next luncheon party.

My plan now is to sail next month for Japan where I shall sit still in Nara for some 3 months in the hope of finishing a catalogue of the Sculpture of the Tempyo period that I have been working on sporadically since before the war. My illustrations are chosen and much of the slender text is finished. At least it should be an introduction for foreigners to the masterpieces of that period. If the job does not take too long and my funds are sufficient I hope to dash over to Peking for a few weeks. In June I suppose you take your family to Pei Ta Ho or the Western Hills but Peking would mean much more to me if I could look forward to seeing you and to meeting Madame.

When do you plan to come again to the wastes of Cambridge? Perhaps we can manage to make them less arid next time.

Looking forward to seeing you then,
before the summer is half over

I am

Always very Sincerely Yours

Langdon Warner

My wife joins me in sending her New Year's
greetings to all three of you.

Peking July 7th 1931

My dear Warner,

About a week ago the ~~pictures~~ pudique-pictures of the Dalai Lama and of the ~~Pentsi Lama~~ Panchen Lama were dispatched to your address. And I am busy ~~copying~~ ~~Those too far~~ of ~~whi~~ I think that the ~~t~~ that I shall (publish the Third pedigree (of the grand Lama pedigree of Peking) in another journal because ~~my the~~ ~~ph~~ the historico-philological commentary which belongs to it will be too long for "Eastern Art". My notes on the two ~~pedigrees~~ pudique-pictures which I hope you have received by now will soon be ready, and I shall despatch them to your ~~address~~ Japanese address before the end of this month, as arranged. —

~~My fourteen boxes containing~~ Taking advantage of your kind permission I have written to a friend who will send my slightly fourteen or fifteen boxes containing ~~statues~~ pictures, books &c. from Stockholm to the Fogg Museum. The catalogue of the collection too will be posted to ~~the Fogg Museum~~ simply to the Fogg Museum, and no ~~my~~ personal name will be mentioned either on the boxes or on the letter. ~~The insurance~~ Everything will be paid for at Stockholm (insurance &c) except, possibly, the freight, which may have to be paid by the Museum. ~~with you~~ be so kind as to I shall

The freight for the boxes cost me twenty two pounds fifteen shillings and four pence from Tientsin to Hamburg (on the British steamer Calchas) and it should cost less from Stockholm to Boston.

May I ask the Museum to advance the freight charges. I enclose a cheque for 115 gold dollars to cover the freight charges. I hope you will be able to explain to the Museum the nature of objects and things. This is a loan collection of things over a hundred years old, which I want for my Harvard lectures. There will certainly be no customs' dues. The boxes will arrive probably some time in August 1931. B. May I ask you to advise the Fogg Museum authorities? 2. Please take the two festive pictures which are to be reproduced. The two polygia pictures, which are to be reproduced in Japan, to trust America and the Museum, and keep them until further notice together with my other things, and excuse me for troubling you rather greatly. Censuring you is anger trouble at Tientsin and that is My wife joins me in sending you our warmest greetings and best wishes. We indeed enjoyed seeing you here, and hope that you will soon return to Peking.

Believe me yours always

P.S. The freight charges will probably be paid in advance at Stockholm. If that should be the case, kindly return the cheque to me.

July 14th 1931

THE NARA HOTEL

NARA, JAPAN

Tel. Nos. 153, 166, 262. NARA
Cable Address "HOTEL" NARA.

My dear V. Stael

Forgive the typewriter, but it is so hot that the ink boils on the paper and I can't manage a red hot pen. Your note (d.h. mein Brief vom 7. Juli 1931) has just arrived and no doubt the paintings will soon follow. I had meant, as I told you, to leave the matter of the reproduction in color till next number as it is too late to get the text done. But now of course I shall do what I can to have them made in preparation for next year while I am in the land of good and cheap reproductions. The only trouble is that of paying the bill out of my own funds - which are pretty low. But there is no way to get the publishers to send me money in advance. If I find it impossible to advance the money I shall be forced to send the pictures direct to America and have them reproduced in black and white — will that disappoint you very much?

This last six weeks in Japan has been pretty steady work with no time off for the usual enjoyments of the country. Happily however, I have largely finished the job of preparing the illustrations for my Tempyo sculpture and they are in the hands of the printer. Whatever may be the matter with the text, at least I can be sure that the illustrations will be pleasing to people who can not hope to study the originals. When the whole mass of material is assembled I think it will surprise the students of Oriental art with its grandeur. As I told you, this book is an attempt to make people in Europe and America appreciate Japanese sculpture and realize that what remains of T'ang does not compare with the contemporary productions of colonial Japan. I would give much to find some really great T'ang Buddhist bronzes such as must have existed in Chang An during its prime. Not being a scholar, I must be content if I can stir up some interest on the part of Europeans and Americans to go deeper into the subject.

Please give Madame my best wishes and tell her how much I enjoyed seeing her salutary effect on yourself. She must bring you and the Bodhisattva to Cambridge before long so that she can see what we are like at home.

If I can do anything for you on this side of the water please be sure to let me know —

Always sincerely yours

Langdon Warner

HARVARD UNIVERSITY
FOGG ART MUSEUM
CAMBRIDGE, MASS., U.S.A.

July 18th 1931.

Dear Von Stael

Did I thank you for your note and acknowledge your cheque? Things are happening so fast and furiously here and I am so absorbed in work that I can be sure of nothing.

I have sent home the cheque and will do "my possible" about your collection. The Lama portraits have not yet turned up, and I leave so shortly that if they don't arrive in time Yamanaka must ship them after me. Happily he is most accurate &

careful in such matters.

As my collotype illustrations can not be done till after Sept. 1st at best, I've decided to dash home at once and relieve my wife at the edge of the nest. She will then have time to visit her brother Nick who is Minister in Buda-Pesth & wants her to play hostess for a month. With luck I shall catch the Prs. Taft on Aug. 1st from Yokohama.

I have a feeling that I wrote you a week ago and that you will curse me for breaking in again on your devotions — However you will forgive in the end.

Be sure to bring over your most engaging family. My regards to them.

Always yours bedesman,
Langdon Warner

My dear Warner,

Many thanks for your letter of July 18th from which I learn that you will reach Cambridge towards the end of this month. Kindly excuse the length and the technical nature of the inclosed article. I could not help putting a number of Tibetan words and adding the diacritical marks to certain letters. If I had omitted them my philological colleagues would have severely criticized me. Mr. J. R. Ware who knows Tibetan will reach Cambridge in September, and has promised to read the all-important proofs of my article and to me especially to mind the diacritical marks. The numerous foot-notes are typed on a separate set of leaves, but (in the ordinary way) they appear, of course, appear at the bottom of the pages to which they belong in the printed article. When I wrote the article in good white ink is unobtainable in Peking. I have, therefore, cut little windows into the enclosed photographs and marked the figures A — Y and α — ο with black ink on the white paper. In the plates which will accompany my article in "Eastern Art" the figures should of course be marked in white letters, which will make the little windows unnecessary. But if you prefer the little window system, I have no objection. Interpolating the originals to your artist in the belief that they would be reproduced in colours, and when I wrote my article I could In my article I do not indicate the colours of the dresses etc. because when I wrote it the paintings had already gone. You might perhaps add a note saying that not when I did not make any notes as to those colours before sending the pictures to Japan, because they were to be reproduced in colours. You might perhaps add a foot-note explaining the absence of Why I do not describe the text colours (except, I think, in one instance). But I do not attach any great importance to such a foot-note. Do not add it, if you

I do not feel ~~that~~ think it ~~necessary~~ superfluous, but please do not delay the publication of the article a minute longer than is absolutely necessary. It is very ~~hot now in July~~ (very hot indeed) It is terribly hot here in summer, the only time of the year, when I am free to write, and ~~if~~ it ~~supports~~ me whenever I have to wait for the publication of any ~~article~~ ~~that~~ ~~disappoints~~ efforts you can imagine how ~~happening~~ terribly ~~disappointed~~ I am whenever an avoidable delay retards the publication of my efforts.

The eighth Dalai ~~lama~~ (lama) ~~was born in~~ The last of the personages represented on plate I, was born in 1758, and he is ~~at~~ at least 15 years old on our picture, which can, therefore, not have been painted before about 1773. The eighth Dalai-lama ~~blo bzań~~ (the last of the personages represented on plate I) was born ~~in~~ dpal ldan ye śes, was born in 1738, and he is about ~~fully~~ 20 years old on our picture, which can, therefore, not have been painted before about 1758.

The Panchen-lama Blo bzań dpal ldan ye śes, was born in 1738, and he is about ~~fully~~ 20 years old on our picture, which can, therefore, not have been painted before about 1758.

I am very glad to hear that you will do "your possible" about my collection. May I ask you to let me know by deferred telegram (this was yesterday) whether it has arrived or not. I enclose a telegram for letters. My cable address is Staelholstein [one word] Angofoo Peking. I enclose a cheque for which will cover that telegram.

My wife and I look forward very much to seeing you again at Peking or in America, and the Bodhisattva who takes great pride in the title conferred upon him by you, joins us and your family in sending you all best wishes and greetings.

Believe me yours sincerely
AvonStaël-Holstein

P.S. I trust that you have by now received the originals of plates I and II, which left here about July 1st/1931. If not, please reproduce the enclosed photographs (I enclose that of each painting). May I have one hundred reprints of the article after its publication? I shall be glad to pay for them.

HARVARD UNIVERSITY
FOGG ART MUSEUM
CAMBRIDGE, MASS., U.S.A.

My dear Staël   September 28th
                                   1931.

Your boxes arrived yesterday (12 of them) and are to be examined by the Customs Officer at his leasure and in the comparative safety of the Museum. The catalogues that you mention in your letter have not put in an appearance. I am cabling you today the news.

The article seems to me a most learned and important document — far too learned for me properly to appreciate. I fear that we go to press tomorrow and that it is too late to be wedged in, but I am sending it post-haste to Philadelphia on the chance.

As I wrote you, I was sorry that you sent the original paintings to Japan. I thought that I had made it clear that no use could be made of them in my absence.

It was necessary for me to be there first to receive them, second to supervise the making of color prints. Now they are adrift on an unfriendly ocean, and Heaven knows where they may be washed up. To what Japanese address did you send them?

Ware has arrived and so has Porter. The former will be pleased & proud to see that your Ms. is not mangled by the American printer. He seems to look forward with joy to the conditions of work that he finds in Cambridge although the Chinese library can not of course equal the combined resources of Peking. I hear, however, that it has vastly improved in the last two years.

Other gossip I have none — at least we have no floods or revolutions, no beatings of C. T. Wang, no active war or stubborn boycott of the Japanese in Cambridge. All of which things seem to be true of poor dear old China.

Please give my regards & kind remembrances to Madame and to the Bodhisattva. My wife joins me in sending them.

Always sincerely yours,
Langdon Warner

```
RECEIVING            中 國 電 報 局              7074
THE CHINESE TELEGRAPH ADMINISTRATION
                      PEIPING                    103
    CFO   29/9
    15   58
         YSCHAN    SHMN

              R91
              CAMBRIDGEDASS      28    5    15S
         LCO
                STAELHOLSTEIN AUGOFOO
                                         PEIPING
COLLECTIONS ARRIVED WARNER
```

My dear Warner,

Many thanks for your letter dated Sept. 1931. I am so glad to hear that you have safely returned to Cambridge, and I am very much obliged to you for having been my collection through the customs. What has happened to the catalogues? I think they must be somewhere at the Fogg Museum. My friend Stackelberg has addressed them to the director of the Fogg Museum and registered the package. Possibly Will you be so kind as to let me know by cable (fifteen words a word Catalohss: StaelHolstein [one word] Angofoo Peking) whether the catalogues have turned up. If not, I shall have to send you one my catalogues (which will mean a few days only to compile from my original notes) *

can await who will try to bring my collection to this country (means one Sir Bexley bonds to be taken away by Mr. Ware) can await who will try to make a suitable company for my collection. Please let me know by cable and state the amount offered. I shall then of course

* I am afraid that the rach of substantial is dying out fast here in America, and we should hurry up. if we still The Estonians before payment, and so do the Chinese (arrears of salary). The Reich has paid me one percent of its debt (bonds) and will never pay any more in final settlement of my claims.

Registered A.R.

Langdon Warner Esq.
The Fogg Art Museum
Cambridge Mass.
U.S. of America

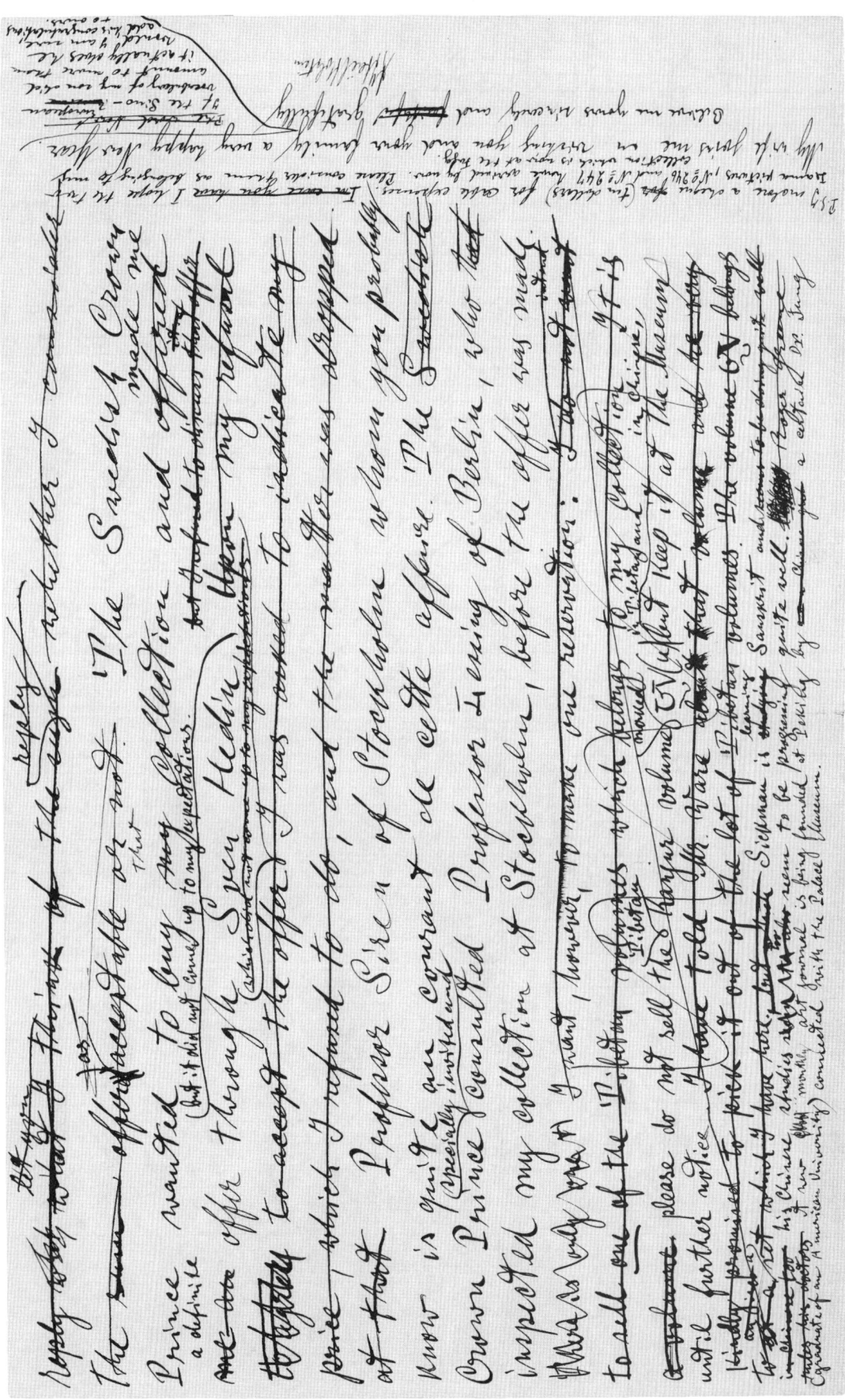

My dear Warner,

Your kind note dated Sept. 3rd reached me only on my return from Darjeen towards the end of that month. I am sorry that I have turned the photos and expected to return to Cambridge immediately, would not state to the catalogue to me. I did not know [...] before returning to Cambridge.

[...] the reply, but I suppose that you then I am very much obliged to you for writing. "I will do my best to sell the collection in America." The fact is that I am still anxious to sell it and that I am rather surprised that I have received no reply whatever to my letter on the 8th of July [...] I sent the latter, the photographs and goods. [...] The [a] catalogue of the collection as well as a long registered letter [...] is a which I gave him details as to the price and [...]

as to the eventual mode of payment [...]

I have exchanged letters with Professor Woods before and always found him an excellent correspondant. Please get hold and find out why he does not reply. That's to say — May I ask you to find time to see him and to let me know the reason of his long silence on this occasion? If he does not want to have anything to do with the matter, please do take it up yourself and use your personal magnetism for getting not to ask Professor Woods in my name to show you my very long letter to him and to let you have the photographs and the catalogue — unless he should object if not for ever for some time — special value to them.

I have also written to my friend Professor A.L. Zucker, College Park, Maryland (but my letters from Washington D.C.) asking him to offer my collection to the authorities of your metropolis. But he is neither an orientalist nor a student of art and has not the opportunities of ascertaining which you possess. I shall be very much obliged to you if you will drop a line to Professor Zucker and suggest concerted action to him. Professor Zucker has written to me and promised to treat us to the matter softly if we do so. He is also in possession of the catalogue and the overtures about which you inquire in your letter and which has been

The former owner of the collection, photographed by Mr. Zumborn, is the late Mr. Gomboyeff, a Buriat of Buriny Junction, Russian who used to be Russian post master here.

You ask me who about Lessing's scholarship. I think it quite up to the mark, and his book on the Lama Temple, which I have read the manuscript of which I have read, would certainly add to the credit of any institution which might publish it. T.F. Lessing is now instructor at the Oriental Seminary of Berlin.

How is Mr. Thompson who so successfully represented the Fogg Museum on our roof garden? I have not heard from him since he left Peking for Soviet Russia. I asked him also to go out with Professor Stroels.

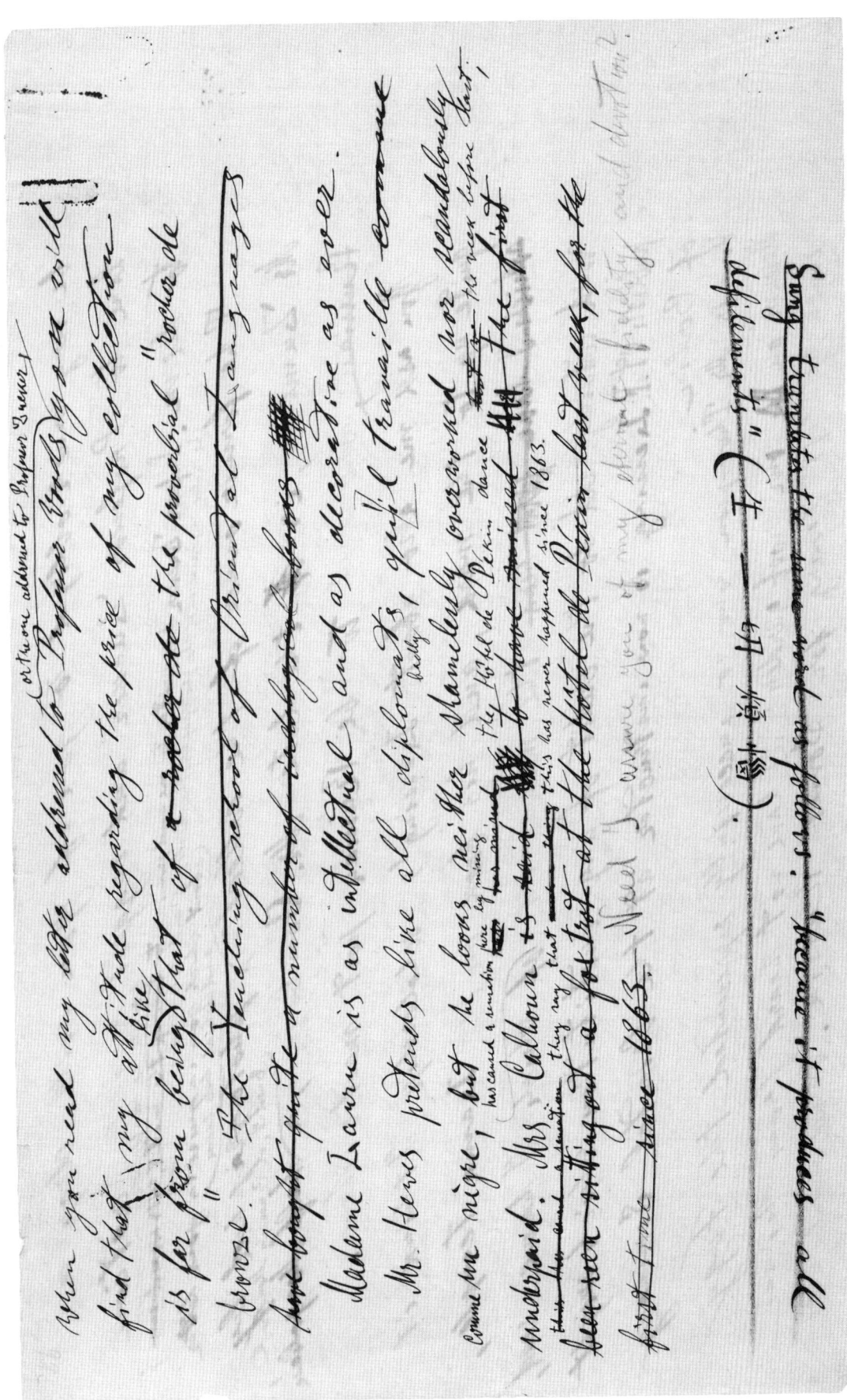

When you read my letter (or the one addressed to Professor Drerup) addressed to Professor Grube, you will find that [any] difficulty regarding the price of my collection is far from being [solved] that [books] the proverbial "rocher de bronze."

The Peking school of Oriental Languages have boast of quite a number of indigenous fools. Madame Laure is as intellectual and as decorative as ever. Mr. Heves pretends, like all diplomats, qu'il travaille comme un nègre, but he looks neither [Bully] overworked nor scandalously [has caused a sensation here by marrying] They Hôtel de Pekin dance [his own] to have amusement the very before last, this has never happened since 1863. Miss Calhoun is [still] they any trust [that] been seen sitting out a fox trot at the Hôtel de Pekin last week for the first time since 1863. Need I wave you of my [utmost fidelity and about time?]

Sung transliterates the same word as follows: "because it produces all defilements" (它 能 生 諸 煩惱).

HARVARD UNIVERSITY
FOGG ART MUSEUM
CAMBRIDGE, MASS., U.S.A.

January 18th '33

My dear von Stael

There is so much to communicate and so many questions to ask that I don't know where to begin. First let me felicitate you on the arrival of an apsara — if indeed that is a correct iconographic description of the happy event. Next let me thank you for thinking of us at new Years time and sending your latest valuable pamphlet for my book shelves.

To report on the extraordinary doings in connection with the article when you kindly sent it to the moribund Eastern Art would require a more skillful hand with iambic pentameters than mine. When it arrived at the bedside of the dying magazine, the doctors made it fairly clear that death was imminent and Jayne sent it off to Norman Brown for an opinion as to its fitness for the *Journal of the American Oriental Society*, as you had suggested in your note that we do. Brown, with commendable good taste, not only did *not* write Jayne any opinion but proceeded to publish the article!

Few scholarly papers in America, or elsewhere, receive such immediate broadcasting as to be published twice, and I imagine that the two editors will have some bitter words to say to each other. Naturally it was not your fault. Jayne has been terribly burdened — being the Director of one Museum and the Curator in another — both without funds to meet many commitments for field work, publication, staff salaries, purchase of collections and all the myriad responsibilities that public institutions

HARVARD UNIVERSITY
FOGG ART MUSEUM
CAMBRIDGE, MASS., U.S.A.

assume nowadays in America. He is, as you know, the most loyal and hard-working person in the world and one of my dearest friends. Please do not threaten him with synthetic magic from your icy Tibetan mountain top in the Austrian Legation.

I never dared write you about the arrival of your flotilla of boxes that I had so cheerfully agreed to store in our small museum. It was a tragedy and at the same time I was constrained to laughter in the privacy of my room. It happened that our familiar government inspector, who has been coming to the Museum for years, was absent. The man assigned to the task was an amazing creature who, in five minutes, had reduced our hard-working staff to unmanly tears. Every box was opened, every object was unwrapped and placed on a table before which he sat. Every object was minutely inspected (and suspected) by him and exhaustive search was made among his lists to find its number and description. He made us responsible for every discrepancy in the lists; all the wrappings must be removed from each object. He never left his chair before the table and he spoke sharply to the hard-working men when they did not hold up an object so that it received a proper light. He was rude to me and to the rest of the staff. Happily, the janitor and his men soon saw that this official must be humored or he could make matters even worse and they soon regarded him as even funny. For three and a half days they labored, and we agreed that other museum work must be practically stopped. I telephoned to the Port of Boston office and was told that I could have him recalled by the Washington authorities, after several days delay. I therefore waited till the work was done & the man gone with a warning from me. I then wrote a formal note of my serious complaint to Boston, a similar one to Washington and got the Bursar of the University to do the same thing. After several weeks I received

HARVARD UNIVERSITY
FOGG ART MUSEUM
CAMBRIDGE, MASS., U.S.A.

most courteous replies from the higher officials and a copy of the order degrading our friend the local inspector. I then provided cigars and drinks to the janitor and his men.

You may imagine that, if there seemed no chance in the old days of finding a purchaser for Lamaistic church paraphernalia, it is quite out of the question today. Museums are not spending a cent in spite of the surprising bargains on all sides and private collectors are trying to sell their treasures. Also it should be recognized that Mongol & Tibetan art has few followers over here and that the spirit behind your collection is that of the iconographist — though it includes many objects of intrinsic beauty. It would be enormously expensive to attempt to store your things or to move them, though I have tried to get them into the basement of the Harv.-Yenching Library. As they have no room in that building I shall do my best to keep them here in spite of the danger that, any moment, the space may be demanded.

As for your friends, the Harvard-Yenching committee, they are gradually seeing the light. They are most anxious to have a resident director to whom they may turn over the management of the whole affair. This person may possibly be Prof. Elysséef who is here for two years lecturing on Japanese history & giving a course in the language. He is pleasant and scholarly and, I believe, would do pretty well for the post, especially as, I am told, he commands the respect of European scholars. My own personal preference would be for a Japanese scholar — but that can never be, nor should it be, in an institution devoted primarily to Chinese subjects.

I plan to give one course in the Summer School and then to rush for Nara where much work awaits me. Naturally, I shall try hard to get to Peking to see the Bosatsu & the Apsara and their delightful mother — not to mention their father who lives in our affectionate esteem and whose wine I have enjoyed in the past. Lorraine joins me in sending you her kindest remembrances

Always sincerely yours
Langdon Warner

HARVARD UNIVERSITY
FOGG ART MUSEUM
CAMBRIDGE, MASS., U.S.A.

Jan. 12th 1934.

My dear von Staël

I was particularly touched by your gift of the little gilt Monju (if indeed it was he) because I had thought that you considered me among the damned. I felt instinctively that you knew that I had taken malicious joy in causing you the embarrassment of seeing your learned article duplicated in two separate magazines and that there were other sins which I could never hope to explain away. As a matter of fact you have been much in my thoughts and on my tongue — and always with admiration for your persevering life of pure scholarship and the high standard you have set for all

of us. I would give much to drop in ²
on your retreat and drag you off to dine
and talk — preferably at your own hospitable
board.

For a year or more now I have meant to
write you seriously on the subject of your
<u>Lamaist collection</u> that is there. As I wrote you,
it happened to arrive under the very worst
conditions when we were all extremely occupied.
For 8 solid days it was unpacked, piece
by piece & each painting fully unrolled at
the command of a peculiarly disagreeable customs
official. It was a wonder to me that our janitor
and his underlings did not resign at once on
such treatment. When it was over I wrote
to the Head of the department & got an answer
after a month's delay apologizing for the man
and saying that – after investigating the matter –
he had been consigned to a mad-house! It was
then repacked as well as might be but the authorities
descended on me and demanded to know by what
right I was storing so many huge cases in a building
where there was not room for our own things.

HARVARD UNIVERSITY
FOGG ART MUSEUM
CAMBRIDGE, MASS., U.S.A.

~~Finally~~ I arranged a place for them that seems safe, but I honestly have not had a moment to open and arrange and check them up. It would take at least a week — especially as the contents of the boxes frequently could not, by any stretch of the imagination, be made to fit your lists.

As you may well imagine, there is no chance of selling such a collection in these dark days of depression. Even when all the world was rich it would appeal to a very limited public. As you pointed out, the things are significant from the iconographic point of view rather than the artistic, and that limits them still further. Harvard of course has a Professor of Buddhist Iconography and (I believe) an Institute for Buddhist Research of international importance. But he & his Institute are not in Cambridge at the moment and neither the art museum nor that of Ethnology nor that of Zoology nor that of Archaeology are equipped to care for such objects. My own feeling is that they should go to the Divinity School where the minds of budding Unitarian Divines would be broadened by contact with some of the grosser forms of Tantric Buddhism. In fact I have always felt, in Unitarianism, a lack of the cosmic urge so admirably expressed by the Lamaistic church.

All of which is merely to emphasize our desire to have you come to Cambridge with your agreeable family and (incidentally) solve the problem of your collections — their storage, their care and their interpretation.

I am just back — 2 days ago — from a short trip to Japan in which I had but 4 months ashore. However, it was extremely interesting though I barely stirred beyond the confines of Nara. My catalogue raisonné of the Tempyo sculpture is now as complete as it can be made and the

HARVARD UNIVERSITY
FOGG ART MUSEUM
CAMBRIDGE, MASS., U.S.A.

collotype illustrations have been finished. It remains only to put some finishing touches to the text and to find some half-witted publisher who is anxious to lose several thousand dollars in bringing it out to the grateful public.

The second half year begins in about a fortnight and with it hard work of a very different sort to what I've been used to lately. I confess that I rather dread it. We are lucky in having Laurence Binyon — just retired from the British Museum — in Cambridge this year as exchange Professor. I have known him for the last 20 years and have a great regard for him.

If you find time to answer this long screed please tell me what has happened to your European estates and don't forget that we

can now offer you a drink in Cambridge
without blushing.

Please give my kindest remembrances to
Madame la Baronne and to the Bodisattva
& to the Apsaras (?)

Thank you again for sending me the
delightful little deity who sits on my
desk as I write.

Always your sincere admirer

Langdon Warner

HARVARD UNIVERSITY
FOGG ART MUSEUM
CAMBRIDGE, MASS., U.S.A.

February ninth
1934.

My dear von Staël

I was delighted at being remembered by you in the tangible form of your learned pamphlet on the Kaçyapaparivatta, which arrived here yesterday. Naturally I can not claim full appreciation of the erudition and labor displayed by it. But I was interested to note the care with which your tangle of references & notes had all been checked and elucidated. Obviously the use of three languages & so many texts

for comparison make the whole
affair one of great significance.

Your little gilt figure stands
on my mantel-shelf at home
and I hope very much that
you can make up your mind
to come, with your family, to
see it there in person.

My wife joins me in sending
her best regards

Always Sincerely
Langdon Warner

P.S. It seems almost certain that Prof. Elisseeff
will take the Directorship of Harv.-Yench. Inst. next
Autumn. What do you think of the appointment?
You may be sure that, in spite of his Japanese
training he is enthusiastically & whole-heartedly interested
in Sinology. On the whole I think he is a good
choice; but I should like your honest comments.

Former Austrian Legation, Peking. Sept. 12ʳᵈ 1934.

My dear Warner,

Very many thanks for your letters! It pleases me immensely to hear that you like the little god I sent you and I am very proud to know that the miniature idol has found a place on your mantle piece. I am ever extremely grateful to your for your great kindness in keeping my collection in a safe place. If it had not been for your having become the collection, I do not know what would have happened to the collection, and it cannot be said that I ought to dispatch my collection it to the Swedish Sweden after having refused the Swedish museum's offer, and it would to sending it back to Peking would be absurd. I do regret that the collection has caused you so much trouble, and I am indeed grateful to you for your successful efforts in getting it through the sh[tuff] American customs. The cosmic urge which, as you say, is so admirably expressed by [PM] some of the Lamaistic divinities, does not seem to have produced a favourable impression upon your particular friend in the customs service. I am very glad to hear that your great work on the Tempyō art is nearing completion. I hope [still] to be privileged by it during my next visit to Japan. I have [I was at Jesu[s]] studying other things during my stay at [Oxford to say]

In your letter you ask me what I think of Stael Holstein's appointment. I am delighted to hear that Stcherbatsky has been elected by the Trustees of the Harvard-Yenching Institute and that the Harvard-Yenching Institute and I heartily approved the appointment you and I heartily approved the choice. You must But I must confess that I am not exactly enthusiastic about Repns — trying to a jurist and farring useless from a younger man who is by no means my something type a specialist in my line certainly of Sanskrit and Tibetan philology. I have not been told wanted to report to Harvard yet, and I parents I venture to hope that I shall never receive such

an order. Could I not, as before, report
to Dean Chase ~~and~~ or to some /other senior/ ~~receive my~~
orders from him? ~~What not are~~ ~~the other~~
The orders will be inspired by Eliséev /it is a man ~~briefing~~ referring to me/ himself
or not, as long as I have not to submit
to his absurd dictation. We were colleagues
as you probably know, /I think I was seniored/
and I ~~submitted report~~ then ~~re-~~ at St. Petersburg
important at that time. I leave sure ~~do~~ more
your invariable diplomacy in order to ~~of~~ what may
save me ~~x possible~~ humiliations, ~~of~~ Stonicoff
~~even hears of my report he will certainly~~ /possibly/
~~hate me, I ~~recognizing~~ careful for years from a close official~~
correspondence between Stonoff and myself.

When I last saw Elisseeff in
When I saw Elisseeff again in 1933 at Peking
he about certain of his Harvard appointment, and his
was
attitude towards myself that somewhat changed,
Now the appointment is a fact, and I fear [Chinese] a
further change of attitude.

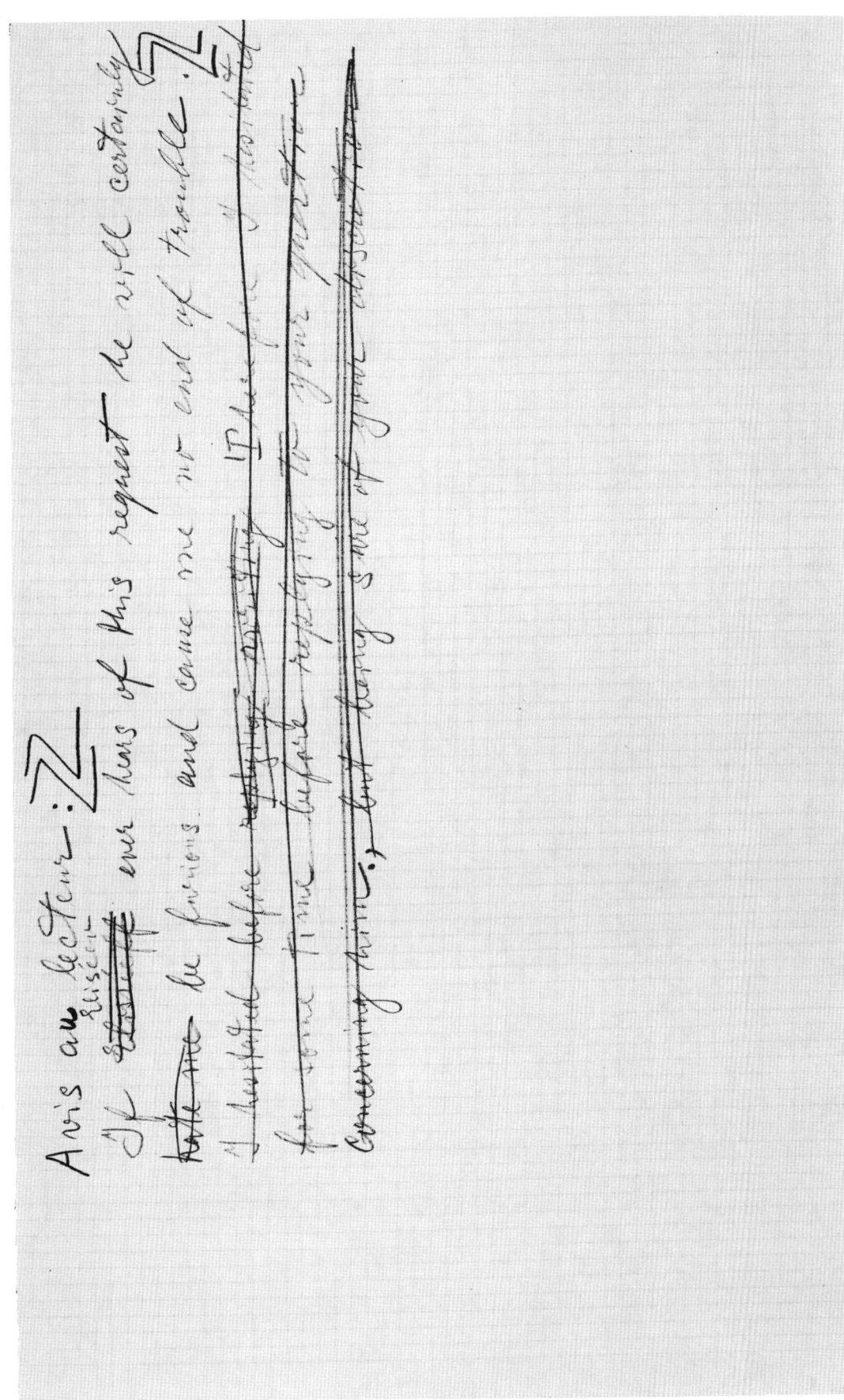

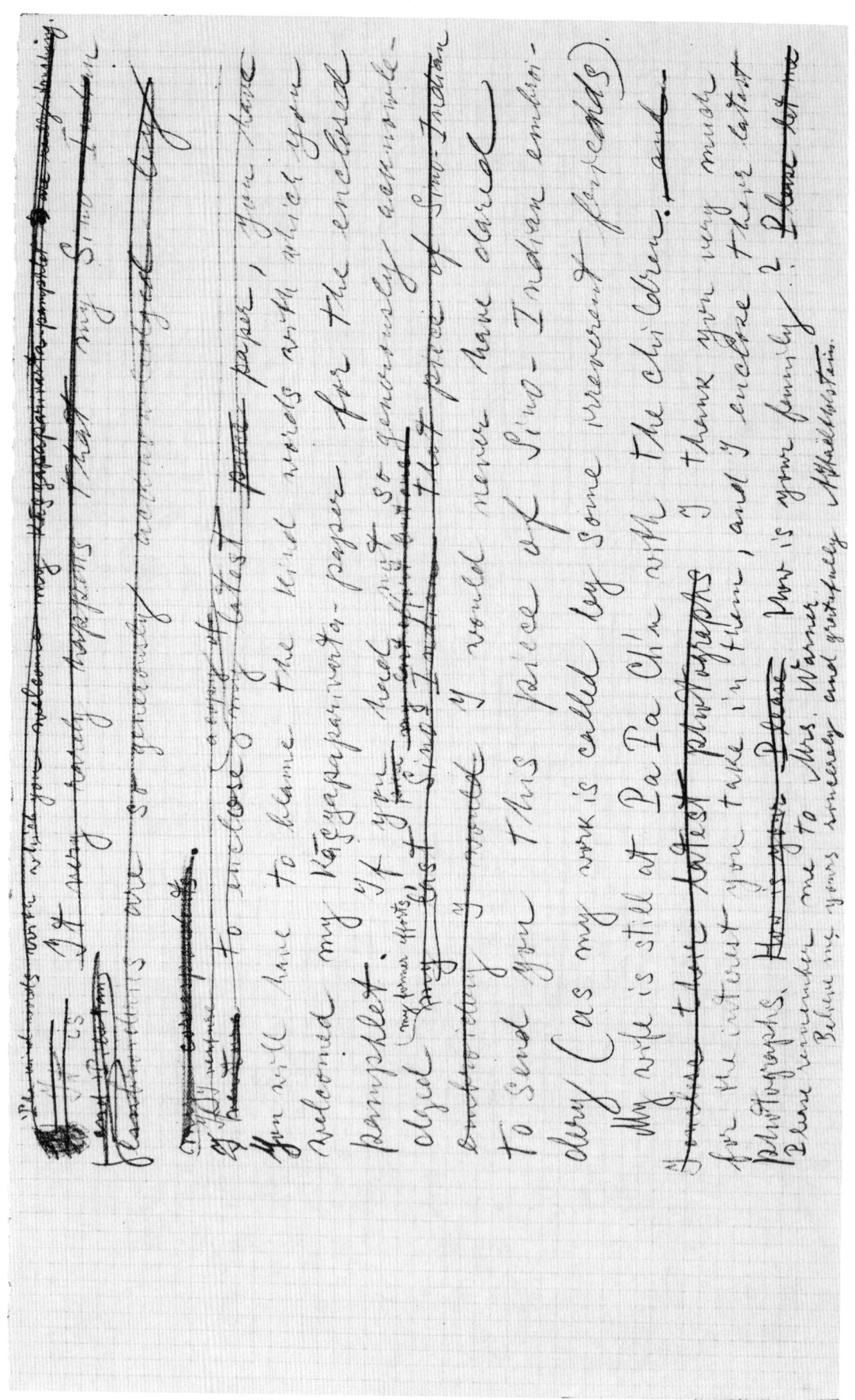

It was very kind of you to enclose copy of my latest paper, you have welcomed my Kāśyapaparivarta-pamphlet. If you would have to blame the kind words with which you welcomed my Kāśyapaparivarta-paper for the enclosed pamphlet. If you had just so generously acknowledged my first Sino-Indian ... that piece of Sino-Indian embroidery I would never have dared to send you this piece of Sino-Indian embroidery (as my work is called by some irreverent friends). My wife is still at Pa Ta Ch'u with the children, and I hope that latest photographs I thank you very much for the interest you take in them, and I enclose the latest photographs. How is your Please What is your family? Please let me been remember me to Mrs. Warner

Before my yours sincerely and gratefully
AvonStaelHolstein

HARVARD UNIVERSITY
FOGG ART MUSEUM
CAMBRIDGE, MASS., U.S.A.

October 1st 1934

My dear von Staël

Your most interesting letter arrived today together with the Kanjur article. For both of these my sincere thanks. If I glean more from the former than from the latter you will understand that it is because my living friends mean more to me than dead gods.

I immediately asked Chase about the status of your private Buddha farm and he confirmed my idea that you have no cause to worry.

The reports you send come to the Education Committee through its chairman. Elyséeff meets with this committee but by no means controls its policy. Further I do not anticipate any desire on his part to try to direct the affairs in a department on which he is no authority. My rather casual acquaintance with him predisposes me to believe that he will not be difficult to co-operate with.

We to the present affairs on this side of the Pacific have suffered from the fact that no committee member know conditions in the Orient or properly understood the problems in a way to make a definite policy possible. With Elyseeff here we shall achieve a certain definiteness even if mistakes are made.

I dare not think of the present state of your collections which had to be moved from this museum to the Germanic for lack of space. If only you could dispose of them it would be a weight off my mind. How about endowing a little museum of Oriental religions in Peking or Cambridge and making me the highly-paid

Curator ? I pass this suggestion along to you, confident that you have but to hear it to agree.

With best hommages to Madame

I am

Always Sincerely

Langdon Warner

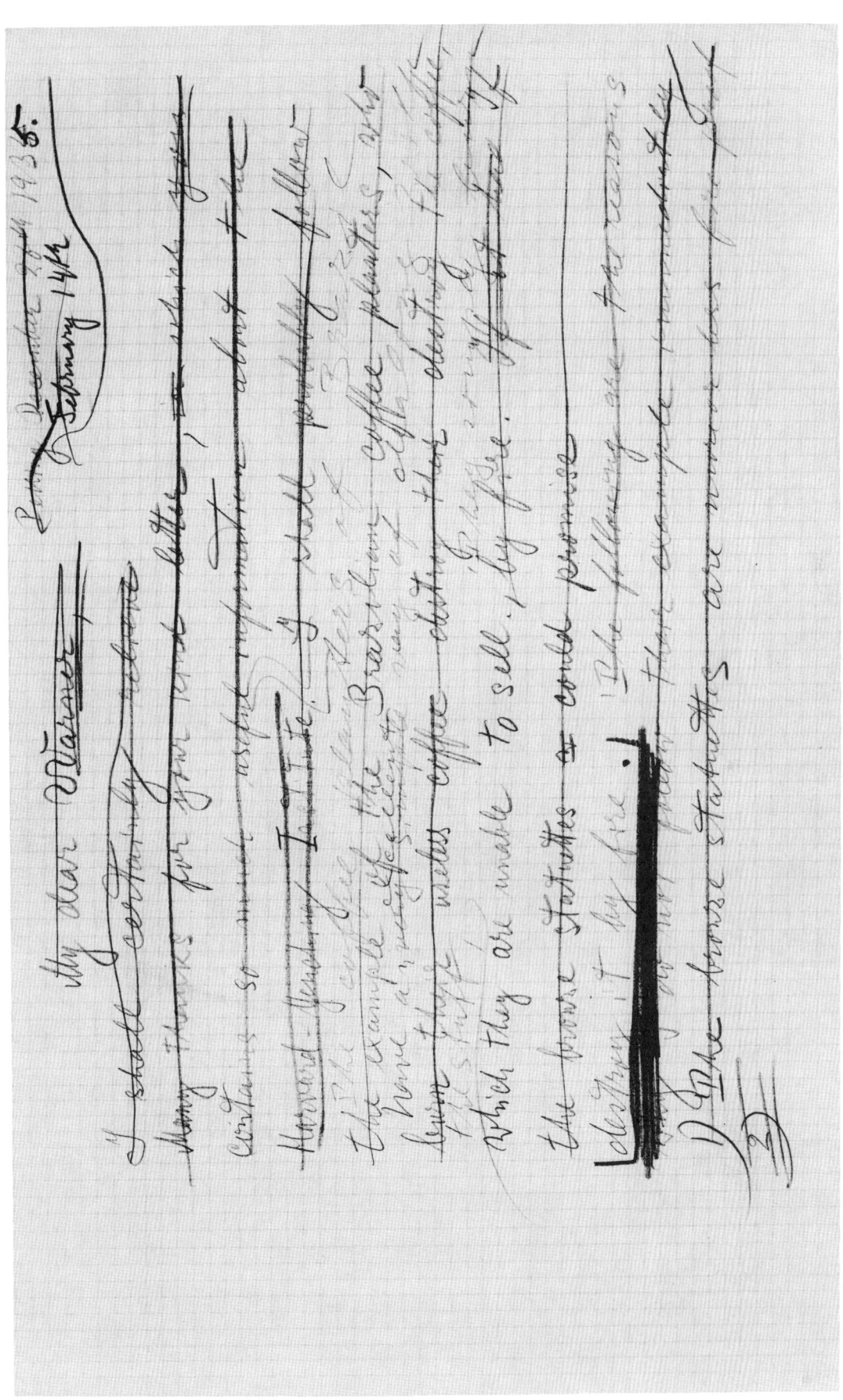

One of the main reasons why I do not follow the Brazilian's example immediately is the fact that the bronze statuettes are more or less fire-proof. Another reason is that I may soon find a more profitable way of getting rid of the objectionable collection. About a year ago a serious representative of an American interested in Tibet, who knew that I had infused the Swedish Crown Prince's and other of my copies offered (to the Swedish Annex) Swedish Museum's offer, asked me whether the collection was still for sale and received an evasive answer. The same representative is expected here

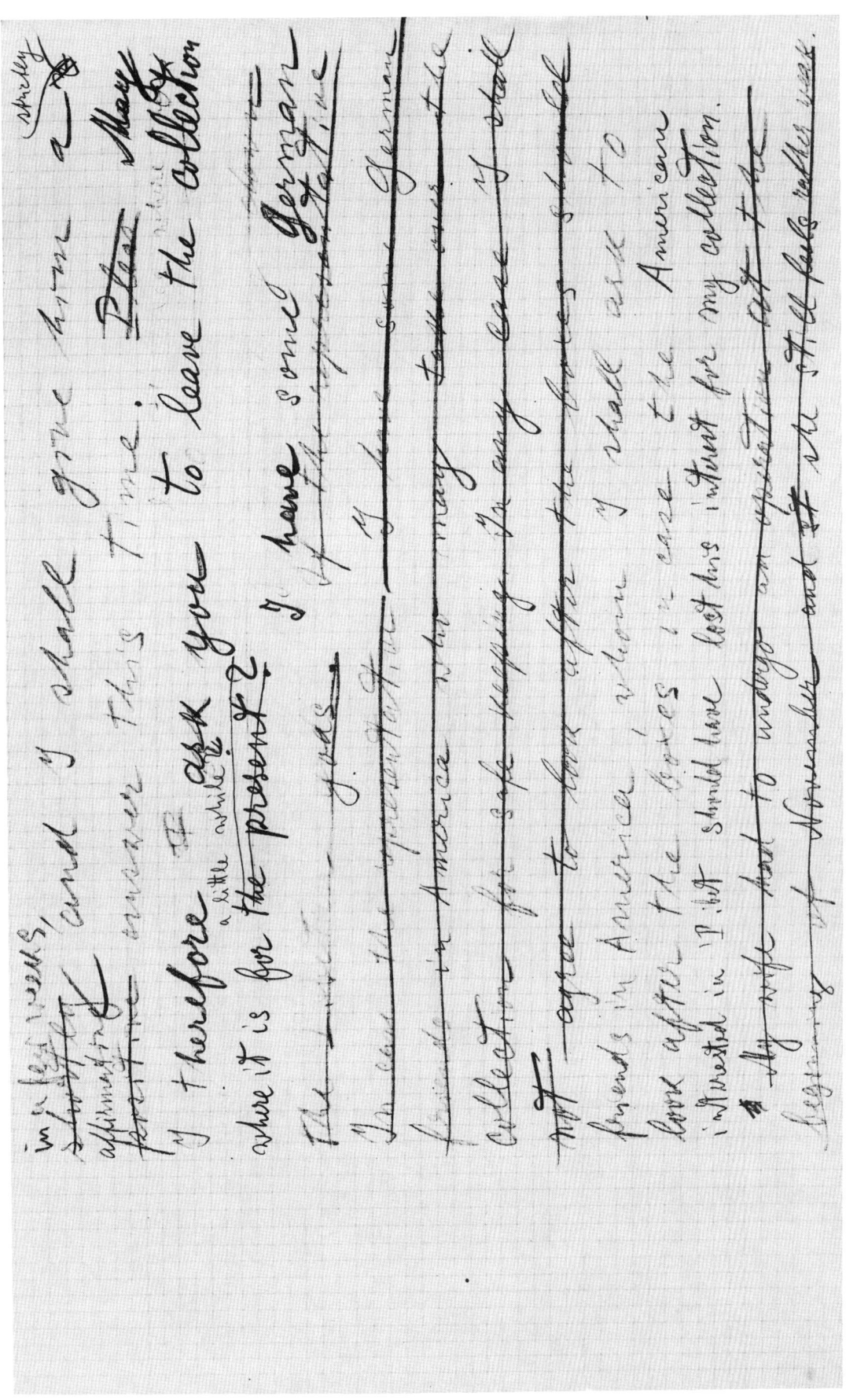

I have been very busy managing my Buddha farm — and especially assisting at the birth of its latest product (an analysis of a hymn addressed to Avalokiteśvara, which I shall a copy of which I shall soon send to you).

I was very happy to make the acquaintance of Miss von Bulberg whose father was a countryman of mine. Her uncle still resides in Riga. She was very enthusiastic about the atmosphere of friendly cooperation, which characterises the Fogg Museum. I do remember this atmosphere with great pleasure, and I shall never forget the friendliness which the authorities of the Fogg Museum showed me during my stay in Cambridge.

Datong. 14.II.35:
abgesandt 14.II.35.

My dear Warner,

My wife had to undergo an operation in November and she still feels rather weak. My son was suffering from diphtheria and has just returned home after spending nearly two months in the hospital. These and some other difficulties are responsible for my delay in answering your kind letter, which I received with many thanks. Please do excuse me for this late reply.

HARVARD UNIVERSITY
FOGG ART MUSEUM
CAMBRIDGE, MASS., U.S.A.

March ninth
1935

My dear von Staël

I am distressed to hear of your family's illness and hope very much that by this time things are normal again and that you are relieved of anxiety.

Please don't think for a moment that I am trying to escape the chance to be of some slight service to you in America. You need have no fear that your treasures are to be thrown out on the street. I merely wanted you to know that they were unpacked under high pressure by a strange savage who, a few weeks later, was confined in an insane asylum but not before I had lodged a complaint against him with the Collector of the Port who sent me a formal letter of apology. If I had space and a fortnight's time I should unpack the boxes and put the contents out on long tables and repack them with care. But there is no room at the Fogg for such an occupation nor are my days long enough to finish the tasks already clamoring to be done. If you have any one seriously desiring to purchase the collections send him to me and I will prove myself an admirable drummer.

This college celebrates next year its tercentenary and I wish you would come over with your agreeable family and meet and talk with some of your colleagues who will come to Cambridge from Europe and Asia. We should not try to keep you across the river in the Business School, but build you a special and appropriate chapel in the middle of the College yard.

Give the Lattimores and Kates my special regards when you meet and remember me most kindly to Madame & the little Bodhisatts.

Always your constant admirer

Langdon Warner

Oct. 22nd 33 —

My dear Warner,

More than a year ago (on Oct. 1st 1932) you wrote to me: "If only you could dispose of them [i.e. of the showing diamant aliments] it would be a weight off my mind." Please excuse me for having afford that weight having so much delayed the lifting operation. Ah I hope that Dr. Ware will soon carry it through. Before he left here about September 1st of he very kindly promised me to relieve me of all responsibility in connection with the end spirits mentioned above.

My family went to Pei Tai Ho for the summer, but I stayed in town spent most of the summer in Peking, hoping to see you here. Somebody told me that you were leaving Cambridge for the Far East in May 1935. To my much regret that you did not come. I wanted to thank you once more, and personally most sincerely, for all the trouble my collections have caused you. 2 Pelliot spent some weeks here this summer and we inspected the new Anyang finds together. Now the winter routine has started again: I am seeing various papers through the press and teaching my Chinese students Sanskrit. May I ask to be kindly remembered to Mrs. Warner? Believe me yours gratefully A v Staël Holstein

[When he is not engaged in archaeology. I am jealous he can still enjoy oriental pursuits etc.]

[while I am by no means prepared (was made a mere burden) I can't —— of my poor self.]

HARVARD UNIVERSITY
FOGG ART MUSEUM
CAMBRIDGE, MASS., U.S.A.

February 17th 1936.

Dear Baron

You are model of what a friend should be. Now at last I can date my Tibetan paintings and read a little more truth into Tibetan history. Up to the present I have despaired of learning enough arithmatic to make the computations that Pelliot's table requires.

I'm just back from a hasty six weeks trip to the great Chinese exhibition at London. Don't let any of your learned colleagues tell you that it was not worth while. Anyone incapable of learning daily from that show is beyond all hope. Of course my 3 weeks in England was all too short. But I included a trip to Cambridge to see Ivor Richards whom you may remember in Peking and to one or two pleasant places in the country to visit friends. The Sinologues and savants were gathered about the exhibition like crows about the corpse of a fresh-killed maiden. Their talk was interesting and their quarrels were delightful. On the whole the bronzes and the pottery comprised the finest part of the show — though I regret to say that some of the Peking Palace bronzes were no more convincing than we used to think them.

At the end of my trip I had 4 delightful days in Paris where I sampled the wine produced in the Province of Burgundy and found it worth my serious attention.

What is the chance of your coming to Cambridge before long? If you don't come and bring your family I shall carry out my threat to come and visit you.

With best regards from myself and my wife to you both

I am
Always Sincerely
Langdon Warner

HARVARD UNIVERSITY
FOGG ART MUSEUM
CAMBRIDGE, MASS., U.S.A.

February 17th 36

My dear von Staël

Your Lamaist collection has been increasingly on my conscience ever since it was repacked after the customs inspection. The cases had to be moved from the Germanic Museum where they were stored, and I decided it was necessary to open them and make sure that the contents had not suffered. This is now in process and we are all sneezing from the familiar Peking dust. Happily nothing seems to have been injured — except an occasional toe or finger that was probably missing when the objects were packed. The paintings, however, have been rolled up for some years and it is essential that they be hung up and aired. This I shall try to do. There may even be a chance to make a small exhibition of them which would greatly benefit their physical condition.

I have written the American Museum of Natural History in New York in the hope that they might wish to purchase your collection to add to the Whitney collection given just before the owner's death. Unfortunately they had neither funds nor space. I shall now write to the Field Museum at Chicago and tell them that the material can be inspected here and that they can communicate with you if they wish to acquire it. I don't have to tell you that the price one can hope to receive nowadays would be small. Few museums and no private individuals could consider sheltering such a comprehensive collection.

The boxes are made out of splintering Chinese pine & hemlock and will no longer hold the nails or be trusted if the collection has to be shipped. To make ten new boxes and properly to pack the objects would be a matter of several hundred dollars gold. This amount I am sorry to say we have not got, though we have already spent more than a hundred on transport.

The photograph albums you sent me represent only part of the collection and show great gaps in the numbering. They are of less service than I had hoped because there is no list or catalogue to be used with them.

<u>Later</u>: I find that it was a good thing to unwrap the paintings because the oil paper, in which they are rolled, had already stained the backs of the pictures. In the course of a few more hot summers the oil would have done serious damage to the surfaces.

Among other things I have come across a series of 9 unmounted rubbings representing Lohan (Arhats)

HARVARD UNIVERSITY
FOGG ART MUSEUM
CAMBRIDGE, MASS., U.S.A.

which are not definitely connected with Lamaism in the form shown. These I have ventured to keep aside as they throw light on the various stages of the stone engravings from which they were taken. Perhaps you would not object if I were to protect them with a paper backing.

March 3rd. The unpacking is now finished and your collection nicely arranged on shelves. Unfortunately it can not always remain in that way because it crowds our own collection out of the necessary space. As I have said, the former boxes are no use. What shall I do? On examining the material I do not find it available except from the point of view of the history of religions and the iconographist. The American Museum of Natural History writes me that the Whitney collection is all that they can handle. My plan of identifying each piece has failed because your lists are incomplete.

That is all the bad news I can think of to send you. For the rest I can only say that I wish more than anything that I could drop in this afternoon to call on you and your engaging family. Perhaps a year from now may see me in Peking for a short visit.

This coming summer I have accepted an invitation to give a course in the Oriental Seminar at the University of California — where the climate is perfect, all the women beautiful and the men are brave. In the autumn I shall come back to Cambridge for the 1st half year and then, with luck sail in mid-January for Japan and China. Please make sure that there is no war or other unpleasantness when I arrive.

With best regards to you and the Baroness

I am always Sincerely yours
Langdon Warner

Leipzig, S.3, Arndtstr.59/III, 19.1.30

Hochgeehrter Herr Baron von Stael-Holstein!

Haben Sie recht herzlichen Dank für die freundliche Einladung, welche Sie mir durch Herrn Dr. Behrsing zukommen liessen. Dass ich Ihnen erst heute antworte, hat seinen Grund darin, dass ich vorher mit dem Herrn Dekan meiner Fakultät sprechen wollte. Dies konnte ich erste nach den Weihnachtsferien tun.

Da ich vom sächsischen Ministerium für Volksbildung und von der philosophischen Fakultät der Leipziger Universität Urlaub erhalten muss, wäre ich Ihnen dankbar, wenn Sie mir die Einladung schriftlich zukommen liessen. Ich wäre Ihnen auch sehr dankbar dafür, wenn Sie die Bedingungen in Ihrem Briefe mitteilen würden, unter denen ich die Stelle bekommen könnte.

Haben Sie zunächst herzlichen Dank für das Vertrauen, welches Sie in mich gesetzt haben.

Ich benutze gerne die Gelegenheit, Ihnen die besten Grüsse des Herrn Professor Hänisch zu senden.

Hochachtungsvoll

Friedrich Weller.

Leipzig, S.3, Arndtstr.59/III, 26.7.30.

Hochgeehrter Herr Baron v. Stael-Holstein!

Ihren Brief vom 8.Juli habe ich erhalten, und ich danke Ihnen bestens dafür. Ich hatte geglaubt annehmen zu sollen, dass die ganze Angelegenheit erledigt sei, wie sehr ich davon überzeugt war, können Sie dem entnehmen, dass ich mich wollte nach Japan austauschen lassen. Der einzige Grund, weshalb ich nicht auf die erste Liste gesetzt bin, ist der, dass ich Herrn Prof. Hänisch gebeten hatte, mir noch etwas Zeit zu lassen. Ich wäre bis Oktober mit einer Arbeit über das Brahmajalasutra(tibetischer Text) fertig geworden, und diese Arbeit vorher abzuschliessen, ehe ich hinausgehe, war mit sehr am Herzen gelegen. Die Arbeit steckt in der Mitte des zweiten Kapitels der Einleitung. Wäre Ihr Brief nur drei Tage später angekommen, so hätte ich vor Ausgang Oktober schwerlich überhaupt etwas unternehmen können, weil diese Woche das Semester schliesst. Wie ich Ihnen schon in meinem ersten Briefe mitteilte, muss ich einen Urlaub durch die Fakultät beim Ministerium auswirken. Ich muss zunächst die Antwort abwarten, ehe ich abschliessend zu Ihrem Briefe Stellung nehmen kann. Denn wenn ich ohne Urlaub losführe, verlöre ich hier meine Stellung, das bescheidene Einkommen, welches ich für einen Lehrauftrag erhalte und könnte nie wieder an meine Universität zurückkehren. Die Sachlage ist für mich deshalb noch besonders ernst, weil mein hochbetagter Vater heute nur einen ganz geringen Geschäftsumsatz erzielen kann. Ich brauche Ihnen keine Zahlen zu nennen, Sie glauben mir die Tatsachen auch so. Hier wusste weder ich, noch sonst jemand---ich habe mich ausdrüklich danach befragt — etwas davon, dass Herr Dr.Behrsing erst im Mai endgiltig abgesagt hat.Da der $ mex.die Fallsucht bekommen hat — er ist nach Auskunft der Deutschen Bank und Diskontogesellschaft heute wert RM 1.01 gegenüber einem Werte von RM 1,58 im Frühjahre und über RM 2.— vor einem Jahre— und ich hier in Deutschland eine Inflation miterlebt habe,so würde ich Sie bitten,mir mitzuteilen,ob es nicht möglich wäre,den Betrag in einer wertbeständigen Valuta festzusetzen,den ich als monatliche Bezahlung erhalte. Schliessen wir auf $ mex.ab,so stehen auch Sie in einem Vertrage drin,und wenn der $ mex noch weiter fällt,so können Sie mir nicht helfen,nicht,weil Sie das nicht wollten,sondern weil Sie juristisch gebunden sind.So,wie die Dinge liegen,erhält jemand bei 400 $ mex.einen um etwa 75.—RM niedrigeren Wert als jemand,welcher vor einem halben Jahre 300.—$ mex erhielt.

Da mir Herr Dr.Behrsing erzählte, dass im Institut weder das Böhtlingksche Sanskritwörterbuch noch sonstige Hilfsmittel vorhanden seien, so würde ich mir einen Handapparat für einen Elementarkurs und den darauffolgenden Textkursus mitbringen,weiterhin die Hilsmittel für eine Einführung ins Prakrit und für zwei Semester Pali.Für eine kurze,genaue Nachricht wäre ich Ihnen sehr verbunden,denn Herr Dr.Behrsing hat mir nichtsdavon gesagt, dass ich einen Teil des Unterrichtes übernehmen soll,noch welchen.Sie sehen damit, dass wir viel weniger unterrichtet sind,als Sie annahmen.

Ueber das wissenschaftliche Leben hier bei uns wird es Sie interessieren,folgendes zu erfahren.In der Indologie geben—wenn ich es auf Formeln bringen soll—— alle Anschauungen, welche unsere Lehrer vertraten, für den Veda und den älteren Buddhismus nach.Für den Veda und Awesta ist durch Johs.Hertels Arbeiten ein Neues aufgestellt worden. Die Umwertung erstreckt sich hier auf die Entstehungszeit und die Inhalte der Weltauffassung, die die vedischen ist.Aber Sie werden gewiss seine Veröffentlichungen in den Indogermanischen Quellen und Forschungen und in der Sächsischen Akademie der Wissenschaften draussen haben.Seine Stellung ist noch umkämpft.Frohe Zustimmung steht harter Ablehnung gegenüber,diese letztere ist sehr viel ruhiger geworden.Auch die Auffassung des Buddhismus wandelt sich.Oldenberg gehört, für uns Junge mit allen seinen Arbeiten über den Buddhismus der Geschichte an. Ich kann Ihnen in Kürze die ganze Entwicklung wohl dahin charakterisieren, dass die junge Generation auf ihre Fahnen geschrieben hat: fort von der ceylonesischen Tradition, sie hat keinerlei geschichtlichen Wert, zurück zu den Texten und zwar zu allen, nicht nur den bisher bevorzugten Pāli-Quellen.

Auch die alten chinesischen Texte geben viel von ihrem altehrwürdigen Ansehen auf. Die Reihe der Untersuchungen wurde m.W. von Pelliot mit einer Arbeit über das Schu-king eröffnet und heute haben die jüngeren auch schon das Schi-ki mit ihrem Zweifel angefallen wie die Rostfäule einen Eisenklotz. Man kann die geschichtliche Lage dahin bestimmen, dass an die Stelle der empirischen, in der Tradition befangenen Exegese die wissenschaftliche Textkritik tritt. Was herauskommen wird, müssen wir abwarten, zeitlich gebunden werden auch unsere Erkenntnisse wie die unserer Lehrer bleiben.

Ich darf Sie um eine Antwort auf meine Fragen bitten. Sobald ich Nachricht vom Ministerium habe, erhalten Sie endgiltigen Bescheid, wenn bis dahin Ihre Antwort eingetroffen sein wird.

Die Grüsse an Herrn Prof. Hanisch habe ich bestellt, und ich sende Ihnen gerne seinen Dank und seine Empfehlung.

Hochachtungsvoll

Friedrich Weller

Leipzig, S.3, Arndtstr.59/III, 22.8.30.

Hochgeehrter Herr Baron v. Stael-Holstein!

                        Der Ordnung halber teile ich Ihnen noch brieflich mit, dass ich meine Zusage abgesandt habe. Sie werden das Telegramm inzwischen erhalten und auch das Reisegeld überwiesen haben. Ich hoffe, dass Sie Freude an mir erleben und wenn ich Sie um etwas bitten darf, dann wäre ich Ihnen sehr dankbar, wenn Sie mir den Einführungskurs im Sanskrit überliessen. Der Grund ist vor allem menschlicher Art. Ich bin ein etwas schwerer, vielleicht auch etwas schwerfälliger Charakter, und da ich zudem meine hochbetagten Eltern in recht bedrückten Lebensverhältnissen zurücklasse, denke ich, dass ich auf diese Weise am raschesten über mancherlei wegkomme. Im Anfängerkolleg ist die Möglichkeit, an junge Menschen heranzukommen, immer am grössten und ich glaube, das wird mir viel erleichtern.

                Inzwischen bitte ich Sie, für mich zu kaufen ein gebundenes Exemplar von Ts'ang, Complete Chinese English Dictionary, The Republican Press, Shanghai und ein English-Chinesisches Wörterbuch, dessen Auswahl ich Ihnen überlasse, da Sie diese Dinge viel besser kennen als ich. Vielleicht Hemeling?? Ich bin mit Ihrer Wahl einverstanden.

                Sonst hoffe ich, dass wir nach dem ersten Jahre meiner Arbeit an Ihrem Institut den Index zum Kaśyapaparivarta fertig haben werden, denn der wird doch wohl drankommen.

                Sollten Sie inzwischen einige Kleinigkeiten mit der Post für mich erhalten, so bitte ich Sie, diese einstweilen anzunehmen.

                Die Beträge für die zwei Wörterbücher bitte ich Sie inzwischen zu verlegen, ich werde sie Ihnen in Peking zurückzahlen.

Hochachtungsvoll

Friedrich Weller

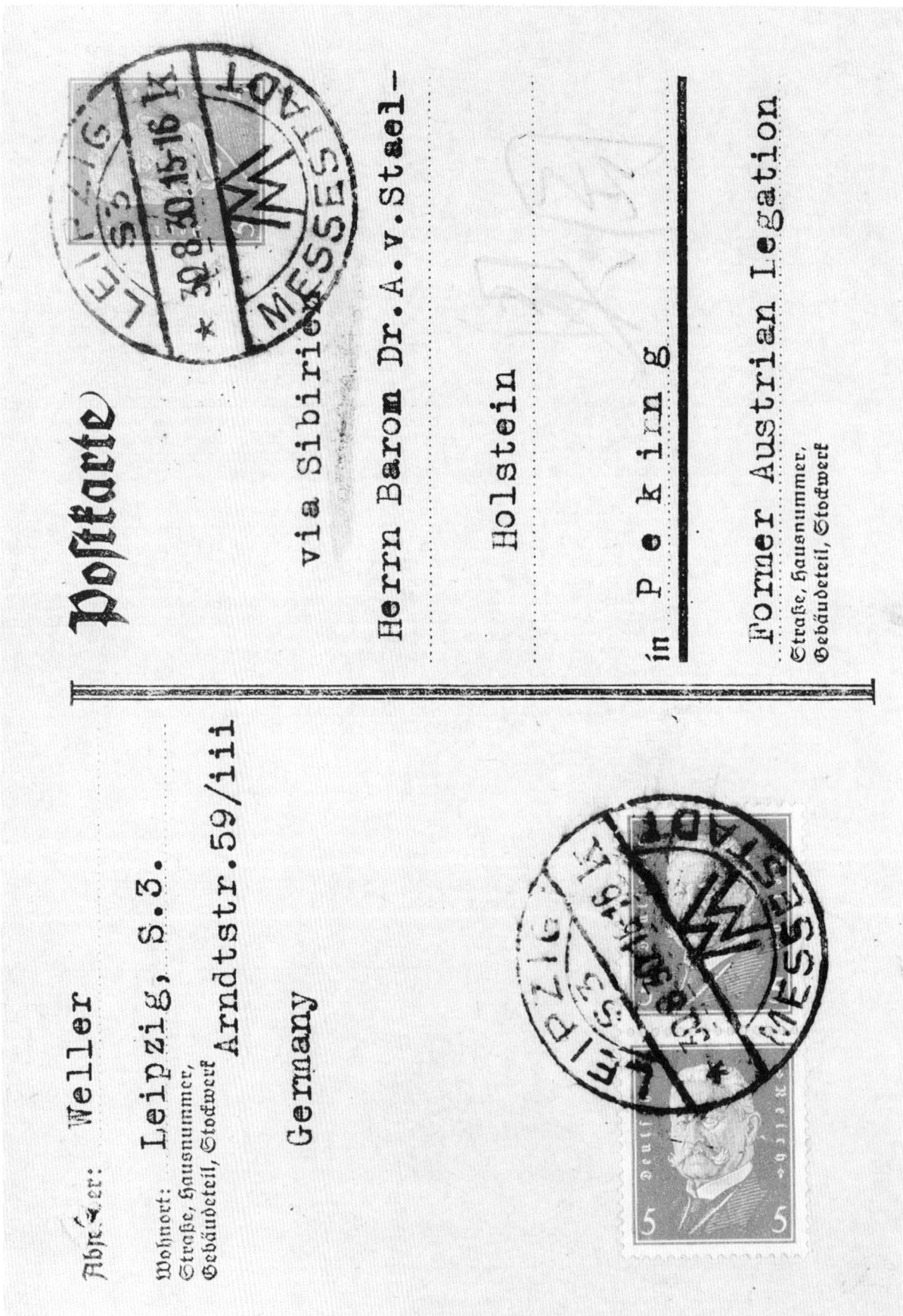

Hochgeehrter Herr Baron v.Stael-Holstein!

Am 28.8.30 habe ich von der Deutsch-Asiatischen Bank in Berlin achthundert Reichsmark erhalten und ich danke Ihnen bestens für die Zusendung.Am 29.8. war ich nach einer Fahrkarte in Berlin im Mitteleuropäischen Reisebüro des Potsdamer Bahnhofes,wohin mich das Auswärtige Amt wegen der Passangelegenheiten gewiesen hatte.Alle Schlafplätze über Warschau-Niegoreloje sind bis Ende September vergeben.Sie waren es bereits gegen die Mitte des August.Ich fahre über Tilsit,Dünaburg,Bigussowo und habe einen Schlafplatz erhalten für die Abfahrt am 14.9.in Berlin. Durch die Leipziger Messe,die Ende August Anfang September stattfindet,ist vermutlich eine starke Nachfrage nach Karten eingetreten.Die Fahrkarte habe ich bestellt und hoffe in der letzten Septemberwoche in Peking zu sein. Es ist in dieser Hauptreisezeit nach dem Fernen Osten alles viel schwieriger,als Sie und ich es dachten.Mein Schiffsgepäck an Ihre Adresse bitte ich anzunehmen.
Hochachtungsvoll

Friedrich Weller,

Friedrich Weller
20 Toh Foo Hsiang   Peking, den 23. November 1930.

Herrn Baron
Dr. A. von Stael-Holstein.
Former Austrian Legation
P e i p i n g.

Hochverehrter Herr Baron,

    Wollen Sie es freundlichst entschuldigen, wenn ich Ihnen auf Ihr Angebot, den Vertrag zu verlängern, aus Mangel an Zeit erst heute Antwort gebe, zumal da ich die Sache reiflich erwägen mußte.

    Die Bedingungen, unter denen der Vertrag weiterlaufen soll, sind, wenn ich richtig verstanden habe, die folgenden: Der Vertrag läuft auf ein Jahr weiter, die Bezahlung beträgt Reichsmark 450.- (vierhundertfünfzig RM.) für zehn Monate, im Ganzen also Reichsmark 4,500.- (viertausendfünfhundert RM.) für das Jahr. Es bleibt hierzu noch offen, welches Honorar für die restlichen zwei Ferienmonate festgesetzt werden soll.

    Ehe ich hierzu endgültig Stellung nehme, möchte ich die ganze Frage zunächst von drei Hauptpunkten abhängig machen:

1) Vorbedingung, ehe ich mich definitiv entscheide, bliebe die Urlaubsverlängerung vonseiten des sächsischen Ministeriums.

2) Ich würde dann noch ergebenst darum bitten, die Höhe des Gehalts einer Nachprüfung zu unterziehen.

3) Die Kosten der Heimreise wären gleichfalls in die Erwägung einzubeziehen; ich bin beider Herreise mit RM. 800.- nicht ausgekommen.

    Für den Fall, daß die Gesundheitsverhältnisse meiner Eltern eine plötzliche Heimreise nahelegen, so möchte ich mir gerne die Freiheit vorbehalten, ohne Vertragsbruch heimreisen zu dürfen, was Sie gewiss menschlich verstehen werden.

    In größter Hochschätzung
    Ihr ergebenster
    Friedrich Weller

Bitte wenden!

P.S. Mir fällt soeben noch ein,daß ich in der Zwischenzeit möglicherweise eine Berufung nach einer anderen Universität erhalten könnte.Obwohl ich in einem solchen Falle alles versuchen würde, um unsere Abmachungen einzuhalten und auch von der neuen,berufenden Universität einen Urlaub zu erwirken,möchte ich doch auch für diese Eventualität um Freiheit bitten,da eine solche Berufung für mich nicht eine vorübergehende,sondern eine Lebensfrage bedeutet (Anstellung auf Lebenszeit).

v. O.

Peiping, den 16. Dezember 1930.
20 Toh Foo Shiang.

Herrn Baron
Dr. A. von Stael-Holstein
Former Austrian Legation
P e i p i n g

Sehr geehrter Herr Baron,

unter Bezugnahme auf mein ausführliches Schreiben vom 23. November 1930 bestätige ich hiermit den Empfang Ihrer gestrigen Notiz.

Da deren Inhalt mit den verschiedenen Punkten meines Schreibens nicht konform geht, so bitte ich, zu entschuldigen, dass ich mir meine Entscheidung vorbehalten will.

Hochachtungsvoll
ergebenst

Friedrich Weller

Patatschu (八大處), 10.8.31
50, Pa betze

Hochgeehrter Herr Baron von Staël-Holstein!

Unserer Verabredung gemäss gestatte ich mir Ihnen mitzuteilen, dass ich telegraphisch benachrichtigt worden bin, dass der Urlaub genehmigt ist, um welchen ich gebeten hatte. Bisher weiss ich noch nicht, unter welchen Bedingungen der Urlaub bewilligt würde. Da somit grundsätzlich die Möglichkeit besteht einen zweiten Vertrag abzuschliessen, bitte ich, im folgenden die gehaltenen Besprechungen und die erfolgten Mitteilungen noch einmal zusammenzustellen zu dürfen. Dabei bitte ich, ein paar

Drucke einer geneigten Prüfung zu unterziehen.

1) Seit meiner Anreise ist der Fahrpreis über Sibirien erhöht worden, außerdem muß ich ein Epbillet kaufen. Soviel ich weiß, beträgt der Preis für das Epbillet sechsundzwanzig Golddollar für die versinkte Strecke. Ich bitte deshalb bei einer Vertragsverlängerung den Betrag für die Rückreise zu erhöhen.

2) Der Vertrag wird abgeschlossen für die Zeit vom 16. Juli 1931 bis 15. August 1932. Dabei sind die Zeit vom 16. Juli 1931 bis 15. August 1931 und vom 16. Juli 1932 bis 15. August 1932 Ferien, für die das vereinbarte Monatsgehalt bezahlt wird.

3

3) Sollten für den neuen Urlaub die einstweiligen Bezüge von der Leipziger Universität wegfallen, so waren Sie, soweit ich verstanden habe, bereit, den Ausfall zu decken.

4) Ich bitte um eine durchgehende Arbeitszeit, etwa von 8-2. Das Institut hat bei einer solchen Regelung zu keinen Nachteil.

5) Die Bezahlung beträgt je Monat 119 (einhundertneunzehn) $ Gold oder 500 Goldmark. Sie erfolgt am 15. jeden Kalendermonates für den folgenden Vertragsmonat.

6) Falls schwere Störungen in der Familie meiner Eltern oder die Möglichkeit, eine feste Lebensstellung zu gewinnen, meine Rückkehr vor Ablauf des Vertragsjahres notwendig machen, soll mir die

Rückkehr offen bleiben, ohne dass ich mich eines Vertragsbruches schuldig mache.

7) Punkt 5 (fünf) gilt unter dem Vorbehalt, dass die unter Punkt 3 (drei) erwähnte Möglichkeit vom Wegfall der einstweiligen Leipziger Bezüge nicht eintritt.

Ich bitte Sie, meine Gestellungen einer Prüfung zu unterziehen und mir eine Antwort zukommen zu lassen, um dann den Vertrag aufzusetzen. Ich bedaure, dass die Angelegenheit sich hingezogen hat, doch bin ich daran schuldlos.

Ich bin in ausgezeichneter
Hochachtung Ihr ganz ergebener
Friedrich Weller.

Hochgeehrter Herr Baron von Staël-Holstein!

Zur Ergänzung meines Schreibens darf ich Ihnen mitteilen, daß nach einer brieflichen Mitteilung der philosophischen Fakultät der Universität Leipzig Punkt 3 und Punkt 7 nur mehr als Eventualkandidaten in Frage kommen.

In ausgezeichneter Hochachtung

Friedrich Weller.

15. 8. 31.
Petschdӣ.

Peiping, Former Austrian Legation, 16.1.32.

Hochgeehrter Herr Baron v. Stael-Holstein!

Da ich Ihre gestrige Erklaerung der Form vidadīyasamjñām zunaechst nicht annehmen kann, gestatte ich mir, Ihnen hierunter meine Auffassung darzulegen. Sie meinten, wenn ich Sie recht verstand, dass vidadīya zentralasiatische Lautform fuer Sanskrit vitathya sei, es ein Adjektiv ist.

Meine Auffassung ist folgende. Es handelt sich um ein Absolutivum, welches vom folgenden samjñām abzutrennen ist. Das Wort ist Schreibfehler fuer nivadīya, welche Form die prakritische Entsprechung fuer sanskritisches nivrtya ist. Auch in der entsprechenden Prosastelle ist statt des Wortes ~~nisrtya~~ nivrtya zu lesen. Damit wird ein klarer Sinn der Textstelle erhalten, ausserdem stimmt damit der Sanskrittext zum tibetischen sgyur ba.

Soweit meine Erinnerung reicht, kommt fuer zentralasiatische Manuskripte eine Lautentwicklung vitathya>vidadīya nicht in Frage, aber da ich hier nur mein Gedaechnis (Gedächtnis) zur Verfuegung habe, und das bekanntermassen immer unzuverlaessig ist, kann mir in diesem Punkte ein Irrtum unterlaufen.

Da wir eine verschiedene Auffassung haben, bitte ich Sie, meine Angaben zu pruefen.

Die Erklaerung der Stelle im Komm. zum Meghaduta halte ich fest. Ich bleibe bei meiner Auffassung von mahābhoga als grossen Umfang habend.

Ich bin mit freundlichen Gruessen
Ihr ganz ergebener
Friedrich Weller

Ueber den Umfang der Indices zum Kāçyapaparivarta
laesst sih folgendes sagen:
1) tibetischer Index, nach Schaetzung der Druckerei, soviel ich
   mich besinne, etwa 22 Druckbogen zu je 16 SS.
2) Sanskrit Index vermutlich 6 - 7 Druckbogen.
3) Chinesischer Index, genauere Schaetzung vorlaeufig unmoeglich, doch wird der Umfang dieses Indexes den des tibetischen vermutlich erreichen oder sogar uebersteigen.
   Verlaessliche Angaben sind fuer diesen Punkt noch nicht
   zu treffen.
13.9.31.

Peiping, 崇文門內老錢局甲二號
16.7.32.

Hochgeehrter Herr Baron v. Stael-Holstein!

Ich gestatte mir Ihnen mitzuteilen, daß ich gestern von der Fakultät die Mitteilung erhalten habe, daß mir das sächsische Ministerium für Volksbildung meinen Urlaub zur Verlängerung des Urlaubes genehmigt hat und zwar um ein Jahr bis September 1933. Nach unserer Besprechung im Herbste letzten Jahres hatte ich ja annehmen müssen, daß ein neuer Vertrag wieder für ein Jahr abgeschlossen würde. Leider haben Sie mir nun neulich mitgeteilt, daß dies in.d. Umständen nicht möglich ist, eine Änderung des Urlaubsgesuches war nicht mehr möglich.

Ich wäre Ihnen zu großem Danke verpflichtet wenn Sie mir mitteilen würden, wann ich Sie sprechen könnte, denn es liegt mir daran, daß der Vertrag abgeschlossen wird.

Ich bin in ausgezeichneter Hochachtung

Ihr ganz ergebener

Friedrich Weller.

Peiping 崇文門內老鎗局甲二號
26.7.32.

Hochgeehrter Herr Baron v. Stael-Holstein!

Der Ordnung halber gestatte ich mir, Ihnen nachfolgend den Inhalt unserer Unterredungen und Abmachungen zu bestätigen.

1) Der Vertrag zwischen Ihnen und mir wird verlängert vom 16. Juli 1932 bis 31. März 1933. Vom 16. Juli 1932 bis 15. August 1932 sind Ferien.

2) Meine Arbeitszeit im Institut beträgt werktäglich sechs Stunden, wobei die Arbeitszeit von 9–12 und 2–5 läuft.

3) Ich kann wöchentlich bis zu fünf Stunden Unterricht am Institut in Sanskrit herangezogen werden. Diese Unterrichtszeit fällt in die Arbeitszeit im Institut.

4) Als Vergütung erhalte ich:
für die Zeit vom 16. bis 31. Juli 1932 $ mex. 250.– (Zweihundertundfünfzig $ mex.),
für die Zeit vom 1. August 1932 bis 31. März 1933 je $ mex. 500.– (fünfhundert $ mex.) für den Monat

5) Für den Fall, daß mir eine Lebensstellung angeboten wird, darf ich, ohne vertragsbrüchig zu werden, auch vor dem 31. März 1933 ausscheiden aus diesem Vertrage zwischen Herrn Baron v. Staël-Holstein und mir. Dabei wird das Gehalt für einen angerissenen Monat mir dann bezahlt, wenn ich über die Hälfte des Monates am Institut tätig war.

6) Für die Rückreise stehen 800.- (achthundert) Goldmark plus Billett zur Verfügung, wenn ich aus dem Institut ausscheide.

7) Sollte ich vor dem 31. März 1933 sterben, so wird Herr Baron v. Staël-Holstein versuchen, das Reisegeld meiner Frau auszuzahlen.

Ich bin in ausgezeichneter Hochachtung und mit besten Grüßen, auch von meiner Frau, Ihr ergebener

Friedrich Weller.

Peiping, East City, Lao ch'ien chü 24, 30.3.33

Hochgeehrter Herr Baron v. Staël-Holstein!

Es drängt sich in diesen Tagen wegen meiner Abreise alles so zusammen, daß ich Sie bitten darf, mich heute einmal zu entschuldigen. Das letzte große Gepäck muß am Sonnabend fort, und vorher muß ich noch einige Dinge erledigt haben, da es sonst zu spät wird. Die Korrekturen, die ich habe, werde ich daheim erledigen.

Ich bin in ausgezeichneter Hochachtung
Ihr ganz ergebener
Friedrich Weller.

NS. Dürfte ich wohl bitten, mir für Sonnabend, den 1.4.33, Nachmittag noch einmal Johnstons Textausgabe des Saundara- nanda zur Verfügung zu stellen? Ich möchte den fünften Gesang abschließen. Wir werden noch 2 Stunden zu arbeiten haben, am Mittwoch sind wir nicht fertig geworden. Sie werden das Buch pünktlich zurück erhalten.

d.O.

PIROSCAFO 16. 4. 33.

Hochverehrter Herr Baron von Staël-Holstein!

Da wir morgen früh Singapore erreichen, will ich Ihnen gerne von da einen freundlichen Gruß zukommen lassen. Hoffentlich sind Sie und die Ihren gesund. Uns geht es gut, wir hatten bislang ruhige See und eine wertvolle Fahrt, wollen wir hoffen, daß der gute Neptun auch wirklich gnädig bleibt.

Arbeiten kann ich auf dem Schiff nicht. Vielleicht ist es ganz gut, daß die force majeure so eingreift. Leider habe ich Sie zu fragen vergessen — es ging die letzten Wochen in Peking wirr durcheinander — ob es wohl möglich wäre, ein complet Exemplar meines Tibetisch=Indischen Indices als Autoren-exemplar zu verschenken. Falls dagegen kein Bedenken bestehen, würde ich bitten, je ein geheftetes Stück an folgende Adressen zu senden:

1) Frau Berta Birnbaum, 北平豆腐巷二十號

2) ~~Herrn Baron A. v. Staël-Holstein,~~

3) " Lin Li-Kuang, Institut.

4) " B. J. Pankratov. "

5) " Prof. Dr. Ferdinand Lessing, Museum für Völkerkunde, Berlin, Stresemann Str. 110

6) " (A. H. Johnston, M.A., The Manor House, Adderbury East, Banbury, Oxfordshire, England)

7) Herrn A. Mostaerts, 北平太平倉二號
   普愛堂

8) Herrn Lou, Academia Sinica, genaue
   Adresse kann Herr Lin Li-kuang
   angeben.

9) Herrn Prof. Th. Ščerbatskoi, Akag. Hayk CCCP.
   Leningrad Truberennenkag nab. 5.

10) Herrn Prof. Obermiller, ibidem.

11) Herrn Prof. Poppe, Asiatisches Museum,
    Leningrad V.-O., Tiflisskaja ul. 1.

PIROSCAFO

12) Herrn Prof. Joh. Hertel, Leipzig-Stötteritz, Denkmalsallee 110.

13) Herrn Priv. doz. Dr. Waldschmidt, Berlin, Universität.

14) „ Prof. Dr. Walter Simon, 北平大取燈胡同三號

15) „ Priv. doz. Dr. Gustav Haloun, Göttingen, Nicolausberger str. 19.

16) „ „ Friedrich Weller, Leipzig S. 3, Arndtstr. 59 II

17.) Herrn Prof. Dr. B. Karlgren, Göteborg, Universität, Schweden.

Ich würde mich sehr freuen, wenn Sie es erreichen könnten, daß meine Bitte erfüllt wird. Wenn ich in Deutschland ankomme, hoffe ich einen Teil Korrekturen des indischen Index vorzufinden, die ich dann gleich erledigen will. Inzwischen aber sende ich Ihnen auch von meiner Frau die schönsten Grüsse mit der höflichen Bitte, uns Ihrer Frau Gemahlin bestens zu empfehlen.

Ich bin in ausgezeichneter Hochachtung

Ihr ganz ergebener

Friedrich Weller.

Leipzig, O.5, Oststrasse 55/iii bei Bachmann, 12.6.33.

Hochverehrter Herr Baron von Staël-Holstein!

Inliegend gestatten wir uns, Ihnen einen Abzug der Aufnahmen zugehen zu lassen, welche wir vor dem Institut gemacht haben. Gleichzeitig möchte ich Ihnen mitteilen, dass ich alle Bücher, welche Ihre Frau Gemahlin und Sie haben wollen, bei Simmel & Co., Leipzig, C.1, Rossstrasse 5 - 7 bestellt habe. Sie werden von der Buchhandlung unmittelbar Nachricht erhalten und die Bücher zugesandt erhalten. Sollte ein Werk den Betrag von 10 - 12 RM übersteigen, so erhalten Sie zunächst ein Angebot. Ich hoffe, dass ich damit Ihre Wünsche erfüllt habe, sollten Sie weiterhin Bücher brauchen, so stehe ich Ihnen gerne zur Verfügung.

Von dem zweiten Index habe ich bisher noch nichts erhalten. Die Seiten 9 - 16 konnte ich erst hier in Leipzig durchsehen, da auf dem Schiffe keine Arbeitsmöglichkeiten bestanden. Ich habe sie an die Druckerei gesandt und hoffe, dass nun der Satz rasch und glatt weitergeht. Meinen Brief von unterwegs haben Sie gewiss erhalten, es wird sich wohl ermöglichen lassen, die paar Freiexemplare zu versenden.

Wir sind gesund, es herrschen hier Friede und Ordnung, die wirtschaftliche Lage ist ernst, die Arbeitslosigkeit ist gross. Es werden gewaltige Anstrengungen gemacht, sie zu meistern. Hoffentlich haben sie den gewünschten Erfolg, es hilft, soweit es nur irgend möglich ist, jeder, aber die wirtschaftliche Lage ist ernst. Trotz allem aber bleibt Deutschland Deutschland.

Bitte empfehlen Sie uns Ihrer Frau Gemahlin und grüssen Sie meine Mitarbeiter am Institut auf's herzlichste.

Ich bin mit schönen Grüssen

Ihr ~~ganz ergebener~~

Friedrich Weller

Leipzig,C.1,Stephanstrasse 12/ii rechts,den 14.7.33.

Hochgeehrter Herr Baron von Staël-Holstein!
Mit gleicher Post lasse ich an Sie die verbesserten Fahnen 17 - 40 abgehen.Sie enthalten leider eine beträchtliche Masse Druckfehler, so viele,dass ich Sie höflichst bitten möchte,mir noch einen zweiten Abzug zugehen zu lassen,wenn es irgend möglich ist.Dabei möchte ich bitten,mir zwei gleichlautende Abzüge zugehen zu lassen.Falls der eine Abzug verloren geht,müsste die Korrektur noch ein zweites Mal gelesen werden.Das kostet mich Tage.Habe ich noch ein zweites Exemplar,so kann ich die Korrekturen in sehr kurzer Zeit übertragen, und es bliebe die Gefahr ausgeschlossen,dass die Korrektur noch ein zweites Mal gelesen werden müsste.Die Fahnen 9 - 16 habe ich bereits vor etwa einem Monate als eingeschriebene Drucksache abgehen lassen, und zwar an die Druckerei.Ich sende sie deshalb nicht noch einmal. Nur Fahne 10 füge ich nochmals bei,weil der angegebene Nachtrag nötig ist.Ich bitte veranlassen zu wollen,dass dieser Einschub noch vorgenommen wird,ich habe das Wort parīksa nur als Titelkopf aufgenommen gehabt,doch ist es der leichten Übersichtlichkeit halber besser auf S.10 noch einzuschalten.
Ich wäre Ihnen,hochgeehrter Herr Baron von Staël-Holstein,sehr zu Danke verbunden,wenn Sie mir die Fahnen 9 - 40 in zweiter Korrektur zugehen liessen,vielleicht kann die Druckerei auch gleich den Rest noch mit aussetzen.Meinen Sonderabzug haben Sie wohl inzwischen erhalten.Für die Weiterarbeit an der Übersetzung brauche ich Ihre Ausgabe des Kommentares,bitte lassen Sie mir ein Stück zugehen.

Bitte empfehlen Sie meine Frau und mich Ihrer Frau Gemahlin und lassen
Sie sich selbst die besten Grüsse senden
von Ihrem ganz ergebenen

Friedrich Weller

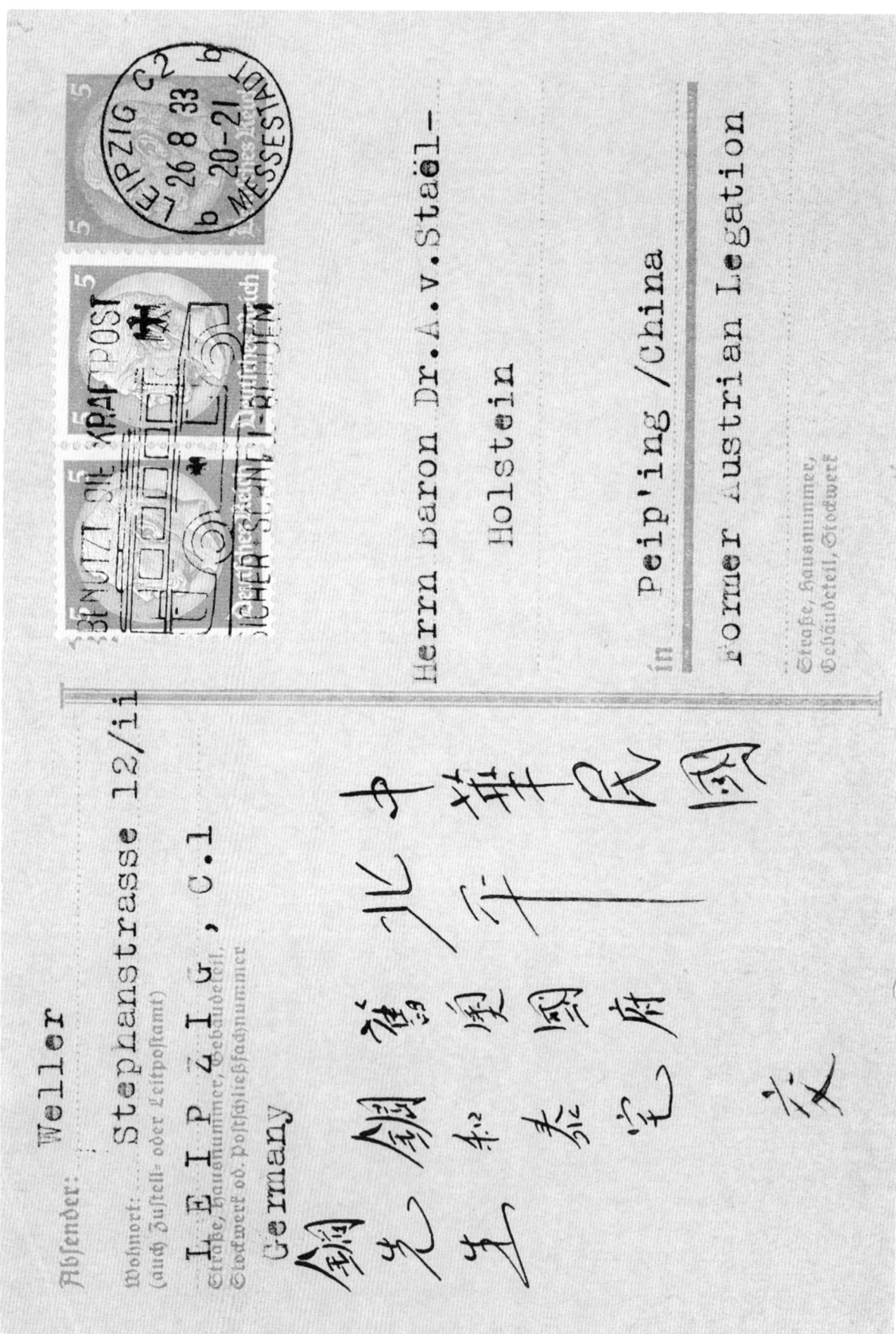

Hochgeehrter Herr Baron v.Staël-Holstein!

für die Zusendung eines Belegexemplares meines tibetisch-indischen Indexes zu Kaśyapaparivarta spreche ich Ihnen meinen besten Dank aus. Darf ich einmal anfragen,ob Sie meiner Bitte haben entsprechen können,ein Exemplar einer Anzahl bekannter Herren zugehen zu lassen?
Die Bücher,welche Sie haben wollten,haben Sie wohl inzwischen alle erhalten.
Ich freue mich,dass das erste Buch nun doch noch fertig geworden ist und hoffe ferne,dass auch das zweite,der indische Index,noch zum Abschlusse kommen wird.

Mit besten Empfehlungen an Ihre Frau Gemahlin von meiner Frau und mir begrüsse ich Sie in ausgezeichneter Hochachtung als Ihr ganz ergebener

Friedrich Weller

25.8.33.

Leipzig,C.1,Stephanstrasse,12/ii rechts,den
16.9.33.

Hochgeehrter Herr Baron von Staël-Holstein!

Hiermit bestätige ich Ihnen,Ihren Brieff vom 29.Juli 1933 erhalten zu haben.Haben Sie recht schönen Dank dafür.Gleichzeitig ging das Exemplar Ihrer Ausgabe des Kommentares zum Kāśyapaparivarta ein. Auch dafür möchte ich Ihnen recht herzlich danken,dass Sie mir ein Exemplar haben zugehen lassen.Ich hoffe,Sie haben inzwischen auch den Sonderabzug meiner Arbeit über das Brahmajālasūtra erhalten und darf Sie vielleicht bitten,den Herren Lin und Pankratov zu sagen, dass ich auch jedem von ihnen ein Exemplar zugesandt habe.Hoffentlich kommen sie an.

Auf Ihren Brief hin,er ging am 14.September ein—die Postverbindung dauert also doch noch 1½ Monat — habe ich gestern eine Anzeige abgefasst ,die ich heute Herrn Dr.Schindler zugehen lasse, um ihn zu bitten,die drei Druckseiten zur Verfügung zu stellen.Ein Schreibmaschinendurchschlag steht Ihnen auf Wunsch zu Gebote.Ich würde mich freuen,wenn Ihnen meine Anzeige von Nutzen wäre,auf alle Fälle hörte ich gerne,was mit dem Institute wird,das würde mich doch sehr interessieren.Vielleicht führt uns das Leben wieder einmal zur Arbeit zusammen.

Da Ihnen unsere Aufnahme gefallen hat,gestatte ich mir, Ihnen noch zwei Abzüge zugehen zu lassen,die wir zufällig da liegen haben.

Für die Grüsse Ihrer Frau Gemahlin danken meine Frau und ich aufs beste, und wir bitten Sie, uns Ihrer Frau Gemahlin bestens zu empfehlen.

Nehmen Sie die herzlichsten Grüsse entgegen von meiner Frau und mir, Ihrem ganz ergebenen

Friedrich Weller

Leipzig,C.1,Stephanstrasse 12/ii rechts,d.26.13.33.-

Hochgeehrter Herr Baron v.Staël-Holstein!

Sie werden inzwischen den Sonderabzug über das Sino-Indian Institute der Harvard University in Peking erhalten haben.Ich hoffe gerne,dass das Artikelchen die erwünschte Wirkung in Amerika auslöst und das Institut trotz der Zeitumstände erhalten bleibt.Der kleine Aufsatz ist in dem 9.Bande der Asia Major erschienen.Das beiliegende Exemplar bitte ich Herrn Pankratov zu übergeben.Inzwischen hat sich ja der Mitarbeiterstab geändert,doch konnte ich da nichts mehr ändern am Tede.Gleichzeitig möchte ich Ihnen recht herzlich für die Zusendung von vier Exemplaren meines Indexes danken,die Stücke sind unversehrt hier angekommen.Ich wäre Ihnen recht dankbar,wenn Sie mir einen Aushänger des indischen Index zusenden könnten, das würde die Korrektur sehr erleichtern,wenn ich die Verweise nachprüfen muss.Ein Exemplar ist da völlig ausreichend..Vielleicht ist es Ihnen möglich,bei Einkäufen von Büchern auch die Antiquariatsabteilung zu berücksichtigen,welche dem Verlage der Asia Major angegliedert ist,ich will mich damit aber in keiner Weise in Ihre Geschäftsführung eingemengt haben. Hoffentlich erfreuen Sie und Ihre Familie sich der besten Gesundheit.Ich bitte Sie,mich Ihrer Frau Gemahlin bestens zu empfehlen und von meiner Frau die schönsten Grüsse zu bestellen.Ihnen selbst auch sende ich gleichzeitig im Namen meiner Frau die besten Wünsche für das neue Jahr und die freundlichsten Grüsse als Ihr ganz ergebener

Friedrich Weller

Leipzig, C.1,Stephanstrasse 12/ii rechts.den 30.4.34.

Hochgeehrter Herr Baron von Stael-Holstein!

Haben Sie recht herzlichen Dank dafür,dass Sie mir Ihre Veröffentlichung:On a Peking edition of the Tibetan Kanjur which seems to be unknown in the West haben zugehen lassen.Es ist dankenswert,dass Sie es unternommen haben,uns mit diesem Kanjur bekannt gemacht zu haben.Ich kann noch nicht überschauen,wie sich Ihre Ergebnisse mit meinen Ausführungen zusammenfügen werden,aber es ist mir ganz klar,dass alle Untersuchungen über die Geschichte der Formung und Überlieferung des Kanjur und auch des Tanjur nur vorläufigen Wert haben,dass unsere Ergebnisse später ergänzt,berichtigt,ausgebaut werden müssen.Auf jeden Fall darf man aus Ihren Ausführungen eine Bestätigung meiner Darlegungen entnehmen,dass diese Geschichte viel verwickelter und langwieriger --wohl auch viel intensiver -- ist,als man sich dies bisher gedacht hat.

Die Korrekturen und die Aushänger habe ich ebenfalls erhalten,ich danke Ihnen bestens für die Zusendung und werde die Korrektur ehestens wieder an Sie absenden.

Die Sonderabzüge,welche ich Ihnen habe zugehen lassen,haben Sie wohl alle richtig erhalten,und ich hoffe gerne,dass mein notgedrungen kurzer Bericht über Ihr Institut Ihren Absichten förderlich gewesen ist.Ich habe geglaubt, mit einem solchem Gesamtberichte sei der Sache eher zu dienen,als mit einer Buchanzeige,ich glaube auch mancher Zuschrift entnehmen zu dürfen,dass ich den richtigen Weg gegangen bin.

Da ich an Sie schreibe,so lassen Sie mich anfragen,ob es wohl möglich wäre,in Ihrer Sino-Indian Series einen Index zum tibetisch-mongolischen brahmaja

Brahmajālasūtra abzudrucken, welchen ich im Manuskripte druckfertig liegen habe. Der mongolisch-tibetische Index ist nach Art meines tibetischen Index zum Kāśyapaparivarta angefertigt, er bringt nicht nur Wörter, sondern die ganzen Wendungen, wie sie sich im mongolischen und tibetischen Texte entsprechen. Im Format und in der Schriftgrösse Ihrer Sino-Indian Series wird er etwa sechs Bogen füllen. Der tibetische Index ist knapper gehalten, er gibt, soweit das möglich ist, die Pāli-Entsprechungen an. Beide Indices zusammen werden den Raum von 7 - 7½ Druckbogen nicht übersteigen, jedenfalls wird die Arbeit keinesfalls mehr als 8 Druckbogen ausmachen.

Kosten für den Druck des Textes und der deutschen Übersetzung des Brahmajālasūtra entstehen nicht, da diese anderweit gedruckt werden.

Ich glaube, es gibt noch keinen derartigen mongolischen Index zu irgend einem Texte, und ohne solche Indices sind auch diese Texte für die Textkritik nicht heranzuziehen, weil das mongolische Wörterbuch dauernd dabei versagt. Ich würde mich freuen, wenn Sie diesen Index in Ihre Indexreihe aufnehmen könnten. Jedenfalls darf ich Sie bitten, mir eine Antwort werden zu lassen. Es wäre doch das beste, man hätte alle dergleichen Indices in einer Reihe zusammen.

Wenn Sie Bücher brauchen, stehe ich Ihnen natürlich jederzeit gerne zur Verfügung, wenn Sie bei einer bestimmten Buchhandlung, etwa Voss oder Harrassowitz, kaufen wollen, werde ich mich selbstverständlich an Ihre Weisung halten, sonst würde ich versuchen, die billigste Quelle ausfindig zu machen.

Ich darf Sie zum Schlusse bitten, meine Frau und mich Ihrer Frau Gemahlin bestens zu empfehlen und selbst unserer beiden herzliche Grüsse entgegenzunehmen. Damit verbleibe ich Ihr ganz ergebener

Friedrich Weller.

Leipzig,C.1,Stephanstrasse 12/ii rechts,den 2.10.34.

Hochgeehrter Herr Baron v.Staël-Holstein!

Zunächst möchte ich Ihnen recht herzlich für Ihren Brief danken.Wir haben uns auch sehr über die Photographie gefreut,welche ihm beilag,und wir hoffen gerne,dass Ihr und der Ihren Leben so voller Sonne sei,wie die Photographie sie für das Pekinger wetter ausweist. Ich kann Ihren Standpunkt verstehen,und ich will Sie gewiss nicht in Unannehmlichkeiten bringen.Was nicht geht,geht eben nicht.Dass ich es schmerzlich empfinde,dass die Arbeit an der Vajracchedikā umsonst getan worden ist,brauche ich ja eigentlich nicht erst noch mit ausdrücklichen Worten zu schreiben.Es bleibt nach solchem Verzicht eben doch eine Enttäuschung zurück,die der Betroffene nicht so leicht verwindet.Es tut mir leid,dass diese Dinge sich so entwickelt haben.Wenn Sie aber einen anderen Index von mir drucken wollten,bei dem sicher keine Konkurrenz entsteht,so könnte ich Ihnen einen kleinen sogdisch-chinesischen Index zu einem veröffentlichten sogdischen Texte zur Verfügung stellen,der Umfang würde vier Druckbogen kaum übersteigen,wenn das Format und die Schriftgrösse der bisherigen Veröffentlichungen verwendet würden.Vielleicht wäre es kein Schade,wenn auch die eigentlichen zentralasiatischen Sprachen in Ihrer Reihe vertreten wären,ich könnte Ihnen auch einen rein sogdischen Index fertigstellen,wenn Sie dies vorzögen.Der erste Index hätte den Vorteil der Kürze,er wird wohl überdem so leicht von keinem anderen geschrieben werden und bis auf die Schlusskorrektur könnten, da der Text klein ist, die Korrekturen in Peking erledigt werden, sodass Ihre Reihe rasch einen Zuwachs hätte. Vielleicht lassen Sie sich meinen Vorschlag einmal durch den Kopf gehen. Mir persönlich wäre es lieb, auf diese Weise mit dem Institute verbunden zu bleiben.

Gleichzeitig sende ich Ihnen die Korrekturen zum Kāśyapaparivarta zurück. Leider hat über diesen Korrekturen irgend ein Unstern gewaltet, den festzustellen mir erst durch die Aushänger Gelegenheit geboten wurde. Ich werde den Eindruck nicht los, dass irgend etwas verloren gegangen ist, wenn ich nach den Unterlagen urteilen darf, die ich hier noch hatte, oder dass irgend ein anderes Missgeschick sich störend eingedrängt hat. Was eigentlich fertig gewesen sein sollte, musste ich in wochenlanger, sehr schwerer Arbeit noch einmal vornehmen, ich bitte es deshalb zu entschuldigen, dass sich die Rücksendung verzögert hat, ich habe die Ferien zu dieser Arbeit haben müssen und fast den ganzen September täglich von früh acht bis abends gegen elf damit zu tun gehabt. Es war eine aufreibende Arbeit, die sich durch die mechanische Aufmerksamkeit auch auf die Seelenstimmung auswirkte, sodass die gleiche Arbeitsleistung im Laufe immer mehr Zeit brauchte. Aber nun bin ich durch. Vielleicht ist es empfehlenswert, wenn die Korrektur in Peking gar erledigt wird, um vor einem neuen Missgeschick verschont zu bleiben. Ich stelle es Ihnen aber anheim, mir die Korrekturen zugehen zu lassen, ich erledige sie selbstverständlich gerne, und es bedarf auch keiner langen Zeit dazu.

Die beiliegende Photographie bitten wir Sie zum Ausdrucke freundlichen Gedenkens anzunehmen, sie ist in Potsdam auf der Höhe aufgenommen, auf welcher Sanssouci steht. Die Anlagen werden Ihnen sicher wieder bekannt vorkommen.

Bitte wollen Sie meine Frau und mich Ihrer Frau Gemahlin bestens empfehlen und sich selbst von uns die besten Wünsche für Ihr Wohlergehen und die schönsten Grüsse senden lassen. Ich würde mich sehr freuen, wieder einmal etwas vom Institute und seinem Gedeihen zu hören. Inzwischen begrüsse ich Sie in ausgezeichneter Hochachtung als Ihr ganz ergebener

Friedrich Weller

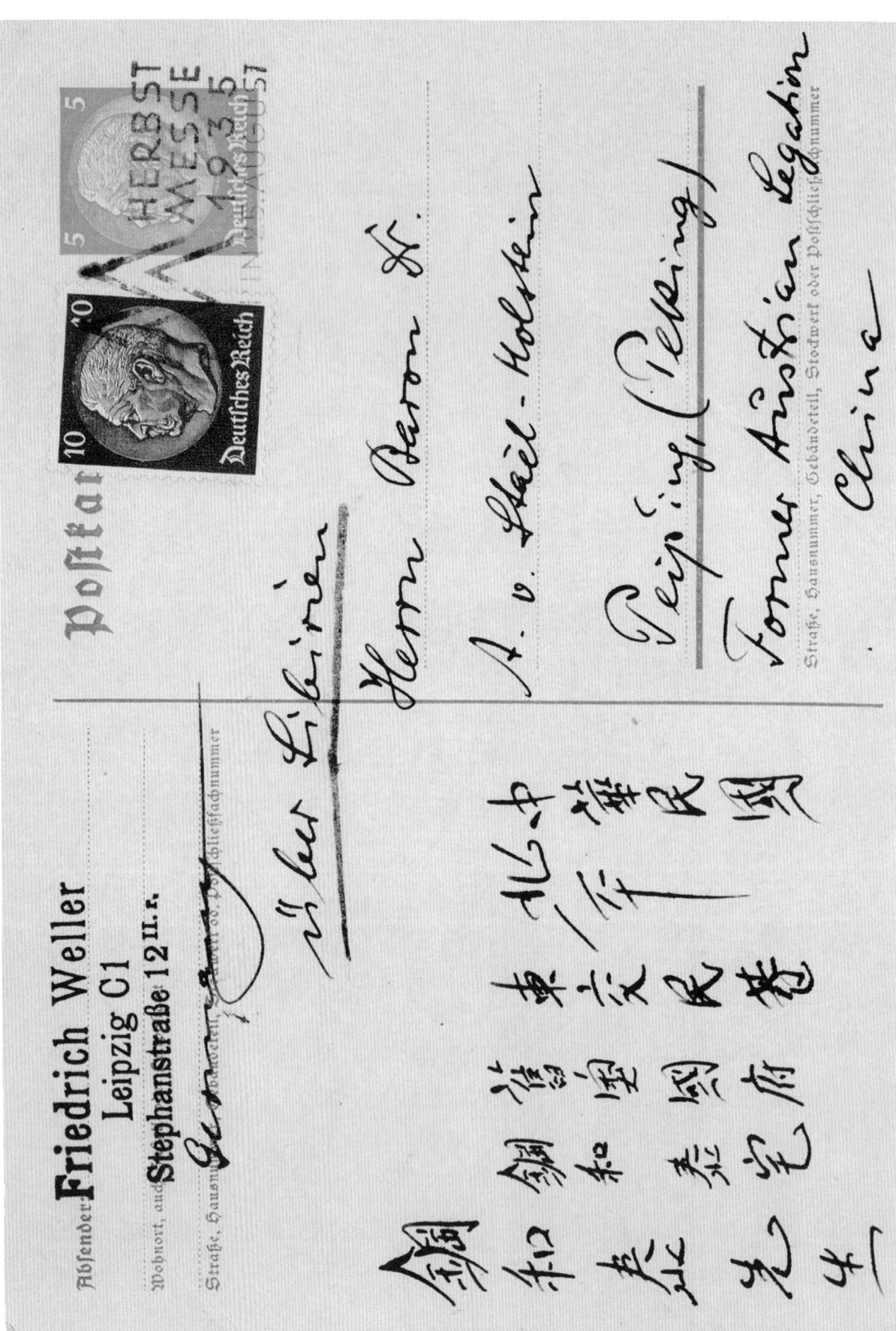

Hochgeehrter Herr Baron von Staël-Holstein!

Heute sandte ich an Sie das darin bezgl. des vorgedr.-chinesischen Indexes zum Sūtrasamuccaya — an Sie ab. Das Ms. umfasst 78 (acht und siebzig) mit Maschinenschrift in rot beschriebene Blätter. Sie paar nötigen Korrekturen habe ich ins Exemplar hineingeschrieben. Bitte bestätigen Sie mir den Empfang.

Mit schönen Empfehlungen von mir u. Frau an Ihre Frau Gemahlin und besten Grüssen an Sie selbst bin ich Ihr ganz ergebener Friedrich Weller.

6. 5. 35.

Leipzig, C.1, Stephanstrasse 12/ii rechts, den 4.6.35.

Hochgeehrter Herr Baron von Staël-Holstein!

Ihr Brief vom 9.Mai dieses Jahres ist am 28.5.hier eingelaufen, und ich danke Ihnen herzlich dafür. Es hat meine Frau und mich recht schmerzlich betroffen, dass Krankheit in Ihrer Familie eingezogen ist. Hoffentlich sind Ihre Frau Gemahlin und Ihr Sohn wieder völlig genesen. Wir wünschen jedenfalls von Herzen, dass Ihre Familie und Sie selber sich einer ungetrübten Gesundheit erfreuen können. Als Ausdruck unserer guten Wünsche bitte ich Sie, das inliegende Brieflein Ihrer Frau Gemahlin mit unseren besten Empfehlungen zu behändigen.

Was den geschäflichen Teil Ihres Briefes angeht, so freue ich mich, dass Sie den kleinen soghdisch-chinesischen Index in die Veröffentlichungen des Sino-Indian Institutes aufnehmen wollen, ich glaube, dass dergleichen Arbeiten wirklich da ihre Heimstätte haben. Das Manuskript werde ich Ihnen in den nächsten Tagen zugehen lassen, Sie können es in Satz geben, denn das kurze Vorwort, welches ich nun in englischer Sprache abfassen muss, ist auf jeden Fall so zu liefern, dass es noch rechtzeitig kommt. Die paar Umsetzungen deutscher Ausdrükke ins Englische, welche notwendig werden, nehme ich am besten bei der Korrektur vor, es besteht sonst die Gefahr, dass sie uneinheitlich werden, weil ich im Ms.etwas übersehen könnte. Es ist dies der kürzeste und sicherste Weg, die Zahl der Fälle ist ausserdem gar nicht ////// ////// gross. Die Lazaristendruckerei kann den Text ohne Frage setzen, da ausser dem lateinischen Alphabet nur wenige griechische Buchstaben benötigt werden,und die sind sicher vorhanden.

Vorläufig danke ich Ihnen recht herzlich,dass Sie diesen Index zum soghdischen Dīrghanakhasūtra drucken.Sachlich darf ich bemerken,dass ohne diese Indices gar keine Aussicht besteht,zu einer gesicherten Deutung der soghdisch-buddhistischen Texte zu kommen.Die Iranisten können diese Texte nur über die Hilfe der Buddhologen aufarbeiten.Ich denke,dass ich Ende der Sommerferien Ihnen den Beweis dafür werde liefern können.Ich bin kein Iranist und werde keiner,ich kann aber doch sehr helfen,diese Texte zu erklären.Es wäre sehr schön,wenn Sie in Ihrer Sino-Indian Series diese Grundlage für die Weiterarbeit schaffen könnten.Soviel an mir liegt,werde ich gerne helfen.

    Ich bin in ausgezeichneter Hochachtung
    Ihr ganz ergebener

    Friedrich Weller.

Leipzig,C.1,Stephanstrasse 12/II rechts,den 1.1.36.

Hochgeehrter Herr Baron von Staël-Holstein!

Für die freundliche Zusendung der Anzeige von Textausgabe, Kommentar und Index zum Kāsyapaparivarta möchte ich Ihnen bestens danken.Sie ist wohl im BEFEO erschienen.Uber meinen Index ist mir noch de la Vallee Poussins Urteil in der Bibliographie Bouddhique V bekannt geworden.Hoffentlich haben Sie alle Korrekturen zurückerhalten.Leider ist der Setzer in seiner ungeahnten Fähigkeit,Fehler zu machen,meinem Bestreben,Fehler zu vermeiden,weit voraus,ich kann leider nicht noch deutlicher schreiben,als es die Schreibmaschine hergibt.Nun,auch das wird vorbeigehen,der soghdische Index ist wesentlich besser gesetzt,was vielleicht einfach daran liegt,dass die Buchstaben grösser sind.Wenn mich die Setzerei nicht wieder länger als ein dreiviertel Jahr warten lässt,bis die zweite Korrektur kommt,so kann die Druckerei versichert sein,dass sie die Korrektur von mir auch umgehend wieder zurückerhalten wird,die Lettern für den soghdischen Index können,soweit ich in Betracht komme,im Februar oder auch noch im Januar wieder frei sein.Ob die Erledigung der Korrektur rasch geht oder lange dauert,liegt einzig an der Druckerei. Ich hoffe gerne,dass ich die zweite Korrektur des soghdischen Indexes bald bekommen werde,das erleichtert auch insofern die Arbeit,als ich dann den Stoff noch lebendig im Gedächtnis habe.

Da ich nun einmal in geschäftlichen Dingen schreibe,so möchte ich mir gestatten anzufragen,ob es nicht möglich wäre,die Veröffentlichung der soghdisch-chinesischen Indices fortzusetzen.Ich könnte Ihnen

in nicht langer Zeit eine Reinschrift für einen zweiten solchen Index
zugehen lassen,das Material für diesen und einen weiteren Index habe ich
fertig im Kasten liegen.Da es für diese Werke noch keine Wörterverzeich-
nisse gibt,könnte man auf diese Weise in der Harvard Series alle buddhi-
stisch-soghdische Literatur der Reihe nach wörterbuchmässig erfassen
und erschliessen;das wäre immerhin eine schöne Teilreihe innerhalb der
Sino-Indian Series.Auch stofflich passte das gut hinein.Vielleicht
lässt es sich ermöglichen,meinen Vorschlag aufzugreifen.Ich darf Sie in
jedem Falle bitten,mir eine kurze Antwort zukommen zu lassen.Möchten
Sie lieber eine andere Arbeit von mir in die Series aufnehmen,so würde
ich Ihnen noch eine Übersetzung eines Mahaparinirvana-Textes aus dem
Chinesischen zur Verfügung stellen können oder auch eine kritische Arbeit über einen soghdischen Text.Beide Arbeiten sind wegen ihrer be-
grifflichen Schwierigkeit in deutscher Sprache abgefasst,was ja aber
nichts ausmacht.Die Harvard University druckt auch sonst deutsche Ar-
beiten.Es läge mir sehr daran,wenigstens auf diese Weise mit dem Institute in Verbindung zu bleiben.Hoffentlich entwickelt es sich im neuen Jah
re recht glücklich;Ich bin mit den besten Wünschen für Ihr und Ihrer
Familie Wohlergehen und hochachtungsvollen Grüssen

Ihr ergebener

Friedrich Weller

Leipzig, C.1,Stephanstrasse 12/11 rechts,den
20.2.36.

Hochgeehrter Herr Baron von Staël-Holstein!

Sie werden inzwischen die Korrektur des soghdisch-chinesischen Indexes erhalten haben.Beigeschlossen sende ich Ihnen nun noch die Titelei und das Vorwort dazu.Ich möchte glauben,dass sich mit dem Manuskripte ein bis vielleicht auf ganze Kleinigkeiten druckfertiger Satz erreichen lässt,sodass ich annehme,der Ausdruck kann Ende April vorliegen.Bitte lassen Sie mir von Vorwort und Titelei einen Korrekturabzug in zweifacher Ausfertigung zugehen,ich muss ja die Korrektur des Indexes noch einmal sehen,die Arbeit wird sehr rasch getan sein,wenn der Setzer sorgfältig korrigiert hat.Ich hoffe gerne,dass Sie sich mit dem Titel einverstanden erklären können.Sie werden gewiss es auch am besten finden,dass alle diese Indices an einer Stätte vereint sind.Es wäre schon eine Leistung,wenn das Institut dies Material geschlossen vorlegen würde.Dem Stoff nach passen diese Indices ja eigentlich wie kaum eine zweite Arbeit in die Veröffentlichungen des Sino-Indischen Institutes hinein,denn hier greifen wirklich Indisches und Chinesisches ineinander wie kaum wieder.Ich würde mich jedenfalls recht herzlich freuen,wenn ich Ihnen den zweiten Band dieser soghdisch-chinesischen Indices zusenden könnte.Konkurrenz haben wir da nicht.Es läge mir doch daran,wenigstens auf diese Weise meine bleibende Verbundenheit mit dem Institute zu erreichen,das mir der Sache wegen naturgemäss doch sehr am Herzen liegt.Die Geschicke des Instutes interessieren

mich doch sehr,denn es ist schon etwas Grosses,dass es eine Stätte gibt,
wo diese Art Forschung gepflegt wird.

Sollten Sie den Titel der Veröffentlichung zu ändern wünschen,so bitte
ich dies zu tun,ohne vorher noch einmal dieserhalb an mich zu schreiben.
Die Arbeit über das soghdische Dhyānasūtra habe ich inzwischen vergeben.
Es bot sich die Gelegenheit,die Arbeit unterzubringen,und so habe ich
zugegriffen,zumal Sie ja schon so andere Arbeiten von mir für den Druck
abgenommen haben und vielleicht noch die übrigen soghdischen Indices
in die Harvard Sino-Indian Series aufnehmen.Ich glaube,dass damit die
Bahn freier wird,weil die Veröffentlichungen dann innerlich geschlossener
bleiben.

Nun möchte ich Sie nur noch bitten,meine Frau und mich Ihrer Frau Gemahlin bestens zu empfehlen.Ihnen selber aber sende ich auch im Namen
meiner Frau die besten Wünsche für Ihrer Familie und Ihr eigenes Wohlergehen.Ich verbleibe mit hochachtungsvollen Grüssen

Ihr ganz ergebener

Friedrich Weller

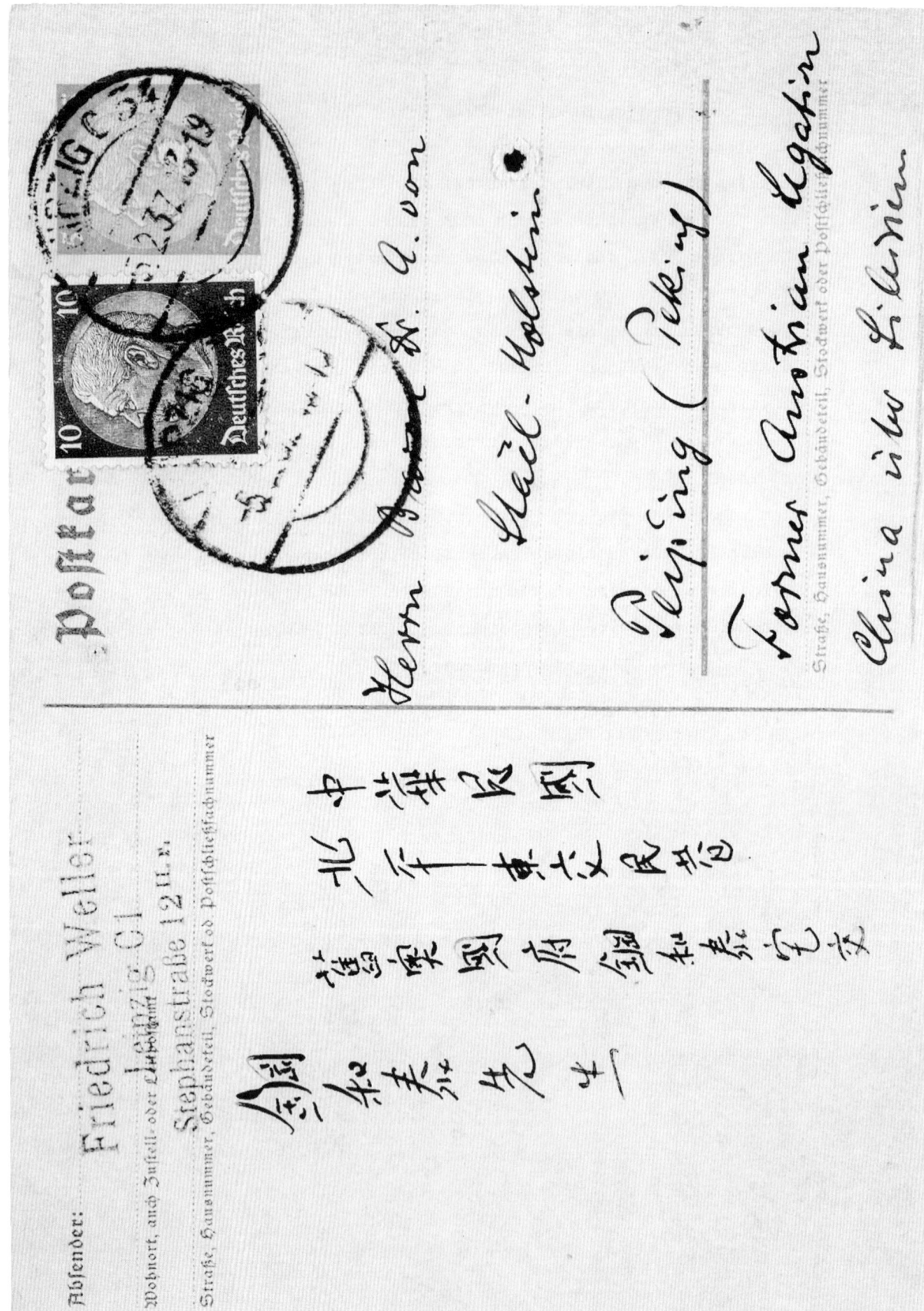

Hochgeehrter Herr Baron von Staël-Holstein!

Mit herzlichem Danke erhielt ich Ihren Brief und die Nachrichten zu haben. Ich bin natürlich einverstanden, daß meine Arbeit als Beitrag eines
Bandes erscheint, wie Ihnen es nur Zeit nimmt, wenn Ihre Arbeit
mit meiner [...]. Die Korrekturen hoffe ich Ihnen in nicht
zu ferner Zeit zustellen zu können, ich denke, daß sie in den ersten
Wochen des Mai abgehen wird, sodaß sie doch dieß in Ihren Händen
sein wird. Für die freundliche Einladung am nächsten Bande mit-
zuarbeiten, spreche ich Ihnen meinen besten Dank aus. Ich werde mir
alle erdenkliche Mühe geben, Ihnen einen Beitrag zu machen.

Sie würden bitte ich Sie, meine Frau, und mich Ihrer Frau
Gemahlin [...] zu empfehlen und und Ihnen [...]
Grüße von meiner Frau? und mir selbst als Ihr ergebener

Stri und Stella.

4.2.27.

Walter

Sehr lieber Professor,

Soeben kürzlich denke ich Ihnen für Ihre Briefe aus Singapur und aus Leipzig) und für das gelungene Exemplar. — das durchaus gelungen gut getroffene Photo — Es freut mich sehr, dass Sie eine angenehme Seereise zurückgelegt haben und glücklich in Leipzig angekommen sind. Die Photographien-plus Ihrer Insel, werde ich verwenden, sobald die Vorstellung die Iksarischten mit die ganze Auflage zurückgenommen haben. Daher habe ich nur einige 120er, Exemplare erhalten. Das eine habe ich Ihnen vor einiger 12er, † 12er,— senden lassen, und das andere ist noch hier. Es ist sehr gütig von Ihnen, dass Sie die Bücher für meine Frau bei Simmel bestellt haben. Bitte ist bitte keines mehr. Die Sendung wird bald hier eintreffen.

In den nächsten Tagen werde ich Ihnen ein Exemplar
meines Kāśyapaparivarta-Commentars zusenden können. Ich
Sie vielleicht Ihren Einfluss dahin geltend machen,
dass die klein (oder die Zeitschrift für Indologie)
über diese Ausgabe und über meine Arbeiten in China
eine kurze Publikationen veröffentlicht? In Halle Russi-
und Sie Mohlig selbst haben meine Besprechung des
Kāśyapaparivarta begründet. Meine Textausgabe des
Kāśyapaparivarta (und ausserdem Japaner begründet haben)
dass ich (es viel weiss), keines gedruckten
deutschen Artikels gewidmet worden. Ich hoffe, dass
Arbeiten meine im Jahre 1932 erscheinenen tibetischen
und chinesischen Commentar-Ausgabe in Deutschland nicht
Erfolg haben werden. Die Harvard-Gelehrten, von
denen meine Zukunft abhängt, haben nicht sehr viel
Interesse für meine Sino-indischen Studien und um

den Bestand <ins>des</ins> <del>meines</del> Instituts zu sichern, muss ich nachweisen können, dass meine Bemühungen zu Erfolge in allen grossen Centren der europäischen Wissenschaft <del>in all</del> <ins>die</ins> Beifall finden. Daher liegt mir sehr viel an einem <del>anerkennenden</del> Worten Ihrerseits <ins>sehr viel</ins>. Es ist nicht die Bitte um die Silfkeit, ohne mich veranlasst, um etwas Major um anerkennende Worte Ihrer Seiten die dann Major zu bitten, sondern Jahre ohne etwas weiteres. <ins>in allem Dingen</ins>

Mit oder Bitte um ich Ihnen Ihre [...] Die Sitzung der Harvard Schule [...] auf [...] Die kommt Die Sitzung [...] Frühjahr 1935 statt [...] Die anerkennenden Worte müssten überhaupt auf Anhalt [...] unter Einstimmung, ohne zu anerkannten Sitzungen [...] nicht nach in Frühjahr zu [...] abzuhalten, will schon im Frühjahr 1934 abgehalten werden. <del>Sie werden</del> <del>Frau</del>

Mit der Bitte, mich Ihrer <del>Frau</del> Gemahlin empfehlen zu wollen, verbleibe ich mit herzlichen [...] Ihr ergebener Meyer Frau [...] Ihnen viele herzliche Grüsse v. Stäel-Holstein

Bitte empfehlen Sie mich Ihrer Frau Gemahlin. <ins>wollen</ins>
Mit herzlichsten Grüssen, auch von meiner Frau, verbleibe ich Ihr ergebener

A. v. Stäel-Holstein.

Unser alter Vertrag wird in vollem Umfange aufrecht erhalten. ~~Für Der alte Vertrag wird aber bis zum 15. Juli 1932 verlä~~ Für die Zeit vom 16 Juli 1931 bis zum 15 Juli 1932 wird ein neuer Vertrag geschlossen. ~~in Monatsgehalt Der neue Vertrag~~ Der Ferienmonat (16 Juli bis 15. August) ~~sind die~~ und alle übrigen Monate des neuen Vertragsjahres ~~nach~~ (16.7.31 – 15.7.32) werden mit je fünfhundert (500) Mark bezahlt. Sonst gelten für das neue Vertragsjahr alle Bestimmungen des alten Vertrages. ~~Sollten Sollten Sie Ihnen bis zum 15 Juli 1931 nicht~~

國立山東大學
NATIONAL UNIVERSITY OF SHANTUNG
TSINGTAO, CHINA

June 9, 1936.

My dear Professor,

I am very grateful to know by a letter from Mr. Chu that you have kindly assented to discuss with me a certain question about Indian script of which I suppose you would probably be not entirely uninteresting.

The question before me is a vowel sign in the Mo-So script. In LES MO-SO by J. Bacot, as you know, there are three kinds of vowel signs in the Mo-So syllabic characters: (1) ～ (2) ～ (3) ～. The first and the second are evidently Tibetan's gNah-Ru and Gi-Gu respectively. The third is, on the other hand, very strange. At first I regard it as only a ～, corresponds to Tibetan's shabs-kyu. More careful examination shows, however, this is not true. Every ～ seems always to be accompanied with three dots. for example, ～ ～ ～ ～ ～ ～ ～. This is found to be the case also in a list of syllabic characters from a friend of mine of Li-Kiang. I conjecture, this kind of writing may probably come in from other script than the Tibetan. But I don't know whether it occurs or not in the manuscripts of ancient Tibetan. Does it occur in the Indian script? I know nothing about them. I can find no trace of it in many scripts I know of Indian origin, such as Siamese, Laos, Burmese, Cambodgien, Ahom, Pa-Yi, etc.. As you are the well-known authority in these regions, I dare to trouble you with this question and wait cordially for your honourable instructions.

Yours respectfully,

Wen yu.

TEL. EALING 2252.

60, MADELEY ROAD,
EALING, W.5.

31st July 1931

My dear Baron Holstein,

You will be surprised to get this note from one of your oldest friends. Since I sent you a cable expressing my congratulations on your marriage I have been in a nursinghome for a very long time, suffering from eye troubles. They are even now very bad and my sight is so impaired that I can hardly read and write.

I am anxious to know how you are getting on and whether I can be of any use to you from here. Sometime ago the question of a professorship in Chinese came up for discussion at the academic board in the School of Oriental Studies here and I took the opportunity to recommend you strongly for this post. I hope the Director Sir Denison Ross has written to you on the subject. -

With best wishes

yours sincerely

M de Z Wickremasinghe

Dear Professor Ware,

The Otialitanistani is, as far as I know, not to be procured in Peking; but I have sent two copies of the Tibetan Sadhanamala to Prof. Clark and one to Prof. Edgerton. Many Thanks for your recent letters. They impress me as highly useful.

Yours sincerely
[signature]

Lieber Herr Wiegert,

Meinen besten Dank für die interessanten Photographien! Mein Neffe wird sie sich zweifellos sehr rühren. Es thut mir sehr leid, dass ich Sie nicht gesehen habe, als Sie so freundlich waren, bei uns vorzusprechen. Herzliche Grüsse mit dem besten Grüssen Ihr ergebener
[signature]

28. VI. 1916.

Mein lieber Herr Baron von Staël!

Zum von fern gekommenen Gaste kann Tokyo leider sehr wenig sehenswerthe Dingen zeigen.

Es gibt in dieser Stadt 大倉美術館 (Kunst-museum von Ōkura), das verschiedenen buddhistischen Statuen von verschiedenen ostasiatischen Ländern enthält. Es ist jetzt eigentlich geschlossen, aber wenn Sie Lust haben die Ausstellung anschauen so werde ich versuchen dass, ob wir es besuchen können.

Wenn man eigentlichen Japan verstanden will so muss man die alten Hauptstädte 奈良 (Nara) und 京都 (Kyoto) besuchen. Dort findet man besonders in Museum altjapanische Kunststücke.

Kyoto ist auch sehr reich an altjapanische von ~~Regierung~~ Regierung besonders beschützten Gebäude.

Es ist ein Buch namens 國寶帖 (Album von volksthümlichen Schätze; kostet 100 yen). Darin findet man Abbilder von allen japanischen werthvollen Kunststücken.

Sind Sie schon 日光 (Nikkō) gewesen? Dort zum Tokugawa Iyeyasu (德川家康) gewidmeter Heiligthum ist eins von sehenswürdigen Sachen in Japan. In 芝 (Shiba) Tokyo findet man auch einige Heiligthümer von 德川家 (Tokugawa-genealogie). Sie sind auch ziemlich berühmt. Sind Sie schon dort gewesen?

Achtungsvollst

U. Wogihara

Tokyo
13. X. 16.

My dear Baron!

From your letter it seems as if I contrived to take money from you by fraud. But look at the catalogue of books published at Jan. 1895 by 其中堂, one of the greatest book-stores in Japan. At page 190 (-九〇) where I have inserted a piece of paper we read: 縮刷大藏經正價金貳百圓也. This evidence rescues me from dishonour. There are many applicants, who wish to have the Tokyo edition. If you know any one, who would sell it at such a surprising cheap price as 120 Yen or thereabout please inform me of him. I should recommend it to the applicant.

5 Fasciculi of Chinese Tripiṭaka and a dictionary, which I left in the Hotel and you kindly sent me back I have just received. The 10th Fasc. of vol. 暑 you can keep so long as you please.

The photogram costed 5 Yen 20 Sen. Wh̃en we come together in Tokyo I shall hand you the bill. I have paid for it. There is no hurry about your repay to me.

Yours sincerely,
U. Wogihara.

Yanaka,
X. 22nd. 16.

My dear Baron,

There are many passages in Chinese Buddhist book, where 振旦 &c. occur, and many of them may exist both in Skt. original and in a Tibetan translation. At present I can mention a passage in 大方廣佛華嚴經 (天三. 22ᵇ) (Avataṃsaka) which work also is rendered into Tibetan, where the characters 震旦 occur.
Again in 佛母大孔雀明王經 (閏 六 71ᵇ) (mahā-mayūrī, one of the pañca-rakṣā) which exist both in the Skt. & Tib. we have the

characters 支那國.

震旦 stands, I think, for Cīna-sthāna, Cīna-tthāna, Cin-tan. The original of 支那國 may be either simple Cīna or Cīna-sthāna or Cīna-deśa or the like.

Yours sincerely,
U. Wogihara.

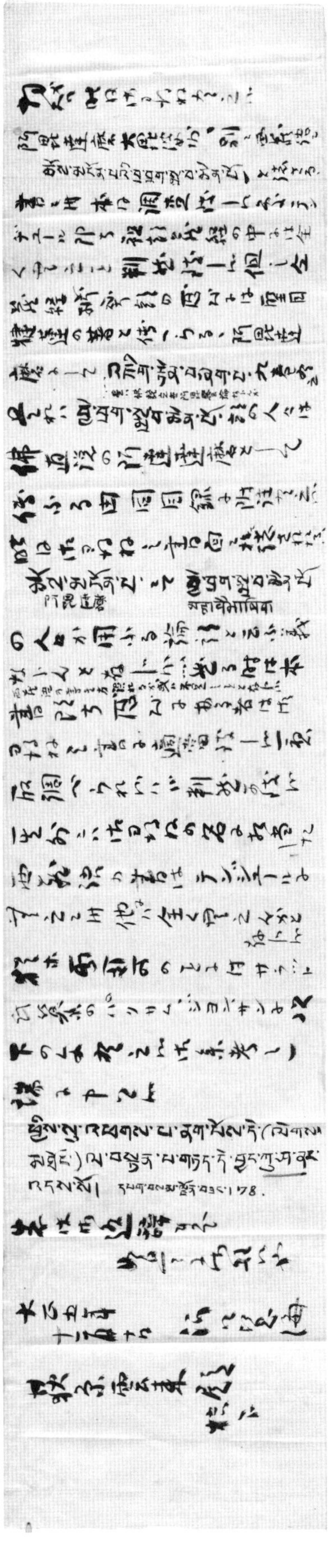

1/2

(局部圖1)

ཕྱིས་སུ་འཕགས་པ་བ་གཤོལ་པོལ་ཏེ། (ལྱགས་
མཉེང་) ལ་བསྩལ་བ་གཅད་དེ། བྱད་ཀྱི་བ་རྫོགས
ར་དས་སོ། དཔག་བསམ་ལྗོ་བཟང་། 178.

With much thanks I have
received a cheque for
¥.15.

Tokyo.
25. Feb. 1917.

My dear Baron!

It is very glad to hear that you can enjoy quite tranquility there and work much better than before. In this semester I read Sukhā-vati-vyūha edited by Prof. M. Max Müller and B. Nanjio, and by the help of its Tibetan version I can make so much improvement of it that e.g. in single page 8 I made 22 emendations!

Hoping your health & happiness,
Sincerly yours
U. Wogihara

農商部地質調查所
The Geological Survey
3, Feng-Sheng Hutung,
W. Peking, China

Peking, Le 15 Juin, 1925.
(China)

Baron A. Von Stael Holstein,

Cher Monsieur:

Notre Collègue au Service Géologique Mr. H. T. Chang m'a fait vous demander certain renseignement sur le Sanscrit.

M. Chang a poursuivi depuis certain temps son étude sur l'origine de l'emploi du zinc et par là du laiton (Brass) en Chine. Il entretient certaine doute sur l'opinion de Laufer qui tend à penser que l'usage du zinc fût introduit en Chine dans la période de Tang de la Perse. Mr. Chang a trouvé maintenant que le mot T'u (鍮) existait déjà dans les livres buddistes beaucoup avant Tang; quelques textes sont copiés et ci-inclus. Pour être sûr de son origine, il veut vous demander si vous voulez lui dire quel était le mot originel en Sanscrit qui fut traduit par (鍮銅) in chinois et comment on le prononçait originellement.

Vous pourrez peut être lui dire aussi quel est l'equivalent sanscrit du mot laiton (brass en anglais (黃銅) en chinois).

En vous remerciant d'avance pour le trouble que je vous cause, je vous prie d'agréer, Cher Monsieur, l'assurance de mes sentiments bien cordiaux.

Wong wenhao

姚秦西曆三九七鳩摩羅什譯妙法蓮華經卷一方便品偈言有云：「鍮鉐赤白銅、白鑞及鉛錫、鐵木及與泥，或以膠漆布，嚴飾作佛像。」鍮鉐 白鑞 梵文音義何为？

吳西曆二二三至二六〇年支謙譯阿難四事經有云：「愚人愚哉，心存顛倒，自欺自誤，猶以金價買鍮銅此。」鍮銅 梵文音義又若何？

mdo 22,74
mdo 22,15
mdo 22,76
mdo 28,233

農商部地質調查所用牋

W. Peking, China

Peking, le 17 Juin, 1925.
(China)

Baron . von Stael Holstein,

Cher Monsieur:

  Notre Collègue du Service Géologique Mr. H. T. Chang m'a fait vous demander certain renseignement sur le sanscrit.

  Mr. Chang a poursuivi, depuis certain temps, son étude sur l'origine de l'emploi du zinc et par là du laiton (Brass) en Chine. Il entretient certain doute sur l'opinion de Laufer qui tend à penser que l'usage du zinc fût introduit en Chine dans la péride de Tang de la Perse. Mr. Chang a trouvé maintenant que le mot T'u (鍮) existait déjà dans les livres buddistes beaucoup avant Tang; quelques textes sont copiés et ci inclus. Pour être sûr de son origine, il veut vous demander si vous voulez lui dire quel était le mot original en sanscrit qui fut traduit par (鍮銅) in chinois et comment on le prononçait originellement.

  Vous pourrez peut-être lui dire aussi quel est l'équivalent sanscrit du mot laiton (brass en anglais (黄銅) en chinois).

  En vous remerciant d'avance pour le trouble que je vous cause, je vous prie d'agréer, Cher Monsieur, l'assurance de mes sentiments bien cordiaux.

P. S. Je vous ai écrit déjà avant-hier c/o Peking Club. M. Hu Hsien m'a donné votre adresse exacte; je vous envoie donc la même lettre une fois de plus.

姚秦 西曆三九七至四一七年 鳩摩羅什譯 妙法蓮華經卷一 方便品 偈言有云：「鍮鉐赤白銅、白鑞及鉛錫、鐵木及與泥，或以膠漆布，嚴飾作佛像」鍮鉐 白鑞 梵文原本音義何如？

吳 西曆二二三至二八〇年 支謙譯 阿難四事經有云：「世人愚惑，心存顛倒自欺自誤，猶以金價買鍮銅也」鍮銅 梵文原本音義又若何？

農商部地質調查所用牋

中國地質學會
The Geological Society of China.
9, Ping Ma Ssū,
W. Peking, China.

Le 29 June 1925

1) ahimsā
2) dāna (hier ist yü oder t'an?)
3) not eating flesh
4) not slandering the...

Cher Monsieur,

Je vous ai écrit le 15 de ce mois pour vous demander quelques renseignements sur l'origine sanscrite (et sa prononciation) de l'expression 鍮銅 ou 鍮石 qui se trouve fréquemment dans les classiques buddhistes p. ex. 妙法蓮華經 (Miao Fa Lien Hua Ching). Mon cher collègue Monsieur H. T. Chang a fait une traduction de "Sino-Iranica" de Laufer avec des notes et commentaires. L'œuvre est déjà imprimée et il attends ces renseignements pour incorporer dans l'appendix. Il est peut-être difficile de remonter à l'origine sanscrite (et sa prononciation) de ce terme Tou-Si 鍮石 qui est en somme peu commun, mais alors Mr. Chang sera heureux de savoir quelle est l'expression sanscrite (et sa prononciation) qui correspond au mot laiton (Brass en anglais, 黃銅 en chinois).

Dans l'espoir de vous entendre bientôt et vous remerciant d'avance pour votre précieux concours, je reste bien vôtre.

Wong Wenhao

[The following paragraph is written upside-down at the top of the page:]

I think that all these facts support the supposition that 倭鉛 ≠ Ka-
mi-nio did not think of Zinc (Chinese 鋅, in Tibet.) He
just down the enamel 琺瑯 but of zinc that metal is hardly
known anything about metallurgy, but if you mention that
I know are Buddha, images, much of copper, bronze, lead,
iron and cadmium but never any word of zinc.

Tib. Separatausgabe des Saddharmapundarīka pag 24 a 4
entspricht Skt ausgabe pag 50, Zeile 15

The materials given in the Tib. text are (after the 夷 nin-chen) 1) Zaṅs = 赤銅, copper

2) h̥khar-ba (kaṃsa, bell metal)   3) ro-m̃e (lead 鉛)   4) lcags   5) sa-yaṅ-ruṅ
                                                                          d   d

I have looked through all the indices and catalogues at my disposal and have also studied
various Tibetan sūtras bearing names similar to the 阿難問事
shih ching (there is no Tibetan sūtra with an exactly corresponding title)
— but in vain. ~~There is not.~~ ~~No exact~~ No counter-
part of the 阿難問事 shih ching seems to
exist in Tibetan and the Sanskrit original is surely lost.

The Tibetan translation of the Saddharmapundarīka
sūtra exists and I have ~~found~~ looked up the passage about
the materials for Buddha statues; the order is exactly the
same as in the Sanskrit original, and the five substances are:
ཟངས (zaṅs, copper) འཁར་བ (h̥khar-ba, bell-metal) ཟོ་མེ (ro-m̃e, lead)
ལྕགས (lcags, iron) and ས (sa, earth).

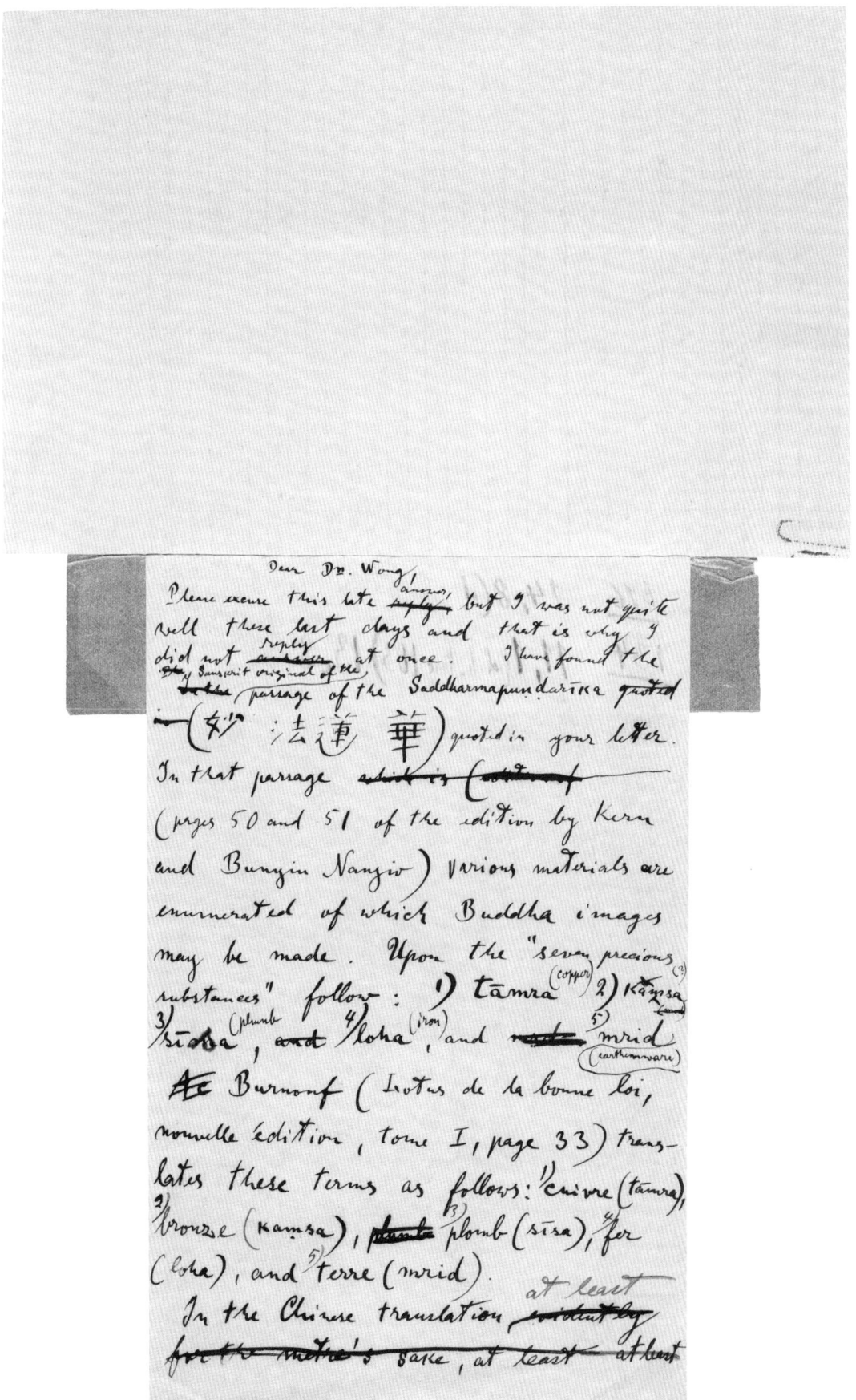

Dear Dr. Wong,

Please excuse this late answer, but I was not quite well these last days and that is why I did not reply at once. I have found the Sanskrit original of the passage of the Saddharmapuṇḍarīka quoted in (妙法蓮華) quoted in your letter. In that passage (pages 50 and 51 of the edition by Kern and Bunyiu Nanjio) various materials are enumerated of which Buddha images may be made. Upon the "seven precious substances" follow: 1) tāmra (copper), 2) Kaṃsa, 3) sīsa (plumb), 4) loha (iron), and 5) mṛid (earthenware).

Burnouf (Lotus de la bonne loi, nouvelle édition, tome I, page 33) translates these terms as follows: 1) cuivre (tāmra), 2) bronze (kaṃsa), 3) plomb (sīsa), 4) fer (loha), and 5) terre (mṛid).

In the Chinese translation at least for the metre's sake, at least

According to the same dictionary raitya means "made of brass, brazen". According to Apte's English-Sanskrit dictionary ~~Calcutta~~ (Bombay, 1914, page 462) the Sanskrit equivalent of the English word "zinc" is dastā.

~~It seems to be quite All the Sanskrit~~ The pronunciation of the Sanskrit words has not changed for the last 2 or 3 thousand years, and if you pronounce tāmra, kamsa etc "à l'italienne" you are sure to get the ~~sounds correct~~ correct sounds.

The Sanskrit original of the 阿難問事經 is lost, as far as I know, and I have not been able to discover any Tibetan translation.

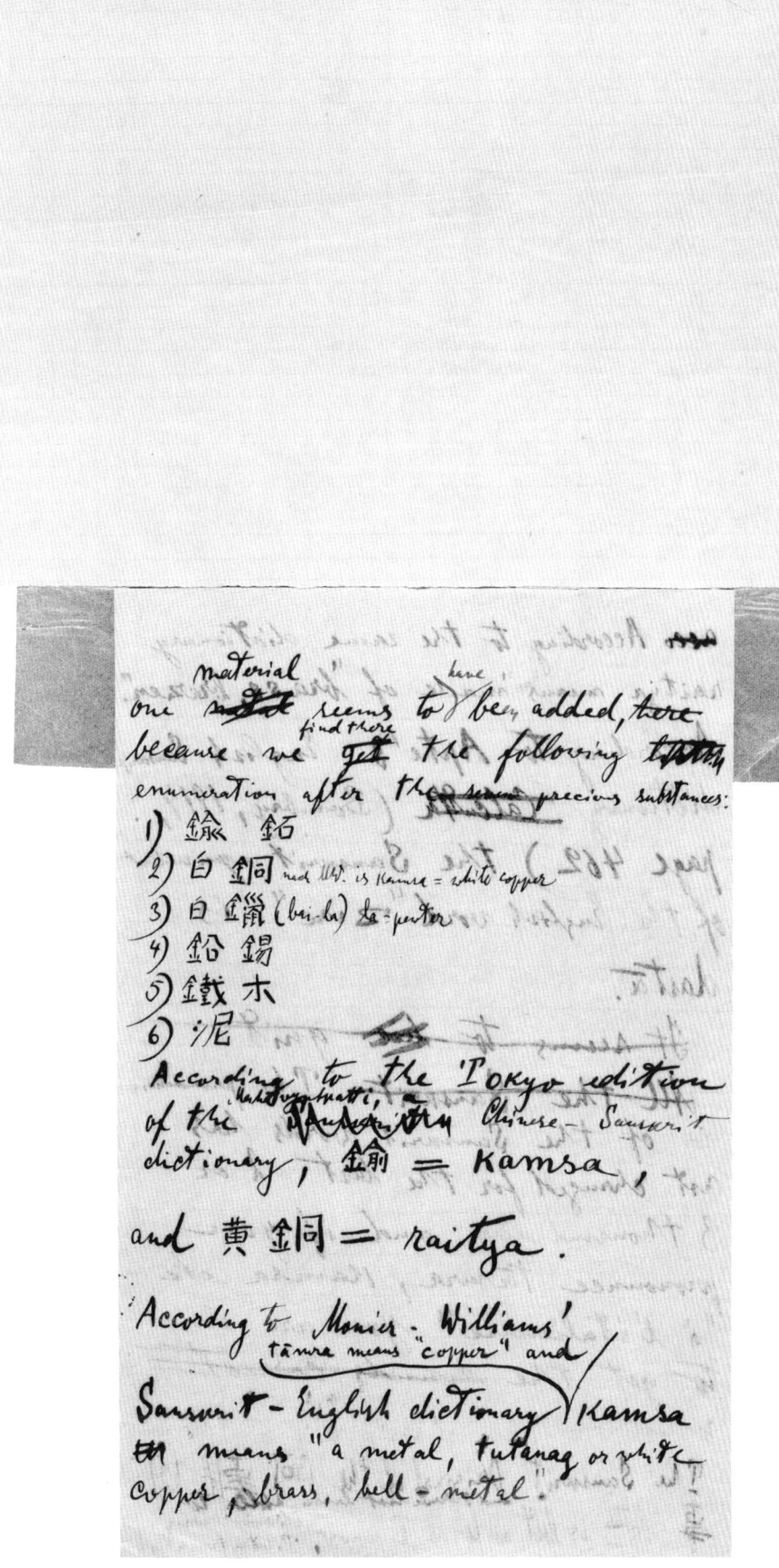

One ~~solid~~ material seems to be added here, because we ~~get~~ find there the following enumeration after the ~~seven~~ precious substances:

1) 鍮石
2) 白銅 (mod Mr. is Kamsa = white copper)
3) 白鑞 (bai-la) = pewter
4) 鉛錫
5) 鐵木
6) 泥

According to the Tokyo edition of the Mahāvyutpatti, Chinese–Sanskrit dictionary, 鍮 = kamsa, and 黃銅 = raitya.

According to Monier-Williams' tāmra means "copper" and Sanskrit-English dictionary Kamsa ~~क~~ means "a metal, tutanag or white copper, brass, bell-metal."

農商部地質調查所
The Geological Survey
3, Feng-Sheng Hutung,
W. Peking, China

Peking, July 8, 1925.
(China)

Mr. Baron Stael Holstein,-
  Pi Kuan Hutung, 7.

Dear Mr Holstein:-

I wish to thank you most heartily for your kind answer to my questions. My colleque Mr H. T. Chang is very grateful for your valuable help and asks me to present you two of his previous works. He has still some other questions which he likes to put before you if it is not to too much abuse you kindness.

1/ Laufer and others were all much puzzled by the Chinese term Tze Mo-king (紫磨金). They did not know what kind of mineral or metal it is. Mr Chang found now that this was used by (法護) to translate a sanscrit term in the 妙法蓮華經卷三 & 卷七 which is also translated as 閻浮那提金, or 閻浮檀金 The original translations are as follows:-

卷三,頁十 授記品記下: 號曰閻浮那提金光如來, 黃金為繩

卷七,頁二 妙音菩薩品下: 閻浮檀金為莖白銀為葉

It seems to Mr Chang that all these expressions refer to one thing; some kind of alluvial gold. He wants to know whether is it possible to have the original term in Sanscrit and what is its meaning.

2/ The Tsi-Pao(七寶) of Buddhist literature is differently translated. According to 妙法蓮華經卷三,頁十, 授記品記下 they are 金,銀,瑠璃,硨磲,真珠,瑪瑙,玫瑰

According to 阿彌陀經 by 鳩摩羅什 they are 金,銀,琉璃,玻璃,硨磲,赤珠,瑪瑙

農商部地質調查所

The Geological Survey
3, Feng-Sheng Hutung,
W. Peking, China

Peking,_____
(China)

玫瑰

Mr Chang suspects that 赤珠 is the same thing than 玫瑰 which means probably the ruby. A Chinese buddhist encyclopedia gives the sanscrit term for 赤珠 as Rohita mukta. Is it correct and what is the original meaning?

3/ 瑟瑟 is one of the Wu Pao (五寶) mentioned both in 法華儀規 (or 成就妙法蓮華經 主瑜伽觀 智儀軌經) and 建立曼荼羅及揀擇地法. Is it possible to find out the original sanscrit word and its significance?

4/ Laufer mentioned a buddhist classic named Jetaka. Have you this book and what is the Chinese translation? It seems that the term 紫磨金 also occurs in this book.

Both Mr Chang and I are really afraid to cause you trouble by asking so many questions. Mr Chang is however so much interested in knowing more about these things that he can not help appealing again to your kindness. He is finishing his translation of "Sino-Iranica" and begins to revise with additions his "Lapidarium Sinicum" of which a second edition will be issued. The matter is not however so much in a hurry and especially as you are not very well. I don't expect to have immediate answer to all these questions. We shall be glad and grateful to hear from you any thing you may find at you convenience.

With renewed thanks for your valuable cooperation.

Yours most sincerely,

Wong venhao

農商部地質調查所
The Geological Survey
3, Feng Sheng Hutung,
W. Peking, China

Peking, July 14, 1925.
(China)

Baron A. Stael Holstein, Esq.,

　　Pi Kuan Hutung,

　　　　Peking.

Dear Sir:-

　　　　I am very much obliged to you for your valuable help for Mr. Chang's study. He feels very grateful for the help so readily given and asks me to forward you the best thanks.

　　　　　　　　　　Yours most sincerely,

　　　　　　　　　　　　Wong wen hao

WHW/H.

To Dr. Wong

Conel!

Could you send me copies of this letter as well as of my previous letter addressed to you? Please do. You evidently have a scribe a type writing clerk, and I possess neither a type writing machine, nor a scribe

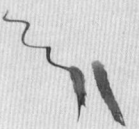

Editorial Department,
Commercial Press, Ltd.,
Paoshan Road,
Shanghai.
April 20th, 1922.

Dear Sir,

Your letter dated March 6th 1922 was received. In reply we beg to apologize that we have asked you to sign the proofs of the pages 1--38 through a mistake. The pages 1--17 with your signature returned to us by express mail was received on February 20th.

We are, herewith, sending you six copies of the corrected proofs (pages 18--38) for your revision and signature as instructed.

Very truly yours,

Y. Tsong

Editorial Department,
Commercial Press, Ltd,,
Shanghai, May 6, 1922.

Dear Sir,

We are in receipt of the returned proofs for the pages 39-59 and your accompanying letter dated April 21st. The mistakes contained in these pages have been corrected. Six copies of the corrected proofs are herewith sent to you for your final reading and signature.

With reference to your first letter dated March 6th, we beg to inform that we wrote you a reply in English on April 20th, when six copies of the corrected proof for the pages 18-38 were sent to you.

Next time please send the returned proofs direct to the above address, to avoid being delivered to our Main Office and consequently delayed.

Yours very tryly,

To the Manager, Editorial Department, Commercial Press Ltd., Shanghai.

Dear Sir

I am in receipt of your letters dated April 20th and May 6th, 1922.

The delay in replying to those letters is partly due to the fact that postal communications between Peking and Nanking were not considered safe until a few days ago when the military situation changed. I enclose the second proofs of the pages 18–59 of the 大寶積經 which I have signed, and some additional corrections. (I beg to be excused for ~~that all of it~~ not all of it.

But I am not responsible for all of them. Lines 4 and 5 of page 30, for instance, were quite correctly printed in the first proofs, whereas they contain mistakes, which I have corrected, in the second proofs. ~~These mistakes~~ are entirely due to The compositor alone is responsible for those mistakes as well as for the mistake on line 2 of page 49 (the words aparūṣma mahānirmāṇa to ākṣari-khinnamanastayā were correctly printed in the first proofs and incorrectly in the second proofs).

Besides adding these new mistakes the compositor has, (which were) I think, ignored some of my instructions written on the margin of the first proofs. I am, unfortunately, not able to prove this, because the first proofs containing the printed text and my corrections have not been sent to me together along with the second proofs. of pages 18-57

May I ask you to be so kind as to send my the first the proofs corrected by myself along with the second proofs in future, so as to avoid misunderstandings? Absolute accuracy is of the utmost importance in an edition like the present one and I hope venture to hope additional that you will kindly see to it that my final corrections are carried out before pages 18-57 are finally printed

Yours very truly
A.v.Staël-Holstein.

TELEPHONE NOS. { NORTH 1555 / NORTH 400 }
TELEGRAPHIC ADDRESS, COMPRESS

ADDRESS REPLY TO
COMMERCIAL PRESS, LIMITED
EDITORIAL DEPARTMENT
PAOSHAN ROAD
SHANGHAI

上海寶山路
商務印書館編譯所

14th June 1922.

Baron Stael Holstein,
   c/o The Peking Club, Peking.

Dear Sir,

In reply to your favour dated 18th ult., we beg to inform you that we have already corrected the second proofs of pages 18--59 as shown and have again sent you, herewith, six copies of the first proofs 60--78 with the originals, for your reading and signature.

                     Yours very truly,

                              Editor-in-chief

COMMERCIAL PRESS, LIMITED
ENGLISH EDITORIAL DEPARTMENT
PAOSHAN ROAD
SHANGHAI

TELEPHONE NOS. { NORTH 1555 / NORTH 400 }
TELEGRAPHIC ADDRESS, COMPRESS

上海寶山路
商務印書館編譯所

4th October 1922

Baron A. von Staël Holstein,
c/o the Peking Club, Peking.

Dear Sir,

We beg, herewith, to forward to you 6 copies of 2nd proof from page 79 to 105 including the 1st set and hope you to acknowledge receipt of same.

Yours faithfully

Kowng

Antwort nebst unterstrichenen Correctur nach Shanghai abgesendet am 6ten November 1922.

TELEPHONE NOS. { NORTH 1555 / NORTH 400 }
TELEGRAPHIC ADDRESS, COMPRESS

ADDRESS REPLY TO
COMMERCIAL PRESS, LIMITED
ENGLISH EDITORIAL DEPARTMENT
PAOSAN ROAD
SHANGHAI

上海寶山路
商務印書館編譯所

20th December 1922.

Baron A. Von. Staïl Holstein,
 c/o the Peking Club, Peking.

Dear Sir,

 For your revision, we send you herewith 5 copies of the 1st proofs of the Pao-chih-ching (寶積經) from Page 106 to 121 together with the original Page 254 – 265, and hope you to acknowledge receipt of same.

 With best compliments of the season.

 Yours faithfully

TELEPHONE NOS. {NORTH 1555 / NORTH 400}
TELEGRAPHIC ADDRESS, COMPRESS

ADDRESS REPLY TO
COMMERCIAL PRESS, LIMITED
ENGLISH EDITORIAL DEPARTMENT
PAOSHAN ROAD
SHANGHAI

上海寶山路
商務印書館編譯所

31st December 1922.

Baron A. Von. Staël Holstein,
c/o the Peking Club, Peking.

Dear Sir,

For your revision, we send you herewith 6 copies of the 1st proof of the Pao Chih Ching 寶積經 from page 122 to 143 together with the original Page 266 – 325, and hope you to acknowledge receipt of same.

Referring to the last dispatch of similar proofs made on the 20th inst., we think it has already reached you in safety.

With best compliments of the season

Yours faithfully

(First part of letter)

Dear Sir,

Many thanks for the second proofs of the pages 106 – 143 of the Pao-chi-ching. I have corrected and signed them and I return them to you (enclosed herewith); I also offer you my apologies for the delay which was caused by my illness. I keep the two title pages which you have sent to me for further consideration. I shall send them to you when the text will be ready.

(third part of letter)

I hope that the second part of the book will be printed a little quicker than the first part. Could you not print the proofs of the entire second part (about 120 printed pages) all at once? That would simplify matters a good deal for you as well as for me. It would save us very much trouble. The expense of preparing a greater quantity of special type (ḥ, ḥ, c etc) is surely worth the great amount of time and labour which we lose by treating the book in small instalments of 30-40 pages.

(second part of letter)

The first part of the book was forwarded to you in 1921 through Dr. V. K. Ting (T) whom I saw in Peking a few weeks ago. He pointed out to you that he had at that time that the pages 1-325 (about one half) of my manuscript constituted the first part of the book and that another part was to follow. I have this day despatched to your address the second part of my manuscript (pages 326-575) under separate cover. When the pages 326-575 will be printed the book will be finished except as regards a short introduction and a few text critical notes at the end (less than 10 printed pages in all).

(fourth part of letter)

The second part of my manuscript contains like the first part a great number of pencil notes; those pencil notes are not to be printed; they are intended for my own information only; please do not print them.

TELEPHONE NOS. { NORTH 1555 / NORTH 400 }
TELEGRAPHIC ADDRESS, COMPRESS

ADDRESS REPLY TO
COMMERCIAL PRESS, LIMITED
EDITORIAL DEPARTMENT
PAOSHAN ROAD
SHANGHAI

上海寶山路
商務印書館編譯所

Sept. 29th. 1923.

Baron A Von Stael Holstien,
c/o The Peking Club,
Peking.

Dear Sir,

Under separate cover we are sending you proof sheets P. 170-188 of the "Pao Chih Ching" together with the original copies P. 398-448.

Yours faithfully,
The Commercial Press,
Per *[signature]*
Editor-in-chief.

TELEPHONE NOS. { NORTH 1555
               { NORTH 400
TELEGRAPHIC ADDRESS, COMPRESS

ADDRESS REPLY TO

COMMERCIAL PRESS, LIMITED
EDITORIAL DEPARTMENT
PAOSHAN ROAD
SHANGHAI

上海寶山路
商務印書館編譯所

November 23, 1923.

Baron A Von Stael Holstien,
c/o The Peking Club.
Peking.

Dear Sir,

Under separate cover we beg to send you 5 copies of the 2nd proofs of the Pao-chi-ching, from page 144 to 188 together with the 1st proofs bearing your correction. Please give these proofs a further revision and return them to us at your earliest convenience.

Yours faithfully,

The Commerciap Press,

Per [signature]

Editor-in-chief.

The Manager, Editorial Department
Commercial Press
Shanghai

Dear Sir,

I enclose the ~~corrected and~~ proofs second proofs of pages 144–188 of the Pao-chi-ching corrected and signed by myself. ~~May I hope that you will~~ I do not consider any further revision by me of the pages 144–188 necessary and I trust that the few remaining mistakes noted on the margin ~~by myself~~ will be carefully corrected ~~at it~~ at your office ~~before~~ the final printing is done.

May ~~I venture~~ I hope to receive the ~~remai~~ first proofs of the remaining pages (188 – about 235) soon and all at once. When those pages will be printed only a few pages containing various readings and notes will remain before the whole book is finished.

Yours faithfully

AvStaël-Holstein.

THE COMMERCIAL PRESS, LIMITED
EDITORIAL DEPARTMENT
PAOSHAN ROAD
SHANGHAI

TELEPHONE NOS. NORTH 1555 / NORTH 400
TELEGRAPHIC ADDRESS, COMPRESS

上海寶山路
商務印書館編譯所

Sept. 29, 1924.

Baron A. von Steal Holstein,
    c/o Peking Club,
        Peking.

Dear Sir,

Under separate cover please find five copies of the second proof of the Pao Chi Ching pp 189-234 together with the first proof corrected by you.

Hoping you will kindly return same to us as soon as possible.

Yours faithfully,

Editor-in-chief.

March 1st 1925.

Dear Sir,

Please excuse my keeping the proofs for such a long time.! The delay is due to two principal reasons. A part of my At first I kept the proofs back because I was afraid that they might be destroyed by on account of the civil war. I was afraid that they might get lost on their way to Shanghai. After that a part of my Peking house was destroyed by fire, and one copy of the proofs perished in the flames. I was, of course, very much upset by the calamity and had to do the work over again. I think I must once more revise the pages 189 – 234. I have not signed the pages 189 – 234, because there are comparatively many corrections to be made and I think consider another revision absolutely necessary. Please send me the next proofs of pages 189 – 234 as soon as possible. May I also ask you to send me a copy of the pages 1 – 188, which are already finally printed? I want the pages 1 – 188 for preparing the preface (only a few pages), the "corrigenda and addenda" and the list of various readings.

```
TELEPHONE NOS. { NORTH 1555    ADDRESS REPLY TO
                 NORTH 400     THE COMMERCIAL PRESS, LIMITED      上海寶山路
TELEGRAPHIC ADDRESS. COMPRESS    EDITORIAL DEPARTMENT             商務印書館編譯所
                                   PAOSHAN ROAD
                                    SHANGHAI
```

March 24, 1925.

Baron A. Stael Holstein,
c/o the Peking Club,
Peking.

Dear Baron Holstein,

    I am in receipt of your letter of March 1st. Under separate cover, I am sending you the new proofs of pages 189-234 of your book for your further revision. As we cannot start printing the book before all the proof sheets have been o.k., I can only send you the o.k. copy of pages 1-188 for your reference in preparing the preface. As these pages are the only copy we have in hand, we have to get them back after you have referred to them.

                        Sincerely yours,

                        Y. W. Wong
                        Editor-in-chief.

Peking Aug. 3/24/1925.

Dear Sir

Excuse me for delaying my answer to your letter dated March 24, 1925.

Please find enclosed herewith:

1) Pages I – XCIV, containing the title page, a Chinese introduction written by Mr. Liang-Chi-Chao 梁啓超, a preface written by myself and some notes to that preface.

2) The corrected proof sheets O.K'd proof sheets of pages 189 – 234 which I have O.K'd now.

3) The proof sheets of pages 1 – 188 which had been O.K'd long ago and which you sent to me on March 25, 1925 for reference in preparing my preface.

In your letter dated March 24, 1925 the following phrase occurs: "As we cannot ~~not cannot~~ start printing the book before all the proof sheets have been O.K.'r. I can only send you the O.K. copy of pages 1-188 for your reference in preparing the preface."

From this phrase I conclude, that I the pages 1-188 have not ~~yet~~ been printed (and that it is still possible to correct certain mistakes which I have only just now discovered. I have consequently corrected those mistakes in pages 1-188, although (and I hope that those corrections will appear in this book when it is finally printed. they had been O.K'd long ago & I think that the entire ~~Chinese~~ text (pages 1-234) may be printed now—

without being further revised by myself, but I ~~should like~~ must to revise the title page, the Chinese introduction (pages I–XCIV), the English preface and the notes before they are finally printed. I intend going to Shanghai for that purpose and I hope that I shall be able to call at your office in a fortnight. I shall be very much obliged to you if you will have the proof sheets of pages I–XCIV ready by that time in order to enable me to finish the revision (without losing too much time at Shanghai) soon and to return to Peking. I am very anxious that the book should appear as soon as possible. ~~Perhaps~~ With many apologies for the delay caused by myself, — P.S. Please call the attention of the type setter to I remain yours sincerely the fact that ~~when~~ the difference between ordinary

May I also ~~shar~~ point out to you that the erasures made by myself on pages 226 and 228 are of special importance.

brackets on the one hand and square brackets ~~[and]~~ on the other ~~is~~ of great importance for the purposes of my ~~p~~ should not be disregarded.

Sept. 19th 1925.

Dear Sir,

In the letter which I despatched to your address on the 1st of September I mentioned my intention of paying you a personal visit at Shanghai about the 15th of this month. I am now very sorry to say that I had to give up that plan, and that I cannot correct the proof sheets of the title page and of the prefaces

May I therefore ask you to send several copies of the proof sheets of pages I – XCIV of the 大寶積經 to my Peking address (c/o the Peking Club) as soon as possible? I am very anxious that the book should appear in the near future.

If you cannot let me have the proof sheets at once, please send me a short note acknowledging the receipt of my manuscript and letters without too much delay.

Sept. 26th 1925.

**PEKING CLUB,
PEKING.**

Dear Sir,

Nearly four weeks have passed since I sent you, in a registered package, the last instalment of the manuscript of the 大寶積經 together with some proof sheets and a long letter. Another registered letter ~~registered like the first one~~ was despatched to your address over a week ago, ~~without having been honoured with a reply~~ but no answer or acknowledgment of any sort has been received here. ~~Please write to me as soon as possible;~~ I am getting apprehensive ~~anxious~~ about the fate of my manuscript, proof sheets and letters. ~~It is I am also very anxious that the book should appear in the nearest future~~

Would it be asking too much if I requested you to send me a ~~since us~~ telegraphic reply upon receipt of this letter? My telegram address is: Holstein Peking Club Peking. If you cannot wire, please write to me at once. I am getting anxious about the fate of my manuscript, proof sheets and letters.

It is of great importance to me that the book should appear in the nearest future.

TELEPHONE NOS. { NORTH 1555
                 NORTH 400

TELEGRAPHIC ADDRESS. COMPRESS

ADDRESS REPLY TO

COMMERCIAL PRESS. LIMITED
ENGLISH EDITORIAL DEPARTMENT
PAOSHAN ROAD
SHANGHAI

上海寶山路
商務印書館編譯所

October 2, 1925

Right Honourable Baron Holstein
c/o Peking Club
Peking

Dear Sir:

Your letters of August 31, September 19, and September 26 and the proof sheets you sent with your first letter have all been received. As you said in your first letter that you would be in Shanghai in a fortnight, we thought it was not necessary to reply to it because we could talk things over with you personally.

The mistakes which you pointed out on the proof sheets have been corrected accordingly. The compositer has carried out your other instructions mentioned in your first letter.

The typesetting of the title page and the Chinese Introduction is now complete and that of the English introduction will be finished very soon. As soon as the latter is finished, we shall send you the proof for pages I-XCIV. The book will be printed when these pages are O.K.'ed.

Yours sincerely,

For The Editor-in-Chief.

BEL:YKP

Oct. 7th 1925

Dear Sir,

Many thanks for your letter dated October 2nd 1925, which relieved me of a great anxiety. I am indeed very glad to hear that you will very soon send me the proof sheets of the title page and of the prefaces. Will you be so kind as to let me have six copies of those proof sheets? The variety of languages used in my book (大寶積經) makes a distribution of the proof sheets among a number of specialists inevitable.

Peking Febr. 18th 1926.

Dear Sir,

I enclose ~~the~~ the corrected proof sheets of the pages I – XXIV of ~~page 100~~. ~~Please print~~ Please do ~~print those~~ ~~Roman (not Arabic) figures~~ ~~whereas~~ adopt ~~the~~ Roman (not Arabic) figures for numbering the pages of the ~~introduction~~ preface, as marked by myself on the proof sheets. It is important that Roman figures should be adopted ~~for~~ for ~~the~~ numbering the pages of the ~~introduction~~ preface, as otherwise great confusion will arise in my notes. Please ask the type setter to see to it that the characters Ă (capital A with a dash above) Ç (capital C with a cedilla) Ẓ (capital Z with a dot underneath) ü (small u with two dots above) ŭ (small u with half moon on top) and ë (small e with two dots above) are correctly set. Most of these characters occur only once or twice ~~more than~~ ~~½~~ three or four ~~times~~ in my preface and they ~~may~~ might perhaps be cut in wood, if you do not possess them in your office. In the proof sheets which you sent me about three weeks ago all these characters appear without the special marks; I have, of course, corrected those mistakes in the enclosed proof sheets. When will you send me the next proof sheets for the final revision, which is absolutely necessary? I waited for the first proof sheets of the preface for nearly five months. I despatched the manuscript to your address on the 1st of September and I received the proof sheets on January 28th.

Please do send me the proof sheets somewhat quicker this time. I shall be very much obliged to you if I get them, say, in a month's time.

THE COMMERCIAL PRESS, LIMITED
EDITORIAL DEPARTMENT
PAOSHAN ROAD
SHANGHAI

June 18, 1926.

Right Honourable Baron Holstein,
c/o The Peking Club,
Peking.

Dear Sir:

We have just received the proof-sheets of the preface of your book, in which, however, pages two to four are not included. Kindly return these sheets to us at your earliest convinence. We shall be pleased, if you would also return us one set of the proof-sheets pp 1-188.

Sincerely yours,

Editor-in-chief.

July 8th 1926.

Dear Sir,

I am in receipt of your letter dated June 18th 1926, in which the following phrase occurs: "We shall be pleased, if you would also return us one set of the proof sheets pp. 1-188". I O.K.'d the proof sheets pp. 1-188 long ago and returned them to you together with my letter dated August 31st 1925. In your letter dated October 2nd 1925 you acknowledged the receipt of those O.K.'d proof sheets and promised to print the book as soon as the title page and the introduction (pp. I-XXV) would be O.K.'ed. I have sent you your letter dated June 11th 1924 already O.K'ed.

II The question as to why you want another set of the proof sheets pp. 1-188 troubles me very much. Should the O.K.'ed proof sheets pp. 1-188 (Stanislas) have been lost after reaching your office? I have only one set of the proof sheets pp. 1-188 left and they are covered with # notes written by me in ink. That is why I prefer not to send them to you. Could you not let me have a new proof sheets of the pages 1-188 for perusal, nor doubt for once useless.

Please send me new proof sheets of the pages 1-188 set up in type by you. I shall correct the mistakes and O.K. them at once unless the corrections be too numerous. I am very anxious that the contents of the pages 1-188 appear soon to know when I may expect the new proof sheets of pages 1-188 and venture to ask you for a telegram informing me of the date, on

Another reason is: That most of those sheets appeared first proofs and do not contain the later corrections which you propose to despatch. (my cable telegraphic address is: StaelHolstein (Klub Peking))

I enclose the O.K.'ed proof sheets of pages I–XXV and a letter addressed to you by Dr. Hu Shih (五月三日).

Sincerely yours

A. vonStaël-Holstein

P.S. Please do not forget to send me the telegram. I am very anxious to see the form in which as soon as possible the uncertainty about must not by the proof sheets' fate.

To the Editor in Chief
English Editorial Department
Commercial Press
Paoshan Road
Shanghai

TELEPHONE No. CENTRAL 8700
TELEGRAPHIC ADDRESS, COMPRESS

ADDRESS REPLY TO
THE COMMERCIAL PRESS, LIMITED
EDITORIAL DEPARTMENT
PAOSHAN ROAD
SHANGHAI

上海寶山路
商務印書館編譯所

August 28, 1926.

Baron Stael Holstein,
c/o Peking Club,
Peking.

Dear Baron Stael Holstein:

I must tender you a thousand apologies for this belated answer to your favor of July 8th, asking that a telegram be sent regarding the proof-sheets pp 1-188 of your work. When your letter arrived here, I was not in office and the same was opened by our Publication Department which forthwith gave instructions to the Printing Department to make new proofs from the press. As a good deal of time had been required to make proof-sheets from the paper matrices, your letter was not turned to me until this morning.

Upon a perusal of your letter, I know how anxious you have been waiting these seven weeks for our telegram. I am very sorry indeed that our oversight has caused you so much trouble. To make most of the situation, I am sending <u>by express</u> the new proof sheets of the entire work. Kindly see if there are errors and return the same to us after they are O. K.ed. We shall lose no more time to have the book printed as soon as the O. K.ed proofs will be received.

Hoping that you will kindly excuse us for our failure to comply with your request,

I am,

Sincerely yours,

Editor-in-chief.

Hage. aug 8. Sept. 1926.

Dear Sirs!

I return herewith the O.K.'ed proofs of the entire book (+ 000). Please print it exactly (as it is) without any further corrections and as soon as possible. I realize that there is a mistake in the pagination of the introduction (the empty page at the back of the title page has not been counted), but I prefer printing the book with that mistake to the inevitable delay of several months which corrections — none of the any further corrections would entail. Corrections which I suggested in the proof sheets returned to you in September 1925 have not been carried out (as far as the pages 1–188 are concerned) and I presume that it is too late to carry them out now. Therefore I have corrected them on two pages of "corrigenda" & "photographs of which I enclose. Please reproduce O.K. of photographs of corrigenda " at the end of the book in facsimile. Setting them up in type (2) pages 255 and 256)

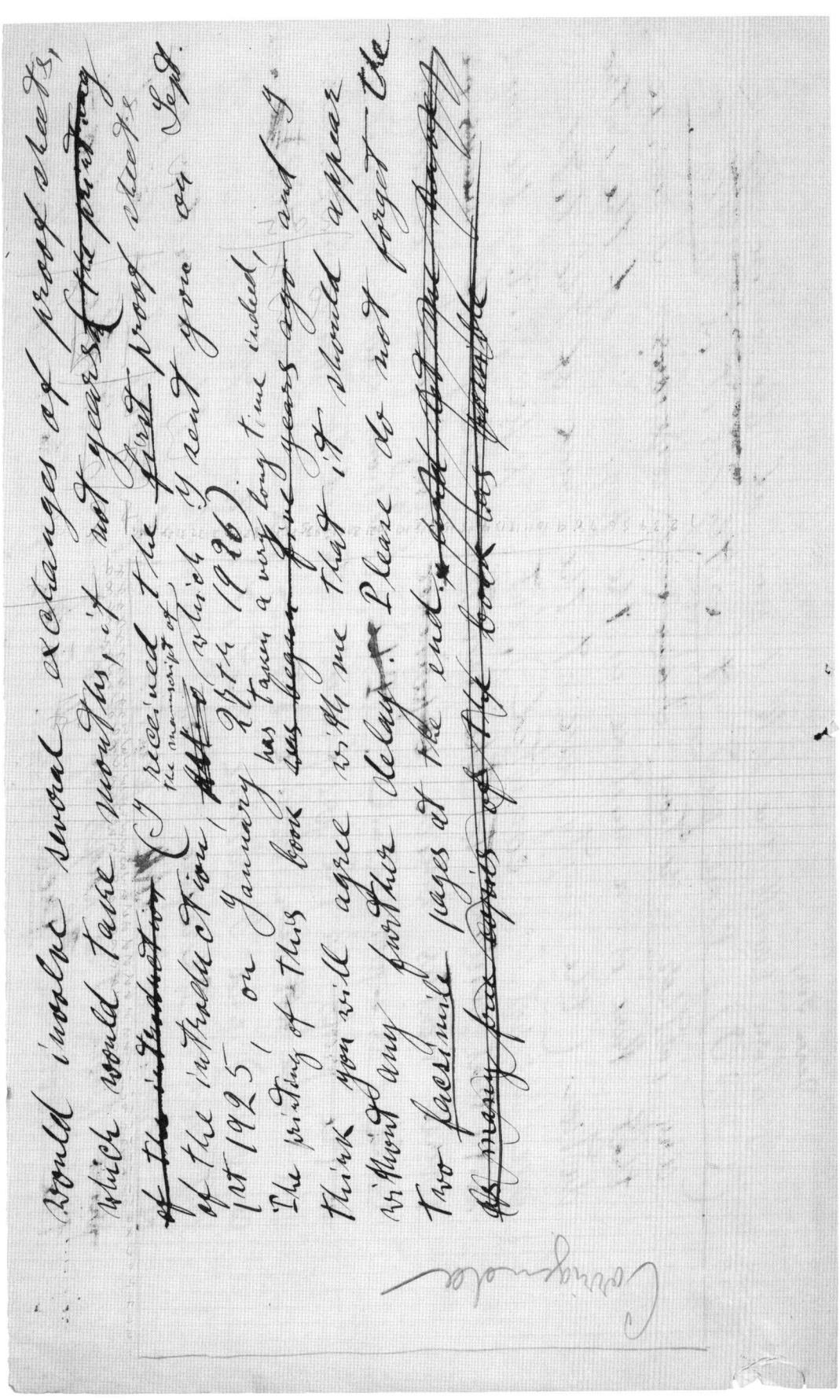

...would involve several exchanges of proof sheets, which would take months; it not yourself the printing of the first proof sheets of the introduction (I received the manuscript of the introduction ##### 27th (1926) of 1925, on January #### 27th (1926) The printing of this book has taken a very long time indeed. I rent you on 29 Sept. has begun five years ago and I think you will agree with me that it should appear without any further delay. Please do not forget the two facsimile pages at the end, ####################### as many free copies of the book as possible.

Carriguola

TELEPHONE NO. CENTRAL 8700	ADDRESS REPLY TO	上海寶山路
TELEGRAPHIC ADDRESS, COMPRESS	THE COMMERCIAL PRESS, LIMITED	商務印書館編譯所
	EDITORIAL DEPARTMENT	
	PAOSHAN ROAD	
	SHANGHAI	

September 18, 1926.

Baron Holstein,
Peking Club,
Peking.

Dear Baron Holstein:

    We have received your letter dated Sept. 8, 1926, together with the proof-sheets of the entire work (大寶積經). The proof-sheets have been handed to the printers and we expect the printing to be finished in two months.

    As a token of our appreciation for the time and energy you have spent in this work, we have recently arranged with Dr. V. K. Ting that sixty complimentary copies will be presented to you, although no renumeration was proposed or asked for at the time when the Manuscript was submitted in view of the fact that the circulation of the book would necessarily be limited.

Sincerely yours,

[signature]

Editor-in-chief.

TELEPHONE No. CENTRAL 8700
TELEGRAPHIC ADDRESS, COMPRESS

ADDRESS REPLY TO

THE COMMERCIAL PRESS, LIMITED
EDITORIAL DEPARTMENT
PAOSHAN ROAD
SHANGHAI

上海寶山路
商務印書館編譯所

Dec. 15, 1926.

Baron A. von Stael-Holstein,
The Peking Club,
Peking.

Dear Sir:

We take pleasure in sending you by separate post a sample copy of The Kacyapaparivarta which is just off the press. The work is in the hands of the bindery and we hope to get out the whole edition in a week or two.

As arranged before, we shall send you sixty complimentary copies of the work after its publication. We shall address them to your address by parcel post as soon as they are ready.

Hoping that the make-up of your valuable work will meet your satisfaction,

We are,

yours very faithfully,

The Commercial Press, Ltd.,

Editor-in-chief.

HARVARD UNIVERSITY
DEPARTMENT OF PHILOSOPHY AND PSYCHOLOGY

Emerson Hall
Cambridge, Massachusetts

February 10, 1921

Dear Baron de Staël:-

I am ordering the books immediately and if you insist I will send you a statement of the expense. It is no trouble whatever. In fact, I am delighted to do anything which brings us a little closer into contact. I spent two years in France during the war at the Sorbonne, but I have not seen Jacobi. Scherbatskoy has escaped to Sweden, and I hope he may pay us a visit here. When may we expect to welcome you? Or must I come to Peking in order to take you again by the hand?

With heartiest greetings,

Sincerely yours,

James H. Woods

Baron Alexander v. Staël-Holstein

HARVARD UNIVERSITY
DEPARTMENT OF PHILOSOPHY
AND PSYCHOLOGY

Emerson Hall
Cambridge, Massachusetts

February 19, 1921

Dear Baron de Staël:

    I am glad to write that the volumes you desired have already started, and as you requested, I send a bill, but I should much prefer that you should drop it into your waste basket.

    Will you allow me to ask whether some one of the pundits whom you know could secure me a Tibetan copy of the Vajracchedikā printed separately in a small volume? I should also be glad if a similar small copy could be found in Chinese, and you might perhaps discover, without too much trouble, whether a Chinese and a Tibetan version of the Suvarṇaprabhāsa can easily be found.

    With most cordial wishes, and the hope that you will tell me a little about your work,

Very sincerely yours,

James H. Woods

Baron Alexander v. Staël-Holstein

HARVARD UNIVERSITY

DEPARTMENT OF PHILOSOPHY
AND PSYCHOLOGY

Emerson Hall
Cambridge, Massachusetts

June 3, 1921

Dear Baron De Stael Holstein:

I am extremely glad to hear from you again and to know that the books reached you. It was quite unnecessary to send the amount of the bill. I thought it might be transferable to some public institution or I would not have sent it.

I have heard from Stcherbatskoy several times and I hope that we can invite him here a little later. How delighted we shall be to have the Kāçyapaparivarta. The son of Roerig the painter has been working very hard with me here. Some day I must send him to you, and I should like nothing better than to accept your invitation to Peking with a chance to enjoy seeing you every day, as we met at Bonn.

Most hearty thanks for the two Chinese texts.

Always faithfully yours,

James H. Woods

Baron Alexander De Stael Holstein

Dear Professor Woods,

About three years ago you asked me to send you one copy of the best Chinese translation of the Vajracchedikā and one copy of the Tibetan translation of the same work. I was ever since under the impression that I had carried out both of your requests. Upon examining your letters I find, however, to my horror, that you acknowledge the receipt of two Chinese books (without mentioning any Tibetan text) from this. I conclude that I either never sent you the 'Tibetan book'. [second] <!-- inserted --> that it is evidently also possible, that either my parcel or your acknowledgment of it should have gone astray. However that may be, I resolved to make [and not multiply & ...] the required text at once and have today despatched to send you the [two copies] of the Tibetan Vajracchedikā, as well as a Chinese translation to your address: one [XX] of the Tibetan [without the printing] One of these copies is not quite complete (the first leaf is missing), but it contains a Chinese [more than] [XXX] [text] interlinear translation (manuscript) [three quarters] of the text.

HARVARD UNIVERSITY
DEPARTMENT OF PHILOSOPHY
AND PSYCHOLOGY

Emerson Hall
Cambridge, Massachusetts
October 21, 1925

Dear Baron de Stael:

You were very good to send me the photographs of the Buddhist statuettes. The Curator of the University Museum was much interested, but he has undertaken some purchases which go beyond his resources for the present. On the other hand, the Boston Museum of Fine Arts and something may come of this.

I am giving this note to Mr. Charles Sidney Gardner who is in Pekin with his wife. He has been a graduate student here of Chinese and is now working on Chinese in Pekin. You will find him an excellent scholar and a most agreeable companion, and I commend him most heartily to you.

Sincerely yours,

James H. Woods

Baron Alexander de Stael-Holstein
Pekin Club
Pekin

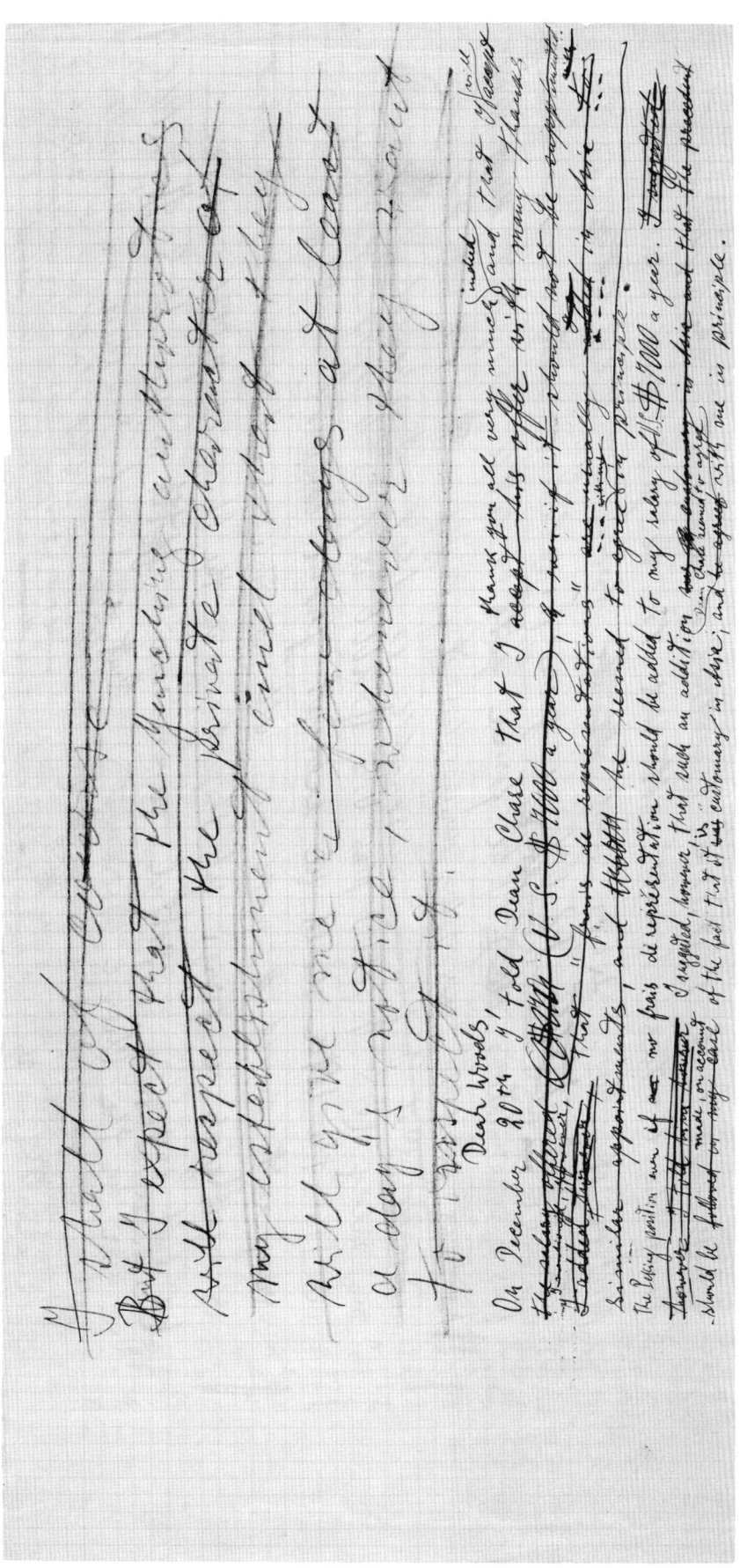

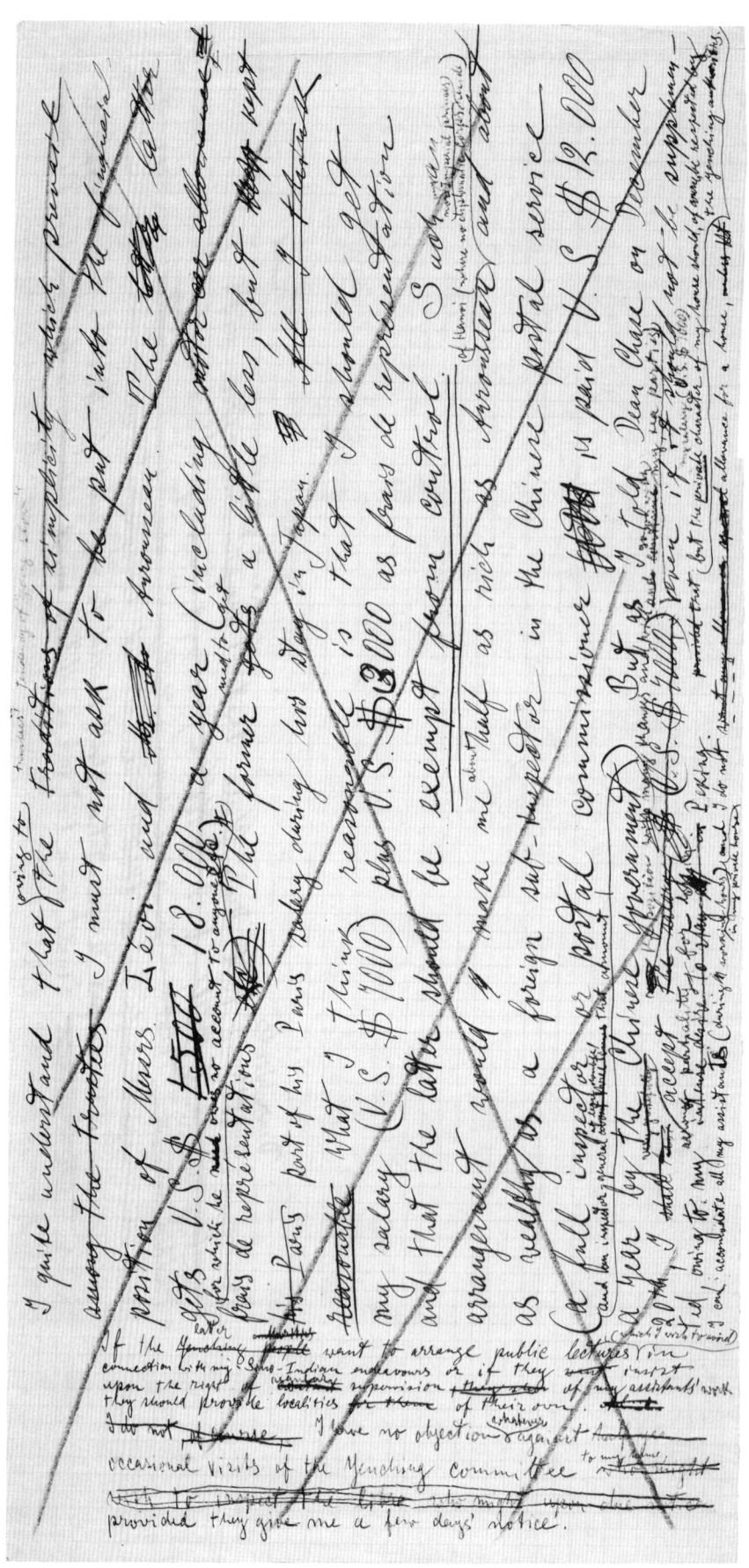

Owing to the fact that I was formerly used to be officially connected with the diplomatic corps I deeply regret many years constantly received invitations from all Peking legations (and have refused their hospitality as I could not reciprocate (was insolvent) (except the Soviet legation), which is very embarrassing). The missionary circles with the foreign diplomats think it unequally that I should mingle with the give bribing diplomats three times daily, and feel that to philologists must of to philology historical science can derive no profit from the contact usually at dinners a world. But they are wrong. The social standing of every foreigner without money in Peking is uncertain (who are not an official at Peking (not at Lawrence). met by this more or less intimate connection with the diplomats. The fact that I am well known at all legations gives me a standing among the higher class of Chinese officials, and it is to the latter that I owe most of my discoveries. The directors of the Palace Museum and of both Research Institutes (all personally) were former ministers who belonged to the former "pronounced aristocracy" of China. which were not a comparable aristocracy director-general The Chair not director of the So Mr Chian, Former Director of the audit department Mr was director of the Palace Museum, Mr. Yeh Kung Chop former minister of Finance, was director of the Research Institute of the National University

Mr. Tsiang Chi Chao, former minister of [struck: ?] [inserted: public] was director of the Tsinghua Research Institute. [struck: I have little hope that] [inserted: To all of these men] I [struck: have (?)] [inserted: owe] it [struck: that] important discoveries and the confidence which they have shown me is at least partly due to my diplomatic semi-diplomatic position. Of I had been able to entertain all these officials [struck: ?] [inserted: suitably] more frequently I would, I am sure, have made many more discoveries. According to Tibeto-Mongolian etiquette practically at [?] is allowed to approach a high Lamaistic dignitary without bringing a present with him. It has been a source of much annoyance to me (and very often a [source] [inserted: of]) during all these years that I have [struck: not] been able to buy any presents for them and I feel quite certain that my [struck: ?] [inserted: archaeological] work has been considerably hampered by my extreme financial position.

[struck: Next of that ??? ???] [inserted: I have ???] Many Lamaistic dignitaries [struck: ???? ??? ???? ??] [inserted: ??? ??? ??? ??? ??? ??? ???? ???] and it is important that one should bring [inserted: something] at the ???? to show the extent of [inserted: one's] hospitality at the psychological moment. If I shall have to obtain the consent of Mr. Tsiang and Mr. Chu [struck: previous] [inserted: ???] many opportunities will surely be missed in each particular [case].

LIBRARY OF HARVARD UNIVERSITY
CAMBRIDGE, MASSACHUSETTS

May 10, 1929.

Dear von Stael:-

    I am writing immediately after the meeting of the Publication Committee and I will enclose the formal vote which I think meets all the problems which we discussed about the publication of Roussel's book. The main point is that you be sure to revise the text and that the execution of the plates is very carefully done to your satisfaction and to that of Roger Greene's.

    I shall write you again about my own affairs very soon.

Very sincerely yours,

James H. Woods

Baron A. von Stael Holstein,
Marco Polo Street,
Austrian Legation,
Legation Quarter,
Peiping, China.

JHW/P
Enc.

HARVARD UNIVERSITY
CAMBRIDGE, MASS.

July 24, 1929

Dear De Stael:

I am not sure whether I wrote you to thank you for the postal cards and also for the happy memories of your visit. I have written to Rousselle. The $3000 has been formally granted. Laufer has been formally called.

May I ask your kind help in reserving rooms for us at the Wagon Lits for about the 21st of September? We leave Vancouver on the Empress of France on August 29. We shall spend about six days in Japan and I expect to take the P & O boat, Mantua, from Yokahama on September 19.

Would it be too much trouble for you to have a rotograph copy made of Asanga's commentary on the Vajra-cchedikā — Nanjio 1167
and Vasubandhu's "   "   " — " 1168

Hollis and I have just written an account for the Times of the desirability of adding you to the list of citizens to whom confiscated property has been returned by the Esthonian Republic. The article in the paper was not couched in such raw terms, but that was the point of the article.

Counting upon seeing you soon,

Very faithfully yours,

James H. Woods

Baron Alexander von Stael-Holstein
Peking Club
Legation Quarter
Peking, China

At the hotel we want preferably two quiet adjoining rooms with bath or one large room with two beds — we care more for quiet than for pretentiousness. By "adjoining" I mean with a door between.

Ex-Austrian Legation, Peking, China, September 4th 1929.

To the Bureau of Harvard University.

Dear Sir,

"page 215, line 2 (N)" May I, ask you to deduct (in pencil) the amount of your bill (No 6) dated May 3rd 1929 and marked "(1) No" from the salary Stael has been promised me by the University? (seven thousand dollars a year minus five per cent for the retiring allowance fund = (six thousand six hundred and fifty dollars a year minus five per cent for the retiring allowance).

Faithfully yours
MüllWalter [Stael-Holstein]

Professor Woods.

Some of my assistants resumed our regular research work, which had almost stopped during my absence, on July 1st. I have been busy with new catalogues since the beginning of June, although the

Empress of France
Yokohama

Many thanks kind letter preparing please write date arrival of Peiping suitable rooms available

Stael

Courses. Besides Mr. Schuster there will be two or three students (two of them Chinese and one Japanese). There will be certainly three of us: Mr. Y. R. Patch (who was invited to Harvard but could not go to America), Mr. Schuster and myself. But there may be two more. I shall never forget your unvarying kindness during the Christmas months I spent at Cambridge. Believe me yours most sincerely and gratefully. MüllWalter [Stael-Holstein]

CANADIAN PACIFIC

Empress of France

S.S. September 6, 1929

Dear De Stael,

Here we are on your last CPR boat within three days of Yokohama and most eagerly looking forward to taking you by the hand again and of paying our best homage to your wife — For we have heard from Chao of the happy event to which you alluded when you were with us at 29 Follen Street — I wish you both the very best of happiness and count upon welcoming both of you in Cambridge.

We stopped for a week in the Canadian Rockies with great satisfaction, alone all in a log-cabin on Emerald Lake close to the forest and the snows and the still glacial water.

Our plans are slightly changed. Instead of taking the P.O. boat Mantua to Shanghai arrives there about Sept 21, we will take the N.Y.K boat from Kobe on Sept 16 and arrive at Tientsin about

September 20 — I do not know whether we can catch the train to Peking on the same day or on the next day the 21st. We should be obliged to you if you could reserve a room with two beds and a bath at the Wagon Lits — It is possible that Stuart will ask us directly to Yenching — He will send some one to meet us — We should however prefer a couple of days at least at the Wagon Lits, if he wants us to be with him.

I hope all your projects are working out well — There will be an infinite amount to talk over and to enjoy together and I send on ahead our most cordial good wishes

Yours always

James H. Woods

I hope all is arranged with Bennett

The Imperial Hotel of Tokyo

September 11, 1929

Dear Dr Stael,

At the last moment we have been compelled to change our plans; and we will now come by Mukden with the expectation of arriving at Peiping on Sept. 22 at 2:38 p.m. I should be obliged if you would change the reservation to that day at the Wagon Lits —

Let me thank, however briefly, while

packing, for the very welcome accounts of your wedding and for the kindness in sending the pictures —

Let me add that I have enjoyed two long conferences with Demiéville. I am impressed with what you write and with your new point of view — Nothing need be said about any new organization until after I see you

With my best wishes and thanks

Sincerely yours

James H. Woods

Dear Woods,

~~A few days ago I sent you a~~

I am very glad to hear from Demié-ville that you will proceed to China without stopping in Japan. Please let me know by wire when we may expect you at Peking. Shall I ~~order a return~~ reserve rooms for you at the Hôtel de Pékin or at the Hôtel des Wagons-Lits. I hope that you have received my letter which should have ~~was to~~ reached you via Paris, but was held up at the Manchurian frontier. It returned to Peking, and was finally despatched to Cambridge via Japan a week or ten days ago.

Looking forward very much to seeing you ~~again~~ and Mrs Woods again soon I remain yours most sincerely

AvStaëlHolstein.

C O P Y.

Peking, Oct. 3. 1929.

Dear President Stuart,

The article in the Standard of yesterday on page 4 gives a misleading account of the Institute and of Baron De Stael"s relations. as Harvard Professor, to Yenching. He is there represented as a "staff member" of Yenching in no wise different from the others. The Trustees of the Institute wish the Harvard professors to be directly responsible to the Board of Trustees and not accountable to the Administrative Committee except for friendly visits and such occasional work with special students as they desire. I mentioned to you the formation of a special committee to deal with the Harvard professors. At present there seems to be no pressing need for such a committee. It might be better to wait for this until we can consult Professor Laufer. Professor De Stael"s assistants would also be responsible to him and not to the Administrative Board.

Article II of the draft of by-laws, which was not formally considered, would need to be radically changed. if it need be adopted at all.

We went over these matters orally just when you were most pressed for time. I think we understand each other and I am grateful for your cooperation. And I am confident that we can adjust this delicate situation, as both you and the Trustees now desire.

With most happy recollections of our welcome to Yenching.

Sincerely yours,
(signed)   James H. Woods.

Owing to the peculiar ramifications of the Baron"s work is it not better to permit no publicity with regard to what he is doing?

I quite understand that you do not want your original researches, which evidently must be considered before later efforts to go for nothing, and I suggest that you keep our manuscript for possible reference in the future.

I was never specially interested in the Vajracchedikā and I shall be only grateful if I shall be able to devote my attention to Pelliot, Bacot.

Peking October 3rd 1929.

Dear Woods,

The enclosed statement is exactly what I feared, and it might will seriously compromise my position in the eyes of my various Peking friends.

I have told everybody that I am here as a Harvard professor "to take" charge of research work in Peking", as President Lowell put it in his certificate. The "Standard" represents me as a subordinate of Mr. Ch'en Yüan of Yenching. I am quite free this morning; please let me know at what time I might come and discuss the matter with you at the Wagons-Lits. Believe me yours sincerely A. v. Staël-Holstein

Dear Woods,

Would not it be a good thing to talk over matters with Mr. Boynton (Trésorier J. Heim) over à trois with Mr. Boynton before his departure for Japan?. I sent him a second (verbal) invitation through Mrs. Roger Greene's brother, Mr. Sieburg ~~who~~ in ~~contrast of opinion that the his soft~~ ~~comes to my house yet.~~ ~~H.Artat party~~ but he has not yet fulfilled his promise to call here. Could you not bring him to my house this evening between 6.30 and 8 o'clock for a cocktail? My "Hall of the Arhats" an important feature of my establishment is not quite ready yet and I think I shall postpone my Chinese party until the completion of the necessary alterations.

My dear Professor Yuan! I have much pleasure in accepting your kind invitation for Saturday October 9th, 10 o'clock. My wife ~~regrets very much~~ sends her thanks you very much for having included her, but regrets that she will be unable to come on account of a bad cold. Believe me yours most sincerely A.Staël-Holstein.

Le baron et la baronne de Staël-Holstein remercient Monsieur et Madame Ed. H. de Tscharner pour leur aimable invitation (dimanche, 13 octobre, 1 heure), à laquelle ils auront l'honneur de se rendre.

Peking le 8 octobre 1929.

GRAND HOTEL DES WAGONS-LITS.
PEKING.

October 22, 1929

Dear Dr Stael,

Roger Greene is leaving for Kyoto on Friday. I suggest that you send him a copy of your budget before then.

On Thursday I go to Peiteiho to spend the week end. May I ask you to send me the copy of the Vajra-cchedikā which I had before? I now have Giles.

And could you let me have Sylvain Lévi's Sūtrālaṃkāra?

Sincerely yours

James H. Woods

Peking, October 24th 1929.

Dear Woods,

There will be no Lama dinner to-night. They will come to-morrow (Friday) at 6 p.m. and I hope you will also be able to come. The Lama dinner will be a men's party.

I have invited the Lattimores for this evening at 6 (a cocktail party) and I hope that you and Mrs. Woods will join us. Please do come!

Experience has taught me that Chinese and Mongolian assistants will only work properly under constant supervision. Therefore I pay my collaborators for the hours which they actually spend at my house. Consequently the pay varies in some cases, and I know only on the last day of the month how much the various men have to get. Then there are special emissaries who look for books, learned Lamas etc. in Mongolia and who have to be paid in advance. How can I pay those men at the right moments if a correspondence with Mr. Stevens Tsai (I think that is the name of the assistant treasurer of Yenching) be needed in every case? The thing is almost impossible. I would have to keep a special secretary for that correspondence.

Some of my assistants are fervent Buddhists - even monks.- How would their names look on the pay roll of an institution, mainly

- 2 -

ly or at least partly concerned with the <u>propaganda</u> of another religion?

Some of my collaborators cannot write English or Chinese. How could they sign the Yenching cheques in a manner acceptable to the authorities of a foreign bank?

I very strongly object to the Yenching detour on many other grounds. Why should the present system not be preserved? <u>I pay for everything</u> out of my own pocket and <u>send the bill</u> with all the receipts to the trustees at the end of the quarter. After having examined the accounts the trustees simply refuse to pay those parts of my bills which they object to. They are thus able to avoid all expenditure which they consider unnecessary or harmful without the slightest difficulty and without much correspondence. Professor Porter comes to my house quite frequently and is in a position to control my budget in every detail.

If the Yenching people insist on the Yenching <u>cheque system</u> I prefer going on <u>without receiving</u> anything from them (they have not paid me anything since my return from America) until the matter be settled by the <u>trustees</u> at Cambridge Mass.

Believe me yours sincerely,

P.S. In very great haste!
I hope to see you this evening at six.

Dairen Kisen Kaisha

S.S. Sakaki Maru

Nov. 14 1929

Dear Dr Stael,

At Chefoo we ran into a student insurrection stirred up by the Commissioner of Education 何思源 who had studied in Chicago and Paris. Students meetings and parades in a highly explosive situation. The students caused the Chinese president to resign, and demand a Chinese dean, better professors of arts, and the separation of the School of Theology. The Medical School does admirable work. The professors are humble, devoted men, with no interests except in their work and their families. The students, unlike those trained in America, go out into the villages as physicians and do not wish to live in cities only. At Tsing-tao we were shown the German batteries and the new university which is in the old German barracks. They spoke of the dignity and fair-mindedness of the Germans in defeat. Eight hundred Germans held the city three months against forty-five thousand Japs and sank two ships.

We are in the muddy waters off the Yang-tze and soon again will be in the thick of engagements. I miss seeing you and count upon our meeting again soon. But before then much remains to be done to clarify the relations with Yenching. At Chelov I discovered some fear that Yenching would encroach upon their freedom

With my very best wishes to you both in which my wife joins
Yours always
James H. Woods

In April 1929, it was settled (Dear Chase, and Dean Donham, agreeing) that 1/2 part of the sums allotted to "Sino-Indian Studies" should be paid to me by Menching on August 1st 1929. But August 1st, September 1st and October 1st passed without any funds reaching me from Menching. That I got anything at all from Menching at that time of course amounted (though rather unwillingly) to admit that the Cambridge orders had ~~the possibility~~ ~~what possibly~~ ~~that~~ Menching and that the delay was due to a misunderstanding. But any such expla such an explanation is excluded in the latest instance of Menching obstruction. On Wednesday November 6th Menching Porter promised me in your presence to send me the long delayed cheque for my ~~travel~~ representation supplementation expenses at once. This his promise was made on Thursday November 11th (without his waiting Furthermore Professor days ago, but no cheque whatever has reached me. Furthermore Porter wrote me a long letter ~~dealing~~ with unimportant matters without mentioning his promise of referring to Eg his promise. This I think constitutes a clear proof of Menching's ~~absolute~~ ~~attitude~~ Of I shall

Excuse this appeal to Cæsar, but things have become very unpleasant for me here since your departure ~~I have made certain promises and~~ I must ~~be certain~~ be sure that I shall be able to keep them. With our kindest regards to you and to Mrs. Woods ~~I remain~~ yours gratefully

H.v.Staël-Holstein

the tone of which evidently lacks the restraint ~~which~~ corresponding to Cæsar's exalted position.

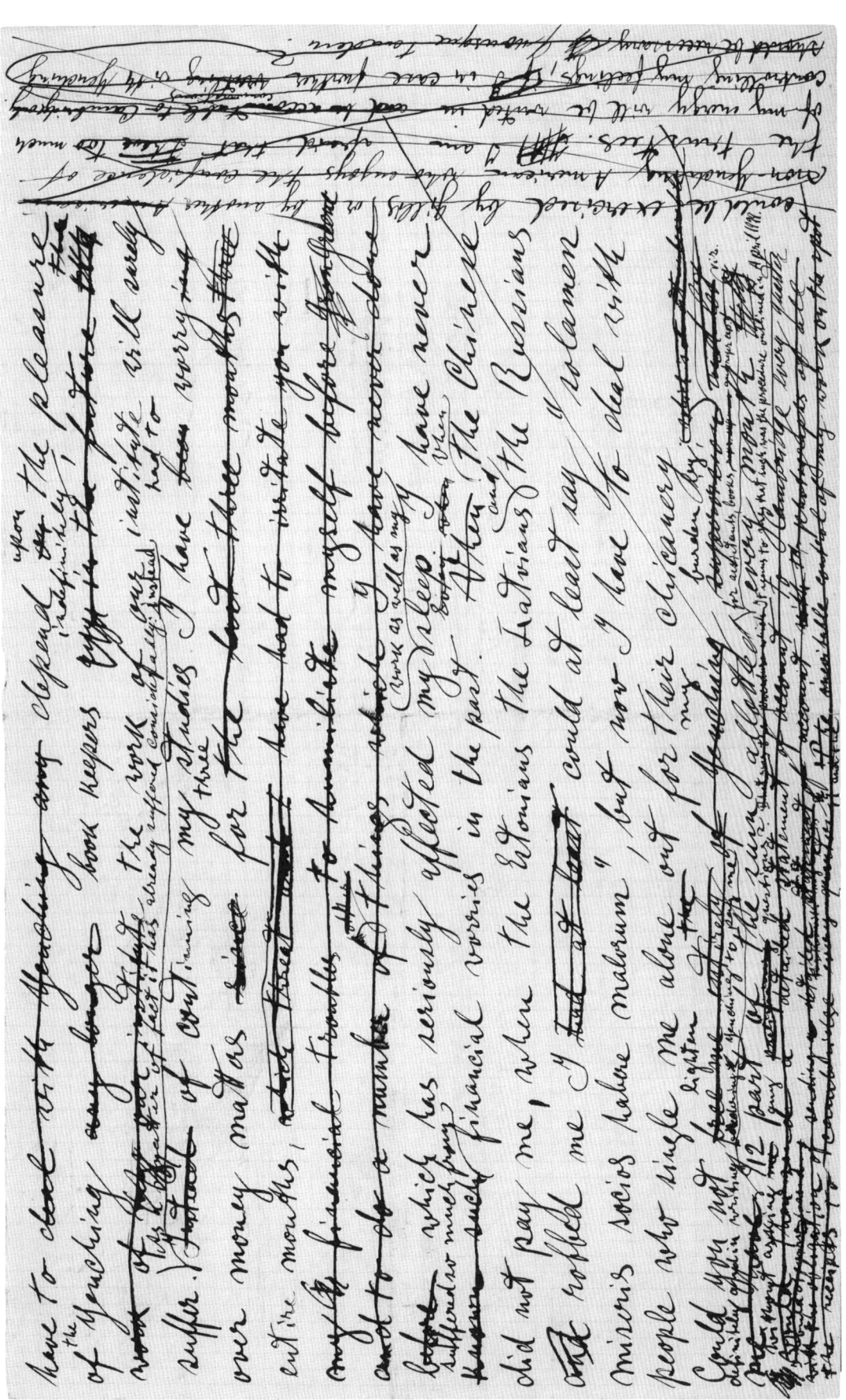

I would of course, send photographs of all the receipts to Cambridge every quarter together with my reports, copies of which would be sent to Professor Porter. Prof Porter could of I'll control my reports on the spot, but he should be theoretically clearly empowered to suspend payments (again) except upon definite orders from Cambridge to do so. I am afraid that too much of my energy will be wasted if the present state of things continues. I was left without any salary for almost four months and had to pay all my expenses. Again even after your kind intervention my expenses which resulted I'd offer this promise of Notary for 6¾ Professor Porter's definite promise of money I hope that the executive committee will be able to discuss more essential troubles for me, they keep to accept my Time Table.

Could you not lighten my burden by definitely promising to pay me 1/12 of the sum allotted for assistants, books and representation expenses ($Mex 26000/12 = $Mex 2166 and cents 66⅔) every month without fail and without raising any preliminary questions? It seems to me that much was the procedure outlined in April 1929.

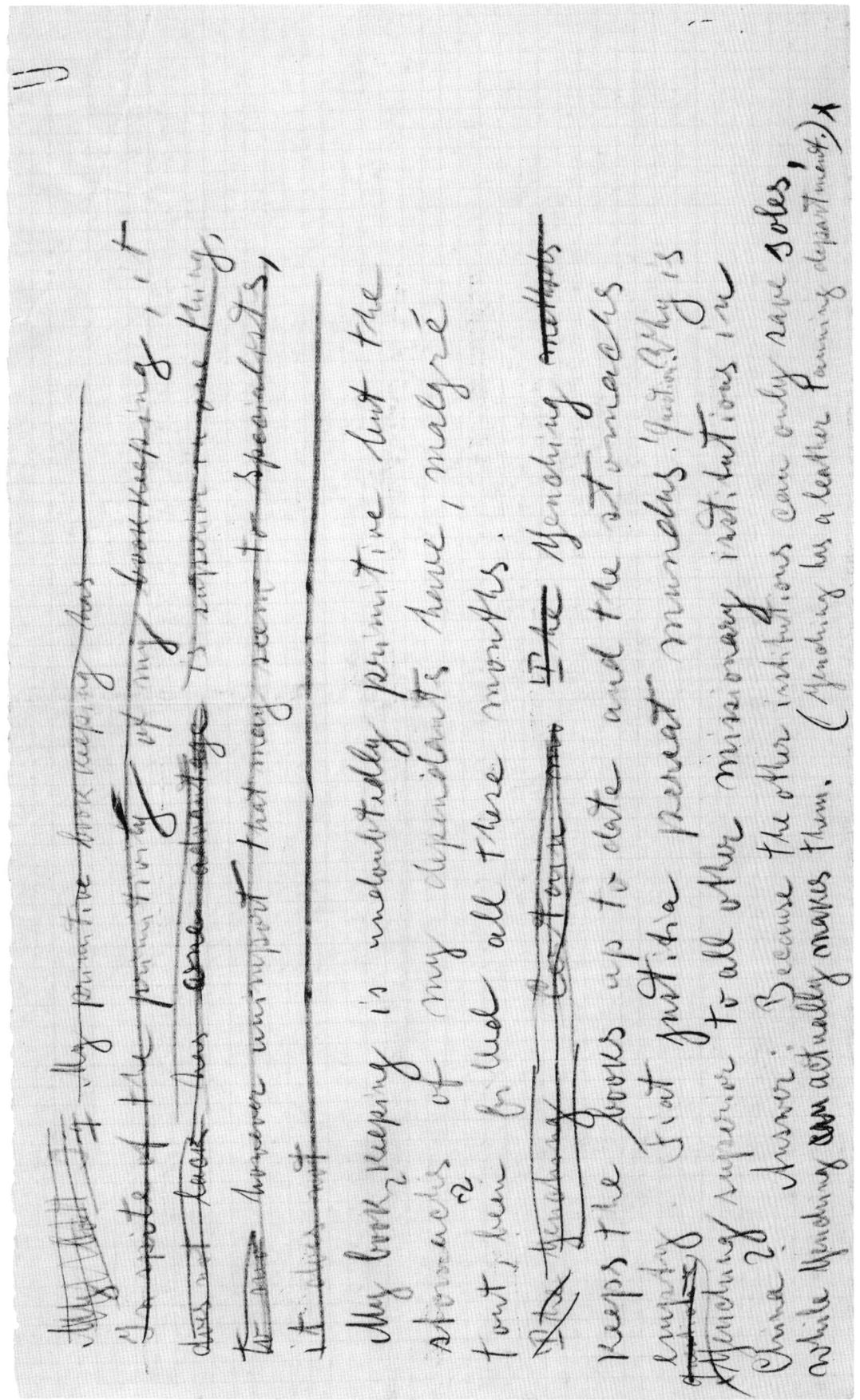

[Copy of a letter sent to Yokoham % the Dollar Line]

Peking December 5th 1928.

Dear Vonds,

Many thanks for your kind letter about the affair which you wrote to me on board the Japanese boat. I have many things to tell you but as I was very much interested in — Thank you

Only a few lines in order to wish your boy a week once more my kind regards. My that day's for assisting me in my fight for independence. Where would I be without your kind help? I would have to obey Mr. Lew's orders and to report to Mr. Yu. All that has been —— These dangers exist no longer, and the outlook is full of hope. The insignificant remnants of Menching imperialism which still stand in my way will, no doubt, also appear before long. I shall write you about that in a few days, and the letter will most probably arrive at Cambridge — bringing more interesting intelligence — about your arrival at Cambridge. I have bought an Imperial Hanger (Six volumes out of 106 are missing). The Mongolian Hanger which we want so very badly will also be got in a few weeks. Then we shall be able to put the finishing touches to our catalogue raisonné of

The Hampir Ratnakūṭa. A few days ago the Porters landed with us, and not nothing unpleasant has occurred and the party arrived with us, and kein Mingsten Trübste ohne erhebende Fieber. "Today I said—and kein zarten Mr. Hui Li Shan — Mr. Pevzratoff has compared The two Tibetan texts of the Vajracchedikā, and a copy of the text adopted by us with all the various readings will be sent to your Cambridge address in a few days. We have discussed and — (Tang) and Chinese translation which we intend publishing along with the six Chinese versions. My wife and I enjoyed your visit very much indeed, and our only regret is that we saw so comparatively little of you both during your stay in Peking (and of Mrs. Luce) We both look forward to seeing more of you during your next visit to China. I saw the German doctor (Professor Krieg) to-day, and he told me that my wife's condition was entirely satisfactory. He said: "die Bauchwand sieht ein physiologisch, und durchaus nicht pathologisch." Many thanks for the interesting letter which you received from the Japanese Shaw. With kind regards to you and to Mrs. Brooks I remain yours gratefully A.V.Staël-Holstein

Bon voyage

Peking, December 10th 1929.

Dear Woods,

The proverb "On revient toujours à ses premières amours" has proved true once more. As you will see from the accompanying photograph the Yenching people disregard our previous agreements almost completely and return to the idea of my being accountable to their Administrative Committee in Peping, malgré tout. Under these circumstances I consider an appeal to Caesar unavoidable, the more so because in your letter from the " Sakaki Maru " I find the words:" much remains to be done to clarify the relations with Yenching."

The Yenching people want (§ 4) me to submit my contractual agreements with the assistants to them which is absurd under the circumstances. I have myself had practically nothing but verbal promises , some of which have been amiably forgotten (Harvard) or deliberately ignored (Yenching). I showed you the Harvard Bursar's letter which deprives me of two months' salary by starting my new financial year on Sept.1st, instead of on July 1st. After the telegram which you so kindly sent to Cambridge in October (asking for four months' salary for me) I thought that the Cambridge authorities would rectify their mistake without further reminders on my part, and let me know by letter. But nothing of the sort happened. I received no communication on the subject from

Cambridge

- 2 -

Cambridge (except the 00 gold cabled to me by Dean Chase) and had to address a long letter to the authorities on December 6th reminding them of their promise of beginning my new financial year on July 1st 1929.

You can imagine how much energy and enthusiasm I lose by having to write such extremely unpleasant letters again and again (not to mention the frequent conversations on the same subject which are even less enjoyable) in order to obtain the sums due to me - and in a foreign language too.

Professor Porter promised on November 6th at the Wagons Lits Hotel in your presence to send me a cheque covering my representation expenses for four months at once. I had to wait for the cheque until November 18th and when it arrived I found that only three months, instead of the promised four had been covered.

No progress has been made with the photostat, since I objected to the Yenching plan of buying the photostat with Sino-Indian money and keeping it at Yenching. I want the photostat very badly for a number of purposes. The most important purpose is: photographing rare manuscripts or prints (like the hitherto un - known Vajracchedikâ Commentary which we are going to publish) which are being lent to me for a limited period and which my various friends would never lend to Yenching. Of what earthly use would a photostat kept at Yenching be to me? If I could have applied to Cambridge for permission to use my savings for buying a photostat,

- 3 -

stat, instead of struggling with Yenching, the question would probably have been solved long ago.

The Yenching people grudge me every penny and use various devices in order to get back part of what they consider their own. Mr. Hsu Ti Shan knows some Sanskrit but certainly not enough to understand commentaries, in spite of which he wants to prepare and publish a Sanskrit-Chinese dictionary. I think his plan foolish (Tschen Yin Koh agrees with me) on account of his philological inadequacy and in view of the fact that the Hobogirin (Demiéville) makes such a publication unnecessary. But he considers me as fellow-subject of the famous "Peping Administrative Committee" and told me a few days ago of his hope that "the authorities" would support his plan against my objections. He knows of course, that in spite of all assurances of independence the Yenching people hold the strings of the purse and can by petty chicanery force me to do almost anything if this appeal to Caesar should prove unsuccessful. As a matter of fact Professor Porter hinted very plainly the other day that the Yenching professor Hsu Ti Shan should be paid out of Sino-Indian funds. I have no use for Mr. Hsu Ti Shan, who lectures at various universities in exactly the diffuse way which I detest. He will never sit at my house for six hours every day (as my other assistants do) - he is much too important for that. If I yielded to Professor Porter's suggestion an exception would have to be made for Mr. Hsu Ti Shan and the rest of my assistants would become as slack as the members of the Yenching

Research

- 4 -

Research institute who meet only for one hour every fortnight.

I quite understand that the Trustees should insist on my expenditure being strictly controlled and I as well as my assistants will answer all questions put to them by Professor Porter, the Trustees' intelligence agent, who might not be satisfied with the photographed receipts which I shall send to Cambridge and to Yenching from time to time. But he should be an intelligence officer only, and not the director of Sino-Indian studies, of which he knows nothing. The Yenching people should be prevented from withholding the funds allotted to me in the future, and they should be strictly ordered to pay me one twelfth of the whole sum (26 thousand Mex. according to the extremely unfavorable exchange rate adopted at present) every month <u>under all circumstances</u>.
Those who object to this plan and who think that I must not be trusted with such enormous sums should remember that my European bridges are burnt and that I am entirely dependent upon Harvard. Whenever they think that I have squandered my employers' funds they can punish me by stopping my Harvard salary. The plan outlined above is the only way out of an impossible situation, and the Trustees should not dismiss it lightly, because a dissatisfied and constantly irritated servant will never be able to perform his duties satisfactorily.

I hope that the Trustees will grant my request and thereby make me forget the extremely irritating treatment which I have received during the last months from their agents. That
<u>treatment</u>

- 5 -

treatment has poisoned my existence, very seriously disturbed my sleep and made scientific work almost impossible. I shall not bore you with any details of the many studied discurtesies which have been shown me, but I must give you some idea of my financial troubles. Before I left Cambridge on May 2nd 1939 it was definitely settled (Deans Chase and Dorham agreeing) that I should receive one twelfth of the sum allotted to me by the trustees on August 1st through Yenching, but August 1st, September 1st and October 1st passed without any funds at all reaching me. For almost four months I had to run my entire establishment without receiving either salary or other sums from my employers' agents who were supposed to look after me, and I daily risked being called upon to pay important sums for books which I had ordered, but which fortunately did not arrive when they were due.* You know how the Yenching people behaved at the end of those four months of anxious writing and endless humiliations. They asked for a preliminary statement of expenses which had never been arranged for at Cambridge, studied it at their leisure (for about a fortnight), paid very reluctantly and seriously reprimanded me for some items like the following: "sent to Mr.Behrsing $ Mex.417". I should have written: "sent to Mr.Behrsing $ Mex.400 plus $ Mex.17 for telegraphic expenses". Photographic reproductions of all the receipts were handed to the book-keepers and words like "see receipt 3901" (which
<u>gives</u>

---

* I have since bought for myself the Imperial Kanjur, no copy of which exists in America. Even the Chinese Government libraries which have been looking for a copy all these years have so far not succeeded in securing one. That collection is of course very important for our work, but I do not expect the H.Y. Institute to pay for it.

- 6 -

gives the desired specification) were added to the objectionable items. They could, therefore, have satisfied their curiosity without any great trouble. But they still consider the missing specifications as much greater offences, than their disregarding the Cambridge orders (which must have reached them) and leaving me without a cent for over three months. Do not you think that my energy should be saved for better things, than such ridiculous quibblings with miserable pettifoggers.

I have again spent two entire days of a very crowded week (lectures, meetings of various committees etc.etc. etc.) in discussing money matters; in order to stop that waste of time please do ask the trustees to issue strict orders to the following effect :

1) Yenching must pay me one twelfth of the sum allotted for Sino-Indian studies every month under all circumstances without waiting for my expense accounts or for any other communications.

2) I must send a detailed expense account with all receipts (as I have done through you for the three months ending on September 30th 1929) in photographic reproductions to Cambridge at the end of every quarter.

3) I am authorized to use what I may save on assistants for buying books which will, of course, remain the property of the H.Y.Institute.

4) All assistants (Westerners and Asiatics alike) will be paid by me directly, and the preposterous Yenching detour will be altogether abolished.

5) During

-7-

5) During the half year ending on December 31st 1929 I shall probably have drawn much less than the 13 thousand Mex. which Yenching has received for me from Cambridge for that period. Yenching must pay me the difference at once and I am authorized to use it for buying a photostat (about 2 thousand Mex.) and for books.

6) Professor Porter may ask questions and may inspect my establishment but must in no way interfere with my direction of Sino-Indian studies.

I do not think that you will consider it advisable to show this letter to many trustees. But I believe that some of the Harvard professors might read it without objecting to the language used. Firstly because English is not my native tongue, and secondly because I have suffered a number of indignities which justify strong expressions. I am proud to be their colleague and they should protect me against the enemies who are, helas, still my masters. Did not the Yenching people use all their influence in order to prevent the passing of my budget last April? Even the hardest boiled of the trustees will have to admit that they owe me an apology for the mess which their agents have caused, and that the latter deserve a rebuke. The best atonement they could offer me would be an immediate acceptance of the plan outlined above.

I hope that you have received my letter in which I thanked you once more for being such a faithful ally and for assisting me in my fight for independence. I sent the letter c/o

the

- 8 -

the Dollar Line office Yokohama.

       With my best New Year's greetings to you both in which my wife joins ,

                      I remain yours gratefully,

Peking Dec. 22nd 1929

Dear Woods,

"Icy-Hot" is the name of a new kind of thermos flasks, but the compound adjective could be equivalent to this language used by Captain Gilly's language equally well apply to what he calls ing when to discussed that the stuff "the missionary tribe." Some elements of that language remind one of the North Atlantic breezes others of That language seems to be composed of two elements: the breezes of the North Atlantic, and the sulphurous vapours of another place noted for its extremely high temperature. During a conversation to you I had with Gilly I had indeed a good opportunity of writing with comparison with my last letter to about two days ago just before I had inhaled a good portion of those vapours, and I am afraid that the tone of my letter was influenced by them. I send you these 5 lines in order to apologize for that tone. Which might

If you think that my letter will produce a bad impression do not show it to any one and forget it. It's contents back

I have had not open conflict with the (where Politik der Nadelstiche" I have used patiently without any similar *Yenching*) *Institute* and Sorbonne quite hostility with them (whenever we meet. Neither Contributors *have that he publishes whenever we meet.* (Tsi-Uhsa have I informed anyone at Cambridge (not even Dean Coolidge) of any conflicts. Besides I hope (my plan

desiderata (regular monthly payments of my salary) to all be present without any <del>further</del> thing for my accounts) *as the most obvious and simple way of dealing with it matter* could be accepted if first suggested to President Stuart and if accepted by him passed on to the meeting of the trustees. As soon as I got a favourable <del>telegram</del> cable from you I will *to Yenching for <del>Sanskrit</del> a Sanskrit assistant* buy the photostat and write to *Yenching <del>Blessing</del>* I have to <del>trouble</del> apply to Gillis now whenever I want photostatic copies which is that extremely inconvenient it forces me to trace
The absence of a Sanscrit assistant *yes. I have not taken any steps* elementary Sanscrit myself. *Yes* *the younger people are* for obtaining a Sanscrit Assistant because the <del>Trust</del> *of very disagreeable* about it and I dare not do anything without their approval <del>to be</del> yes.

I have seven students in my elementary class: Schuster, (Kaufmann), (a Dutch ethnologue), Dr. Rene, and four Chinese. I also don't have my Sino-Tibetan studies with Schuster and Pockert. I shall in a few days send you the Tibetan text of the Vajracch- — which you might compare it with the Tibetan text in your possession. Our Tibeto-Tibetan edition of the 5 are texts (one Sanscrit, one Tibetan and one Sanscrit and Chinese texts) are now quite ready for print, including all the various lections.

Many thanks to you and to Mrs. Woods Hocking for your charming Christmas card from Japan.

My wife and I send you both our heartiest greetings.

Yours very sincerely
MWalleschmidt

P.S. The most important points of my plan are:
1) That hindering should pay me one-tenth of the entire sum [approximate rate of exchange adopted according to the authority at present] (26 thousand doll. [with my circumstances] [waiting for my statements of accounts] any other communications)
2) That I should be authorized to use whatever I may need for assistants, for buying books which will, of course, remain the property of the H.Y. Institute.

3) That the money which I should be authors 2nd to use two thousand Mk. surf divisity on half year wiley on Dec 3rd 1929 Mk. for buying a photostat which is to remain the property of the H.-Y. institute. If I had not thus for Yenching, it makes me previous to think that I but for Yenching interference of Yenching friends I might already have possess a photostat and not just Sanscrit assistant would slowly to have to to try say I love very much time teaching the beginners and then going to Gilby with my manuscripts. I have been extremely busy all these days with me preparing my lectures, lecturing and even replying to Sino-Indian questions addressed to us from America, Europe, India, Japan and China. But we are becoming an important centre of studies — in magnum harmonine gloriam!

4) All assistants (lecturers and Asiatics alike) will be paid by me directly, and the preposterous Yenching detour will be altogether abolished. Yenching may act as an observer of my activities, may ask questions and may report my sins to Cambridge, but must never stop payments on its own initiative.

Dear Woods,

Messrs. Greene and Porter have simply ignored my very broad hint at the representation expenses (2000 gold a year). ~~It would be rather embar~~ That may be due to genuine avidy a ~~ignorance~~ and not to "mauvaise volonté". ~~But~~ In any case ~~it would be rather embarrassing~~ for me ~~to take up~~ taking up the question again with an unprepered Porter ~~about~~ (~~during~~ at wednesday tomorrow's conference, Vagous-Ls its 5 p.m.) I would be extremely ~~very~~ ~~highly~~ embarrassing. If you ~~should~~ see Professor Porter before tomorrow's conference (will you), please tell him that the "account lessness" of the representation expenses was all settled at Cambridge, and that he must not wait for any bills before paying me the sums in question. ~~Thus~~ I shall be so grateful to you if you will assist me in removing this last vighna.

P.S.

I am, ~~naturally~~ of course, extremely anxious to know ~~what role ~~~~has you regard~~ whether you regard the modus vivendi outlined in this letter is acceptable. May I ask for the favour of a wire indicating in a few words how my proposal has been received by ~~the~~ the trustees or by the Cambridge executive Committee? My ~~telegram~~ address ~~is~~ for cables is:

StaelHolstein (one word) ~~Australeg~~
~~is~~ Augofoo Peking

I owe him much gratitude and ~~feel~~ feel a great sympathy for him, but I do not want even Professor Porter to be our food dictator, because he is, after all, a servant of ~~Yenching~~ our Yenching enemies.

What I want to avoid ~~at all price~~ is that Yenching should be able to starve me into submission. It must be laid down definitely that they may report ~~what~~ my sins to Cambridge but that Cambridge alone should be entitled to suspend payments. A regular income is the first ~~condition to~~ requirement which ~~directors~~ educators of ~~good~~ book keepers should fulfil. ~~If that condition~~ ~~h~~ If the trustees want to make a good book keeper of me let them order Yenching to pay me one twelfth every months regularly without waiting for my statements of account or any other communications.

The authorities of the National University of Peking owe me three years' salary, but I am not half as angry with them as I am with the Feuchtwang[?]. The former simply cannot and will not pay anyone, while the letter singles me out for Chicanery. At our conference on November 6th Professor Pelsing[?] definitely promised in your presence to pay me certain sums (333.33½ Dollar) regularly in future at the end of every month. As I already wrote you the period the accumulated sums for July August and September on November 18th but failed to keep his promise concerning the October payment which I did my best he still withholds. I thought that he might pay me let me have for the issue the first the October November and December sums together at the end of December, but he has not done so.

The 25th is the Yenching pay day, and I have received nothing, although Penkraeff's Scheque did arrive promptly. The Yenching people probably want me to wait for the money. It would probably take me to remind me of their right to (without ? most urgent ?) probably want me to ask for the money that would give them a chance to remind me of Mr. Hsü T. Shen whom they want to force me into any collaboration. But I shall not go to freeing my request I have tried. But I cannot do that because they are not aware my request of ... reminding me of Mr. Hsü T. Shen whom they want to force into my establishment, or rather into my payroll. I cannot ask the Yenchingese to pay up, because that would enable them to ask as soon as I do — they will certainly retort by reminding me of Mr. Hsü T. Shen whom they want by way of reply into my establishment of any validity — must go rather into my payroll. Therefore I would be ??? you with a ...
I shall not ??? I insist upon the adoption of the plan outlined in my letters of Dec 10th and Dec 22nd
as many financial worries in my life as during the last five months.

Since August 1st I have constantly been beseeching for some overdue payment or other (would be made) I hope I shall not have to trouble ↄ

I hope that I shall be able to direct my attention to (more or) less ~~Buddhistic~~ annoying problems in the future.

With kind regards from us both to you and to Mrs. Woods

I remain yours sincerely
AlvonStaël-Holstein

Worrying takes time and the Aoerting things cause Whenever I succeed in getting rid of my rambling Yunching thing ets, the Peking and the rest of the world do not appear to me as to still appears to me as the best of possible cities. LeonerStaff and I have made as All my assistants are doing extremely well, not except the lamas who are not as good as my old Lama friends. But one of the latter is expected to return soon

I lectured on ~~those~~
~~In addition to those~~ lectures which were delivered at my home I ~~those~~ taught at the National University of Peking where

~~That~~ During the academic year 1929/1930 I ~~##~~ conducted two classes: 1) Sanscrit grammar for beginners (2 hours) 2) Comparative study of the Purāṇamālinā in Sanscrit, Tibetan and Chinese (4 hours) 3) ~~History of~~ Indian religious history (2 hours).
~~Of~~ 1 and 2 were ~~held~~ The classes 1 and 2 were held at my house, but the lectures on Indian religious history were delivered at the National University of ~~##~~ Peking. ~~##~~ Since my return to Peking, about eighteen months ago, The National University of ~~##~~ has paid me the equivalent of about twelve hundred U.S. dollars. I consider ~~these payments~~ (on account) that sum as a payment of the debt which The National University owes me, rather than as a remuneration for ~~those two weeks~~ my lectures. The National University failed to pay me for three years (July 1925 – July 1928).

I believe that critical editions of Chinese Buddhist texts can only be prepared by Sanskritists together with [the best] Chinese groups of specialists. Each group of specialists. If we apply the standards of Western criticism of Buddhist to the Chinese Buddhist texts edited by Chinese scholars alone we find that [they are] not satisfactory even [in] the [most] [Biographies] [of] faultline. Therefore We find that the editions are far from being faultless. The Japanese editions are far from being faultless. Therefore the collaboration of Western Sanskritists with Chinese [scholars] is necessary. that they Buddhist contain the various readings of the different sources, but they frequently from a Japanese scholars is necessary of compounding of [the meaning of a text] as they can has been [either] hopelessly unintelligible or out of [text] is not. Therefore reproducing a Chinese Buddhist text its commentary should be not only be acquainted with Sanskrit Pitakas and Chinese but should also have complete knowledge of [the] 第(?)入 the wrong readings. Only a Sanskritist & Chinese or Japanese scholars well read in Buddhist & Chinese [but chiefly] [Chinese] [scholars] unacquainted with Buddhism [navigates] [or] [utopia] [integrated] but such can satisfactorily [can] chose the correct reading [in most] cases. Brightly Sankrit oriental and I think that consequently [the] vista and its commentary should not be [ ] Fan text.

Jan. 4th 1930.

On Saturday I went to Yenching and paid Chancellor Stu[art] as well as a number of other dignitaries my New Year's visit.

The enclosed letter addressed by Mrs. Porter to my wife shows also that I am trying to keep on good terms with Yenching.

Yesterday Mr. Ch'en gave the director of the Research School of Chinese Studies on the Harvard-Yenching Institute Foundation lunched with me and arranged I showed him. I introduced him to some of my assistants. I also showed him some of my Japanese Buddhist books which are not to be found in the Peking libraries and which the professor had never seen before. I said that I knew nothing about the history of Christianity in China, and suggested that it would be more

I suggested that we should meet periodically from time to time at Peking where we could use my books for the solution of Buddhist problems which might interest him. He agreed with my view that such meetings would be more fruitful than my attendance of the ordinary Sino-Indian gatherings organised throughout [?] are very glad that I need not go to Yenching. That will now [?] meetings [?] [?] what are [?] [?] time and unable me to avoid being mixed up with [?] what they call the Sino-Thing [?] [?] concerned with [?] [?] [?] [?] as chairs, asking support William Hung's Hsin[?]... [?] Sino biographies [?] [?] the balance of power [?] [?] [?] [?] [?] proofs [?] find more jobs for his relatives [?] [?] [?] [?] [?] and is trying to get more support [?] [?] [?] in America [?] [?] [?] during the Hung brothers absence in America [?] [?] [?] I am very glad that I need not [?] for Yenching during each expedition to that nest of learning that cuts me off three days. I hope you have received my four December letters. No financial news from Yenching. The solemn agreement of November 6th is still being ignored. Ch'in Hsien is very much dissatisfied with the Yenching magnate [?] [?] [?] [?] [?] [?] [?] [?] [?] [?] [?] The present state of things is unstable [?] Hardly [?] [?] [?] [?] yours sincerely
regime negotiating both here and there. [signature]

With kind regards to you and to Mrs. Hoult from us both Yours sincerely

This name is Fieldward (Comp. the Yenching University Directory for 1929-30 which has just been issued.

Dear Woods,

Only a few lines to thank you for having spoken to President Stuart about our funds. He has sent to Professor Porter who called here with the telegram a few days ago — as a result of that telegram Pantsratoff received his January cheque on yesterday (February 5th). Professor Porter tells me that it is ~~very~~ ~~~~ ~~~~ ... and that the ... I got ... numerous delays. The ... of the remaining amount of Porter of this ... on the arrival of January. He said that it may tell the treasurer's fund ... ~~~~ Delone ~~wondered~~ ... to be ... may be to blame for the delays. The letter's ~~wonderful~~ is certainly an ... a good thing. In itself, but I think ... ~~~~ constantly for ~~~~ fragments. ~~~~ to ask ...

I hope you have received the Tibetan text of the Vajraćchedika. We have the original ~~copy~~ of it here (in Roman characters for (transliteration) (two pencils)), and I send you the copy, as arranged, with the various readings, in order to enable you to compare it with your Paris notes.

Rosenthal's book (the Chu Pien) I have so far received only two chapters of the Chu Pien Chuan (Rosenthal's book), (rest of the manuscript to be when I get the full manuscript) and the photographs none of which have received me yet, I shall be able to return a report of the work. I hope to write to Rosenthal. Narita is busy I ought to be able to send you suggestions as to

I shall let you have my suggestions with regard to that edition. Narita is reviewing the two chapters first chapters (Wiesbaden) and I have written to Rosenthal for the remainder of the work. It should have been here long ago.

November 30, 1930

29 FOLLEN STREET
CAMBRIDGE

Dear Dr Staël,

I have looked over your Vajracchedikā — I was a little surprised that you sent it to Chase instead of to me, and still more surprised at some of the remarks in your introduction —

I am unwilling to give up my original plan of publishing the text of the commentaries as well as the translation, and had begun to work upon them in Peking with the help of the book one of your men was kind enough to prepare for me. You remember we talked of my plans here and in Peking. I had expected to publish the text of the Vajracchedikā itself, and indeed had done much work on it, so that it was almost ready — I consented to let you and your men do it at your request. But I had no desire to turn over the commentaries as well — This of course does not apply to Kamalaçila which Pankratoff discovered — That I should be glad to incorporate in my book as his work, or to have him publish it separately if he desires —

Your introduction does not do justice to all the facts ~~concerned~~ involved in the case — I should like to have you mention that I have been and am planning to publish both text and translation of the commentaries or to omit all mention of the commentaries altogether —

I am sorry not to have kept in
better touch with you this year —
My work has been unusually pressing —
And you know that I am a notoriously
bad correspondent — But we often
speak of you, and hope that all goes
well with you both —

My wife joins me in best wishes

Sincerely yours

James H. Woods

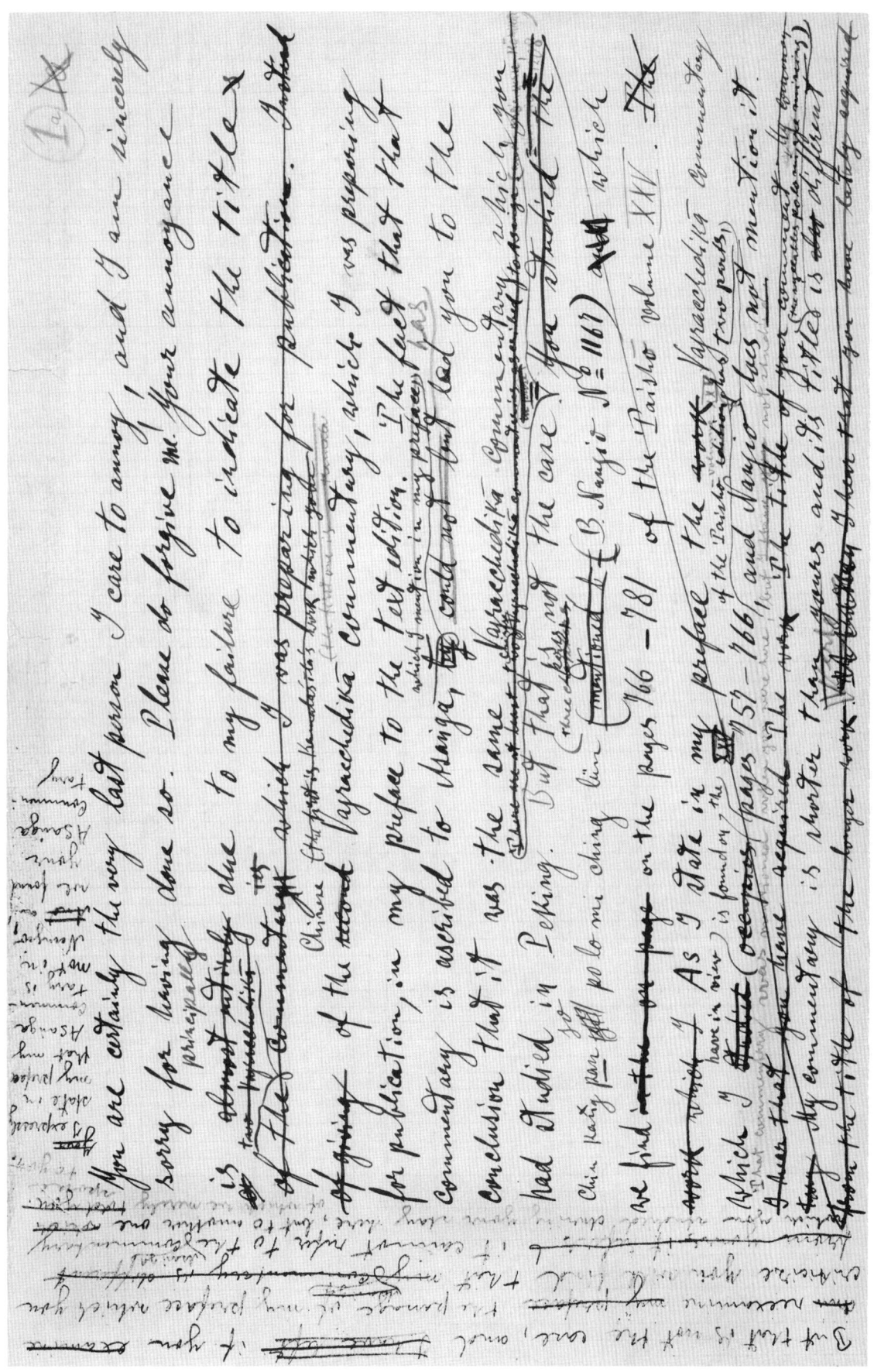

The title of the shorter work (which I studied) is. and the title of the longer work (which you studied) is. The two commentaries differ, no doubt, much in grammar (eg for instance the introductory words and the first few lines Suh), but there are, as the Japanese edition shows, very great differences (大綱同示).

If you examine the part of my proper introduction for which you criticize me, you will find that this statement that The Asaṅga commentary which I was preparing for the press is not in Nanjio. The Asaṅga commentary, a text of which is described by Nanjio (№1167) and we obtained the text for you asked us to find it from a text of which you studied at Peking the first Nanjio number (1167) for you according to that number which it bears in Nanjio and which you indicated to me in your letter dated July 24th 1929.* My preface further fixes the identity of "my thing" without any possible doubt volume by indicating the Taishō pages XII, 757–766) without any humble doubt that or on which it is printed. Your commentary that is found on the Taishō pages XII, 166–781. My commentary

* That letter lies before me. In it you ask us for copies of "Asaṅga's commentary on the Vajracchedikā", Nanjio 1167, and Vasubandhu's commentary on the Vajracchedikā commentary №№ Nanjio 1168." There are more than eighty three Vajracchedikā commentary texts six of which are supposed to be translated from Sanskrit

Asaṅga

Your commentary bears the title Ch'in Kang Pan Jo Po Lo Mi Ching Lun has three chapters and is longer than my Asaṅga commentary which is named/designated by a different name: Ch'in Kang Pan Jo Pô Lo Mi Ching Lun, and has two chapters only. The Ch'in Kang Pan Jo Po Lo Mi Ching Lun has three chapters and the Ch'in Kang Pan Jo Lun (Besides these two prose commentaries there is a third Chinese Vajracchedikā commentary in verse (Kārikās) ascribed to Asaṅga (Nanjio 1208).

I hear that you have lately acquired a copy of the Taisho edition of the Chinese Pripitaka. ## You can therefore easily verify my statements by comparing your copy of the Vyakhyayukti Commentary (by Asanga) which you took with you from Peking to Cambridge with vol. XXV of the Taisho edition. The Asanga Commentary is the only one of the numerous Vyakhyayukti commentaries which has Komatasila's Commentary has been known to Tibetan scholars for many years. It is mentioned by Bodhi... (another [?] commentary of [?] ... specially interested in the Vyakhyayukti and shall do nothing things apart from studying ## its commentaries. ## its notes you submit unless I receive definite instructions from you about study its commentaries again ! unless you obstinately tell us to do so. If it is not right to devote two or three months exclusively to the Vyakhyayukti, of [?] apply to [?] I devoted roughly 2 months perhaps to have sufficient time to enable me to complete [?] no longer than 10 to 15 hours a day in order to finish the notes etc. by before the last of September. If you do not wish it we shall send you the Chinese ## Pripitaka. Please ... In your letter you suggest as a [?] that I should either finish that you are planning to publish both text and translation of the commentaries ## omit all mention of the commentaries altogether.

26

I am not especially interested in the Vyākaraṇa'ka, and if it was only in order to please you that I devoted the time I devoted some time to it with the sole purpose of pleasing you. In that I regrievously failed and that failure has imput me to [find extent that] at my own fuge will you never replied to my letters I shall never study the Vyākaraṇa'ka [commentaries], or its commentaries anymore.

Again in regards to [Indian that] [definitely] my [important] one to abzar. I cannot off will [one that] glad if he can devote [this time to [photography painting and dramatic iconography]] rather than to the to devote his Time to his own fields

of philosophy which he never studied before, never studied before, and which he will be only able to speak [of] superficially, leaving seriously [alone]. [crossed out] The ruby which he has gave me that [crossed out] I am extremely pleased [with] not say the very best [crossed out] I [could] say the very [best] [crossed out] But the time and some of my [crossed out] of the material which he [collected] [crossed out] If you could manage to rear it Both of the material of the materials which are collected my [crossed out] corr for another visit to Peking as useful [and] fine Some things like [crossed out] [crossed out] Shaolin Some of them [crossed out] at first the materials which are collected and thrown [crossed out] interesting and useful to [crossed out] a documentarian more like the [one] I [sent] in [October] from [crossed out] Somefield [crossed out]

from their value for the history of the commentaries, naturally, facilitate the task of modern translators, and we are very glad to hear that Professor J. H. Vooks is not

The Chinese more than eighty Vajracchedikā commentaries

At present most of these eighty Chinese translations of the
J. H. Vooks is preparing editions of the

In your letter you suggest that my preface should either mention that you are planning to publish both text and translation of the commentaries or omit all mention of the commentaries altogether. There are more than eighty Chinese commentaries of the Vajracchedikā six of which have been translated from the Sanskrit of Asaṅga (3) Vasubandhu 王圓什 (Vajrasi?) and Kumārajīva 戊戊 (Kumārajīva?). Under these circumstances I prefer not mentioning any commentaries in my preface, and suggest that the changes indicated on the accompanying sheet should be made in my preface.

The present volume has no index, because the texts collected here and containing commentaries, which Professor J. H. Vajracchedikā

Wogihara is preparing for the press, form a group, induced in one volume, to be published, which should be treated as one separate whole. A separate

attached index dealing with some words, thought Words. The English translation of the Vajracchedikā upon which Professor Wogihara is engaged at present will be as it is Professor Wogihara has already been prepared, has

We are very glad to hear that Professor Wogihara will shortly publish translations of 3 three commentaries as well as of the text of the Vajracchedikā.

Please cancel the passage written in black and substitute the passage written in red for it.

I am not specially interested in the Vaiśeṣika and I devoted*) to it with the sole purpose of pleasing you. In that some time to it with the sole purpose of pleasing you. In that purpose I egregiously failed, and that failure has upset me to such an extent that I should never, of my own free will, study the Vaiśeṣika, or its commentaries, again. I believe that Pankratoff too will be glad to devote his whole time to his own field, rather than to a philosophy which he never studied before.**)

*) It has never been pointed out before, as far as I know, that (Simplicīn attadmnation) both versions of the Vaiśeṣika sūtra**** in the three languages (Skt., Chin., and Tib.), and accompanying all the various readings [...] a considerable task. [...] took me several months. [...] and abandoned [...] the holiday trip which I had [...] account of the Vaiśeṣika. My assistants also [...] arrived [...] before [...] they had practically [...] and I thought [...] Sanskrit and Tibetan [...] I found that [...] the Sūtra manuscripts as well as the handwritten copies kept [...] different [...] that an texts (completeness and position) had never, as present, [...] been [...] and that the notes had to be entirely rewritten.

**) In your letter dated Nov. 30th 1930 you mention Kamalaśīla's Vaiśeṣika commentary "which Pankratoff discovered". Pankratoff will hardly claim Kamalaśīla's commentary as his discovery. Kamalaśīla's commentary is described in Cordier's catalogue and I mention that fact as well as the year (1915), in which Cordier's catalogue appeared, in the part of my paper which you criticize.

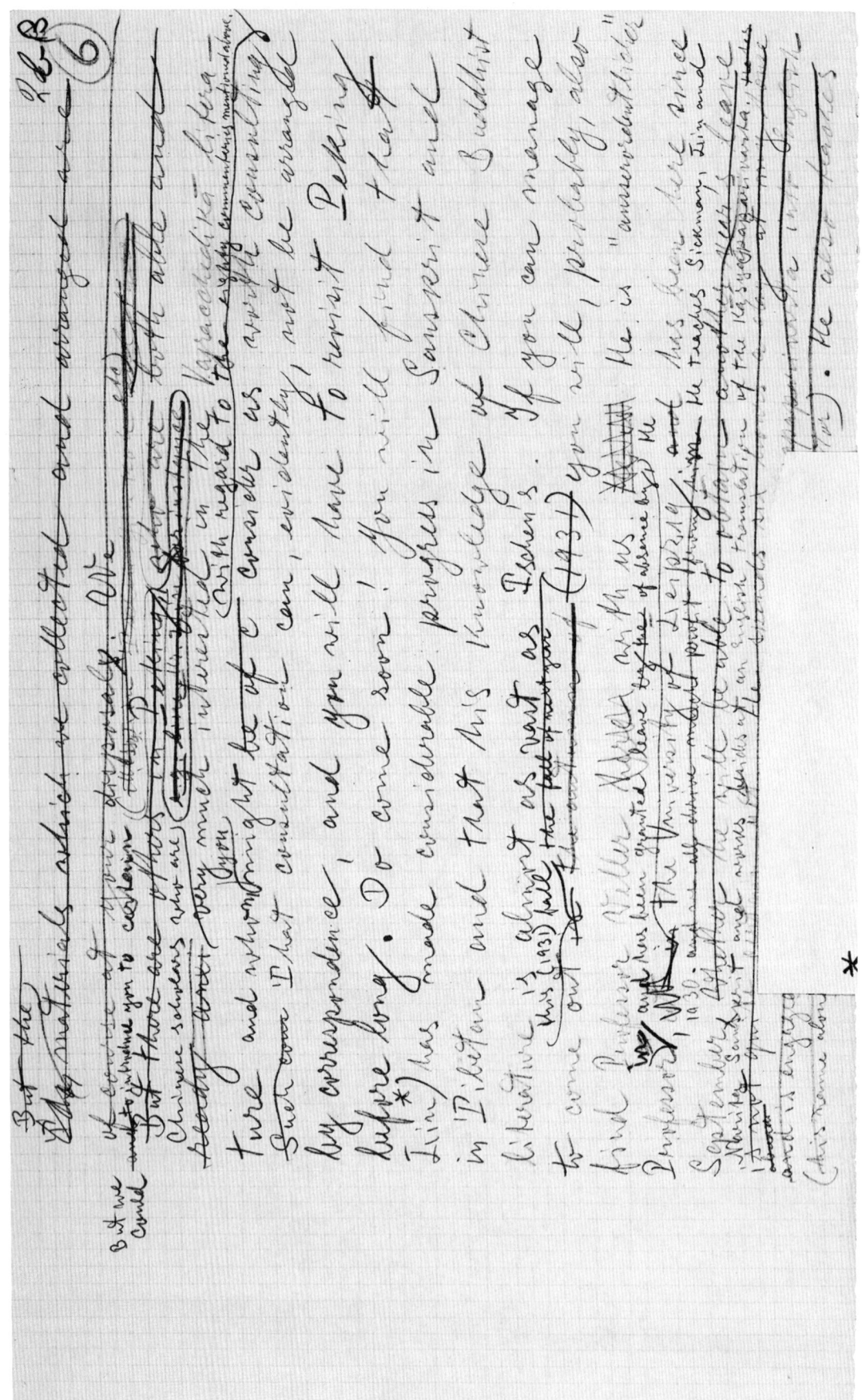

6) P.8

But the
~~But we could~~ ~~the source of~~ materials which we collected and arranged are ~~of your disposal~~. We ~~But~~ there are ~~lots~~ of ~~the who are~~ Chinese scholars who are ~~studying~~ {studying Tibetan in Peking} etc., already very much interested in the Vyākaraṇika literature and who might be of consider as ~~with~~ the eighty commentaries mentioned above with regard to some "That consideration can, evidently, not be arranged by correspondence, and you will have to revisit Peking before long. Do come soon! You will find that {Lin) has made considerable progress in Sanskrit and in Tibetan and that his knowledge of Chinese Buddhist literature is almost as vast as Ischen's. If you can manage to come out ~~to~~ this (1931) ~~half the~~ {the fall of} ~~autumn~~ (1931) you will, probably, also find Professor Zieler Müller with us. ~~He is~~ He is "unverheiratet". ~~My~~ and has been granted leave by the of absence by the University of Leipzig and has been since September, 1930, ~~and is~~ ~~all rim~~ most put through ~~him~~ his tragic sickness, Lin and Ischen, ~~could~~ ~~and~~ will be able to potatoes ~~amplify~~ very large Sanskrit text works in an orient translation of the 149 gagatanika notes and is enjoying Chinese akin ~~grad~~ imprints the 1937.
(An come ahead*) He ~~will~~ takes

*

* Jin seems to have ~~made~~ dis- covered important Chinese ~~documents~~ bearing on the Tokharian question, ~~which has interested~~ in which I have been interested for many years. But I have not yet been able to study the great amount of material, which he has collected, properly. ~~I am~~ I am now working at the edition of the Kāśyapa commentary. ~~Pankratoff is con- tinuing to~~ Pamcratoff teaches ~~to~~ Jin and Narita Tibetan, and continues his Dahurian studies ~~not~~ ~~yet. The Dahurian language~~ before ~~that dialect~~ had not been investigated and Pamcratoff hoped to publish the first Dahurian grammar, until he learned that ~~a~~ Mr. Poppe of Leningrad had just published ~~his ~~ ~~I have been trying to get~~ ~~a copy of the~~ ~~Poppe's work for months but have not yet succeeded~~ Verte

Vix one a few months ago. We have just received a copy of Poppe's work ~~to who~~ and we find that ~~by~~ Poppe describes ~~with~~ a Dahurian dialect which is not identical with Pankratoff's dialect. Pan- ~~kratoff~~ will, however, have to rewrite a great part of his grammar.

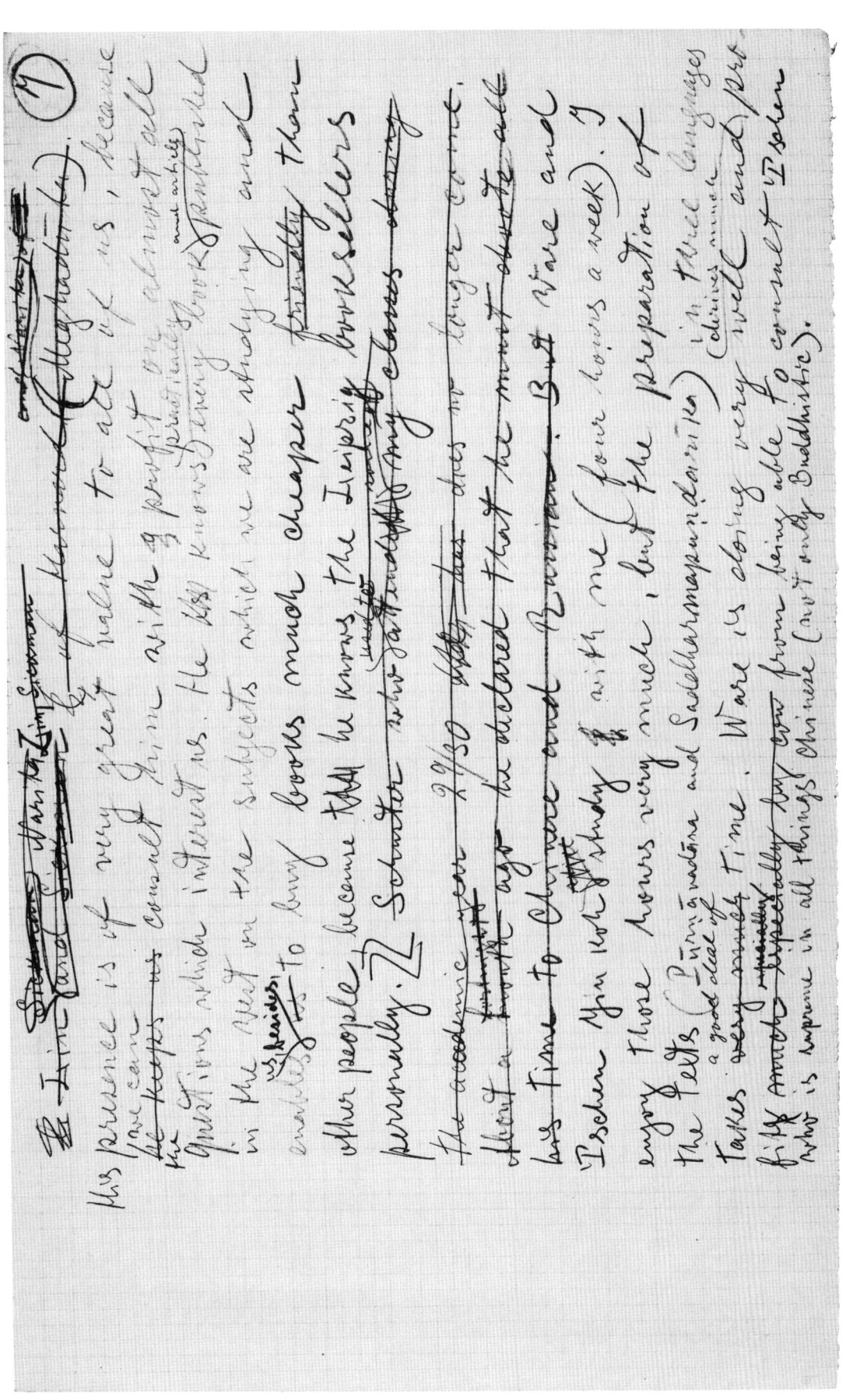

It is my aim to keep in touch with all the Western 8 and Eastern authorities on Buddhism. Müller is the officier de liaison with the West, Tschen (represents China, "in—in other—it is not other" and Mongolia,) Narita — Japan, and our Lamas — Tibet. These men also help us in building up a Sino-Indian Library which does not exist anywhere in China. Owing to the liberality of the H. Y. Institute we have succeeded in making a good start. We have acquired the Mongolian Kanjur. But it will take (immense work) years to complete the task. Many Tibetan (many works out of hand) works are out of print and obtaining editions like the Mongolian Kanjur is a proposition in itself, which requires months of bargaining and of diplomatic negotiations. It's a result of our labours to develop into a really competent Institute / Academy of Buddhist history, philosophy etc. many Chinese, Tibetan, Japanese and Western scholars. We receive letters and visits almost every day from representatives of various countries and almost everybody knows that what we are doing for Buddhist international public is due to the support which we receive from Harvard University.

*.

Leningrad ~~only~~ is said to possess a complete copy of the Mongolian Kanjur, the Paris copy is incomplete. The copy which Gillis and I bought some months ago with H.Y. money is complete. ~~The ge Most of the volumes are in the vaults of a neighb~~ It is now in my keeping, and I hope you will ~~let us keep~~ allow us to use it here for some time to come. I keep most of those very rare volumes in a brick vault.

9

Dear Friend,

You might consider other changes
[illegible] Some more changes might be necessary because the various readings
of the Tibetan texts which you consulted at Paris [illegible]
can't be found. If you like to change or to supplement
some of my Tibetan notes, please do so. Such changes
might be necessary because you frequently have consulted sources,
it unknown to me at Paris. I proposed I wrote you about
a year ago about those various lections and sent you a copy
of the Schilling Tibetan text with. The various readings
contained in the Kanjur. Did that letter Did you receive
that letter and the book containing the Tibetan text in
transliteration?

Please do make all changes in my edition (totts) (preface text and notes)
which you consider necessary desirable without consulting me beforehand.
I agree to all your of emendations manner and expect not to see them
before the publication of the volume.
I wrote the same thing to Clark but my letter was of course, intended
[illegible] it to Clark because I thought that you were under a
[illegible crossed-out text]

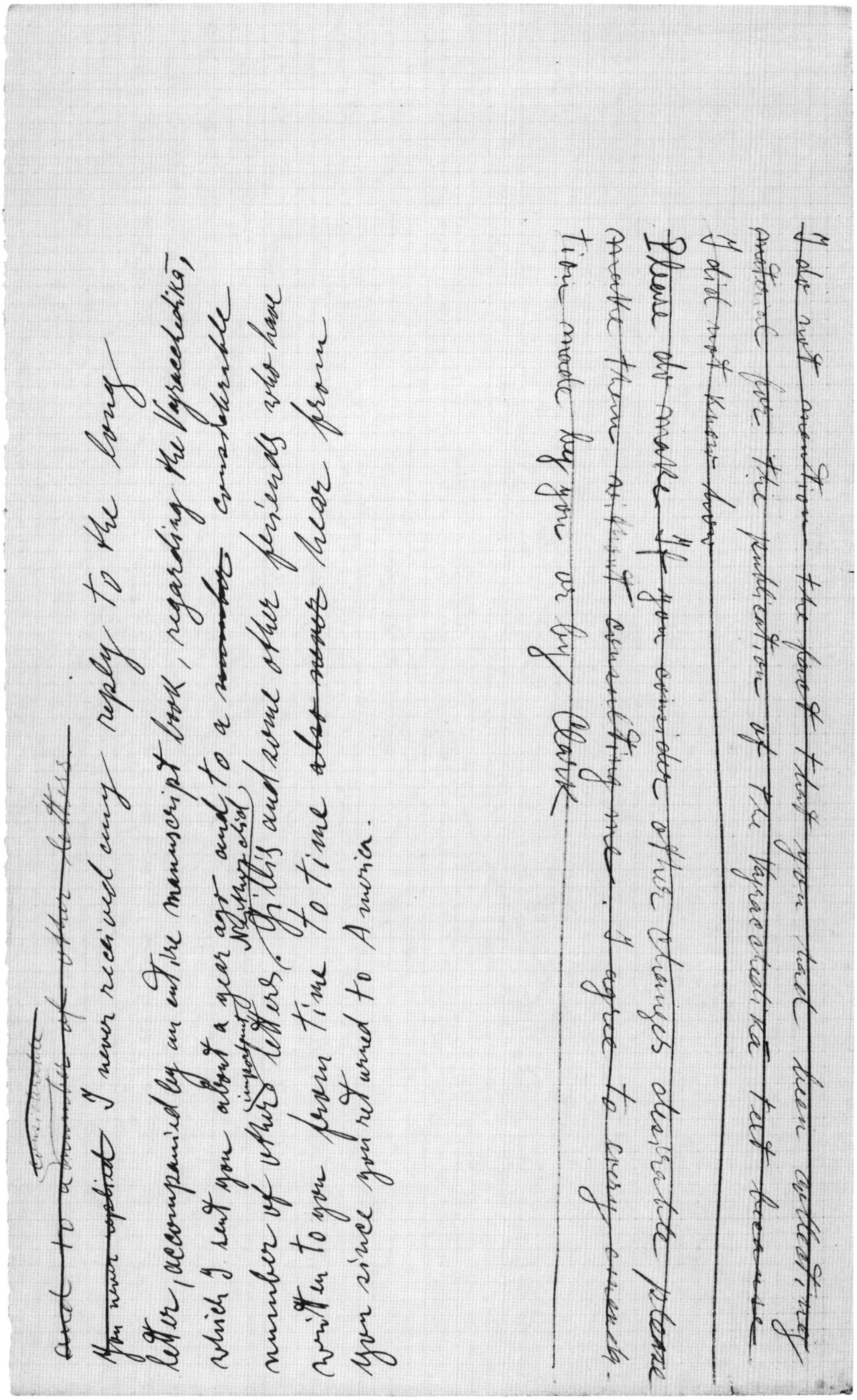

~~and to a ~~considerable~~ number of other letters.~~
~~You never replied~~ I never received any reply to the long letter, accompanied by an entire manuscript book, regarding the Vajracchedikā, which I sent you about a year ago ~~and~~ to a ~~number~~ considerable number of other important letters. Neither did Gillis and some other friends who have written to you from time to time ~~also never~~ hear from you since you returned to America.

~~I do not mention the fact that you had been collecting material for the publication of the Vajracchedikā text because I did not know how~~
~~Please do make If you consider other changes desirable please make them without consulting me. I agree to every emendation made by you or by Clark~~

As I already wrote to thank your silence does not make us forget. But one practically everything to you, and we ~~feel~~ all feel the deepest gratitude to our ~~rather~~ perfect friends, thy wife and I are very much ~~thank~~ thankful to you, and to Mrs. Woods for your charming Christmas card, and we hope that our New Year's greetings reached you in time.

Believe me yours sincerely
Staël-Holstein

My wife and I send you and Mrs. Woods our best New Year's greetings, and I remain yours sincerely

I shall regard it as a great favour if you will send me a deferred Telegram indicating in a few words that the fire of your indignation ~~matters~~ (Kopjagni) Boston, is no longer blazing as ~~fiercely~~ wildly ~~as~~ did on November 30 July 1930. I know how busy you are, and that I cannot look forward to a letter from you in the near future. But even an immediate reply by letter would ~~happen~~ ~~mean~~ ~~it~~ ~~suppose~~ ~~the~~ take ~~much~~ a magnitude to reach me, and would ~~keep me~~ ~~me~~ mean another month of anxiety. ~~I have~~ Please. By sending me a telegram you ~~may~~ might ~~clearly~~ ~~duly~~ (mention the period of anxiety which began ~~for~~ ~~us~~ when your letter ~~reached~~ ~~us~~ ~~by about a month.~~ My ~~the~~ cable address is: Staëlholstein (one word) Angusfoo Peking.

THE STAFFORD HOTEL
BALTIMORE

April 19, 1931

Dear Stael,

I had thought that I could write you sooner in reply to your last letter. But the longer I try to discover the right answer, the more I am at a loss. For whichever way I decide, much damage must be done.

Accordingly I am going to take more time until I can adjust my plans and see more clearly what I wish to do. I will write you again.

Elizabeth joins me in best wishes to all three of you. We enjoyed the picture which you sent us at Christmas and thank you heartily for it.

Sincerely yours

James H. Woods

Former Austrian Legation Peking, November 18th 1931.

Dear Woods,

The Roman Catholic monks of the Pei T'ang monastery (Roman Catholic Peking) possess a printing press which has been enlarged and perfected during the last few months. They now are able to print Chinese texts and excellent Phags-pa font and are also able to print transcribed Tibetan as well as Sanskrit texts with all the diacritical marks in a most creditable way. Please (Comp. the two enclosed sample pages) do allow us to print the following books which are quite ready at the Pei T'ang: [NEW paragraph!]

A Tibetan-Sanskrit index to the Kāçyapaparivarta, compiled by Professor Vallée (Mr. Lin is making the Chinese index in collaboration with Professor Vallée). It will consist of three parts:

a) Sanskrit
b) Tibetan
c) Sanskrit f, and Chinese f.

The Tibetan part is the most important. I agree with Professor Vallée in thinking that the three parts should be issued as separate books.

Samuzi.t
Chagz.bcod
Kaçyapaparivarta

2.

The Tibetan part is the most important one because for the Chinese Buddhist terms are to

The Tibetan part is of the greatest importance for the study of the Tibetan Buddhist literature, because it enables us to ascertain the Sanskrit equivalents of the many Tibetan terms which we did not understand so far sufficiently comprehensive on account of the lack of Tibetan-Sanskrit glossaries. I am sure you agree with me in holding that *practically* every phrase of the Tibetan Buddhist writings has to be retranslated (at least mentally) into Sanskrit in order to be properly understood by Western students. Professor Vallée Poussin's Tibetan index has been ready for months, that and I intended sending it to America for your approval (unavailable at the University) I send you merely the two enclosed pages became we cannot entrust manuscripts which was the single copy for many months to the post office. Canby be trusted. if it is too bulky the post office canby be trusted to compile to the post office at the present moment.

* The Sanskrit and Chinese indices are not quite ready yet. Each one of the three indices will form a separate volume. That will not be much more convenient than for binding them all at once for comparative studies, than having them all in one volume. The Sanskrit and Chinese indices are not quite ready yet.

The Manchu and Mongol indices to the 360 Chu To P'u Sa Shêng Hsiang (as my data and a vocabulary are T'ibetan) have been printed about three years ago, which were sent to America by post got lost even in 1929, at a time when no political complications existed. All manuscripts written in two languages whatsoever (except those are especially liable to disappear because the copyists that is they represent but matter (political manuscripts may have been taken a T'ibetan manuscript book which I sent to the Soviets and Chinese in spite of my repeated enquiries, once or oftener. All manuscripts written in more or less unknown languages are liable to disappear because the copyists regard them as coded political or military messages. Manuscripts but they have also been made copies of slips that in the form of slips exist in the form of slips but have not yet been copied.

Another work which we want to print at the Pei P'ing (with your kind permission) Daguriun (Nonni dialect) grammar by Poncrattoff. It is quite ready for print

4

and I enclose the typewritten introduction to it as a part of type written beginning of it for your approval. [crossed out] Another work of ours which is quite ready on slips is a complete (catalogue of the works the Contents [crossed out] (our index) (these things) the supplement to the Chinese Pri-piṭaka (Mi Dzang) is also ready on slips. It consists of two parts — the first one catalogue is arranged alphabetically and the second arranged alphabetically with an index to it (of two parts of slips. It enables the reader to find it on the first part the titles and authors (titles and authors). We must print it soon, because Messrs. Peng and his son have worked at it for many months. a very long time and has cost If you will allow us to print it at the Pei Tang, please do not doubt too much delay we shall be very grateful. If we delay the publication too long

5

We must try our utmost. We must hurry with this publica-
tion, because to forgets because that the possibility of its meeting with the fate of our Kanjur index is by no means excluded. We had finished a considerable part of the latter, when we learned that the Otani University of Kyoto magnificent copy of the Kanjur had prepared an Ōtani Chinese Kanjur index (two parts have been published in 1930 and 1931, the third one will follow soon). What has happened to the Buddhist Pantheon photographs of which certain not some notes and indices prepared by Baking brought to Cambridge in 1928. According to the last I heard about them was that they would be ready in the fall of 1930. I wrote to Professor Clark a long letter to Professor Clark, but never received a reply. That letter was dated the fall of most probably which I sent to Cambridge but has remained unanswered to this day.

I hope that the edition will not be delayed much longer because otherwise the Chinese might edit the materials themselves and ~~the scripts~~ and all our ~~attempt~~ in which case labour would be lost.*

* I spent many months first in obtaining the permission to photograph the Palace Buddhas etc. (Comp. Journal Asiatique, Janvier-Mars 1928, page 140) from the higher authorities, then in photographing them in the presence of extremely hostile gendarmes, and later in compiling indices as well as some notes. The Palace Committee asked me some time ago to sell them the plates, but I refused, and the plates are still here (from Austrian Legation). The Committee possesses the originals, and may photograph them again for publication at any moment.

I spent many months first in obtaining the permission
to photograph the Palace Buddhas etc (Comp Journal Asiatique
Janvier Mars 1928, page 140) ~~from~~ from the higher authorities
(and later ~~many months~~ in compiling indices as well as some notes)
in the presence of extremely hostile gendarmes
The Palace Comm.tt. asked me some time to sell them the plates but
I refused. The plates are still here (Austrian Legation) but
photograph them again for publication at any moment

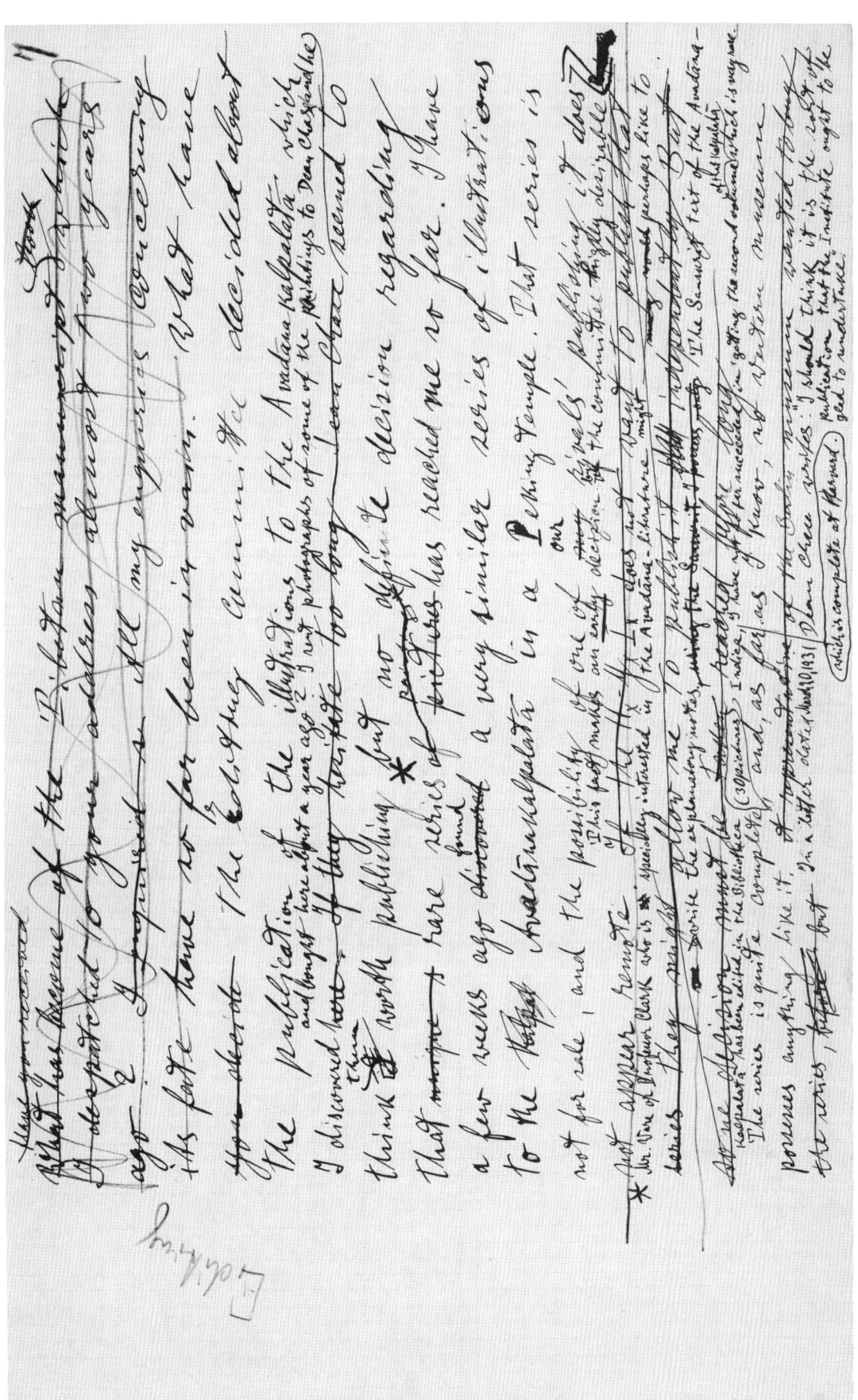

I also think that your edition of the Vajracchedikā text should appear without any further delay, because (up to the words Tadyathā dāsoṭsyat in our chapter 10) (one Skt one Tib. and six (Chinese Texts)) only one tenth part only of the polyglot Vajracchedikā edition has so far appeared in 大日本 (大日本續藏經) The rather obscure Japanese monthly "Mahāyāna" (大乘) 雑誌, 雜誌, the edition has evidently been compiled which is published a periodical devoted to religious propaganda rather than to philological research. I have reason to believe (the editor of) that polyglot Vajracchedikā edition has been largely influenced (the printed Skt. text of which is) by my Kāśyapa edition, the plan of which he simply adopts, that is to follow (though) for the various lections which he entirely neglects). He has, however, entirely neglected the various readings, and does not seem to know that I printed in addition to the Sanscrit textus ornatior (published by Müller) a Sanscrit textus simplicior (discovered by Stein and edited by Pargiter) exists. Neither only the Schilling's Tibetan text I have reason to think that the Japanese and Kanshur Tibetan texts referred to. The Japanese editor has evidently given up his edition, because the last installments of the Vajracchedikā have appeared in The "Mahāyāna" since May 1930 (the last number of the Mahāyāna which I have seen appeared 17 September 1931) and I

It is very hot here in summer, (the only time when I am free to write) and you can imagine how terribly disappointed I was when I heard that your article (on the history of the Dalai Lamas and Pan Chen Lamas) which I wrote in July 1931 would probably not appear before December 1932 in an American journal (the editor book (Eastern Art). The article reached the editor through no fault of his or mine too late for this year's publication. In order not to lose face among other editors that published of mine though the Chinese I must have another anything else. I suspect this is to you in order to show how difficult it is July the July edition of the Kāśyapa commentary which is being edited by the Peking Metropolitan Library was partly printed before I left for America and which is being paid for by the Peking Metropolitan Library and Peking University. It is not quite ready yet. More than a hundred pages of that very difficult text (Tibetan and Chinese only) must still be turned have a number of articles

The two enclosed pages that have been printed of the Pei Lang and show the type

In addition to the publications mentioned above we have a number of works in preparation (but not ready for print.) Mr. Lin besides studying Sanskrit, Tibetan and Indian religious history under Professor Keller, Mr. Parkeroff and myself has made a complete translation of the Jarbhasutras (Nanjio column 13) from Chinese into English. Both works exist in Tibetan translations as well, English and Russian before publishing the translations the Tibetan versions must be analyzed carefully, prepared a complete concordance of the Tibetan and Chinese versions so far. The Sanskrit texts are lost. The most voluminous work which we have produced is Mr. Lin's Treatise on the

He has collected a great amount of Chinese material on that question.

Tokharians ('Pa Hu'e). He has succeeded in finding a good deal of Chinese material which had escaped the attention of the Westerners who have written on the subject. But numerous that [word] and detailed question being incompetent to weigh the evidence collected by Mr. Lin properly, I have decided to count for Pelliot, who is expected here shortly, apparently what he thinks of Mr. Lin's work, before recommending it for publication.

But of all that is "Zukunftsmusik." What we stand in most urgent need of is your consent to publish 1) The indices to the Kāśyapaparivarta 2) the Daguria n grammar and 3) the index to the Hsi' Tsang. three The indices to the Kāśyapaparivarta of which I enclose two sample pages will cost about three thousand dollars (about two hundred airland eight hundred pages, five hundred copies, paper like sample). The Dagurian grammar (about two hundred three hundred and fifty pages, five hundred copies, size and paper like sample pages of the indices) will cost about one thousand and four hundred two hundred dollars that

13

Pek dyy The two parts of the index to the Hūi Dzong ~though partts ~~tastly exist on slips only~~ will probably not occupy more than three hundred pages of the same size and cost about one thousand two hundred dollars. Yet ~~I do not~~ I suggest the following title for the first volume:—

A Tibetan Index to the ~~Kaçgapapariñaarta~~ Kāçyapaparivarta
~~compiled~~
of the Sino-Indian Library of Peking
by Dr. Friedrich ~~Weller~~
Dr. Friedrich Weller
and ~~published under~~ the
Patronage of the Harvard-Yenching Institute
of
Cambridge, Massachusetts

14

to that second introduct I do not think it attractable
Today. If it must be, The books could be published
as numbers 1, 2 and 3 of an Sino Indian series.
Original
But I think that looks too pompous rather
superfluous. Why not give Why should we not
content ourselves with titles like the following:

A Tibetan Index to the Kagyapapariyesta
at the Sino-Indian Library of Peking

by

Dr. Friedrich Weller

Compiled and published under the
Patronage of the Harvard-Yenching Institute
of Cambridge Mass.
by the Sino Indian Library of Peking

Peking 1937.

Sall ot.

By But I have But I can But I can But we can afford [15]
to wait until your directions as to the title pages arrive
by ~~letter~~ by mail, if only you allow us to ~~begin~~ ~~printing~~ ~~at least~~
the Tibetan index, ~~and~~ (and the Man-tsang index)
the Dagurian grammar at once
by cable. We have been telling everybody about our
forthcoming publications, and more than two years
almost 2½ years have passed since the inauguration
(and temporary adjournment)
of our Sino-Indian Library. Without any visible results.
That state of things is ~~very~~ rather humiliating for
my assistants and for myself. I quite understand
that you insist ~~very~~ on seeing works like the history of
the Tokharians before having them published by your authority +
indies   ~~ouptique~~ ~~done~~   and at your expense,
but the three ~~publications~~ Tibetan index and the Dagurian
grammar contain ~~only~~ mostly material in oriental languages
                                               and very little
English text. As to the latter, ~~opposite~~ Mr. Roger Greene promised
to look it through himself or ~~delegate~~ to some other competent
persons to look it through before the final publication of the books.

In suggesting that some of our publications should be issued without having first been submitted to you in their entirety we are merely ask for a privilege which Professor Hung etc. already posses. They have a few months ago published "Harvard-Yenching" indices which, as far as I know, were never sent to Cambridge Mass. for approval. Please do not delay your answer too long, and remember that however much you may think necessary, with all respect due to the learned members

* Preparing two copies of all our manuscripts (one for Cambridge Mass. and one for Peking) is evidently not impossible, but it would take weeks to reproduce all the Chinese characters and diacritical marks correctly, and the work would have to be done by the authors themselves.

Unless we ~~can~~ (if you do not allow ~~here~~ us) to print ~~doters you enable~~ something, we shall pass for sluggards among our confrères in America, Europe and Asia, and I do not think we deserve such a reputation. All my assistants spend six hours ~~by~~ (9-12 and 2-5) daily ~~in~~ ~~tim~~ working or teaching in our Sino-Indian Library (former Austrian Legation), and our only vacations are the Chinese New Year (ten days) and the rainy season (one month). ~~~~ ~~Owing to your kind recommendation~~ Your kind recommendation and the liberality of the Trustees have enabled me to realize ~~~~ what seemed but a dream ~~three~~ four years ago, and I hope that our publications will not disappoint our generous friends when they appear in print.

Believe me yours sincerely and gratefully

Former Austrian Legation,
Peking, November, 18th, 1931.

Dear Woods,

The French monks of the Pei T'ang monastery (Roman Catholic), Peking, possess a printing press which has been enlarged and perfected during the last few months. They have an excellent Chinese font and are also able to print transcribed Sanskrit as well as Tibetan, Mongolian etc. Texts with all the diacritical marks in a most creditable way (Comp. the two enclosed sample pages). Please do allow us to print the following books at the Pei T'ang:

An index to the Kaçyapaparivarta compiled by Professor Weller (Mr. Lin is making the Chinese index in collaboration with Professor Weller). It will consist of three parts: a) Tibetan, b) Sanskrit, c) and Chinese. The Tibetan part is of the greatest importance for the study of the Tibetan Buddhist literature, because it enables us to ascertain the Sanskrit equivalents of many Tibetan Terms which we did not understand so far on account of the lack of sufficiently comprehensive Tibetan-Sanskrit glossaries. I am sure you agree with me in holding that practically every phrase of the Tibetan Buddhist writings has to be retranslated (at least mentally) into Sanskrit in order to be properly understood by Western students.

Professor Weller's Tibetan index[*] has been ready for months, and I intended sending it to America for your approval. I send you merely the two enclosed pages printed at the Pei T'ang, because we cannot entrust manuscripts which have taken many months to compile to the Post office at the present moment. The Manchu and

[*] Each one of the three indices will form a separate volume. That will be much more convenient for comparative studies, than having them all in one volume. The Sanskrit and Chinese indices are not quite ready yet.

- 2 -

Mongol indices to the Chu Fo P'u Sa Shêng Hsiang Tsan as well as a very rare Tibetan block print which were sent to America by post got lost even in 1929, at a time when no political complications existed. The same fate may have overtaken a Tibetan manuscript book which I sent to your address about two years ago and the receipt of which, in spite of my repeated enquiries, you never acknowledged. All manuscripts written in more or less unknown languages are liable to disappear because the censors regard them as coded political or military messages.

Another work which we should like to print at the Pei T'ang with your kind permission is the Dagurian (Nonni dialect) Grammar by Prakratoff. It is quite ready, and I enclose the type written beginning of it for your approval.

Our index to the supplement to the Chinese Tripiṭaka (Hsü Tsang) is ready on slips. It consists of two parts (titles and authors), and Messrs. Teng and Ku have worked at it for many months. If you will allow us soon to print it at the Pei T'ang, we shall be very grateful. We must hurry with this publication, because the possibility of its meeting with the fate of our Kanjur index is by no means excluded. We had finished a considerable part of the latter, when we learned that the Otani Daigaku Library of Kyoto had prepared an analytical index of the Kanjur (two parts have been published in 1930 and 1931, the third and last one will follow soon).

What has happened to the Buddhist pantheons photographs of which with some notes and indices prepared at Peking I took to Cambridge in 1928 ? The last I heard about them was that Professor Clark's edition of the materials would be ready in the fall of 1930. I hope that the edition will not be delayed much

- 3 -

longer because otherwise the Chinese might edit the materials themselves in which case all our labour would be lost.[1]

What have the Editing Committee decided about the publication of the illustrations to the Avadānakalpalatā which I discovered and bought here about a year ago ? I sent photographs of some of the paintings to Dean Chase and he seemed to think them worth publishing but no definite decision regarding that rare series[2] has reached me so far. I have a few weeks ago found a very

[1] I spent many months first in obtaining the permission to photograph the Palace Buddhas etc. (Comp. Journal Asiatique, Janvier - Mars 1928, page 140) from the higher authorities, then in photographing them in the presence of extremely hostile gendarmes, and later in compiling indices as well as some notes. The Palace Committee asked me some time ago to sell them the plates, but I refused, and the plates are still here (former Austrian Legation). The Committee, however, possess the originals, and may photograph them again for publication at any moment.

[2] Mr. Ware or Professor Clark who is specially interested in the Avadāna-literature might perhaps like to write the explanatory notes. The Sanskrit text of the Avadānakalpalatā has been edited in the Bibliothica Indica, which is complete at Harvard. I have not so far succeeded in getting the second volume of that kalpalatā which is very rare. The series is quite complete (30 pictures) and, as far as I know, no Western museum possess anything like it. In a letter dated March 20, 1931 Dean Chase writes: " I should think it is the sort of publication that the Institute ought to be glad to undertake".

- 4 -

similar series of illustrations to the Avadānakalpalatā in a Peking temple. That series is not for sale, and the possibility of one of our rivals' publishing it does not appear remote. This fact makes an early decision by the committee highly desirable.

One tenth part (up to the words Tathāgato draṣṭavyaḥ in our chapter 10) only of the polyglot (one Skt. one Tib. and six Chinese texts) Vajracchedikā edition has so far appeared in the rather obscure Japanese monthly "Mahāyāna" (大乘), a periodical devoted to religious propaganda rather than to philological research. I have reason to believe that the editor of that polyglot Vajracchedikā edition of which I first heard early in 1931 has been largely influenced by my Kāçyapa edition (the first of its kind), the general plan of which he adopts. He has, however, entirely neglected the various readings, and does not seem to know that in addition to the Sanskrit textus ornatior (published by Müller) a Sanskrit textus simplicior (discovered by Stein, and edited by Pargiter) exists. Neither are the Schilling and Kumbum Tibetan texts referred to. The Japanese editor has, evidently given up his edition, because no instalments of the Vajracchedikā have appeared in the "Mahāyāna" since May 1930 (the last number of the Mahāyāna monthly, which I have seen, appeared in September 1931), and I think that the edition has been stopped by the Japanese, because they heard that a more elaborate edition than theirs was being prepared at Peking. The small part which has appeared in Japan may be

* I am very anxious to know about the reasons owing to which the Editing Committee hesitate to publish our manuscript which I sent them over a year ago. Please do give me a detailed account of the mistakes which you must have found in our Vajracchedikā, so that we might improve our ways in the future. I have done everything I could in order to avoid mistakes: I revised all the texts and notes several times with the help of Pansratoff and Tsin, and before sending the manuscript to America I submitted it to Professor Weller who arrived here from Leipzig just in September 1930, in time to pass judgment on our work. We went through the whole of it very carefully, and Weller agreed with practically every line of our manuscript. I did not know before 1931 that the "Mahāyāna" monthly existed.

- 5 -

safely ignored by any future editor, but the latter, whoever he may be.* should hurry up. The Japanese may at any moment resume the publication of the text. It is very hot here in Summers, and you can imagine how terribly disappointed I was when I heard that a rather elaborate article (on the history of the Dalai and Pan Chen Lamas) which I wrote in July 1931 would probably not appear before December 1932 in an American year book (Eastern Art). The article reached the editor the year book, too late for this year's publication.

In order not to lose face among the Chinese I must see another publication of mine through the press before taking up anything else. My edition of the Kāçyapa commentary which was partly printed before I left for America and which is being paid for by the Peking Metropolitan Library and Tsinghua University, is not quite ready yet. More than a hundred pages of that very difficult text (Tibetan and Chinese only) must still be revised.

*From your letter dated November 30th 1930 I concluded that you would publish our Vajracchedikā text. In that letter you write: "I consented (in October 1929) to let you and your men do it (i. e. the Vajacchedikā text edition) at your request" and suggest that a passage in my introduction should be changed. I sent you the desired emendation forthwith in a letter dated January, 1931 and you acknowledge the receipt of it in your letter dated April 19th 1931. You do not, however, say in that last letter when and where you will print our Vajracchedikā text. A long letter which I wrote to Professor Clark on the subject in 1930 as far as I know has never been answered.

In
The addition to the publications mentioned above we have a number of works in preparation which are not yet ready for print. Mr. Lin besides studying Sanskrit Tibetan and Indian religious history under Professor Weller, Mr. Pankratoff and myself has translated the two Garbhasūtras (Nanjio column 13) from Chinese into English. Both works exist in Tibetan translations as well, and before publishing the English translations the Tibetan versions must be carefully analysed. I have merely prepared a complete concordance of the Tibetan and Chinese versions so far. The Sanskrit texts are lost. The most voluminous work which we have produced is Mr. Lin's treatise on the Tokharians (Ta Hsia). He has succeeded in finding a good deal of Chinese material which had escaped the attention of the numerous Westerners who have written on that much debated question. But being incompetent to weigh the evidence collected by Mr. Lin properly, I have decided to ask Pelliot, who is expected here shortly, what he thinks of Mr. Lin's work, before recommending it for publication.

But all that is "Zukunftsmusik". What we stand in most urgent need of is your consent to publish 1) the indices to the Kāçyapaparivarta 2) the Dagurian Grammar and 3) the index to the Hsü Tsang. The three indices to the Kāçyapaparivarta of which I enclose two sample pages will cost about three thousand two hundred dollars Mex. (about eight hundred pages, five hundred copies, size and paper like sample). The Dagurian Grammar (about three hundred and fifty pages, five hundred copies, size and paper like the sample pages of the indices) will cost about one thousand and four hundred dollars Mex. The two parts of the index to the Hsü Tsang will probably not occupy more than three hundred pages of the same size and cost about one thousand

- 7 -

two hundred dollars Mex.   If it must be, the books could be
published as numbers 1, 2 and 3 of an Oriental series. But
I think that rather superfluous.   Why should we not content
ourselves with titles like the following ?

A Tibetan Index to the Kāçyapaparivarta

by

Dr. Friedrich Weller

compiled and published under the

Patronage of the Harvard-Yenching Institute

of Cambridge Mass.

But we can afford to wait until your directions as to the title
pages arrive by mail, if only you allow us to begin printing
the Tibetan index, the Dagurian Grammar and the Hsü Tsang index
by cable. We have been telling everybody about our forthcoming
publications, and almost 2½ years have passed since the inauguration
of our Sino-Indian enterprise without any visible results. That
state of things is rather humiliating for my assistants and for
myself.   I quite understand that you insist on seeing works
like the history of the Tokharians before having them published by
your authority and at your expense, but the indices mentioned
above and the Dagurian Grammar contain mostly material in
oriental languages and very little English text.   As to the
latter Mr. Roger Greene promised to look it through himself
or appoint some other competent persons to look it through
before the final publication of the books. In suggesting that
some of our publications should be issued without having first

- 8 -

been submitted to you in their entirety ✱ we merely ask for a privilege which Professor Hung etc. already possess. They have a few months ago published "Harvard - Yenching" indices which, as far as I know, were never sent to Cambridge Mass. for approval. Please do not delay your answer longer than is absolutely necessary. If you do not soon allow us to print something, we shall pass for sluggards among our Confrères in America, Europe and Asia, and I do not think we deserve such a reputation. All my assistants spend six hours (9 - 12 and 2 - 5) daily at the (Former Austrian Legation), and our only considerable vacations are the Chinese New Year (ten days) and the rainy season (one month).

✱ Preparing two clean copies of all our manuscripts (one for Cambridge Mass. and one for Peking) is evidently not impossible, but it would take weeks and weeks to reproduce all the thousands of Chinese characters and diacritical marks correctly, and the work would have to be done by the authors themselves.

Mr. Bodde has arrived and studies Sanscrit with Professor Weller

Dear Woods
On account of the Magdalenian crisis great
The Peking climate is, in spite of all, great moment
reigns everywhere in China, but if we meet Professor
is wonderfully quiet and we can henceforth [undisturbed] devote our [attention] to the
Sino-Indian study of Sino-Indian problems. It is very
privilege, which is largely due to your [kind] kind offices, and
[...] and you [...] my last Christmas greetings.

If the Sino-European vocabulary of my son did amount to more than
it actually does, he would, I am sure, add his congratulations to mine.
I think he should found a [...] with R. J. Char's children and
perhaps some others, who [...] are as much obliged to you as
he is. [...] That not would surely ask you to accept the
position of their Patron Saint.

Believe me yours sincerely and gratefully
A. v. Staël-Holstein.

P.S. A few days ago I sent you a very long letter and enclosed [...] parts
of [...] long letter with our proposed publications. Has it arrived?

HARVARD-YENCHING INSTITUTE

29 Follen Street,
17 BOYLSTON HALL
CAMBRIDGE, MASSACHUSETTS

December 28, 1931

Dear De Stael:

Thank you for your Christmas card: we were both glad to hear from you. I am much interested in the report of your work, and shall take up the various items with Blake as soon as possible. I certainly see no objection to your publishing them all, and hope to be able to cable you to that effect in a few days.

I am sorry to have let so long a time go by without writing to you. I have been waiting, hoping to see clearly what was best to do about the publication of your Vajracchedikā text. I think that now, at any rate, I can tell you how I feel about it, and that between us we can find some sort of a solution.

Here are the facts: You knew from the start that I was working on the texts, and brought me a number of Chinese versions, as you remember. You knew too that I was planning to make later a comparison and interpretation of the commentaries of Vasubandhu and Asaṅga. In Peking I asked your men to paste some of the variants on paper for me, and they became interested in the thing and wanted to take it over. I consented, as you say, telling you that I did not want to give up the plan of doing the commentaries myself. But it certainly did not occur to me that in allowing you to complete the collation of the texts, my own work on them was to be quite overlooked and thrown away, and that I should have nothing to do with writing the preface, which I had been planning. I think that my readings should be incorporated in the book, and some reference made in the preface to the fact that the plan of making such a collation, though carried out by your men, was originally mine. How this can best be managed, I do not know. Shall I send you back your manuscript with my readings?

Your remarks on the commentaries seem to me misleading. Surely, the fact that there are many commentaries is beside the point - you knew it was Asaṅga and Vasubandhu, in whom I was interested. Nor is a bare translation of this or that commentary of importance, but rather the interpretation and comparison of several: so that to publish two separate commentaries of Asaṅga would have been futile. As you know, I have definitely planned for years to work on the texts and on these commentaries after I have given up some of my duties at Harvard, and while the plan has lost much of its interest because of all these misunderstandings, I am not yet ready to give it up. But it must be for the future, and any reference in your preface to the translation of commentaries or

— 489 —

#2

text is premature.

     I am sorry this matter should have hung fire for so long a time. It seemed impossible to write about it, partly because I was confused about what it was best to do - it was very startling, to say the least, to find that you had so completely overlooked the plans I had often discussed with you - and partly because I was deeply hurt. I have counted on your friendship for a great many years, and still do, in spite of all this.

Later:
2/

     We approved the three projects which you described to me,- the Dagutian Grammar, the Index to the Hsü Tsang, and the indices to the Kaçyaparivarta on condition that one-half of the expense be met out of the appropriation for the Sino-Indian Institute for either this year or next.

     I will write suggestions as soon as Blake returns.

     With all good wishes of the season to you and all your family,

                          Yours very sincerely,

                              James H. Woods

Professor de Stael-Holstein,
    ex-Austrian Legation,
        Peiping, China.

HARVARD-YENCHING INSTITUTE

17 BOYLSTON HALL
CAMBRIDGE, MASSACHUSETTS

January 18, 1932

Dear de Stael,-

I forwarded you a cable on December 28th:

"Conditionally approved. Await letter",

and I wrote you on the same day.

I now wish to add a statement of the opinion of the Publication Committee with reference to the indices to the Kāçyapa Parivarta, the Dagurian Grammar, and the Index to the Hsü Tsang. The committee felt that, because of the financial depression throughout the world and here also, it ought to ask you to find one-half of the sums necessary for these publications out of this year's appropriation for the Sino-Indian Institute or out of the appropriation for some following year. The condition of the exchange makes this less onerous for you.

The committee also thought that there should be a format for the series to conform to your edition of the Kāçyapa Parivarta. The title suggested for the series would be the "Harvard-Sino-Indian Series or the Sino-Indian Series of the Harvard-Yenching Institute. With reference to the indices of the Kāçyapa Parivarta, could a smaller type and smaller numbers be used, and could the space between the lines be reduced so that there will be more words on the page? This may not be so simple for the fonts of the Pei T'ang, but the size of the page could remain the same as that of your edition of the Kāçyapa Parivarta.

With regard to the title of Dr. Weller's index, would it not be more logical to say "Index to the Tibetan Translation of the Kāçyapa Parivarta, by Dr. Friedrich Weller, Volume -- of the Harvard-Sino-Indian Series, published by the Harvard-Yenching Institute"?

There is no reason why you should delay printing the index to the Hsü Tsang. You might send us the title page for approval. This will prevent much confusion and inconsistency in the different series.

We were very glad at last to have definite suggestions about printing, and we have answered as soon as we could get the various expressions of opinion which are necessary from the Financial and Educational Committees.

Professor de Stael-Holstein, #2

    We have also approved a project by T. L. Yuan, and we should be very glad if you could speak to him of this and tell him how glad we are we can co-operate with him and with the National Library.

                      Sincerely yours,

                        James H. Woods

Professor A. de Stael-Holstein,
    Sino-Indian Institute,
        ex-Austrian Legation,
            Peiping, China.

Shall be delighted to hear from you and hope to meet soon again

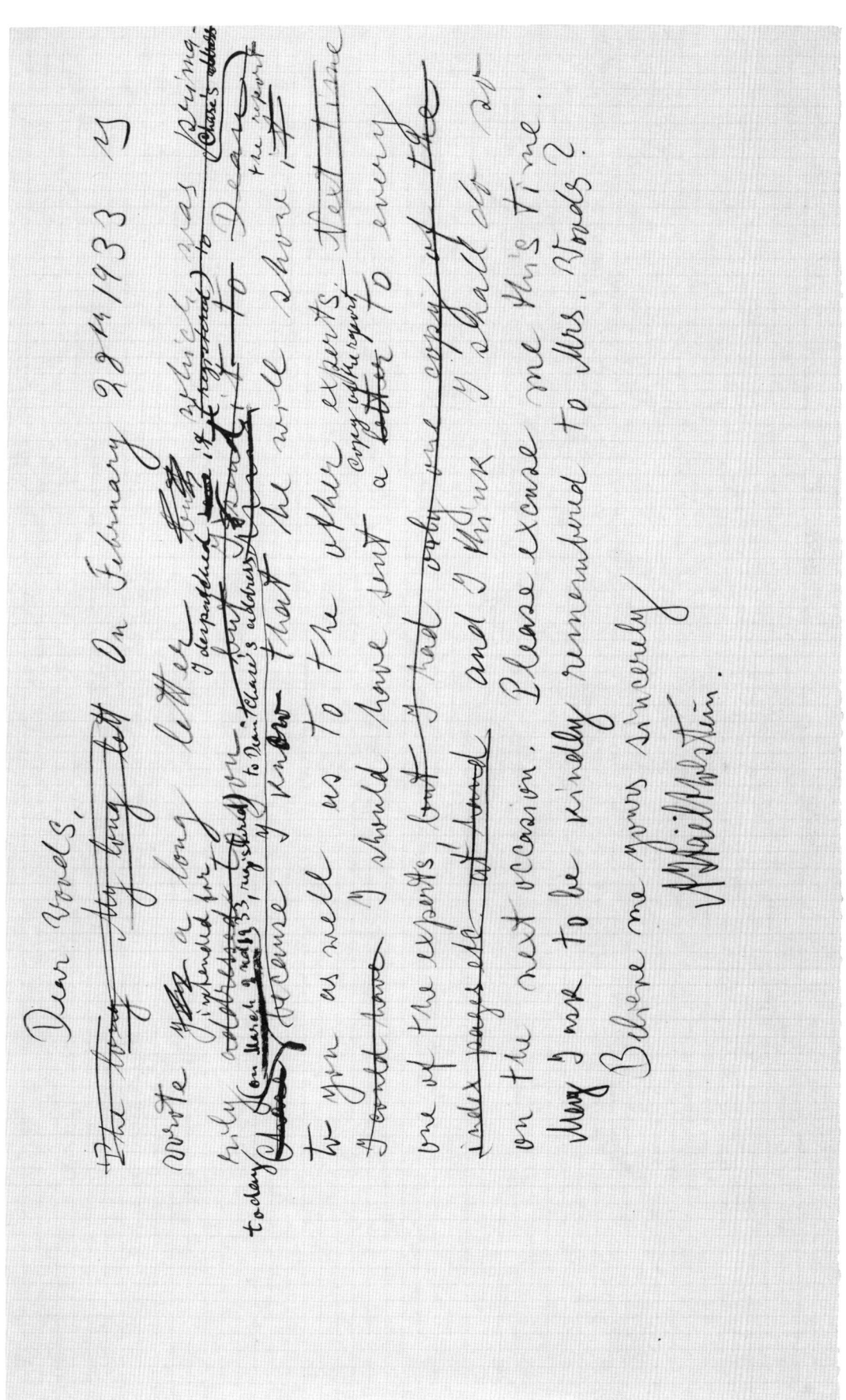

Peking, 1st February 27th 1934.

Dear Mrs. Woods,

We were so glad to get your charming Christmas card, and we thank you as well as Professor Woods very much for your good wishes. May the new year bring you nothing but happiness!

Today Peking has obtained — We are still in mid-winter and the whole of Peking is white with snow, but in less than a month's time we shall certainly have summer weather. There is hardly any Real Spring weather in North China. Real Spring is practically unknown in North China. Believe me, yours most sincerely Olga Stael.

HALEKULANI
AND BUNGALOWS ON THE BEACH AT WAIKIKI
HONOLULU, HAWAII

Dec. 4 1934

Dear de Staël,

Few things could be more welcome to me than your message by the cable, and at the same time, word from Ware of your remembrance of my birthday in lapidary form — I cherish them both because they reveal to me that our friendship is deep and strong enough to survive the shocks to which circumstances expose it. I was distressed because my plan of work for these last years and the accumulations of texts and the labor of months was suddenly snatched from me — I knew of course how much better you and your staff could do the work than any individual and especially such as sciolist as I am — But now I am making other plans and all the painful surprise has passed away — I should be very unhappy without your friendship — And I hope now that our friendship has been tested by fire that it will be closer and more enduring than ever — And the delight of feeling that we are working together would be very keen —

Tomorrow we take the boat for Japan — I have been attempting to collect instances from Buddhist books of the causes and the cure for ~~dis~~ disintegration of consciousness — The problem is almost invariably just the opposite, the unification of consciousness by the unification of the object of perception — Perhaps you have a string of passages up your sleeve that will illumine my path for me —

HALEKULANI
AND BUNGALOWS
ON THE BEACH AT WAIKIKI

HONOLULU, HAWAII

Existence here, for the past month, has been most pacific and invigorating, few problems, many glimpses into the new situations of international politics —

I shall miss the chance of taking you by the hand — There is so much to talk over — And I am much disappointed not to look forward to seeing the Frau Baronin and your son — But we shall have the opportunity — My wife joins me in heartiest greetings

In alter Treue

James H. Woods

~~Dear Woods,~~ means

I think I need not take up your time today with the Chu T'ien chuan. I think I shall manage to get the book out without any assistance from the H. Y. Institute. Another question Dear Woods,

~~I think we shall get the Chu T'ien Chuan out somehow without giving~~ After a renewed consideration ~~I have considered~~ of Mr. Rousselle's ~~telegram again (which I enclose)~~ enclosed telegram, I have come to the conclusion that his book (Chinese Text and English translation of the Chu T'ien Chuan with many plates) will ~~certainly~~ be printed, even if he should receive no assistance from America. His father ~~family~~ is very wealthy and ~~that~~ will will surely sacrifice a considerable ~~more than~~ ~~the sum~~ ~~two thousand dollars~~ rather, than see his son's labour wasted. Furthermore ~~I made an agreement~~

I feel sure that Tschen will again ~~call up our~~ hold our regular Sino-Indian meetings next autumn and I hope that you and Schuster will also come

Extracts an Baldur 1
Dennéev 2
Taxel 3
Holst 4
Wrangell 5
Blandi 6
Tippelsk 7
Rosen 8
Sachs 9
Clark 10
Langdon 11
Blake 12
Chase 13
Donham 14
P. Ivy 15
Lucinda 16
Tsampa 17
Ungern-Sternb 18
Pauli 19

Mon cher Comte,

Comme c'est aimable de votre part de nous envoyer un si joli cadeau! Le bronze est ravissant, et nous vous envoyons nos remerciements les plus sincères.

Croyez, cher Comte, à l'expression de mes sentiments bien dévoués.

Peking November 21st 1931.

Dear Mrs. Woods,

We remember your stay here with great pleasure and hope to see you again soon.

Please accept our best New Year's wishes and believe us your sincerely yours ~~sincerely yours~~

A Stael Holstein

A Stael Holstein

Reverend A. v. Mañjuśrī, Professor of Philosophers

To Professor J. H. Woods
29 Follen Street
Cambridge Mass
U. S. of America

Mr. & Mrs. Birkhoff
———————— Bingham
———————— Chases Kinder
———————— Lattimore
———————— Gardner

promised me long ago, that in return for the material, collected by myself, and the help received by him from my Chinese assistants, he would bear all the costs of the publication. As no sum was mentioned in the promise, I have the right of insisting upon the publication without any subsidy, and that is what I will do. In view of all this I need not take up your time this morning at 10 as arranged.

LÉGATION DE RUSSIE.
BANGKOK

le $\dfrac{21\ \overline{VI}}{4.\ \overline{VII}}$ 1917

Cher Baron,

J'ai reçu Votre lettre du 6. $\overline{VI}$; je Vous en remercie beaucoup; cela m'a été un grand plaisir d'avoir de Vos nouvelles. J'espère que Votre vie à Pékin est toujours encore aussi agréable que lors de mon séjour à la Légation. Mais surtout j'espère que Vous ferez l'excursion à Bgk, qui, j'en suis sûr, Vous intéresserait beaucoup. Le voyage n'est pas du tout fatigant, au moins comme moi je l'ai fait. Les bateaux norvégiens de la "Siam-China-Nav. Cy" vont de Hongkong – via Swatow, à Bangkok 10 jours. J'étais le seul passager de I cl., j'avais une bonne cabine et prenais les repas, préparés par un excellent cuisinier, avec le capitaine, un norvégien très instruit et très aimable. – Ici j'habite la Légation et je ne crois pas que je prendrai une maison pour moi tout seul. Il y a ici plusieurs hôtels, dont le plus grand est "l'Oriental", où Plançon a passé 4 mois et M. Arnold, le Chargé d'affaires d'Amérique, ami de Behr, une année entière. On paie 250 ticaux par mois. Au „Trocadero" qui est près de la legation on trouve aussi de bons logements. — Le climat de Bgx, dont on m'a tant parlé, paraît tout-à-fait agréable; à la longue il est probablement fatigant, mais pendant des mois, je pense, on peut le supporter sans difficulté et même le trouver très agréable. — Quant aux objets de Vos études, je pense que Vous trouveriez ici beaucoup d'intéressant; l'Université n'est pas encore ouverte, mais elle doit être inaugurée bientôt. Il y a une grande bibliothèque nationale, des couvents et beaucoup de temples de la plus grande beauté et très différents de ce que j'ai vu à Pékin. —

Comme le Ministre n'a pas encore reçu ses lettres de créances, nous menons une vie très retirée. Le Prince et M.me de Phitsanoulok sont encore à la campagne et je ne leur suis pas encore présenté. Nous voyons souvent quelques diplomates, surtout M.r Arnold, l'américain, qui est tout à fait charmant. —

Je viens de recevoir une lettre du 24.IV où l'un de mes collègues m'écrit qu'il a vu Baldur, qui est parti pour le front, ayant été élu chef de l'escadron. — Wolkonsky était très occupé et continuait son travail avec autant de zèle comme avant.

Je Vous remercie, encore une fois, pour Votre lettre et les nouvelles de notre province; ici les journaux arrivent très tard et nous n'avons que ceux de Pgd. — Je Vous prie

de saluer Dmitri, et les autres secrétaires à Pékin, et de me croire Votre très dévoué

N. Wrangell. —

Bangkok, le 3 Février 18.

Cher Baron,

J'ai reçu, il y a longtemps votre aimable lettre du 17 Septembre, et je vous demande pardon de ne pas encore y avoir répondu. Comme vous me demandiez, dans cette lettre, quels étaient mes plans et si nous ne pourrions voyager ensemble, je voulais bien vous donner une réponse plus ou moins précise. Mais voilà déjà 4 mois que je ne puis faire aucun plan et que j'attends ici le moment où je pourrais rentrer. Les nouvelles que j'ai reçues de chez nous sont bien tristes. La dernière lettre que j'aie reçue est datée de Reval, le 4/17 XII. Ma famille est allée à R. parceque la vie à la campagne est devenue tout à fait insupportable; il y avait des militaires aussi à Ruil, mais ils se conduisaient décemment, tandisque Iffer, qui après la mort de mon oncle Magnus, appartient à ma mère a été pillé et complètement brûlé; de même on m'écrit que les biens de mes parents Toll et Wrangelstein ont été pillés. Pastfer / Cr. Maydell a subi le même sort. –

Ne sachant combien de temps je resterai ici, j'habite toujours encore la Légation. J'ai fait quelques excursions – à Petchaburi, à Hua-Hin, et dernièrement à Savankaloke et Pitsanuloke. Le pays et la ville sont charmants, le peuple Siamois le plus sympathique et aimable que je connaisse, et la vie au Siam serait la plus agréable, s'il n'y

eût pas eu nouvelles de notre pays. —
Je regrette que Vous ne soyez pas encore
venu, Vous auriez trouvé ici, j'ose penser,
des matériaux inépuisables pour vos études,
et nombre de gens s'y intéressant et
sympathiques. J'ai fait la connaissance
du Chef de l'Université Chulalongnorn,
S.A.R. le Prince de Jainad (Rangsit) qui
a fait ses études à Heidelberg. Il y
a aussi bien des Siamois, élevés en Russie,
tous sympathiques et aimables. — Ceux
qui viennent de passer par Pékin, me disent
qu'ils ne Vous ont pas vu, de sorte que je
pense que Vous avez fait de nouveau une excursion; le Consul à Hongkong m'écrit
d'ailleurs que Vous n'y êtes pas encore arrivé.
J'espère que cette lettre Vous parviendra et que
j'aurai aussi de Vos nouvelles. —

Je Vous prie de me croire, cher Baron,
Votre si sincèrement dévoué NNWrangeh.

Dorpat, den 11. XI. 28.

Lieber Baron,

Für Ihre freundliche Karte aus Kioto, über die ich mich sehr gefreut habe, sage ich Ihnen vielen Dank. Ich hätte Ihnen schon früher geschrieben; doch wollte ich gern Ihnen gleichzeitig die neue Adresse meiner Schwester mitteilen, welche lautet:-
Mrs. H. A. Kursell, 412 No. Broadway, Yonkers, N.Y. —
Vielleicht sehen Sie Kursells, die sich jetzt ganz in New York, d.h. in Yonkers eingerichtet haben, einmal. Sie würden sich gewiß sehr freuen, Sie wiederzusehen.

Seit d. September halte ich mich wieder in Dpt. auf und setze meine estn.-französ. Studien fort. — Es hat mich sehr interessiert, neulich Ihre Dokumente, mit Hilfe meines Lehrers, ins Estnische zu übersetzen. Auch einen Band der Ovgrünewaldtschen Erinnerungen habe ich eben zum Druck vorbereitet. Er umfasst die Jahre 1860-81; in allernächster Zeit muß er erscheinen.

Neulich lernte ich hier in der Ressource K⁺ Walter Maydell kennen, der 5 Jahre lang in Bonn Sanskrit studiert hat. Er erzählte u.a., daß Щербамский ein Tibetanisches

Dokument veröffentlicht hätte, in welchem „die ganze Philosophie Kants" enthalten wäre. Ins Deutsche oder eine andere europ. Sprache wäre es nicht übersetzt worden. Falls sich WM. nicht irrt, ist Ihnen das aber wohl längst bekannt. — Ihre Frau Stiefmutter sah ich neulich auf dem 50-j. Jubiläumsfest des Evang. Vereins J. Männer; sie machte gerade mit viel Interesse die Tagung des Intern. Versöhnungsbundes mit, zu der auch die Baronin Pilar aus Pernau gekommen war.

Hoffentlich verbringen Sie eine angenehme Zeit in Amerika, in einer Umgebung, die gewiss ganz anders ist als die, in welcher Sie die letzten 13 Jahre verbracht haben. —

Mit bestem Gruss
Ihr ergebener
M Wrangell. —

Wrangell

Lieber Baron,

Meinen besten Dank für Ihren Brief vom 17. XI. 33, der so viel Interessantes Wichtiges enthielt, denn ich aber leider garkeine Nachrichten über Ihr eignes Leben fand. Bitte schildern Sie mir in Ihrem nächsten Brief recht eingehend was Sie und die Ihrigen im alten Zu guten Reval fühlen.

Wie geht es Tante Kira, Axel Roth, Otto Wrangell, Dr. Kügelgen (Reval) und Stoël—Sommer. Womit beschäftigen sich seine Söhne (oder hat er nur einen?)?

Viele herzliche Grüsse von Ihrem ergebenen Alhdl.

P.S. Könnten Sie mir ???? eine Photographie des Öbilds schicken, das nach dem Inhaberaufnahmen hergestellt worden ist?

Ihrem

Brucker

Ich habe furchtbar lange nichts von Ihnen und Ihrer Familie gehört und ich zweifle doch sehr, wie das Schicksal sie Ihnen gegenüber verhält. Ich gönne Ihnen von Herzen ein gutes Jahr. Ich hoffe sehr, dass es Ihnen in diesem letzten Jahre (oder letzten Jahre) ein ganzes Jahr gewesen ist.

Mit der Bitte, mich Ihrer Frau Gemahlin zu empfehlen (und in der Hoffnung, dass Sie mir bald schreiben werden)

Ihr ganz ergebener

v. Wallenstein.

Peking, June 20th 1934.

Dear Dr. Masumura,

I have been studying Buddhist history for many years* and, I am assisted in my researches by a number of Chinese as well as Chinese scholars who, like myself, work in that the house situated in the # South East corner of the Austrian Legation compound. The fact (have lived through lectures here for the last five years) that a number of Japanese scholars hear daily their horn signals for 5-6 hours every day.

*
The enclosed reproduction of a page from the "Young East" proves that my researches are appreciated in Japan.

a few yards from the house where we work is ~~it~~ cannot, of course, be a matter of indifference to us. ~~It you~~ Will you be so kind as to ask the authorities to ~~soldiers~~ whether they could not practise a little farther away ~~to practice elsewhere~~ ~~where those ever exciting sounds from this we-still~~ be very much obliged to you. ~~The soldiers~~

This is not the first time that the military musicians interfere with our studies. A year ago they ~~did~~ our researches were

I succeeded in we were similarly afflicted, but the soldiers stopped musicians went elsewhere to practise after I had appealed to Mr. Suma, the first secretary of the Imperial Japanese Legation as well as to Mr. Thurbure the Royal Netherlands minister as well as Mr. Thurbure Both Mr. Suma and are at present absent from Peking and I cannot ask them to help us. I venture to address this appeal to you because I know that you are interested in historical studies. Believe me yours sincerely A Staël-Holstein

Friday, June 19th 1925.

Dear Mr. Yü,

I hear that all the teachers of the National University are contributing to the Shanghai fund. I ~~shall do the same~~ want to join my colleagues in that matter, but before doing so I must see you for a few minutes. You will be able to tell me, or to inquire for me as to ~~how~~ where the payment is to be made etc. Please come and see me as soon as possible.

Yours sincerely
A v Staël Holstein

1.

D. C. Yü
Yung-Huo-Gung

~~Dear~~ Baron,
    I am very sorry that I have not yet succeeded to get that commentary of Kaçyapa. I urged Mr. Ku again, but he only said: "I shall ask them again when I see them. It is unpleasant to see that they do not say frankly ~~that~~ they don't want to give, but ~~only~~ try to procrastinate by excuses. For a long time they have been grumbling about, why the other copies are not yet returned, and now there is another chance for them to grumble before me." So I did not urge him persistently, for he is bearing the grudges of both sides; it is

2.

not fair to press him too much.

I have not yet been able to copy the commentary very much by the writing machine. The machine does not belong to any friend of mine, but I rent it from a typewriting school. I have to pay them two dollars, if I use their machine one hour a day for one month, and I have to use it at definite hours, ~~all~~ the other hours being occupied by other men. I have paid them two dollars some time ago, and now if I wish to type more than one hour a day I must pay more according to the proportion. On the machine

3.

which I use, there are still three hours in the morning not yet occupied. I have told them that I would take that three hours for ten days and pay them two dollars. They consented, but after I came back from their school I discovered that I have only three dollars left with me, of the money which borrowed from my friend; and the time for me to pay for my room is also coming. If I pay one of these, I shall go without money for food in three or four days at most. So I hesitated and paid neither of them, and in the meantime I went about and tried to borrow some more from my friends. You know I have

4.

very very few friends in Peking; in fact not more than a dozen, and among this few, only one or two I can call intimate, and from whom I can borrow money sometimes, but they are all poor. Yesterday I went to one of them, I talked with him for some time, and hinted that I am in need of money now, but he made no reply, so I know he is also in difficult, and said nothing further.　To-day I went to another one; I directly told him my difficulty, but in reply he told me his, so I came back without any result. Since I cannot pay for the machine, I

5.

think to-morrow I shall copy it with hand again. But I cannot copy very much a day, as it is straining my body and eyes more than with a machine. I will use the machine as soon as I succeeded in getting the money to pay for it.

    I regret very much that I asked about money that day, because I did not realize how much trouble it would give you. I hope you will pardon me for it, because necesity made me bold.

                  Your Student
                      D. C. Yü

1.

Yii Dao Chuan
Yung-Huo-Gung.

6th. Oct. 1925.

Dear Baron,
I received your letter with ten dollars this morning. Thank you so very much for your kindness; but since my impudence of that day has given you enough trouble, I do not wish to give you more, so I send the money back by post.

For me, to see that others are distressed for my sake is more painful than to suffer from poverty or even starvation. Before the moon festival I received a letter from a friend, saying that he had run into debt recently; and he had a very hard time, now, because in China the moon festival is the time for every one to clear his debt. As I owed to that friend money, which I got from him before I came to Peking, it tormented me greatly to think that I was also responsible for his trouble, I hesitated for sometime, and at last I wrote and told him that I would pay him the money which I owed him for so long; although at that time I had no idea where I could get the money to send him. Before; you servant has been always very obliging to me. When-

2

ever he noticed that I was in need of money, he would ask me: "Yü Sien Sheng, are you in need of money now? If you are in need of money at any time, please tell me frankly; I have got money to lend you." But at that time I had already borrowed thirty four dollars from him at three times. The first time I got fifteen from him, he was as obliging as before. The second time I got another fifteen from him, to pay a debt which I owed to a friend in Yenching University; although my friend did not ask me to pay him, but it was time for him to pay his tuition fee, and I knew very well that he was in difficulty to get the money for it. But when I got this fifteen dollars from your servant, he was not so prompt as before; and from that time he never asked me whether I was in need of money or not. A few days after I was obliged to borrow another four dollars from him, and this time I had to ask him, and although he give me the money, but I noticed that he was apperently unwilling. So after I wrote to my friend, I soon realized the difficulty of the task as

3

to where I could get the money to send him. At first I thought I would tell my situation to your servant, ask him to get thirty dollars from some of his friends, and I would be glad to pay interest to him. But when I went to your house, your servant tried to shun me, and would not permit me any time to talk to him — evidently he was afraid that I should ask about money again. Then I gave up my hope to get money from him.

But the thought that my friend was in difficulty for my sake, and the thought that I had promised him to send him the money before the moon festival, continued to torment me. Then I began to think the work which I did for that institution. I thought I had copied some fourty leaves for them, so they may not afraid that I would get the money and do no work. I thought if I ask my teacher to tell Dr. Hu, certainly he would be willing to help me out of this awkward situation, as it makes not very much difference to them, if they pay me a few weeks in advance. I thought about this for several nights days and nights and at last determined

4.

to tell you about it when I see you. But when I saw you that day I became very nervous. After some hesitation, I asked about the money abruptly. Then you told me that I better ask from them when I have finished the whole thing. Then I lost my courage to say any thing further.
When I came back that day, very much discouraged and disappointed, I was almost sleepless the whole night. I thought again and again about the problem before me, until my head began to ache. At last I determined to muster my courage to ask you again the next day, and proposed to tell you the situation I was in. But when I came before you the next day, I became very nervous again, and in telling you my difficulty I became so rude and impolite from excitement. It tormented me immensely to think that my teacher was so much distressed by my rudeness, and thoughtlessness. When the idea first occured to me, that the manuscript which I copied could help me out of the awkward situation, I only thought about my own side. I did not know that Dr. Hu was not in Peking, and I did not realize that even he were in Peking it is not proper to ask for money before I finish

5.

my work. I know my teacher is distressed by economic difficulties. Your servant has often told me, with great sympathy, how much do you suffer from short of money. If others do not understand your difficulties, your servant and I certainly do understand them. So, when I asked about money that day, I did not expect that you should give me out of your own purse. When I got the money it pained to notice that my teacher was distressed. I hesitated for a whole day before I changed the cheque and sent the money to my friend. I sent him at last, becaused he was also distressed for my sake and besides I had promised him.

But now the only thing which pains me is the trouble which I inflicted upon my teacher. If I cannot do anything to lessen my painful burden, I would certainly not increase it by giving more trouble to you. I am still well off now. I will try to solve my present question by giving trouble to no one if I can.

Yours obediently

Yii Dao. Chuan

PALACE MUSEUM

PEIPING, CHINA.

26th February 1930.

Dear Dr. Holstein,

As requested I am sending you a copy of Mr. John D. Rockefeller's letter to Mr. Yeh Pei Chi, our Director General dated 23rd January 1930. and by the way I take pleasure in sending you 10 pictures of Tzu Ning Kung Garden before repaired and 6 pictures of the same after repaired.

Sincerely yours,

(T. K. Yu)

北平故宮博物院
PALACE MUSEUM
PEIPING, CHINA.

29th October 1932.

Dear Baron Holstein,

With reference to the robe of Panchan Lamma of Chien Lung period as desired, I have been reported that there is an old priest's robe laid up in Fang Chung Lao near Yu Hua Ko, but no identification has been discovered.

Moreover as to the history of the said robe I have instructed the Historical Dept. to make an investigation to the effect. I will let you know if something along that line can be found.

Yours truly,

J. K. Yu

My Dear Professor Hum,

I am very much interested [obliged?] to you for the tickets. I have not started to read them yet, but I shall do so before long in order to consult what remains of the Tibetan Kanjur owned by the Palace Museum.

I have distributed most of the sixty copies sent of the commentary which I received from the Commercial Press. Among the persons and institutions which have to must by now have received copies of the book are the following:

Prof. Thomas (Oxford) Prof. Konow (Oslo) Prof. Karlgren (Göteborg) Prof. Morgenstjerne (Göteborg) Prof. Lüders (Berlin) the Royal Asiatic Society (London) Prof. de la Vallée Poussin (Brussels) Prof. Waldschmidt (Berlin) Prof. Tucci (Rome) Prof. Demiéville (Paris) Prof. Vogel (Leyden) Prof. Rahder (Leyden) Prof. Przyluski (Paris) Prof. Bacot (Paris) Prof. Lévi (Paris) Prof. Ecole Lessing (Berlin) Prof. Weller (Leipzig) Prof. Haenisch (Berlin) The École française d'Extrême Orient (Hanoi) Prof. Blare (Harvard) Mr. Ware (Harvard)

Prof. Chase (Harvard), Prof. Clark (Harvard), Prof. Woods (Harvard), Prof.
Prof. Hackin (Paris), Prof. Simon (Berlin), Prof. v. Zahn-apps (Königsberg)
Prof. Porter (Yenching), Mr. Martin Fischer (German Leg. Peking) M.
Prof. Pelliot (Paris) and the Société Asiatique (Paris), and
Sir Denison Ross (School of Oriental Studies, London).
I shall be very grateful if you will send copies to
President Stuart (Yenching), Professor William Hung (Yenching),
the President of Harvard University (China in summary?), the All American Council
of Learned Societies, the Mr. Indge (Freer Gallery
Washington D.C.), Professor Edgerton (Yale), Professor Williams
Jackson (Columbia), the Asiatic Museum (Academy of Sciences,
Leningrad), Prof. Fu Ssŭ-nien, and the Library of the Deutsche
Morgenländische Gesellschaft (Halle, Germany), the President
of Santiniketan University (Bengal, India) and to the University
of Dr.Ox of Calcutta and the President of the Asiatic
Society of Bengal (Calcutta), Professor Takakusu (Imp. Univ. Tokyo) and
Prof. Haneda (Imp. Univ. Kyoto) and Prof. Yabuki (Taisho University, Tokyo).

故 宮 博 物 院
IMPERIAL PALACE MUSEUM
PEKING

June 13, 1929.

Baron A. von Stael-Holstein,
Hotel de Pekin,
Pekin.

Dear Baron:

I take pleasure in sending to you herewith your appointment as adviser to the Imperial Palace Museum signed by the Director of the Museum, Hon. Yi Pei-Chi, Minister of Agriculture and Mines at Nanking.

Minister Yi highly appreciates the services you have rendered to the Museum in the past and hopes that your cooperation in the future will contribute greatly to the growth of this institution.

Yours very sincerely,

TLY:L

Dear Woods,

Would not it be a good thing to talk over matters with Mr. Boyden (tomorrow, Thursday) over à trois with Mr. Boyden before his departure for Japan? I sent him a second (verbal) invitation through Mr. Roger Greene's brother, yesterday afternoon in anticipation of agreement, but he has not yet fulfilled his promise to call here. Could you not bring him to my house this evening between 6.30 and 8 o'clock for a causerie? The "hall of the Abbot's" — an important feature of my establishment — is not quite ready yet and I think I shall postpone my Chinese party until the completion of the necessary alterations.

My dear Professor Yuan,

I have much pleasure in accepting your kind invitation for Wednesday October 9th 10 o'clock. My wife requests me to add her very much thanks for having included her, but regrets that she will be unable to come on account of a bad cold. Believe me yours most sincerely, vStaëlHolstein.

Le baron et la baronne de Staël-Holstein remercient Monsieur et Madame Ed. H. de Tscharner pour leur aimable invitation (dimanche, 13 octobre, 1 heure), à laquelle ils auront l'honneur de se rendre.

Peking le 8 octobre 1929.

故宮博物院
IMPERIAL PALACE MUSEUM
PEKING

March 7, 1930.

Baron A. von Stael-Holstein,
Ex-Austrian Legation,
Peping.

Dear Baron Stael-Holstein:

On behalf of the Palace Museum we want to thank you for your good offices in securing the splendid gift from Mr. John D. Rockefeller, Jr., which has enabled us to restore four Lamaistic temples in the Imperial Palace. The Lamaistic images are now preserved from destruction, a fate that had threatened them for some time, and will be available to students in the days to come. We would also request that you would be kind enough to convey our thanks to Mr. Rockefeller, Jr., for his timely donation.

It is most gratifying to us to be able to inform you that as a result of Mr. Rockefeller's gift, which was the first of its kind received by the Palace Museum, other friends were moved to make gifts to help us in our work. President Chiang Kai-Shih gave a large sum toward the repairs of the gate, towers, etc., which have greatly improved the approach to the Museum. Sir Percival David and Mr. Joy Morton have contributed toward the repairs of the halls used for exhibiting porcelains and bronzes. When we think that these gentlemen were influenced by the example of Mr. Rockefeller, our gratitude to him is all the greater. In conveying him our thanks, kindly inform him that his gift has not only enabled us to make repairs to the Lamaistic temples, but has also served as an impetus to others to make similar gifts.

Assuring you of our keen appreciation of your constant interest and assistance, we remain,

Yours sincerely,

Associate Director of the Library,

Associate Director of the Art Museum.

National Library of Peiping

Peiping, China.

June 17, 1932.

Baron A. von Stael-Holstein,
Peiping.

Dear Baron Stael-Holstein:

With reference to the three invoices in photographic reproduction which you sent me yesterday, I write to say that we shall be glad to have all the books except "The Jataka" which we have already had in our Library. The postage for Simmel's invoice dated April 15 is to be divided by two, RM29.40 for "The Jataka" and RM29.40 for the other two publications, and I trust this will be agreeable to you. We are writing to authorize the Deutsch-Asiatische Bank to pay you RM681.80 for the books.

Yours very truly,

TLY/W

Acting Director.

P.S. Will you kindly let the bearer have the books?

Peking July 18th 1932.

Dear Dr. Yuan,

Many thanks for sending me the list of reference books, I shall ~~have~~ the list of books which I have studied with great interest. ~~I have~~ I highly appreciate ~~your~~ the suggestion, that I should call your attention to important books still missing in your collection, and I have ~~noticed~~ already chosen the titles of some such ~~copies~~. In a few days I shall personally take these notes to your library.

Believe me yours sincerely

Peking, August 28th 1933.

Dear Professor Yuan,

I enclose two copies of Professor Willer's index. May I ask you to keep one of them and to present the other one to the National Library?

In accordance with your instructions I have asked the Lazarists to send you only 240 copies of the cover & the title page and 3) the introduction (to the commentary) as well as the bill (for 500 copies).

Believe me yours sincerely and gratefully

A. v. Staël-Holstein

I have personally received sixty copies of the commentary and of the text (from the Commercial Press) which you so kindly promised me.

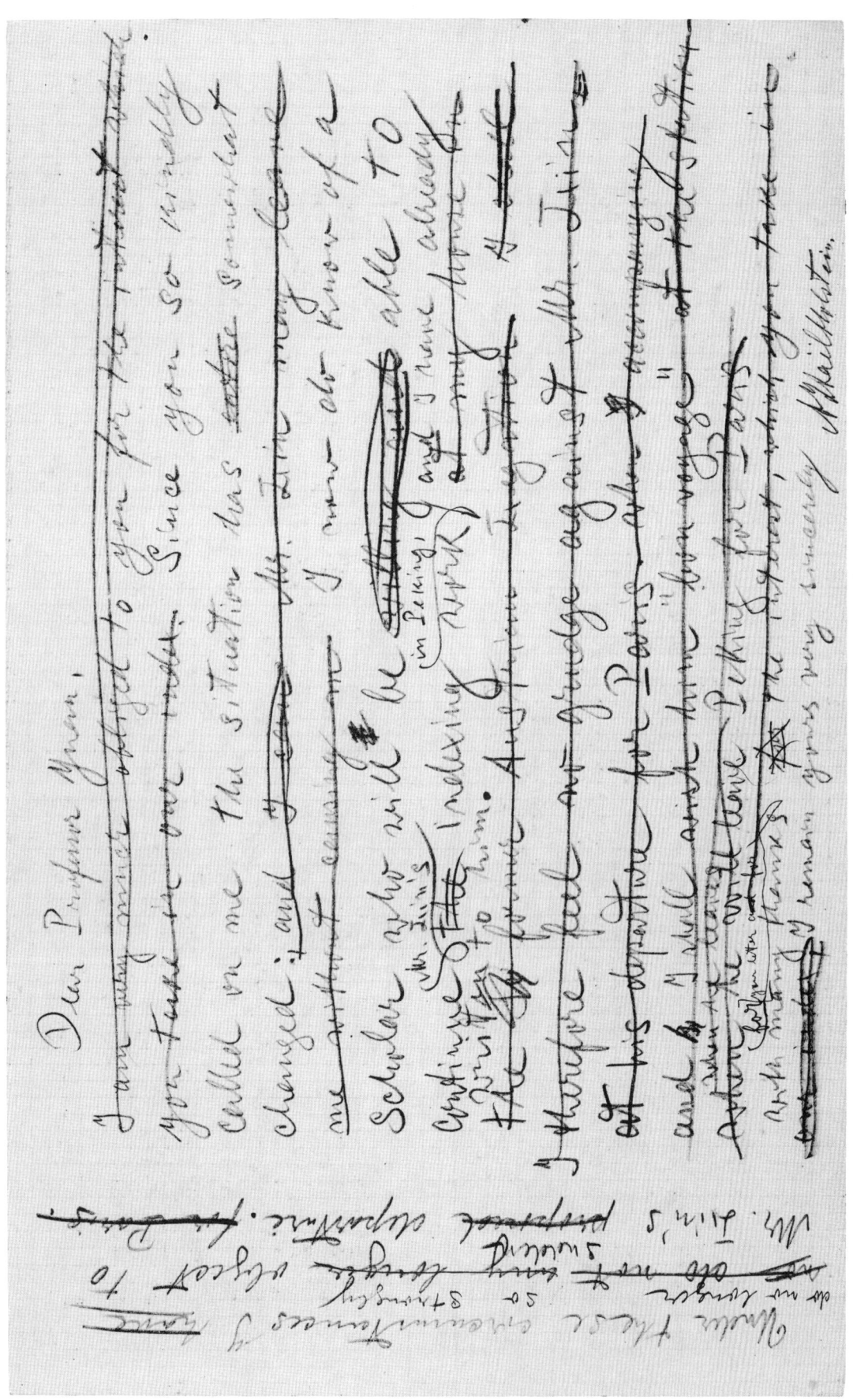

Dear Professor Yuan,

Many thanks for your note. I have sent the manuscript of my various notes (10 pages) to the printers, and they have acknowledged the receipt of the 48 pages. As soon as the letter will be printed I hope to send the manuscript of my introduction to the Ching Hua Hsin Chi.

Believe me yours sincerely
AvStaël-Holstein

Note 31.

Comp. Schulemann, op. cit., pages 98 and 143, Köppen, op. cit., II,

Note 32.

Waddell, Lamaism, page 232.

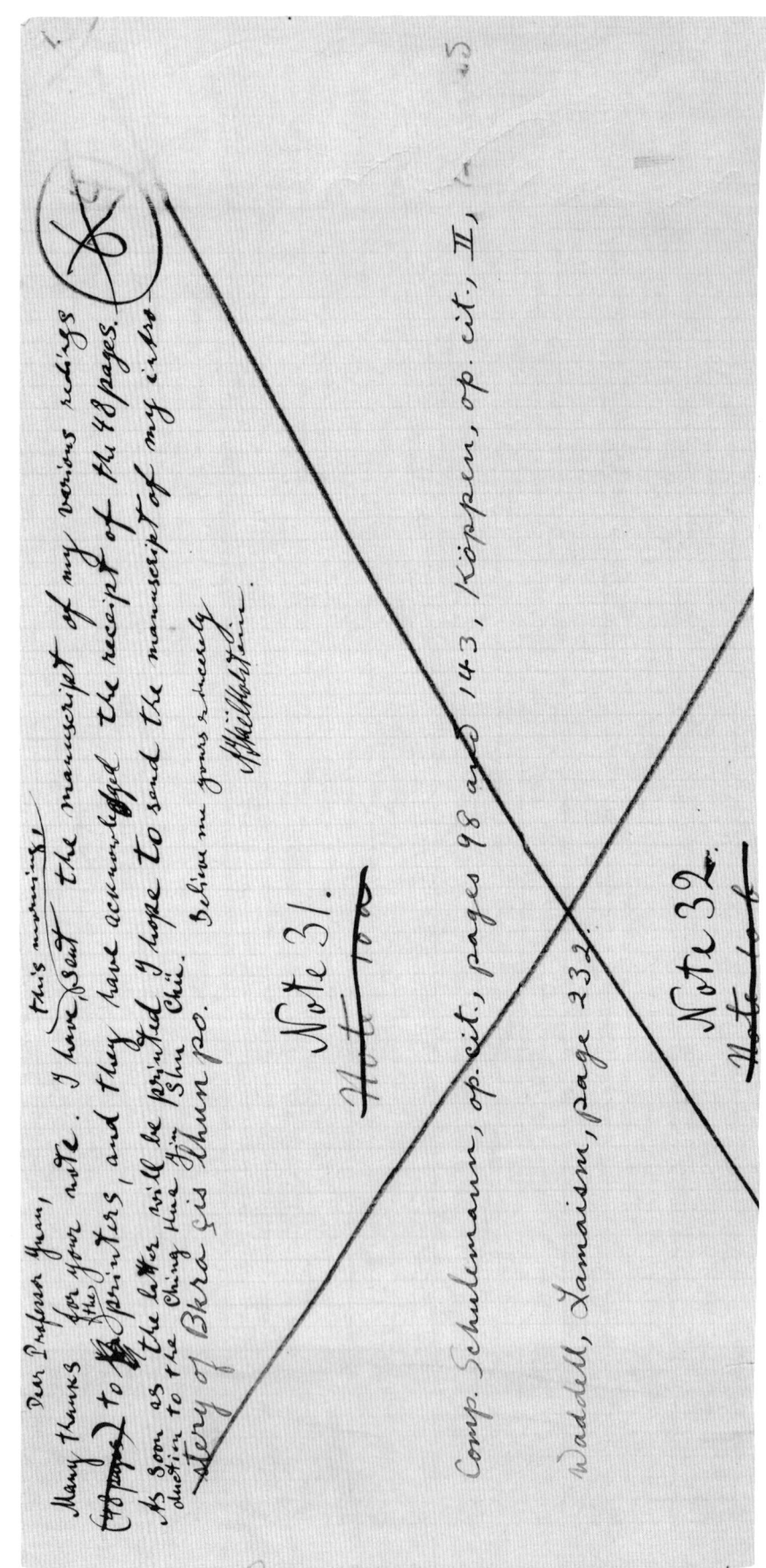

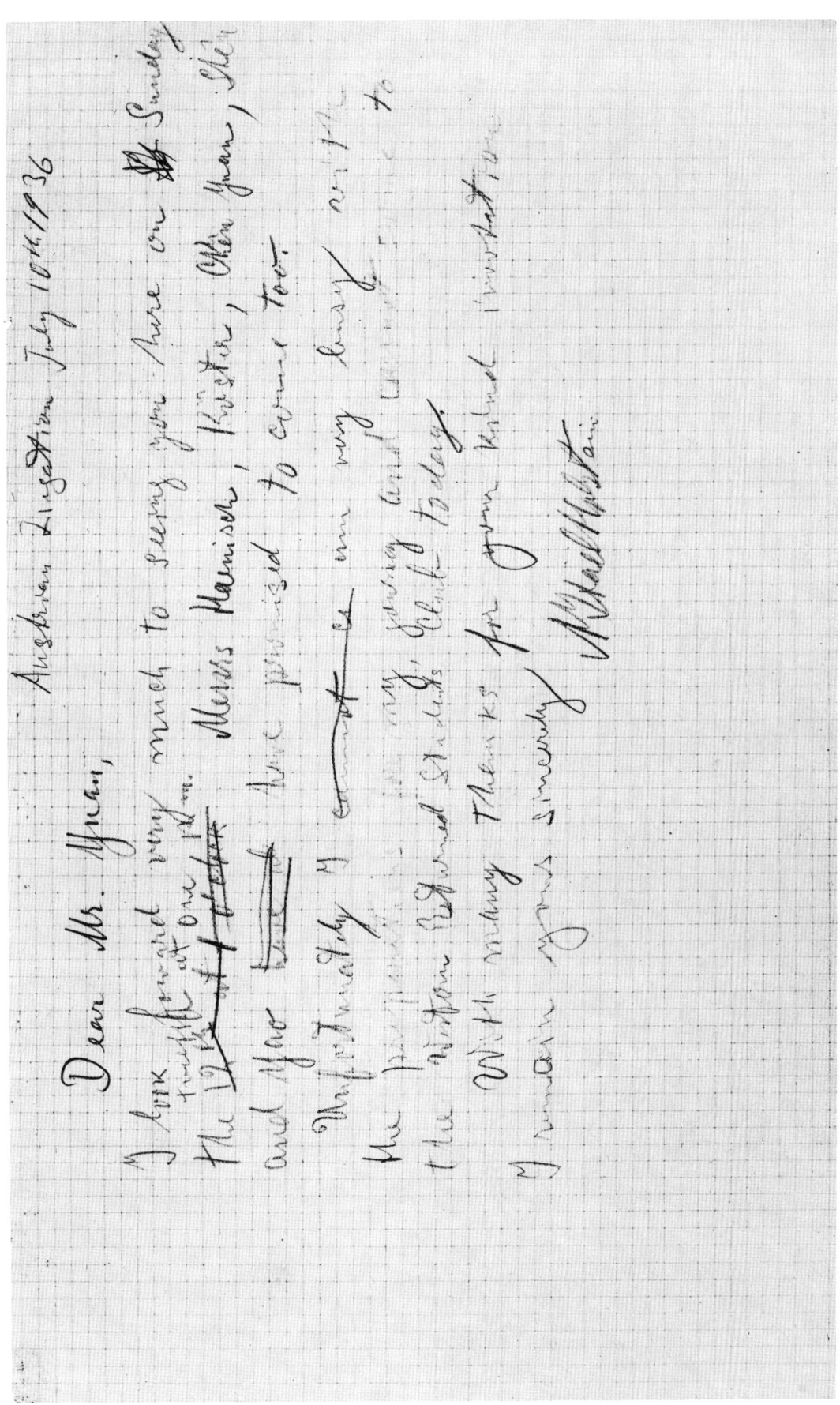

Austrian Legation July 10th 1936

Dear Mr. Gran,

I look forward very much to seeing you here on Sunday. I thought at one time the Messrs Harrison, Krötsche, Otto Franke, Eller and Mrs. [?] have promised to come too. Unfortunately I cannot [?] am very busy with the [?] in my journey and wish to finish Buddhist Studies Vol II today.

With many thanks for your kind invitation

I remain yours sincerely
A v Staël-Holstein

My dear Professor Grieg, 3

After several unsuccessful attempts at getting in touch with a reliable picture restorer I have succeeded. A friend of mine who is a great collector of ~~folks~~ told me that he has had about two hundred ancient pictures restored by a certain specialist whom (The man who has not appeared yet but as) he promised to send to my house ~~soon as~~ ~~he comes~~ I will send him on to you with my card. So far he has not come yet.

Believe me yours sincerely

à Monsieur Alphonse Monestier
hommage de l'auteur

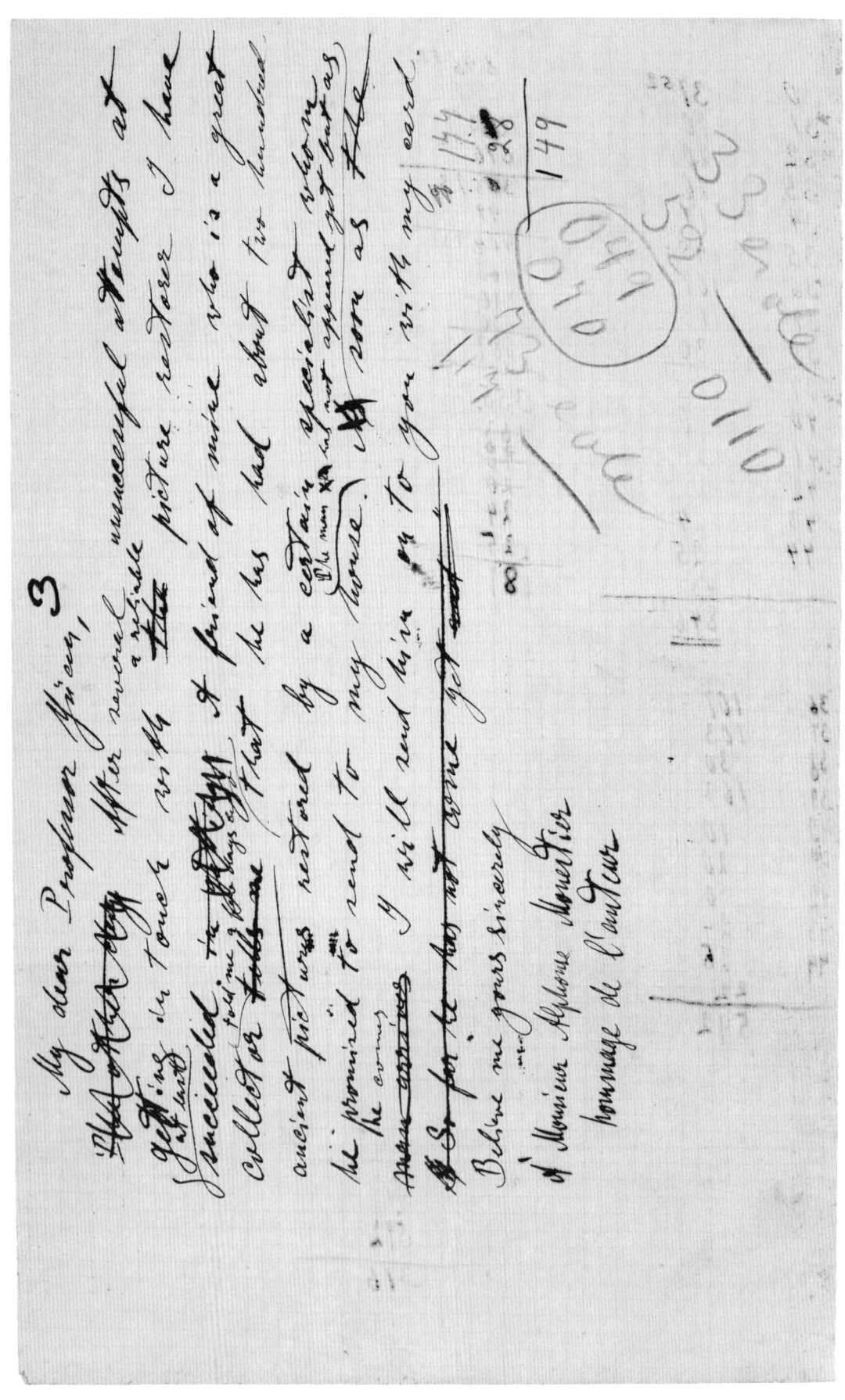

Societeit „De Harmonie"
Batavia

Batavia-C., 23rd June 1936
Weltevreden, Gang Kadji 39

No.

Dear Sir,

I have just received the sad tidings of the death of Rev. F.X. Biallas, which fill me with deep sorrow. In him I lost a dear friend, who always showed sincere sympathie with my sinological studies. It is not very long time ago that he promised to publish within this year in the Monumenta Serica my translation of Tufu's poems book I-IV. As you are associate editor of this journal, I should be very much obliged to you, if you were kind enough to let me know, if those translations have appeared or will appear, and if reprints could be sent to my above-mentioned address.

At the same time I venture to ask you, whether the plan of the Harvard University to compile a great Chinese-English Dictionary is on the point of being carried out. As I take great interest in Chinese lexicography (cf. the preface of Giles' Chin. dict. 2nd edition), I should like to join the staff of this enterprise, although I am an old man (65 years) and a bad linguist. Could you perhaps inform me about any prospects I may have.

Trusting you will give me an early answer,
I remain, dear Baron von Staël-Holstein,

Yours sincerely
Erwin Zach

Пекинъ 28 Февраля (н.сг.) 1917 г.

Глубокоуважаемый
Василій Васильевичъ,

Кончина Карла Германовича, о которой я узналъ случайно, ~~терпимъ~~ ~~тица мия~~ меня очень опечалила. ~~Уже какъ кромѣ личной дружбы я~~ ~~нитралъ въ немъ~~ "для друзей покойнаго!" Какая потеря для науки! ~~Теперь некого будетъ спрашивать~~

О. И. Щербатскому я писалъ почти ежемѣсячно, а Вамъ по крайней мѣрѣ два раза — въ Ноябрѣ и Декабрѣ. ~~Академія имъ выслала книгъ~~

С. Ф. Ольденбургу я написалъ письмо въ началѣ ~~Янв~~ Февраля новаго стиля. Кромѣ того я послалъ въ комитетъ двѣ копіи ~~и~~ (одну на Ваше имя а другую на имя С. Ф. Ольденбурга) и фотографическіе снимки среднеазіатскихъ древностей хранящихся въ Сеулѣ. Эти фотографіи были также отправлены

С. Ф. Ольденбургу. Освоемъ ра-
ботаѣ въ Японіи я писалъ
Вамъ, О. И. Щербатскому и
С. Ф. Ольденбургу. Здѣсь я
исключительно занимаюсь
китайскимъ языкомъ и по-
вослѣдствіи вернусь въ Японію.
~~Беру на себя смѣлость просить Васъ о высылкѣ мнѣ~~
~~Пожалуйста вышлите мнѣ~~ ~~ту~~
~~туда~~ какъ можно скорѣе и
какъ можно больше денегъ.
Мой адресъ: Императорское Россійское
Посольство Токіо. жизнь
~~на дальнемъ востокѣ стано-~~
~~вится дороже съ ~~~~ кажды~~
~~днемъ. и я былъ Кроме того Я~~
былъ бы Вамъ весьма благодаренъ за
письмо. Отъ Васъ ~~и~~ и отъ С. Ф. Ольденбурга
я ~~никакого письма не~~ ни одного письма
не получилъ, а отъ О. И. Щербатского всего
двѣ открытки. Послѣднее письмо отъ
О. А. Розенберга, ~~было послано~~ которое я
получилъ, было послано въ Октябрѣ мѣсяцѣ
а завтра у насъ 1ое Марта по поводу счита...
~~искренне~~ преданный Вашъ А.Шталь

Hoshigaura (Dairen)
17 Yurimachi.
d.19.Oktob.27.

Hochgeehrter Herr Baron,

Ihr freundlicher Brief v.27.Juni kam erst vor paar Wochen in m/Besitz;da die S.-A.m/Miscell. Buddhica unterwegs verloren gegangen waren, konnte ich die von Ihnen aufgestellten Fragen nicht sofort beantworten.

Ich erinnere mich nicht mehr,ob ich Dharmaraksas Uebersetzung,mit Hilfe m/japanischen Schülers,verglichen habe.Der Umstand,dass die Erklärung d.Namens "Avalokiteśvara" dort fehlt könnte gegen meine Auffassung reden.-Was die tibetische Version betrifft,so ist sie doch allzu spät (VII Jahrh frühestens),um in Betrtracht kommen zu können.-

Ich beeile mich Ihre Aufmerksamkeit auf

ein marma zu richten: die Form "Avalokiteśvara" steht bereits im Horyuji MS.von Prajñāpāramitā-hṛdaya,von Bühler,-wie Sie wissen- 500-550 datiert.Deshalb müssen m/Ergebnisse korrigiert werden:p.252(5) "in the sixth cent."statt"7th", ebenso p.274(d).Ich kann es nicht begreifen, auf welche Weise ich dies Datum (Horyuji MS.) nicht herangezogen habe;ein entsetzlicher lapsus. -

Was die Vaitulya-Vaipulya Frage angeht, so bin ich ausser Stande auf d.Gebiete d.Sinologie (wo Sie doch zu Hause sind!) eine selbstständige Meinung zu äussern;ich gestehe pp. 24I,n.I,und 254,n.2,dass ich Chinesisch nicht kenne und das ganze Chin.Material m/Japanischer Schüler verdanke.Ich wage aber die folgende "Hypothese" aufzustellen (ohne jegliche Verantwortlichkeit!),-aus Rosenbergs Wörterbuch

(Intro. to the study of Buddhism, Tokyo, 1916, – das Buch besitzen Sie wahrscheinlich), herausgefischt.

Könnte das 2te Zeichen (jih 日) für 旦 (tan) verschrieben worden sein ? (v. Ihre Gaṇḍīstotra 204 Rosenberg, p. 233, 7). – Andererseits könnte man auch das Zeichen 白 (pai, po, – Ros. p. 335, N° 106) vermuten.

Das Ite Zeichen (tan) würde auf ein verschriebenes Vaitulya, das 2te – auf ditto Vaipulya hindeuten.

Das ist nur ein ajñānalalitam! –

Jedenfalls, scheint eben die Unbestimmtheit der Transkription der von Ihnen angeführten Uebersetzung aus d. 2ten Jahrh. nicht gegen m/Auffassung zu sprechen.

Wie Sie bereits wissen, bin ich nach Dairen gekommen, wo ich bis auf Weiteres bleiben muss.

Meine Japaner geben mir eine 4-monatliche Reise nach Ceylon, die ich Anfang (oder Mitte)

November antreten werde.

HabenSie dort (Ceylon) einige Bekannten ?

Ich würde Ihnen für ein paar Empfehlungen höchst dankbar sein.

Wahrscheinlich habenSie m/S-A.von"Dignāga's Nyāyapraveśa etc."(<u>served up cold</u> !) erhalten.

Dieser Brief ist deutsch geschrieben,teils weil ich Ihre Freundlichkeit erwidern und <u>Ihrer</u> Muttersprache mich bedienen wollte, teils um Ihnen die Entzifferung meiner scheus-slichen Handschrift zu ersparen. Deswegen wollenSie mir die Maschinenschrift verzeihen;ich weiss wohl,dass es <u>awfully bad form</u> ist.

Mit herzlichen Gruss
Ihr ganz ergebener
W. [signature]

Pékin le 2 septembre 1929.

Cher Monsieur et Collègue,

Je vous suis infiniment reconnaissant pour votre intéressante étude sur le cheval Balaha. Excusez-moi, je vous en prie, de ne vous remercier que maintenant. ~~Я у меня есть~~ Je suis tout à fait confus de ne pas vous avoir répondu plus tôt, mais je suis allé en Amérique, chercher de l'argent pour mon Institut, ~~j'ai été absent pendant quelques mois en Amérique~~ à près et puis je me suis marié. Tout ça ~~prend~~ du temps. Est ce que mon rapport, dont vous avez bien voulu accuser la réception, va être publié bientôt? Мои денежныя дѣла были въ ужасномъ положеніи; китайцы мнѣ должны за три года, эстонцы и латыши тоже не платятъ и ожидавшаяся изъ Ганоя сумма, болѣе или менѣе опредѣленно обѣщанная почти два года тому назадъ, ~~тоже~~ до сихъ поръ не пришла. Въ будущемъ мы будемъ жить исключительно на американскія деньги, но по долгамъ надо расплатиться. Если приложенное письмо на имя директора не безусловно любезно, не передавайте его пожалуйста по адресу.

Искренно преданный Вамъ и благодарный А.Сталь.

1 Pu tu ssu chien hsiang, Nan chih tzu
3.Mai 32

lieber Baron Staël,

können sie mir vielleicht eine korrekte Übersetzung des beiliegenden Zitates verschaffen? Es stammt aus einer längeren Steininschrift. Die Kenntnis eines gebildeten Chinesen genügt in diesem Fall nicht, es muss jemand sein, der buddhistische Texte zu lesen versteht. Besonders kommt es mir auf den einen Satz an: "Der alte Meister (die alten Meister?) der Hua yen-Sekte haust (hausen) an einem Ort mit 3 Stufen." Ich gebe unten die Übersetzung, wie ich sie habe, aber ich bin nicht ganz zufrieden, vor allem nicht mit dem erwähnten Satz. Haben Sie nicht einen Chinesen zur Hand, der mir den bewussten Satz deuten kann? Ich wäre Ihnen sehr dankbar und bitte um Entschuldigung ob der Störung.

Mit besten Grüssen Ihr erg.

Perzynski

;;;;
Ein alter Buddha (alte Buddhas?) aus glasiertem Ton steht (stehen?) dort. Der Kuanyin pusa haust in einer Grotte der w. Klippe. Der alte Meister (die..?) der Hua yen Sekte haust (hausen?) an einem Ort mit drei Stufen. Die Buddhagestalten der ö. liegenden Berge sind jede in einer Grotte.

28. XII

Многоуважаемый Барон
Александр Августович

Год тому назад я покинул Россию и перебрался на свою родину в Польшу, где стараюсь продолжать во Львовском университете свою востоковедную работу (в более тесном контакте с Европою). В последнее время я несколько раз натолкнулся на Ваше имя, счёл это счастливым предзнаменованием и вот пишу Вам, чтобы переслать Вам искренний привет а вместе с тем и попросить Вас о товарищеской услуге.

В T'oung Pao (Mars 1924, N 1) я прочёл заметку P. Pelliot, основанную на сообщении Kouo Kio ki k'an, о том, что в Пекинский университет передано большое количество документов за время правления манджурской династии для разбора и изу-

чения; вероятно, имеется в виду составление очередной династийной истории („Цинъ-ши"). Pelliot по этому случаю указывает, что часть документов этой эпохи разошлась по частным рукам, и действительно до меня дошли также сведения о том, что порядочное количество актов на манчжурском
письменном
яз. находится у одного (Бахшира — по профессии маньчжура (я сожалению, имя его я в данную минуту забыл).

Меня, как маньчжуриста, все эти известия интригуют в весьма сильной степени. Самый старый памятник манчжурской письменности, какой нам известен, относится к 1641 г. (памятник около Сеула в Корее); от прежней эпохи дошли только легенды (очень нечеткие и грубые) на монетах, а между тем прежняя манчжурская письменность должна представлять много особенностей, так как манчжуры с 1599 по 1682 г.

употребляли так наз. письмо без точек и кружков: [монгольский текст] тонки фука аку херген-и битхе (иными словами, это было обычное неуленанное монгольское письмо), а до 1599 г. маньчжуры пользовались не только монгольским письмом, но и языком.

У пол-мнутой баикира есть образец письма без точек и кружков; я думаю, что он должен был бы находиться и в том, что передано Университету; быть может, отыщется и где что написанное по-монгольски. Так как среди Пекинских профессоров имеются люди весьма просвещенные, то они должны обратить внимание на указанные много обстоятельства и, вероятно, могли бы дать Вам, как своему коллеге, необходимые разъяснения. Если бы мои предположения оказались верными, мне очень хотелось бы получить возможность ознакомиться с старыми документами въ подлинномъ видѣ, либо по фотографическимъ снимкамъ. Особенно хотѣлось бы получить какой-нибудь цѣлостный актъ, напр., какую-либо грамоту с печатью за время до 1632. Конечно, расходы, которые потребовались бы на это дѣло, я с полной готовностью немедленно бы покрылъ.

Слышалъ я также, что покойный бар[онъ] предполагалъ издать маньчжурско-китайско-джурчжэнь-японский словарь. Не слышали ли Вы что-нибудь объ этомъ дѣлѣ? Подобный словарь былъ бы для меня чрезвычайно важнымъ приобрѣтеніемъ.

Очень смущаюсь, баронъ, что я Васъ безпокою этими просьбами, но дѣло для меня чрезвычайно важное, а болѣе обратиться мнѣ не к кому.

Надѣюсь, что Вы пребываете в добромъ здравіи и имѣете возможность работать в родной для Васъ области.

Съ наилучшими пожеланіями остаюсь

В. Котвичъ

Władysław Kotwicz
Uniwersytet, Lwów (Poland).

敬啟者茲訂於本月九日（星期六）正午十二時半在
敝寓（燕大東門外蔣家胡同三號）便飯後開燕京學
報委員會商量學報進行事宜務懇
撥冗蒞止是幸此致

鋼和泰先生

顧頡剛敬啟 廿二、十二、二

敬啟者前得博蓀兄先生電話告
先生特為拙作在燕京學報發表至佳幸
擬不到在十五期第一篇如此文
先生尚未蓋印而名立下得校校貝兒鬼一引
以接印所答壽校對當以最快一定鴿送上
審勘也並告示之
賜覆乃幸此上
鋼和泰先生大鑒

欣悌詢弟稽首
百廿一

國立北京大學用箋

鋼和泰先生

茲奉上檔案文件二幅謹祈

先生將此兩種文件之名稱譯出以

便檔案會填寫目錄此專此敬頌

教祺

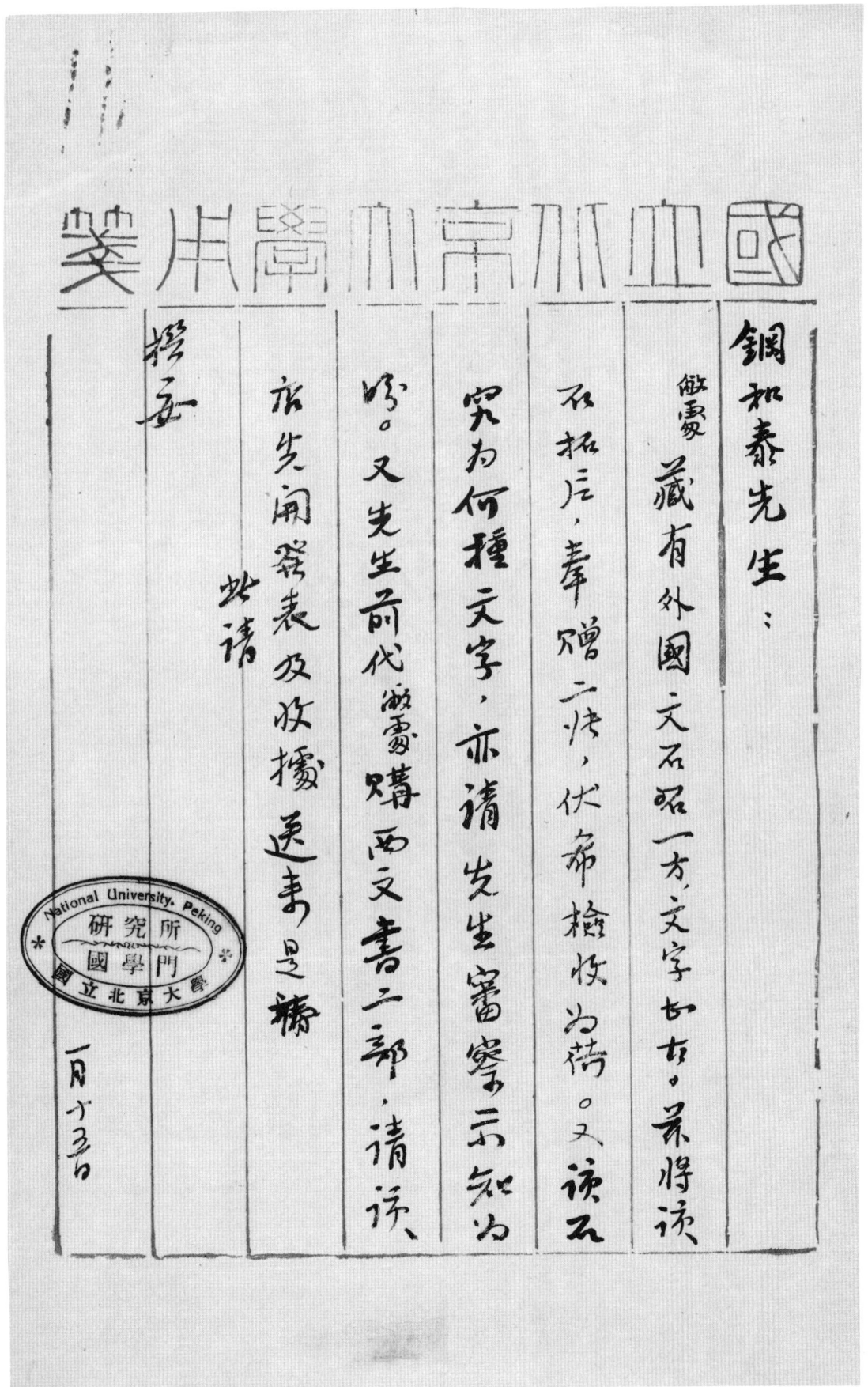

鋼和泰先生：

今天特將本學門檔案會外國文影片一份(共八張)本學門考古學室外國文拓片一份(共三張)送你，請你查收，又附送外國文影片一份，外國文拓片一份，請你轉交貴友中能認識這種文字的，指教這些影片拓片到底是甚麼文字。再者檔案會現在又發見一個蒙藏文件，本學門皆不知是甚麼文告，請你到有空的時候，到本學門指示大畧以便

國立北京大學用箋

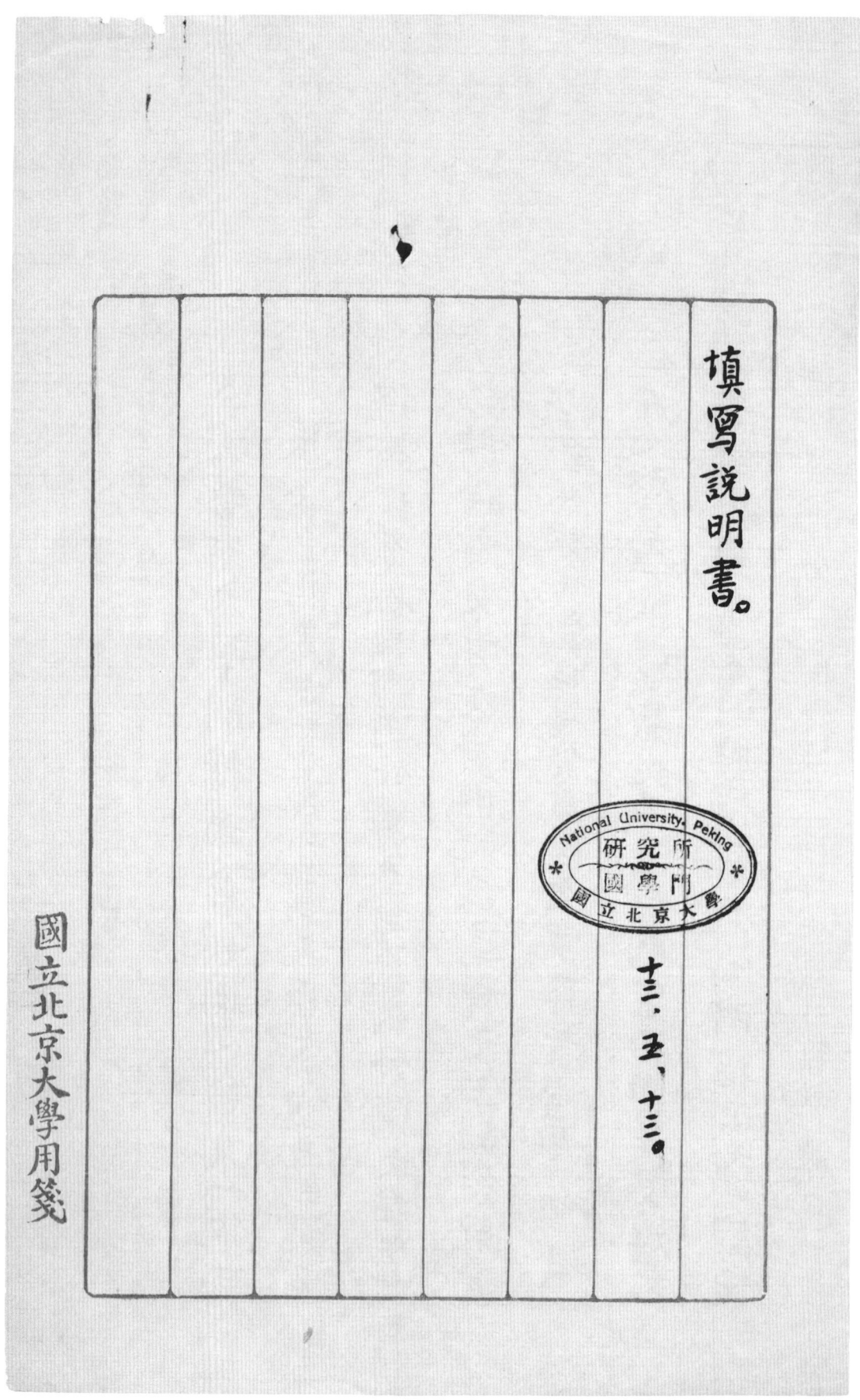

鋼和泰先生大鑒。頃奉上之佐沙文（即疏勒文）影片。

後查知其尖次地名，在新疆巴楚（漢名瑪拉巴什）東二日程。漢人名曰托和沙拉。營地即在喀什

噶爾河新滩旁。漢人呼北城為喀王城，譯文書中名此城為攔你。獲悉坦回地同。在鉎綫一七度緯綫三九·五〇

凡由阿克蘇至喀什循大道走者必徑于此要之。

鄉花此秦發現尚有泥塑佛像，坐織兄，陶小銅錢。

又若殘低同穴出土者，有陶器、木器（有彩）等；。當

視督為情，唐向物，距現在約五一千三百餘年前後。

殷切希望 先生速將此文件研究有結果，究欠為何也。

又荀瞎相違之先生，三字寄高僧何中有論及譯經中滿香語事，特抄出奉上，俾作參攷。

又吐魯番之晨光發見文日內將去，再奉交潘先生收到研此矣。專此申谢

署安

蕭文郭 敬上 六十八日

鋼先生大鑒久未聆
教馳念良殷辰維
起居多福為頌日前由鄧先生交
到佛教圖像照片一張係薩之像
尊示囑弟查明此是何薩之像
其下方又手所捧者究是何物
弟現正在文書籍中考查如何
尚不能查明弟以意度之中

國所流行之佛菩薩之像有多手者惟准胝菩薩及觀音菩薩兩種據日本富田斅純所編之秘密辭林 Himitsu jirin 第五七三葉謂准胝菩薩 Sunde 面有三目又身有十八臂其中有二手結印置於胸前右邊第二手施無畏印第三手劍第四手數珠第五手微若布羅

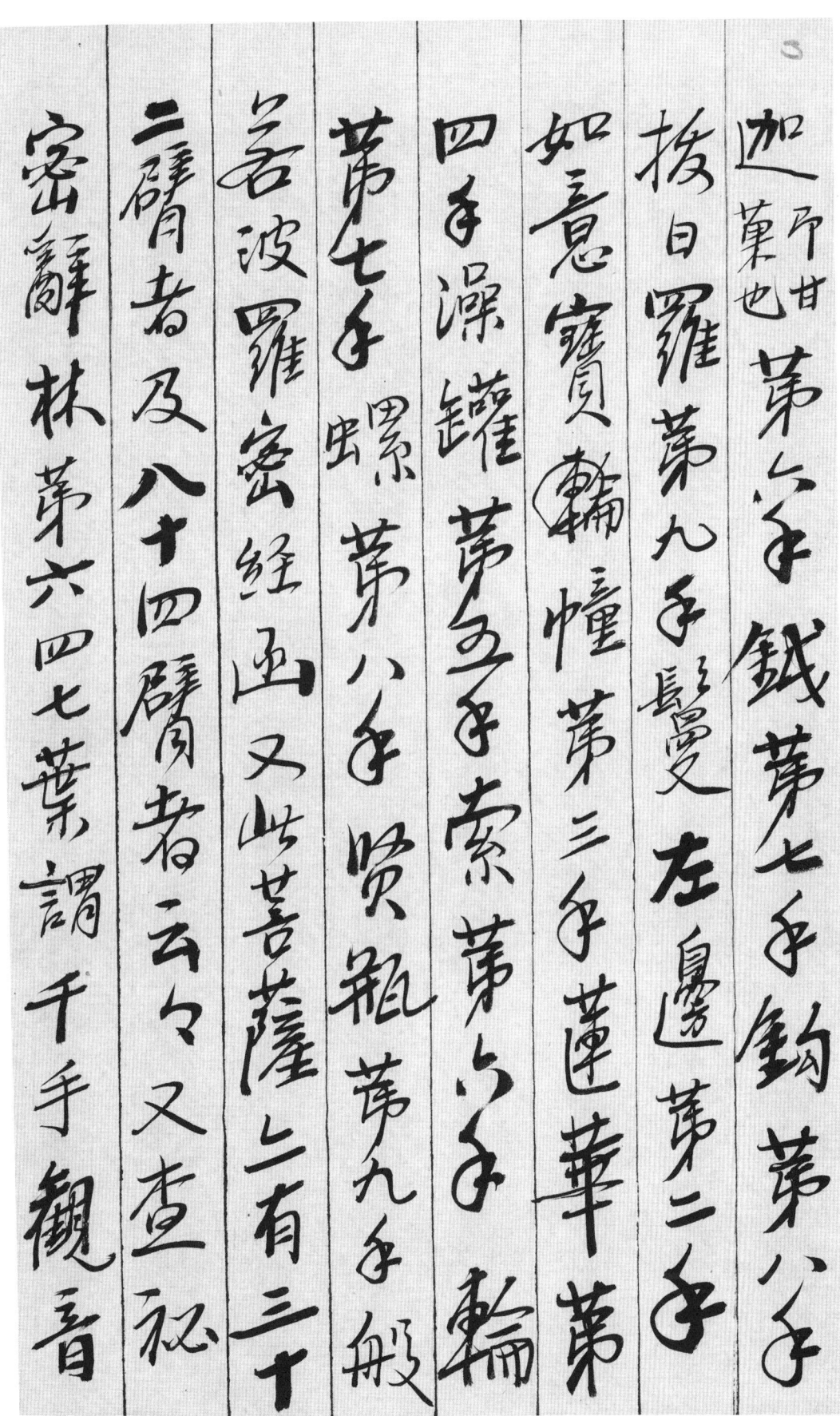

迦菓也第七手鉞第八手
按曰羅第九手鬘左邊第二手
如意寶輪幢第三手蓮華第
四手澡罐第五手索第六手輪
第七手螺第八手賢瓶第九手般
若波羅蜜經函又此菩薩上有三十
二臂者及八十四臂者云々又查祕
密藏林第六四七葉謂千手觀音

Sahasrabhujasahasranetra

有四十臂 其中有兩手當胸合掌 又有兩手結定印 置於臍下 此八手則右之十八手執青蓮花、錫杖、化佛、日輪、金鈎、劍、鏡、三股杵、寶印、鉢、髑髏幢、梵經、五色雲、箭、蒲桃、胡瓶、念珠、與願、左之十八手則執白蓮花、三股戟、宮殿、月輪、紅蓮、白拂、弓、梵篋、法螺、寶瓶、羂索、玉環、又謂結定印之二手上置一寶鉢 云々 李查此秘密辭林一書在 O. Rosenberg 編之佛教研究名辭集中心常被引用則此書所載當為可信既云結定印之二手上置寶鉢則此次

兄所欲知者，所臍下如，手所捧者或者即是寶
鉢矣，乎又查禪林象器箋 Zenrin
shōkisen 第八百十四葉謂鉢之容量
大鉢受三斗小者受斗半中者
知據此言之則此像中之鉢其收
精高上未嘗無理矣又此禪林象
器箋一書乃呉平無著道忠
禪師所編又名禪宗辭典上營

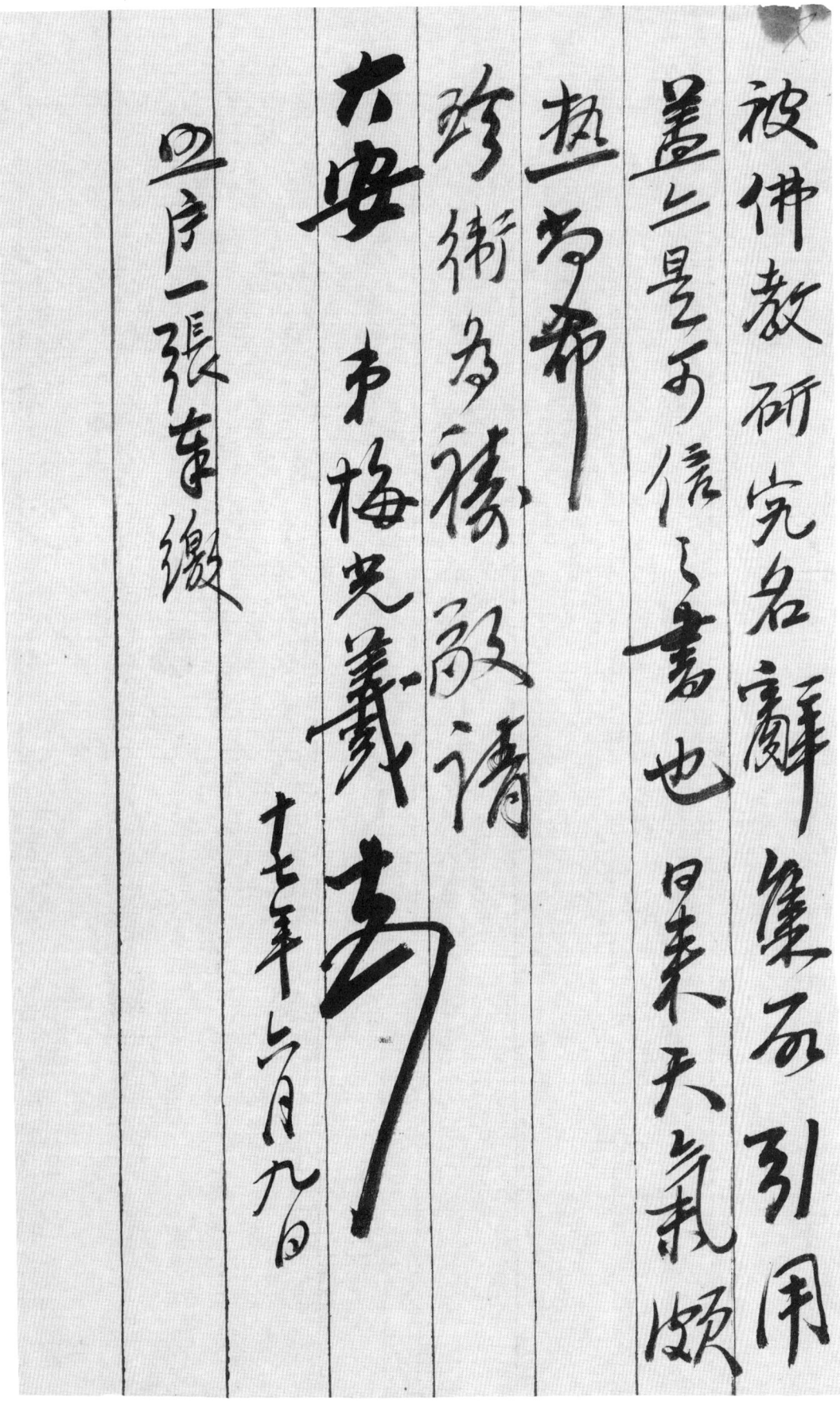

逕啟者茲訂于九月十九日（星期三日）下午六時在敝寓（燕東園廿四號）開燕京學報編輯委員會商量學報進行事宜

會議後聚餐務希

撥冗出席是幸此致

和泰先生

容庚敬啟 九月十二日

Mittwoch den 19. 6 Uhr

廣東地方警衛隊編練委員會用箋

鋼和泰先生侍右：我們是此天念書時

得

先生種種善誘陸教而少我們對於印度

學本業也很想致力所完于是回程之同伴

予從不就同北平將印度學的所究暫時中止

並而我們對於這門学問仍些不能忘懷之暑

常之想念起

先生不逢我们返粵以後糊之逢之過了幾

中華民國　年　月　日

廣東地方警衛隊編練委員會用牋

年什麼成績都一班沒有花々勢要想寫信給
先生但一执筆西自去都撂擱浮很就把筆停
下了
日昨专意中在上海湖志报看見先生主持
的中印研究院的相片一張我們覺得先生
及邹念親先生兩位绕知到先生已成立了
這樣的一個研究學術的機囙不禁爲之歡
喜无玩我們很想知到這佣中印研

廣東地方警衛隊編練委員會用牋

先生院的情形如果這個研究院有印刷品很
望先生寄些給我們看看以慰我們的渴
念玉將研究的才針由容及問題示知則尤
感慰我們現立的情形不甚足述不過同敝
付你民慶閱讀内典可是不甚方便參攷的
設備又不足等俟友指導攷之什麽研
得了這是我們自己覺得很欠憾的事此致候

特祉

生周用
梁寶麗 仝上十月二日

中華民國 年 月 日
周用現寓廣州市大北直街西華二巷三十八號

北平近代科學圖書館用箋

敬啟者本館籌備期間承
學術界先進暨各文化機關諸同志熱心贊助竟能
於短期內完成實深欣幸所得巨帙名著美不勝收
雲天高情感佩兼極茲定於十二月五日下午三時
在王府大街九號本館舉行開幕典禮敬希
駕臨指導藉匡不逮為荷此致

鋼和泰先生

北平近代科學圖書館代理館長 山室三良謹啟

十一月廿六日

出席與否請覆

Beim Pantschen Lama.

Europa pocht mit aller Macht an die Tore Asiens, und selbst das geheimnisvollste aller Laender, Tibet, erschliesst sich der westlichen Zivilisation - freilich nicht westlicher Kultur! - unter Fuehrung seines Priesterkoenigs, des "Priesters der Weltmeere", des sogenannten Dschamtso Rinpotsche oder Dalai Lama. Einfluesse der britischen Politik spielen dabei mit, denn der Aufmarsch der Weltmaechte auf dem Glacis Hochasiens hat begonnen. Aber auf der anderen Seite ist eine aeusserst starke Gegnerschaft gegen die modernistische Politik des Potala, des tibetischen Vatikan, vorhanden. Als Fuehrer der konservativen Gruppe ist kein Geringerer anzusehen als das "Grosse Lehrerjuwel" des lamaistischen Buddhismus, der Pantschen Rinpontsche (oder Taschi Lama, wie ihn die Mongolen nennen), der offiziell die Stellung eines Hohenpriesters und eines Lehrers des Dalai Lama einnimmt. Nach dem Inkarnationsdogma des lamaistischen Buddhismus steht der Pantschen Lama sogar ueber dem Dalai Lama, denn er ist die Verkoerperung des hoechsten "Buddhas des unendlichen Lichtglanzes", waehrend der Priesterkoenig nur den davon abhaengigen Bodhisatva, den "gnaedig Herniederschauenden" verkoerpert. Beide zusammen sind die methaphysischen Kraefte des vierten Weltzeitalters, die bewirkt haben, dass auf Erden erschien der indische ERleuchtete: Gautama Buddha, der Shakya-Sohn. Die Staerkung der konservativen und antienglischen Partei, sowie die Hebung des Ansehens des Pantschen lassen sich uebringens sowohl die Chinesen, wie auch die Russen sehr angelegen sein. Als die Spannung zwischen dem Dalai Lama und dem Pantschen Lama, zwischen koeniglichem Amt und Lehramt, zu gross wurde, zog es der Pantschen vor, seine Residenz Taschi-lhunpo, den "Segensberg", zu verlassen und nach Norden zu ziehen. Freilich verhinderte die chinesische Regierung, dass er zu seinen getreuen Mongolen zog, wohin ihn ein Kirchenkonzil

zwecks Einsetzung eines neuen "Lebenden Buddha",und somit Fuersten der Mongolei,gerufen hatte,und lud ihn dafuer nach Peking ein,wo er vom Staat mit den Ehren eines Souveraens empfangen worden ist.Der Oberstzeremonienmeister der Regierung liess ihn durch die Tore der Stadt im gelben Wagen fahren,um wieder gut zu machen,dass Kaiser Chien-lung vor etwa hundertfuenfzig Jahren den damaligen Pantschen Lama,der ja nach dem Inkarnationsdogma ein und derselbe wie der heutige ist,an den Toren Pekings hatte aussteigen und zu Fuss durch die Tore gehen lassen. Die chinesische Regierung hat dem Pantschen einen taeglichen Ehrensold ausgesetzt und schickt ihm Tag fuer Tag einige erlesene Gerichte.Er aber,strenger Ordenssitte getreu,nimmt nichts zu sich ausser Tee mit zerruehrter Butter und einfaches Brot.Er reist nun nach dem Sueden zur Erholung von den Pocken,an denen er hier leicht erkrankte.Merkwuerdiges Schicksal! denn auch der Vorgaenger unter Kaiser Chien-lung befiel hier die gleiche Krankheit sogar mit toedtlichem Ausgang.Der Pantschen reist zunaechst nach Shanghai,dem Wohnsitz uebrigens des japanischen Lordabtes Grafen Otani,des Exponenten der Buddhistisch verbraemten Expansionspolitik Gross-Nippons,und von Shanghai weiter zu der heiligen Insel Putoshan im chinesischen Meere,wo er den Sommer verbringen wird - gleichweit entfernt und gleichweit nah zu allen politischen Machtzentren Ostasiens,Aber nicht nur der Staat hat den hohen Kirchenfuersten mit hoechsten Ehren empfangen,sondern ebenso der Bund der Religionen.Es existiert hier in Peking naemlich ein Schutzverband aller Religionen (Griechisch-Katholischer, Protestanten, Buddhisten,Lamaisten, Taoisten,Konfuzianer,Mohammedaner usw.).Dieser Schutzverband begruesste
  ̶ ̶ ̶ ̶n Lama anlaesslich seines Aufenthalts in Peking mit einer
      nischen,weltumspannenden Ckarakters.Es war Ostersonntag,
      schen Priester sangen erst tibetische Litaneien mit wunder-
)enen,der Griechisch-katholische Kirchenchor und ein pro-
      sangen."Also hat Gott die Welt geliebt...."und

die "Kreuzigung".Gilbert Reid,ein amerikanischer Theologe,hielt die Begruessungsrede,und der Pantschen Lama erwiderte in liebenswuerdiger Weise,indem er die Gelegenheit benutzte,mit kurzen Strichen die Lehre des Buddhismus darzustellen.Er ging von dem metaphysischen Gesetz der Widervergeltung des Guten und Boesen aus und beschwor die tausendkoefige Menge,endlich deoch allem Leid bei sich und anderen Wesen,die Tiere eingeschlossen,ein Ende zu machen durch Beschreitung des Pfades der Tugend.Bei dieser Massenbegruessung vom Pantschen Lama einen persoenlichen Eindruck zu erhalten,war natuerlich unmoeglich,das ist nur in einer Privataudienz moeglich.

Baron Staël-Holstein, dem bekannten Buddhologen und Kenner des Sanskrit, Tibetischen und Chinesischen, Professor Lessing, dem Meister aller wichtigeren Sprachen Asiens, und mir war es vergoennt, durch Vermittlung des chinesischen Ministeriums eine Audienz beim Pantschen Lama zu erhalten. Wir wurden durch das grosse Suedtor eingelassen, das zu den Palaesten am Sued- und Mittelsee fuehrt, dem heute "Praesidententeil" genannten Abschnitt der verbotenen Stadt. Nach Durchschreiten der Torhalle steht man vor einer gewaltigen Geistermauer, die den Blick auf den Suedsee abhaelt. Wir gehen an ihr links vorbei und erblicken nun den gewaltigen See, und wie ein Maerchen-koestlich, wie es nur diese uralte Kultur Chinas hervorbringen konnte- leuchtet üeber die Wasser herueber die "Insel der Seligen" mit ihrem Palast. Dieser Yingtai-Palast ist Wirklichkeit gewordener Traum. Hallen und Pavillons zeigen eine Grundlage von weissem Marmor und Alabaster, purpurrote Mauern, Rotlacksaeulen, koestliches Holzwerk und als Kroenung Daecher mit gelben, blauen und gruenen Ziegeln. Im weiten Bogen zieht sich das Westufer hin, und wir muessen ganz herum bis zur Nordseite gehen, immer berauscht von dem Anblick der traumhaften Insel. Dieser Palast liegt so schoen und verlockend da, dass man ganz vergisst, dass seine Raeume unendliche Qualen gesehen haben. Hier wurde der unglueckliche Kaiser Kuang-hsu von der alten Kaiserin-Witwe gefangen gehalten und schliesslich, als sie schon selber im Sterben lag, zum Tode gezwungen. An dieser merkwuerdigen Staette nun weilt heute als Gast des Reiches der Mitte der geistliche Vater der Lamaisten, der Pantschen-Lama. Eine Marmorbruecke fuehrt weiter zur Insel und eine breite Freitreppe, die ganz allmaehlich nur ansteigt, fuehrt zum Palasttor. Vom Tuersturz wehen Tuecher in den heiligen Farben gelb und rot. Im ersten Hof stehen viele Hunderte von Wallfahrern, die von Lamas zu einem Zuge -einer hinter dem anderen- geordnet werden. Wir durchschreiten eine Halle. Im zweiten Hof steht dieser Pilgerzug geduldig wartend und zieht ganz langsam - ein Pilger nach dem anderen - in die grosse Halle zum dritten Hof,in der ein feierliches Hochamt gelesen wird.Da drinnen schreiten die Pilger ueber Teppiche,die aussen einen schwarzen, dann einen gelben Rand und innen ein rotes Mittelstueck zeigen.Dort sitzt auf hohenpriestelichem Throne (fuenf Stufen,sieben Kissen) der Pantschen-Lama.Die Wallfahrer sind von weit,weit her wochenlang gepilgert,jetzt koennen sie gerade einige Sekunden lang das Ziel ihrer Sehnsucht erblicken,sich ehrfurchtsvoll niederwerfen,waehrend an dem Altare seitlich die heilige Handlung vollzogen wird,und schon muessen sie weiter.Im dritten Hofe setzen sie sich auf den Boden nieder und verfolgen lauschend,betend,besinnlich,noch ganz benommen,den weiteren Verlauf der Messe.Wir sind durch ein Seitentor in den dritten Hof eingetreten und betrachten die Pilgermenge.Ein buntes Bild ! die meisten stammen aus der Mongolei und sind in ihre prachtigen Farben gekleidet,meist rot ,aber auch vielfach gelb,rotbraun,violett,dazwischen sieht man auch das Blau von Mandschuren und Chinesen.Koestliche Haartrachten erblickt man bei den Frauen,geziert mit schwerem Silber,Korallen und anderem Geschmeide und in kunstvollen Zoepfen geflochten. Alte und Junge,Kranke,von anderen gestuetzt,Kinder,von ihren Muettern getragen,Reiche und Arme,Priester,mongolische Adlige,Kaufleute und gewoehnliches Volk.Alles ist hierher gewallfahrt,den seligen Augenblick zu erleben,einmal den geistlichen Vater von Angesicht zu Angesicht zu sehen und mit seinem Segen gestaerkt ,getroestet,beruhigt wieder in die weite Heimat zu ziehen.

  Wir warten das Ende der Messe in einer Seitenhalle,einem alten kaiserlichen Empfangsraum ab.Ein mongolischer Herzog -in blauer und schwarzer chinesischer Kleidung- unterhaelt sich mit uns auf Chinesisch mit weltsicherer Alluere.Da werdwn wir zur Audienz gerufen. Man fuehrt uns durch den innersten Hof zum Empfangsraum der letzten

Halle.Ein Streifen aus kaiserlich gelber Seide ist durch den Hof gelegt,ein Vorrecht des hohen Kirchenfuersten.Vor dem Eingang werden durch den Vorhang nach alter Sitte erst unsere Ehrengeschenke gereicht, sodann werden wir eingelassen,Seine Heiligkeit zu sehen.Da steht er, aber kein Kirchenfuerst,sondern - ein Heiliger,der "Shakya-Moench aus Taschi-lhupo",wie er sich selbst bescheiden nennt.Sein weises,unendlich guetiges Auge ruht auf uns mit tief ins Herz dringenden Blick,der doch gleichzeitig waermend umfasst.Er ist so liebenswuerdig,nach westlicher Sitte uns zu begruessen:stehend mit kurzem,festem Haendedruck,jeden mit den grossen,braunen Augen umfassend.Voll voelliger innerer Freiheit benutzt er aus Ruecksicht auf uns die abendlaendischen Formen,eine leichte Handbewegung,wir duerfen uns setzen.Er selber nimmt auf einer doppelbreiten,geschnitzten chinesischen Sitzbank Platz.

Die einleitenden Worte werden gesprochen,und ich habe Musse,ihn zu betrachten.Ein kraeftiger Mann,Mitte der Vierziger,nicht hager,nicht beleibt,mit voellig ebenmaessigem Gesichtsausdruck.Die grosse Stirn ueber den dunklen,hochgewoelbten Augenbrauen zeigt kaum merkliche Falten,die Zeichen des Denkers,aber ueber alles das breitet sich eine wundersame Glaette des Gesichtsausdrucks,die eine voellige Abgeklaertheit und Weltueberlegenheit strahlt.Wohl sieht man auch bei uns im Westen Priester und Weise,deren Wesen vollendete Vergeistigung zeigt,aber nie wohl sieht man diesen Ausdruck souveraener Kampflosigkeit fern von jeglicher,auch der leisesten,Verkrampfung.Dies Merkmal,Disziplin ohne Zwang,Zucht bei voller Freiheit der Seele,ist das eigentliche Erbe asiatischer Priesterweisheit und das Geheimnis dieser eindrucksvollen Persoenlichkeit.Dazu hinter runden Brillenglaesern diese wundervollen,grossen braunen Augen von einer solchen Guete,wie ich sie noch nie bei einem Menschen sah.Er laechelt mir zu und sein unendlich gewinnendes Laecheln laesst eine Perlenkette blendend weisser

Zaehne sehen,die noch um so schoener wirken,als die Oberlippe und
Mitte der Unterlippe durch einige wenige schwarze Barthaare,ein Zeichen der aelteren Priester,geziert werden.Der ebenmaessige Kopf besitzt
ein wohlgebautes,gerundetes Kinn,das umso staerker die vorhandene,
aber voellig beherrschte,Energie ins Auge fallen laesst,als der Kopf
nach Priestersitte glatt geschoren ist und daher seine ganz gleichmaes-
sige Kontur zeigtxxxx.Auch die Backenknochen treten kaum merklich her-
vor,wie denn ueberhaupt sein Rassentypus nur von der Seite sichtbar
ist.So auch die geradlinige Nase mit gleichmaessig breitem Ruecken
und abgerundeter Spitze.Von vorne dagegen ueberwiegt durchaus das
Charakteristische seiner vergeistigten Persoenlichkeit.Die Ohren sind
vollendet harmonisch gebaut.Der Gesamteindruck zeigt Souveraenitaet
des Wesns,ruhigen Willen und unendlich tiefe Guete.Die Gewaender sind
lediglich die ueblichen der hoeheren Geistlichen.Die Fuesse stecken in
weissen,mit Brokatstreifen gezierten Schuhen,das Untergewand blitzt
manchmal koestlich in herrlichem rotgoldenem Brokat.Aber ueber alles
das traegt er - in Togaform geschlungen - den tiefroten Ueberwurf,wie
ihn der einfachste Priester traegt.Kein Abzeichen zeigt die hohepries-
terliche Wuerde an.Die durchgeistigten Haende bewegen sich mit jener
Leichtigkeit,wie sie nur Kindern oder ganz reifen Menschen eigen ist.
Kein Schmuck beschwert das feine Spiel der Finger.Lediglich ein Rosen-
kranz schlingt sich in dreifacher Kette um das linke Handgelenk.-

  Baron Stael-Holstein zeigt ihm die Abschrift einer tibetischen Urkunde,die ein Vorgaenger des Pantschen Lama im 18.Jahrhundert
ausgestellt hat,und bittet um Erklaerung einiger Fachausdruecke der
Theologie und des kanonischen Rechtes,die unserer Wissenschaft bisher
gaenzlich unbekannt sind.Der Pantschen Lama laesst sich einen Schreib-
stift geben und ist so liebenswuerdig,eigenhaendig unter alle fraglichen
Stellen des Dokumentes seines Vorgaengers einen tibetischen Kommentar

zu schreiben.Professor Lessing stellt einige Fragen aus dem Gebiet der lamaistischen Kunst.Meine Fragen beziehen sich zunaechst auf a denA den Aufbau der tibetischen Messe und Kommunion,weiter auf den Parallelismus des Ritus mit den Stufen der Meditation,dem Pfad des Menschen, den kosmischen Ebenen.Nun geht die Unterhaltung ins Religionsphilosophische und wird erheblich schwierig.Der Pantschen Lama schreibt mir zunaechst eine Erklaerung des Namens der Tuisol-Messe auf.Selbstverstaendlich wird die Messe nur dann richtig vollzogen,wenn sie gleichzeitig Meditatonserlebnis des Priesters ist.Wir uebersetzen Meditation mit einem gelaeufigen chinesischen Wort,aber der Pantschen Lama ist dieser Ausdruck nicht recht.Im Moment entsteht eine geradezu babylonische Sprachverwirrung,alles sucht in Sanskrit,Tibetisch,Chinesisch,Mongolisch und Deutsch eine Verstaendigung.Der Pantschen Lama ist ploetzlich wie ein Gelehrter genau,er laesst sich das grosse Viersprachenlexikon (Tibetisch-Mongolisch-Mandschurisch-Chinesisch) bringen und schlaegt in seinem wissenschaftlichen Eifer selber mit einer geradezu erstaunlichen Lebendigkeit nach bis er die einfache chinesische Transkription des Sanskritwortes a/ySaMaM"Samadhi"gefunden hat.Er will nicht,dass die buddhistische Meditation mit anderen chinesischen Meditationsarten restlos gleichgesetzt wird.Bei dem Nachschlagen Im Viersprachenwoerterbuch,ist seine dunkelrote Priestertoga etwas zurueckgerutscht und laesst seinen rechten Arm sehen,der nach uralter Ordenssitte gaenzlich unbekleidet ist.Auch hierbei ist geradezu erstaunlich das Ebenmass der Glieder,das die vollendete Harmonie seines Geistes widerstrahlt.Die ploetzlich entfaltete Lebendigkeit erst zeigt,welch jeder Zeit verfuegbare Energiemenge in diesem ueberlegenen ruhigen Manne steckt.Ich habe noch einige Fragen,der Pantschen Lama sagt mir ,um dies zu verstehen, muesse man viele Jahre die heiligen Buecher studieren und ausschliesslich diesem Studium leben.Dann aber geraet er ploetzlich in Nachdenken und sinnt,waehrend sein Oberkoerper sich leise von rechts nach links

und links nach rechts bewegt wie beim Meditieren der heiligen Sutras.
Eine Stille-beinah hoerbar- fuellt den ganzen Raum.Dann taucht er wieder aus der Versenkung zurueck,sein Blick leuchtet auf,und er spricht:
"Weisheit laesst sich nicht aus Buechern lernen,Weisheit ist ein goettliches Geheimnis".Dann ein ploetzlicher Entschluss,er laesst einen
Priester hereinrufen,der vor ihm zum Segen niederkniet,und der Pantschen
Lama gibt ihm die Anweisung,mein Lehrer zu werden.

  Zwei Stunden sind wir beim Pantschen Lama gewesen,wir verabschieden uns.Er laesst sich von einem Diener die Chadags,die Ehrengeschenktuecher aus hellblauer Seide reichen,in deren Faeden Buddhabilder glaenzen,und ueberreicht jedem von uns eines.Er haelt sie mit
beiden Haenden in der Form eines lamaistischen Segensgrusses,die Daumen von der Seide umwickelt.Wir nehmen nach feierlicher Sitte mit tiefer Verneigung in seine hohenpriesterlichen Haende die Seidentuecher
entgegen,fuehren sie nochmals zur Stirn und verlassen rueckwaertsschreitend den Raum,er selber steht wieder da wie im Anfang.Ganz schlicht,
kein Kirchenfuerst - ein Heiliger,der "Shakyamoench aus Taschi-lhunpo",
wie er sich selbst bescheiden nennt.Sein weises unendlich guetiges
Auge ruht auf uns mit tief ins Herz dringendem Blick,der doch gleichzeitig waermend umfasst.-

  Wir verlassen den Palast auf der Insel der Seligen,gehen
ueber die Marmorbruecke zurueck rings um den See herum.Von Ferne ueber
die Wasser gruessen die gelben,gruenen und blauen Daecher.Ich muss
immer an diesen vollendeten Menschen denken.Wie war es doch?"Weisheit
laesst sich nicht aus Buechernerlernen,Weisheit ist ein goettliches
Geheimnis......"

Erwin Rousselle
6. April 1925.